TIME SERIES
Forecasting, Simulation, Applications

MATHEMATICS AND ITS APPLICATIONS

Series Editor: G. M. BELL

Emeritus Professor of Mathematics, King's College, University of London

STATISTICS, OPERATIONAL RESEARCH AND COMPUTATIONAL MATHEMATICS Section

Editor: B. W. CONOLLY,

Emeritus Professor of Mathematics (Operational Research), Queen Mary College, University of London

Mathematics and its applications are now awe-inspiring in their scope, variety and depth. Not only is there rapid growth in pure mathematics and its applications to the traditional fields of the physical sciences, engineering and statistics, but new fields of application are emerging in biology, ecology and social organization. The user of mathematics must assimilate subtle new techniques and also learn to handle the great power of the computer efficiently and economically.

The need for clear, concise and authoritative texts is thus greater than ever and our series endeavours to supply this need. It aims to be comprehensive and yet flexible. Works surveying recent research will introduce new areas and up-to-date mathematical methods. Undergraduate texts on established topics will stimulate student interest by including applications relevant at the present day. The series will also include selected volumes of lecture notes which will enable certain important topics to be presented earlier than would otherwise be possible.

In all these ways it is hoped to render a valuable service to those who learn, teach, develop and use mathematics.

Mathematics and its Applications

Series Editor: G. M. BELL

Professor of Mathematics, King's College London, University of London

series continued at back of book

TIME SERIES
Forecasting, Simulation, Applications

GARETH JANACEK, B.Sc., M.Sc., Ph.D.
and
LOUISE SWIFT, B.Sc., Ph.D.
School of Mathematics, University of East Anglia

ELLIS HORWOOD
NEW YORK   LONDON   TORONTO   SYDNEY   TOKYO   SINGAPORE

First published in 1993 by
ELLIS HORWOOD LIMITED
Market Cross House, Cooper Street,
Chichester, West Sussex, PO19 1EB, England

A division of
Simon & Schuster International Group
A Paramount Communications Company

Printed and bound in Great Britain
by Bookcraft, Midsomer Norton

British Library Cataloguing in Publication Data

A catalogue record for this book is available from the British Library

ISBN 0–13–918459–7

Library of Congress Cataloging-in-Publication Data

Available from the publishers

Table of contents

Hugo, Sophie and Pam
and Paul, Mum and Dad and Peter

Preface

My spelling is wobbly.
Its good spelling but it wobbles and the letters *get in the wrong place*
$\qquad\qquad\qquad\qquad\qquad\qquad\qquad$ *Winnie the Pooh* (1926), A.A. Milne

We began this project when we found that all the existing introductory time series texts were (a) totally theoretical or (b) practical—usually adhering to one particular package—and/or (c) usually concentrated on one particular type of model only. Most texts seemed to be at research level, or were very basic introductory forecasting manuals. They also do not appear to be very statistical. We have written with final-year undergraduates or non-specialist practitioners in mind, for instance operational researchers or economists who find they have to 'dip their toes in the water'. As such we assume some prior knowledge of statistics and mathematics—perhaps the equivalent of the first-year maths and statistics course of a science or social science degree course. We require a basic level of matrix algebra, probability, calculus—including Fourier series—and some experience of the linear regression model. While the required background is not very extensive, we assume a certain level of doggedness in working out the details.

In this book we aim to provide the reader with a broad introduction to time series analysis from a viewpoint midway between the practical and the theoretical. Our feeling is that too many texts concentrate on one particular class of models, and in consequence, for the novice at least, the central ideas common to all time series models are easily lost. To this end where possible we consider the analysis and forecasting of state space models. This has the advantage that we can use the Kalman filter for estimation and that the ideas readily extend to multiple models and missing values. The Kalman filter is difficult at first, but we give an intuitive derivation which the reader does not need to understand in detail. We have also noticed confusion in students caused by what appear to be a plethora of conflicting estimation algorithms. Our view is that all these are approximations to maximum likelihood, and so we use exact likelihood estimation via the Kalman filter, but emphasize that the reader will obtain broadly similar results by using whichever procedure. Enough detail is supplied for the reader to write their own exact likelihood program, although the reader is encouraged to use whatever software he or she has available.

The bulk of the book considers only univariate time series. Chapters 1 and 2 introduce time series models and provide the mathematical background for the later chapters. The book then forks into two streams, either of which may be studied separately, as Chapters 1 and 2 are the only prerequisites. Chapters 3–6 present a time domain approach to linear models from a state space viewpoint, whereas Chapters 7–9 consider spectral methods. Chapter 10 gives a brief introduction to some more complex topics, including multiple time series.

The ideas common to all time series models—estimation, prediction, model selection, and evaluation—are introduced in Chapter 3 via three simple models of different types. In Chapter 4 we introduce the state space model in a general form, so that Harvey's structural models and ARMA models can both be represented as special cases. We give a practical description of the Kalman filter algorithm, with enough detail for the reader to write their own likelihood maximization program. Chapter 5 treats ARMA models—again as a special case of the general state space model. We have included standard ARMA methodology in parallel, as so much software is ARMA based. In Chapter 6 we provide an introduction to the class of structural models developed by Andrew Harvey at the London School of Economics.

Frequency domain ideas are introduced in Chapter 7, while Chapter 8 introduces the spectrum and its ramifications. Chapter 9 covers spectral estimation. The frequency domain treatment is fairly basic, but we have found that it takes newcomers some time to assimilate the concepts involved, and we aim to keep our treatment reasonably simple.

The final chapter leads into some more complex issues in time series analysis, and provides references for further work. We consider multiple series, in time and frequency, the inclusion of exogenous variables, the use of transformations, and how to deal with missing values. Long memory and non-linear models are touched upon.

Throughout the book we have provided a mix of exercises which can be done by hand and those requiring software. Some (a minority) require access to exact likelihood estimation programs.

Our thanks to Simon Peters for his advice on programming the state space estimation. Anyone who reads this book will recognize the debt we owe to others in the field. We have acknowledged our debt in cases where we can be explicit, but there is no doubt it goes very much further. The errors, omissions, etc. are of course ours alone.

1

Introduction

Time is the simplest thing.

C. Simak

We begin by defining a time series as *a record taken through time*, that is a sequential set of data measured over time. The central idea is that of a *sequence* of observations. A mathematician might talk of a function $F(t)$ of time t, but such classical functions with no random element are not our main interest; instead we wish to look at 'random functions' or records which contain a random component. We can just think of a time series as a random sequence, not necessarily through time, as we shall see in Chapter 2, but for the moment we stick to our original definition.

We cannot avoid examples of time series; they arise whenever we take records, and examples abound, for example

the number of unemployed in the EEC each month
the temperature in the core of a nuclear reactor
the signal from a distant stellar object
daily rainfall readings
the amplitude of a radar return signal.

Figs. 1.1 to 1.5 give illustrations of such series.

To make our task easier we shall concentrate almost exclusively on discrete time series in which measurements are taken at equally spaced discrete time points. Since we shall be applying computational techniques, this is not unreasonable, and indeed often data are only available at monthly, weekly, or millisecond intervals. However, in some situations it does imply that a 'continuous trace' has been sampled or digitized. In engineering terms we look at *discrete* or *digital* signals, not analogue ones. For further detail see Chapter 7.

We begin our study of time series with this chapter in which we take an overview of some informal methods of examining such series. Our aim will be to model time series and hence gain insight into their generating mechanisms, perhaps to forecast or perhaps to construct a larger theory. This informal introduction will, we hope, motivate the definitions and approaches that arise when we look at probability and more complex

models. Nevertheless, one should not underestimate the power of these simple techniques; they can be most useful, and indeed in X11 and other seasonal adjustment
packages, they are still widely used.

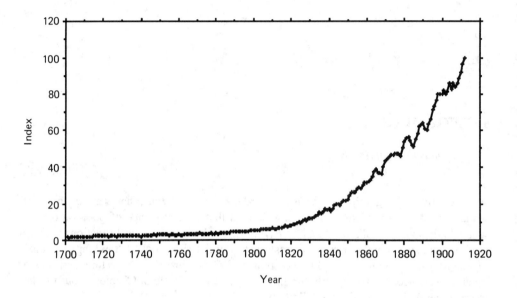

Fig. 1.1. UK index of industrial production.

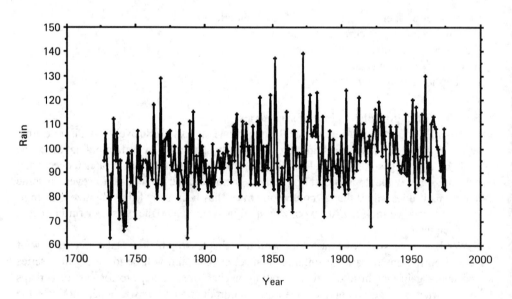

Fig. 1.2. Annual rainfall.

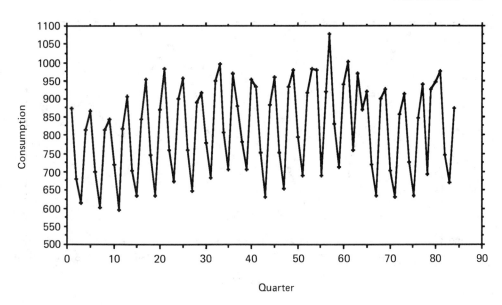

Fig. 1.3. UK primary fuel consumption.

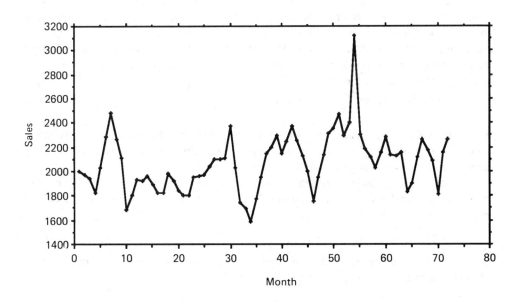

Fig. 1.4. Sales of jeans in the UK 01/80 to 12/85.

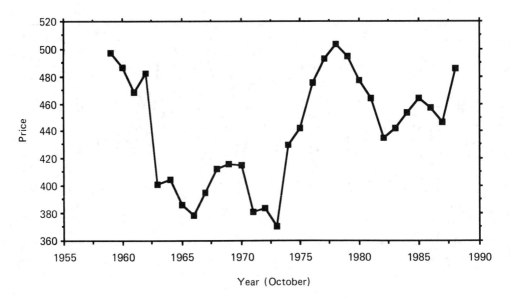

Fig. 1.5. Austin Mini prices (in 1959 pounds).

1.1 SMOOTHING AND SEASONAL ADJUSTMENT

Examining the traces in the figures above, we can see evidence of some patterns. Series are often described as having 'trends', 'seasonal cycles', or 'seasonal effects'. Many series have cyclic patterns which are not seasonal; the sun spot cycle is a good example, as is the outfall of the river Orinoco. To understand such series it can be helpful to disentangle these effects, and this is our first aim. Since our emphasis is on building a model given a time series $X(t)$ we shall think of it as being generated by a model, for example a simple one of the form

$$X(t) = T(t) + S(t) + R(t) \qquad t = \ldots -1, \ 0, \ 1, \ 2, \ \ldots . \tag{1.1}$$

Here $T(t)$ is the trend, $S(t)$ the seasonal term, and $R(t)$ is the irregular or random component. Economists and others may go further and add a further 'cyclic' term, but for us the above has more than enough complexity for the moment.

To make things a little more precise we shall define a constant level to be a (zero) trend, and we shall assume that the seasonal effect, when it exists, has period s; that is, it repeats after s time periods

$$S(t + s) = S(t) \qquad \text{for all } t. \tag{1.2}$$

In fact it is convenient to make the further assumption that the sum of the seasonal components over a complete cycle or period is zero,

$$\sum_{j=1}^{s} S(t + j) = 0. \tag{1.3}$$

This is tantamount to a scale change; indeed, it is comparable to the 'sum of zero' assumption for the treatment effects in the analysis of variance. The assumption that the seasonal effects are constant over time is a larger one, but it may well be reasonable; as we often have only a few cycles worth of data it may be the only possible assumption, given the data.

Consider the data on fuel consumption given in Table 1.1. The full series is given in the data appendix and a plot of the series in the table is given in Fig. 1.6.

Table 1.1. UK primary energy consumption (coal equivalent).

Year	1	2	3	4
1965	874	679	616	816
1966	866	700	603	814
1967	843	719	594	819
1968	906	703	634	844
1969	952	745	635	871
Means	888.2	709.2	616.4	832.8

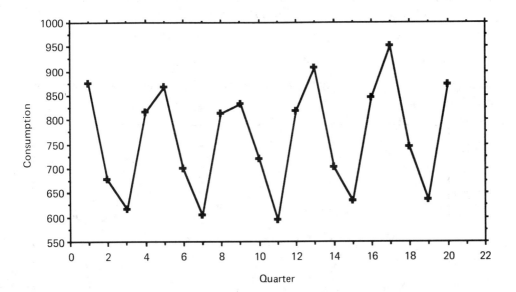

Fig. 1.6 Primary fuel consumption '00,000 tons.

As one might expect, there is considerable seasonal variation, which is just the effect of consumption following the UK seasonal variation in temperature. Overplotting the years (a useful trick which we recommend) shows a reasonably stable seasonal pattern, as can be seen in Fig. 1.7.

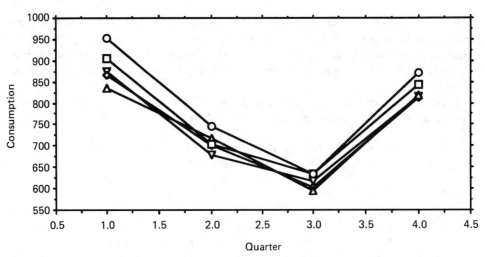

Fig. 1.7. Fuel consumption for five years.

If we assume a model of the form (1.1), then we can attempt to estimate the various components. A simple approach is to average the seasonal values over the series, and use these, minus the overall mean, as seasonal estimates. Since the overall mean of the data above is 761.65 we have as estimates of the four seasonal values

$$S(1) = 888.2 - 761.65 = 126.55 \qquad S(2) = 709.2 - 761.65 = -52.4$$
$$S(3) = 616.4 - 761.65 = -145.25 \qquad S(4) = 832.8 - 761.65 = 71.15.$$

Subtraction of these values from the original series leaves the trend plus irregular terms as plotted in Fig. 1.8.

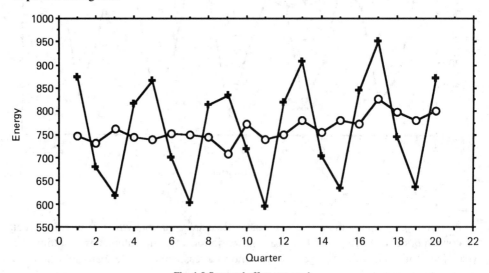

Fig. 1.8 Seasonal effect removed.

This technique, in general, works well, as we can see, on series having linear trends with small slopes. To see why, we consider a linear trend $T(t) = a + bt$ and a seasonal of period s viz. terms $S(1), \ldots, S(s)$. Then for the case of $N = ms$ observations, if we ignore the irregular component, the overall mean is given by

$$\frac{1}{N}\sum_{j=1}^{N}\{T(j)+S(j)\} = \frac{1}{N}\left\{Na + b\frac{N(N+1)}{2}\right\} + \frac{1}{N}\sum_{j=1}^{N}S(j)$$

Since the sum of the seasonal effect is zero from (1.3) while the sum of the kth seasonal terms is

$$\frac{1}{m}\sum_{j=0}^{m-1}\{T(k+sj)+S(k+sj)\} = a + bs\frac{(m-1)}{2} + \frac{1}{m}\sum_{j=0}^{m-1}S(k+sj) + bk,$$

we have for fixed seasonal effects a difference after subtracting the mean

$$bk - b\frac{(s+1)}{2} + S(k). \tag{1.4}$$

Consequently the adjusted series obtained by subtracting the seasonal estimates has itself no seasonal effects, but there is some distortion to the trend from the adjustment process. When b is large or the trend is not linear, then this process may not work very well. In many cases one finds that locally a trend may be well represented by a linear function; problems may arise, however, when one attempts to fit a 'global' trend over a long time scale.

An alternative is just to look at the averages for each complete seasonal cycle (the period), since the seasonal effect over an entire period is zero. The problem here is that one can lose a lot of data unless we use a *moving average*. This is just the series of averages

$$\frac{1}{s}\sum_{j=0}^{s-1}X_{t+j}, \quad \frac{1}{s}\sum_{j=1}^{s}X_{t+j}, \quad \frac{1}{s}\sum_{j=2}^{s+1}X_{t+j}, \ldots$$

These will give a series with the seasonal effect removed since each of the sums covers all the seasonal periods and, as above, we recall that the sum of seasonals is zero. These averages correspond to the trend and irregular terms at times $t + (s-1)/2$, $t + (s-1)/2 + 1$, $t + (s-1)/2 + 2$, ... Looking at a linear trend as in the case above will illustrate this point.

$$\frac{1}{s}\{a + b(t+j) + S(t+j)\} = a + bt + b\frac{(s-1)}{2}.$$

This is a problem when the period is even, since we have the adjusted series values at time points which do not correspond to the original series. A look at the computations laid out below for the energy data will convince you of this. To overcome this problem the simplest solution is to take a moving average of order 2 on the offending series. This so-called *centred moving average (CMA)* brings us back to the correct time points. The other small point is that we lose some data at the ends of the series; some adjustments are available for this, but we shall ignore them and refer the reader to Kendall (1973) for details. The computational procedure for the fuel series is laid out in Table 1.2 and plotted in Fig. 1.9.

Table 1.2. Calculation of the moving average.

Quarter	$X(t)$	MA	Centred MA
1	874		
2	679		
		746.250	
3	616		745.250
		744.250	
4	816		746.875
		749.500	
5	866		747.875
		746.250	
6	700		746.000
		745.750	
7	603		741.750
		737.750	
8	814		740.125
		742.500	
9	834		741.375
		740.250	
10	719		740.875
		741.500	
11	594		750.500
		759.500	
12	819		757.500
		755.500	
13	906		760.500
		765.500	
14	703		768.625
		771.750	
15	634		777.500
		783.250	
16	844		788.500
		793.750	
17	952		793.875
		794.000	
18	745		797.375
		800.750	
19	635		
20	871		

Given the centred moving average, a simple way of estimating the seasonal effects is to look at the differences between the MA and the original series. To estimate the kth quarter seasonal we just average the kth quarter differences. Thus in the case above we have as seasonal estimates

$$S(1) = 128.594 \quad S(2) = -46.487 \quad S(3) = -142.000 \quad S(4) = 65.000$$

which you will notice sum to 5.107. Since we require the seasonals to sum to zero we add a correction factor of

$$\frac{-5.107}{4} = -1.254$$

to the values above to give

$$S(1) = 127.340 \quad S(2) = -46.487 \quad S(3) = -143.254 \quad S(4) = 63.746.$$

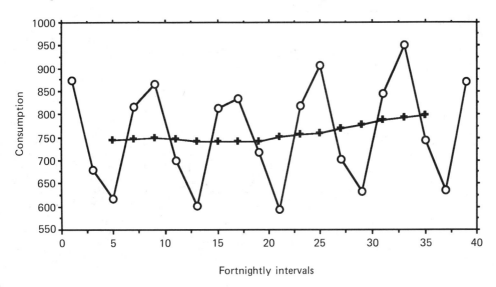

Fig. 1.9. Fuel consumption and centred MA.

We can then examine the irregular component of our series which we estimate by subtracting both the centred moving average and the seasonal effects. A plot of this component is given in Fig. 1.10.

Thus we see how it is possible to estimate the three components of our model and hence 'decompose' the series into its component parts. Fig. 1.11 shows a plot of the three components which are obtained from the model and which make up the fuel series.

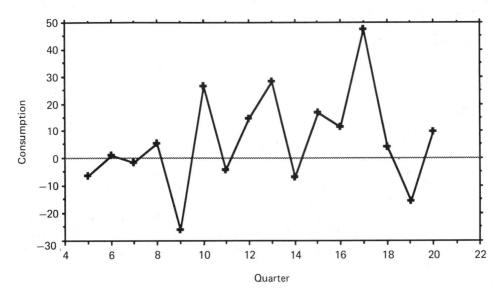

Fig. 1.10. Irregular component.

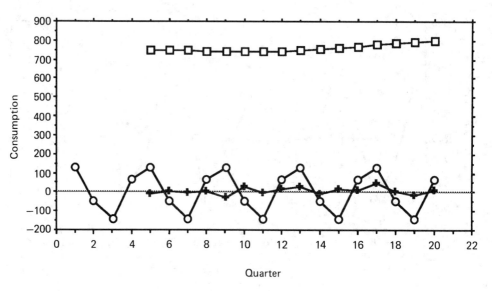

Fig. 1.11. Decomposition of fuel series.

While such decompositions have their own interest they also enable one to do some-thing more—make predictions, since if we are satisfied that our model (1.1) is appropriate then we might as well use it to make predictions. For example, given the 20 quarters in Table 1.1 we might ask for predictions of the next year's values. The model equation is

$$X(t) = T(t) + S(t) + R(t), \qquad t = \dots -1, \ 0, \ 1, \ 2, \ \dots,$$

and a sensible predictor might be

$$\hat{X}(t + k|t) = \hat{T}(t + k) + \hat{S}(t + k).$$

We have estimates of the seasonals, and so all we need to do is to predict the trend. If we fit a line

$$T(t) = a + bt$$

to the centred moving average we have

$$\hat{T}(t) = 713.376 + 3.647t.$$

The fit is not very good, but for illustration will suffice. Then for predictions we obtain the values in Table 1.3. A plot of the forecasts made at time $t = 20$ is given in Fig. 1.12.

The model outlined above is not the only one. A possible variant on (1.1) is a model with a multiplicative seasonal effect, viz.

$$X(t) = T(t)S(t)R(t) \qquad t = \dots -1, 0, 1, 2 \dots, \tag{1.5}$$

Table 1.3

Period t	Trend T	Seasonal S	Predicted $\hat{X}$	Actual X
21	789.963	127.340	917.303	981
22	793.610	−46.487	747.123	759
23	797.257	−143.254	654.003	674
24	800.904	63.746	864.650	900

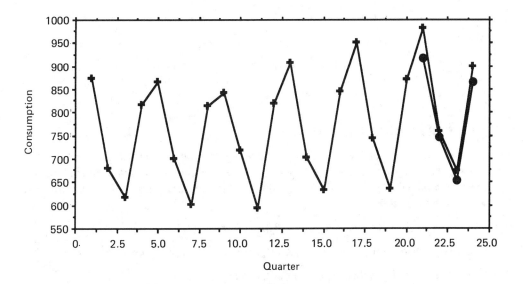

Fig. 1.12. Actual and forecast fuel consumption.

where once again T, S, and R are the trend, seasonal, and irregular components. One might prefer such a model if the plot of the series showed that there was a trend and the amplitude of the seasonal peaks was increasing, such as in Fig. 1.13.

The model in (1.1) can have its parameters estimated by the 'ratio to moving average' method, which entails finding the smoothed centred moving average series $X^*(t)$ in exactly the same way as above and then computing the ratios $X(t)/X^*(t)$ *instead* of the differences. These ratios are then averaged to obtain an estimate of the seasonal effects corresponding to the sums in the additive model (1.1). The authors admit that they find that just taking logarithms and working with the transformed quantities is a rather more attractive approach.

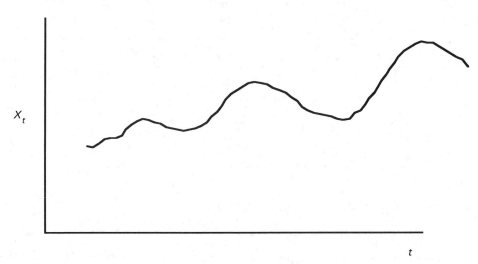

Fig. 1.13. Increasing amplitude of seasonal peaks.

1.2 REGRESSION METHODS

There are many alternatives to the moving average methods outlined above. An attractive one for the case of a linear or slowly moving trend is the use of dummy variables in a regression model. To illustrate the procedure we use the fuel consumption data. Suppose we consider the model

$$X_t = \beta_0 + \beta_1 t + \beta_2 d_1 + \beta_3 d_2 + \beta_4 d_3 + \beta_5 d_4 + \varepsilon(t)$$

where the $\varepsilon(t)$ are 'errors' and $d_1, d_2, ..., d_4$ are dummy variables where

$d_1 = 1$ if it is the first quarter of the year,
      0 otherwise

$d_2 = 1$ if it is the second quarter of the year
      0 otherwise,

etc. Notice the more natural notation X_t.

   As will be clear to those of you well versed in regression methods this model is over parametrized, and we need to remove a parameter. There are two possible alternatives:

(1)   to set the first quarter to a zero level and in consequence all the other quarters are measured by using this as the reference value,
(2)   to use a regression model with a zero intercept.

We choose (2) and try the model

$$X_t = \beta_1 t + \beta_2 d_1 + \beta_3 d_2 + \beta_4 d_3 + \beta_5 d_4 + \varepsilon(t).$$

Using a standard regression package (say MINITAB) we have for the regression equation

$$X_t = 3.38t + 858.83d_1 + 675.45d_2 + 579.28d_3 + 792.30d_4. \tag{1.6}$$

As can be seen from Fig. 1.4 this technique also appears to work well.

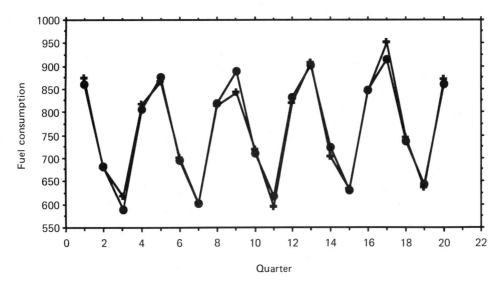

Fig. 1.14. Regression model and actual.

An obvious alternative to the use of dummies is to cope with the cyclic effect by fitting regressions with sinusoidal terms, for example

$$E[X_t] = \mu + \sum_{j=1}^{m} \left\{ \alpha_j \cos(\omega_j t) + \beta_j \sin(\omega_j t) \right\},$$

the aim being to model the cyclic oscillations by the sines and cosines. For this model, if we think in terms of the general regression model

$$\mathbf{Y} = \mathbf{X}\beta + \mathbf{e}$$

then the design matrix $\mathbf{X}$ has a leading column of 1's and then columns containing either sine or cosine terms. Note that if we choose the frequencies ω_j to be the *Fourier frequencies* $2\pi j/N, j = 0, 1, \dots N$, so that the columns are orthogonal since

$$\sum_{t=0}^{N-1} \cos(\omega_j t) = 0 \qquad j \neq 0$$

$$\sum_{t=0}^{N-1} \sin(\omega_j t) = 0 \qquad j \neq 0 \tag{1.7}$$

$$\sum_{t=0}^{N-1} \cos(\omega_j t)\cos(\omega_k t) = \begin{cases} N/2 & \text{if } j = k \neq 0 \text{ or } N/2 \\ N & j = k = 0 \text{ or } N/2 \\ 0 & j \neq k \end{cases}$$

$$\sum_{t=0}^{N-1} \cos(\omega_j t)\sin(\omega_k t) = 0$$

$$\sum_{t=0}^{N-1} \sin(\omega_j t)\sin(\omega_k t) = \begin{cases} N/2 & \text{if } j = k \neq 0 \text{ or } N/2 \\ 0 & \text{otherwise.} \end{cases} \tag{1.8}$$

In this case the estimates become

$$\hat{\mu} = \frac{1}{N}\sum_{t=1}^{N} X_t$$

$$\hat{\alpha}_j = \frac{2}{N}\sum_{t=1}^{N} X_t \cos\left(\frac{2\pi j}{N}t\right)$$

$$\hat{\beta}_j = \frac{2}{N}\sum_{t=1}^{N} X_t \sin\left(\frac{2\pi j}{N}t\right). \tag{1.9}$$

Since we have orthogonality we have a simple computational problem, and inference is very much easier. If we do *not* choose the Fourier frequencies, the above simplicity is lost.

We return to the fuel data discussed above as an example of cyclic data. Here we have 20 observations, so the Fourier frequencies are of the form $2\pi j/20$, but since the cycle is clearly of period 4 quarters it is probably only worth using with only one sine and cosine term with that period, viz. a model of the form

$$X_t = \mu + \alpha \cos\left(\frac{2\pi}{N} \times 5\right) + \beta \sin\left(\frac{2\pi}{N} \times 5\right) + \text{error.}$$

The result of fitting this model by using least squares gives a fit of the form shown in Fig. 1.15, which seems is quite good. This approach will be discussed in greater detail in Chapters 7 and 8.

The advantage of the regression model approach is that one has both very clear and explicit components for the model, and, in principle at least, one has a great deal of statistical inference at one's disposal. This is not quite true, for, as we shall see, the irregular component or the errors are highly correlated in many interesting cases. A further drawback is that we assume that a functional form, here linear, can represent the trend or the seasonal over the whole time period.

One way around this latter problem is to fit a series of local functions to the series and describe the trend by this series of smoothed functions. Rather surprisingly, one way of doing this is to use a moving average with unequal weights. Suppose we decide to fit a

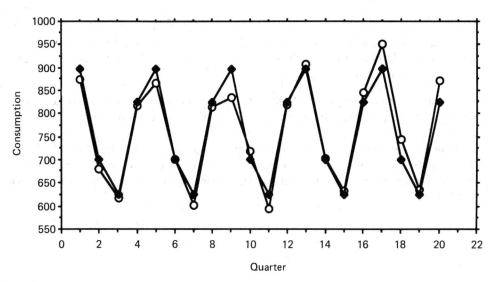

Fig. 1.15. Fuel consumption and fitted model.

cubic curve to five successive series values. There are, as always, advantages to recoding, so let us relabel the time axis and describe the five points as X_{-2}, X_{-1}, X_0, X_1, X_2. If we fit

$$X_t = a_0 + a_1 t + a_2 t^2 + a_3 t^3 + \text{error} \tag{1.10}$$

we have

$$\sum_{-2}^{2} t^2 = 10, \qquad \sum_{-2}^{2} t^4 = 34, \qquad \sum_{-2}^{2} t^6 = 130,$$

giving normal equations.

$$\sum_{-2}^{2} X_t = 5a_0 \qquad\qquad +10a_2$$

$$\sum_{-2}^{2} X_t t = \qquad 10a_1 \qquad\qquad +34a_3$$

$$\sum_{-2}^{2} X_t t^2 = 10a_0 \qquad +34a_2$$

$$\sum_{-2}^{2} X_t t^3 = \qquad 34a_1 \qquad\qquad +130a_3.$$

Solving for a_0 gives $\frac{1}{35}(-3X_{-2}+12X_{-1}+17X_0+12X_1-3X_2)$, and from our coding we note that this is the midpoint of the regression curve. The usual notation for a moving average of this form is to write the coefficients between square brackets with any + signs omitted, viz. $\frac{1}{35}$[−3, 12, 17, 12, −3].

We can compute a sequence of these midpoints and hence smooth a data sequence. Using the moving average above on the UK migration data gives the results laid out in Table 1.4.

As in the cases above, a plot of the moving average against the original data is shown in Fig. 1.16. Choosing 7, 9, or more points or a higher order polynomial gives similar moving average results. For more detail and examples the reader is urged to consult Kendall (1973).

Table 1.4. UK migration figures.

Migration from UK	Smoothed series
284.00	
302.00	
309.00	299.49
278.00	290.60
293.00	290.34
291.00	280.29
240.00	250.03
233.00	231.80
246.00	250.63
269.00	258.63
238.00	240.83
210.00	215.74
209.00	202.74
192.00	192.09
189.00	198.26
229.00	217.26
233.00	248.43
259.00	235.43
185.00	200.00
164.00	162.29
174.00	179.91
213.00	
210.00	

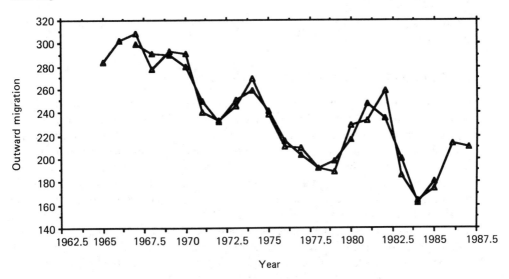

Fig. 1.16. UK migration.

1.3 THE BACKWARD DIFFERENCE OPERATOR

At this point we shall find it useful to define the backward shift operator B. This is simply defined as

$$Bf(t) = f(t-1) \quad \text{with} \quad B^{-1}f(t) = f(t+1).$$

Another related operator is ∇ defined by $\nabla = 1 - B$ or

$$\nabla f(t) = (1 - B)f(t) = f(t) - f(t-1).$$

These operators are widely used in the literature to indicate operations on time series. There are some obvious reasons for wishing to manipulate series; for instance if X_t has a linear trend when ∇X_t does not. This is easily shown, since writing $X_t = a + bt$ gives

$$X_t - X_{t-1} = a + bt - a - b(t-1) = b.$$

The extension that

$$\nabla^2 = (1 - B)^2 = 1 - 2B + B^2$$

removes quadratic trends is also easily demonstrated. The reader might like to try their hand in the case of a polynomial trend of order p.

After some algebra one can express moving averages in terms of the difference operator which can prove useful at times. Thus for a cubic on seven points we obtain the moving average $\frac{1}{21}[-2, 3, 6, 7, 6, 3, -2]$, which is equivalent to

$$X_2 - \frac{1}{21}\left\{9\nabla^4 - 9\nabla^5 + 2\nabla^2\right\}X_{t-3}.$$

We shall use these operators extensively when discussing the Box–Jenkins models of Chapter 4.

1.4 FORECASTING AND MOVING AVERAGES

Suppose that we wish to forecast a time series given some past history $X_1, X_2, ..., X_N$. In many cases it may well be possible to visualize a model of the form (1.1) above, but one may be reluctant to assume that the trend term or the seasonal is fixed; thus the techniques above may not be appropriate. In addition, if many forecasts have to be made, say for predicting demand in a fashion warehouse, it may be important that any forecasting process does not required too much computation. We can make some progress with this problem if we think of our series as having a memory. In that case it may be reasonable to assume that the relationship between X_t and X_{t-k} becomes weaker as the value of k becomes larger. Naturally, if there is no memory we have considerable problems and might perhaps contemplate other options. A rather attractive method of forecasting series based on the idea of a memory decay is exponential smoothing. We shall see how it may be applied here, and discuss its theoretical implications later.

Suppose that we observe $X_1, X_2, ..., X_N$ and wish to model the series sufficiently well to make forecasts at times $N + 1, N + 2, ...$, etc. For simplicity we shall begin by assuming that there is no trend or seasonal effect, and we have our usual irregular sequence of observations. To make a forecast we might construct a smoother series $\{M_t\}$ which we aim to use at any time point t as a 'local approximation'. One possibility is

$$M_t = \alpha X_t + (1 - \alpha)M_{t-1} \quad |\alpha| \le 1, \tag{1.11}$$

that is

$$M_t = \alpha X_t + (1 - \alpha)M_{t-1} = \alpha X_t + (1 - \alpha)\{\alpha X_{t-1} + (1 - \alpha)M_{t-2}\}$$
$$= \alpha X_t + (1 - \alpha)\{\alpha X_{t-1} + (1 - \alpha)\{\alpha X_{t-2} + (1 - \alpha)M_{t-3}\}\},$$

giving

$$M_t = \alpha \sum_{j=0}^{t-1} (1 - \alpha)^j X_{t-j} + (1 - \alpha)^t M_0. \tag{1.12}$$

If we assume that the initial value M_0 is chosen to be X_0, an initial value of the observed series, then the smoothed value is just the weighted sum of the previous observations. At time t the memory of previous values of the series can be made faint by choosing a large (near to 1) value of α, while small (near zero) values of α give a relatively large weighting to past values. This smoothing process is known as *exponential smoothing*, and, given this smoothed series, one possibility is to use it to make forecasts. Explicitly we forecast X_{t+1} at time t using M_t. It will help to introduce some notation here since we shall be doing a lot of forecasting and we need to be clear as to quite what we mean. Let us write the *forecast* of X_{t+k} given $\{X_{t-j}, j = 0, 1, 2, ...\}$ as $F_t(k)$. Then the smoothed series forecast described above is given by $F_t(1) = M_t$ or

$$F_t(1) = \alpha X_t + (1 - \alpha)F_{t-1}(1), \tag{1.13}$$

or if we write the forecast error as $e_t = X_t - F_{t-1}(1)$ then from (1.13)

$$F_t(1) = \alpha e_t + F_{t-1}(1). \qquad (1.14)$$

Thus if we are making a series of projections the exponential smoothing forecast requires very little computation (on the assumption that α is known) and only knowledge of the last forecast and its error. This means it can be very useful in cases where we need to make a large number of forecasts, say in a stock control system with many lines, or for some reason we have very little computational support. We can examine the effects of applying exponential smoothing on the centred moving average of the fuel data. For the moving average of the fuel series we have computed the smoothed series for the two cases $\alpha = 0.9$ and $\alpha = 0.1$. The calculations are given in Table 1.5 and are plotted in Fig. 1.17. We have set $F_2(1) = X_3$ to start off the calculations. As can be seen, 0.9 gives a very good fit!

Table 1.5. Exponentially smoothed fuel moving average.

Quarter t	Actual series X_t	Smoothed series	
		$\alpha = 0.9$ $F_t(1)$	$\alpha = 0.1$ $F_t(1)$
3	745.25	745.25	745.25
4	746.88	746.71	745.41
5	747.88	747.76	745.66
6	746.00	746.18	745.69
7	741.75	742.19	745.30
8	740.13	740.33	744.78
9	741.38	741.27	744.44
10	740.88	740.91	744.08
11	750.50	749.54	744.73
12	757.50	756.70	746.00
13	760.50	760.12	747.45
14	768.63	767.77	749.57
15	777.50	776.53	752.36
16	788.50	787.30	755.98
17	793.88	793.22	759.77
18	797.38	796.96	763.53

The choice of *discounting parameter* α is not altogether obvious; large values of the discount factor α make the smooth series react rather quickly to changes, while small ones smooth the process. We take the view that a sensible strategy is to initialize the smoothed series with the first known data value and then to minimize

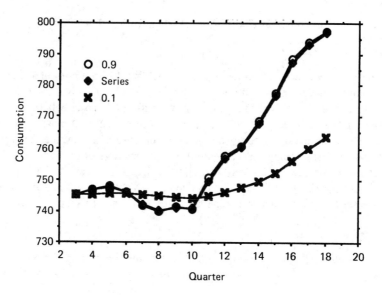

Fig. 1.17. Exponentially smoothed fuel series.

$$\sum_{i=1}^{N}\left(X_t - F_{t-1}(1)\right)^2 \tag{1.15}$$

with respect to α. This requires some computation, but it is not a difficult numerical problem. Using the series above we found that the optimum value of α is 0.7.

It is not difficult to show that the smoothed series has the same mean as the original when the series is long enough; however, a more interesting case arises when there is a trend. Take for example the case where the series has a linear trend say, $X_t = a + bt$, then,

$$M_t = \alpha \sum_{j=0}^{t-1}(1-\alpha)^j X_{t-j} + (1-\alpha)^t M_0; \tag{1.16}$$

substituting for X_t and approximating the finite sum as

$$\sum_{j=0}^{t-1}\beta^j = \frac{1}{(1-\beta)} \quad \text{and} \quad \sum_{j=0}^{t-1}j\beta^j = \frac{\beta}{(1-\beta)^2}$$

gives

$$M_t = a + bt - \frac{(1-\alpha)}{\alpha},$$

assuming $M_0 = 0$ or t very large.

So it follows that the smoothed series *lags* the original series. In a similar way it is reasonably straightforward to examine the behaviour of the smoothed series, given a variety of time series. Details are given in Brown (1963).

In consequence if we have series with a trend we must do something to make the exponential smoothing form acceptable. Brown (1963) made several suggestions (see also Exercise 1.10), but here we restrict ourselves to one option which has proved very successful. That is, to introduce a trend term thus giving two smoothed series

$$M_t = AX_t + (1-A)(M_{t-1} + T_{t-1}) \quad |A| < 1 \tag{1.17}$$

$$T_t = C(M_t - M_{t-1}) + (1-C)T_{t-1} \quad |C| < 1. \tag{1.18}$$

The forecast based at a time t for time $t + k$ is then given by

$$F_t(n) = M_t + kT_t \tag{1.19}$$

It is straightforward to generalize these models to include a seasonal effect. If we denote the jth seasonal as S_j and take the period as s, then for an additive model of the form (1.1)

$$X(t) = T(t) + S(t) + R(t), \quad t = 1, 2, 3, \dots$$

we have

$$\begin{aligned}
M_t &= A(X_t - S_{t-s}) + (1-A)(M_{t-1} + T_{t-1}) & |A| < 1. \\
T_t &= C(M_t - M_{t-1}) + (1-C)T_{t-1} & |C| < 1. \\
S_t &= D(X_t - M_t) + (1-D)S_{t-s} & |D| < 1.
\end{aligned} \tag{1.20}$$

with the forecast of X_{t+k} made at time t being

$$F_t(k) = M_t + kT_t + S_{t+k-s}. \tag{1.21}$$

When one prefers to use the multiplicative model

$$X(t) = T(t)S(t)R(t), \quad t = 1, 2, 3, \dots \tag{1.22}$$

the corresponding equations are

$$\begin{aligned}
M_t &= A(X_t/S_{t-s}) + (1-A)(M_{t-1} + T_{t-1}) & |A| < 1 \\
T_t &= C(M_t - M_{t-1}) + (1-C)T_{t-1} & |C| < 1. \\
S_t &= D(X_t/M_t) + (1-D)S_{t-s} & |D| < 1,
\end{aligned} \tag{1.23}$$

with the corresponding forecast

$$F_t(k) = (M_t + kT_t)S_{t+k-s} \quad k = 1, 2, \dots, 5. \tag{1.24}$$

Authors have reported considerable success in the use of models of this type for prediction. The usual procedure is to set up initial values of the seasonal, and trend effects, and then to find optimal smoothing constants, using a known segment of data. An excellent account is given in Granger & Newbold (1977) and in Chatfield (1978).

To illustrate the method we go back to the fuel series given in Table 1.1. We take the first year's worth of data to set up the initial values and then use the first three years of the series to find the optimal parameter values. We take the linear additive model and set $M_0 = 746.25$, the first year mean, while we estimate the seasonal effects by taking the seasonal minus the overall mean, giving

$$S_1 = 127.75, \quad S_2 = -67.25, \quad S_3 = -120.25, \quad S_4 = 69.75.$$

The trend is set to zero for simplicity. The optimum values of the discount parameters were found; we used a simple, minimization procedure on a PC, and the optimal values proved to be $A = 0.531$, $B = 1.000$, $C = 0.003$. The forecast can be seen plotted in Fig. 1.18.

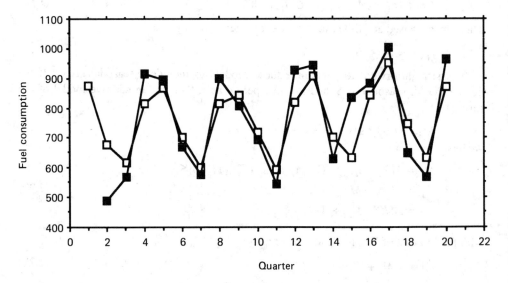

Fig. 1.18. Forecast fuel consumption (■, forecast; □, actual).

The results appear to be quite good despite our rather simple model. There are many further wrinkles one can attempt to improve the moving average model, but we prefer to move on to discuss more complex models.

While the techniques described in this chapter are relatively simple they can be very effective, especially when used with insight rather than being regarded as a black box.

EXERCISES

(1)   The table below gives the numbers of people migrating into the UK in thousands.

i) Find the trend in the data, using a global regression model, and comment on your results.

(ii) Smooth the data, using an appropriate moving average. Can you give any reasons to justify your choice?

Year	Number	Year	Number	Year	Number
1965	206	1975	197	1985	232
1966	219	1976	191	1986	250
1967	225	1977	163	1987	212
1968	222	1978	187		
1969	206	1979	195		
1970	226	1980	174		
1971	200	1981	153		
1972	222	1982	202		
1973	196	1983	202		
1974	184	1984	201		

(2) The death rate per thousand people is given in the table below for England and Wales.

Decade	Quarter ending in			
	March	June	September	December
1841/50	24.7	22.0	21.0	21.7
1851/60	24.7	22.1	20.3	21.9
1861/70	25.2	21.8	21.0	22.1
1871/80	23.7	20.9	19.6	21.3
1881/90	21.6	18.7	17.3	19.1
1891/00	20.7	17.6	17.0	17.7
1901/10	17.7	14.6	13.8	15.4
1911/20	17.2	13.6	11.8	14.9
1921/30	15.5	11.7	9.5	11.8

Suggest and fit a simple model to the series.

(3) The data below give the sales of a company for each quarter from 1965. Use a suitable moving average to decompose the series into trend and seasonal components. Hence or otherwise forecast the sales for 1971–72.

Year	Quarter			
	1	2	3	4
1965	323	144	474	821
1966	408	248	625	925
1967	434	259	681	1274
1968	831	434	940	1639
1969	1222	592	1054	2001
1970	1278	768	1405	2417
1971	1260			

Which is the most appropriate model for these data in the sense of providing the better forecast?

(4) A time series $\{X_t, t = \dots -1, 0, 1, 2, \dots\}$ is believed to be well represented by the model

$$X_t = f(t) + g(t) + \varepsilon_t$$

where $f(t)$ is a smooth slowly changing trend and $g(t)$ is a seasonal component of period $n = 2m$. Assuming ε_t has zero mean, show that

$$X_t^* = \frac{1}{2m}\left\{ \sum_{s=-m+1}^{m-1} X_{t+s} + \frac{1}{2}X_{t-m} + \frac{1}{2}X_{t+m} \right\}$$

is an unbiased estimate of $f(t)$ when $f(t)$ is well represented by a linear trend.

(5) If the moving average $[w_{-m}, \dots, w_0, \dots, w_m]$ is used to determine trend, what is the value of the sum of the coefficients?

(6) Suppose that B denotes the backward shift operator defined as $BX_t = X_{t-1}$, and $B^{-1}X_t = X_{t+1}$. Interpret the operator

$$A(B) = a_n B^n + a_{n-1}B^{n-1} + \dots + a_1 B + a_0.$$

Show that such operators obey the normal rules of arithmetic and deduce that the result of applying a sequence of moving averages to a series is independent of the order of application.

(7) If B denotes the backward shift operator in (6), define $\nabla = 1 - B$ so that $\nabla X_t = X_t - X_{t-1}$. Show that

$$f(t) - \frac{1}{5}\sum_{s=-2}^{2} f(t+s) = \frac{1}{5}[\nabla^4 - 5\nabla^3 + 5\nabla^2]f(t-2).$$

(8) Find the value of a which minimizes

$$Q = \sum_{j=0}^{\infty}(X_{t-j} - a)^2 \beta^j.$$

Show that this estimate of a at time t is just the simple exponentially weighted smoothed series.

(9) If we define the smoothed series M_t, find the response of M_t to the following inputs:

(a) The step $X_t = 0, t < 0$; $X_t = 1$ otherwise.
(b) The impulse $X_t = 1$ when $t = 0$ and zero otherwise.
(c) The parabola $X_t = t^2$.

(10) Suppose that X_t is well described by $X_t = a + bt$. Define two smoothed series

$$M_t = \alpha X_t + (1-\alpha)M_{t-1}$$

and

$$S_t = \alpha M_t + (1-\alpha)S_{t-1}$$

Find the response of M_t and S_t to the original series X_t. Hence show how one might estimate a and b and forecast the series. This concept was both introduced and extended by Brown (1963).

(11) Suggest an exponential smoothing form to forecast the data in the table below.

Year	Annual rainfall (in)	Year	Annual rainfall (in)
1960	130	1970	100
1961	97	1971	91
1962	87	1972	97
1963	94	1973	84
1964	78	1974	108
1965	110	1975	83
1966	113		
1967	109		
1968	108		
1969	101		

Hence or otherwise predict rainfall for 1976.

2

Stationarity

What I tell you three times is true.

L. Carroll

2.1 INTRODUCTION

Up to now we have taken a fairly informal, even cavalier approach to the study of time series. To get further we now need to look at the probabilistic structure of time series, and in consequence we need to be precise about some of the mathematical details. As we shall see in later chapters, there are considerable benefits to be gained from a diversion into mathematical detail. We begin by looking back over our informal definitions, and a good start is the definition of a time series itself, so some definitions.

A *random process* is a sequence of random variables X_t indexed on the set T, symbolically $\{X_t : t \in T\}$. We shall reserve the term *time series* for series where the index is time, but as usual when it is convenient we shall take some liberties. When we actually make an observation of a time series we obtain a sequence of outcomes of the random variables. This sequence is called the *realization* or the *sample path*. The set of all possible sample paths is the *ensemble*. We are in the position of the statistician who has a vector valued random variable $\mathbf{X}$ and obtains a realization $\mathbf{x}$, which is also a vector. The set of all realizations, here vectors $\mathbf{x}$, gives the sample space, which is just the ensemble. The problems for a time series are a bit more complex since we have to bear in mind the *order*, and our vector may have infinite dimension. As an example, consider the sequence of independent identically distributed variables $\{X_t : t = \ldots -2, -1, 0, 1, \ldots\}$ where

$$p(X_j = 1) = p(X_j = -1) = \tfrac{1}{2}.$$

Then one possible realization is just $\{\ldots -1, -1, 1, -1, 1, 1, -1, \ldots\}$ obtained by flipping a coin; the set of all such realizations gives the ensemble.

At this point we need to consider a problem which is of real concern to probabilists. If we have an infinite sequence of random variables and hence an infinite dimensional distribution is it possible to define probability distributions for all combinations of X_t's in the time series, and vice versa? This is a real point of practical interest since it is clear that we are unlikely to have an infinite set of members of the sequence to play with. The problem was resolved by Kolmogorov, who showed that we may specify the behaviour of the complete process by restricting ourselves to the behaviour of $\{X_t\}$ at a finite number of points. This will suffice for our needs, but the interested reader will find a clear discussion of these points in Priestley (1981).

The class of random processes that we have looked at so far is very wide indeed, in fact rather too wide for us to make much progress in modelling a real series. We now try to restrict the class of processes so as to make modelling possible. As we have been thinking in terms of distributions it seems natural to start here. One possibility is to require that the process looks much the same in any time segment, or is the same no matter what the choice of origin. More explicitly we shall say that $\{X_t\}$ is *completely stationary* or *strictly stationary* if the joint distributions of

$$(X_{t_1}, X_{t_2}, \ldots, X_{t_n}) \quad \text{and} \quad (X_{t_1+h}, X_{t_2+h}, \ldots, X_{t_n+h})$$

are the same for all $t_1, t_2, \ldots, t_n$ and $t_{1+h}, t_{2+h}, \ldots, t_{n+h}$ belonging to the index set T. *Thus we require the distributions over the ensemble to be identical.* This is both a severe restriction and one that is difficult to handle. Another, more tractable, possibility is to consider the moments rather than the entire distribution. (Fig. 2.1).

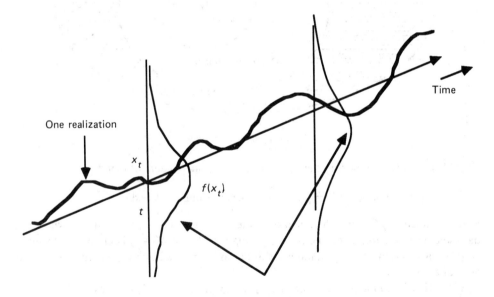

Fig. 2.1. Density at single time points.

We say that $\{X_t\}$ is *stationary to order m* if all the joint moments up to and including m exist for both

$$(X_{t_1}, X_{t_2}, \ldots, X_{t_n}) \quad \text{and} \quad (X_{t_1+h}, X_{t_2+h}, \ldots, X_{t_n+h})$$

and the corresponding moments are equal. That is,

$$E\left[X_{t_1}^{\alpha_1} X_{t_2}^{\alpha_2} \ldots X_{t_n}^{\alpha_n}\right] = E\left[X_{t_1+h}^{\alpha_1} X_{t_2+h}^{\alpha_1} \ldots X_{t_n+h}^{\alpha_n}\right]$$

with

$$\sum \alpha_j \le m$$

for all n and all admissible values of t_j and h. In practice we set $m = 2$ and restrict our attention to just the first two moments in much the same way as one does in traditional statistical practice.

In the case $m = 2$ (Fig. 2.2) we say the process is *second order stationary, weakly stationary*, or (sloppily) *stationary*. From now on unless explicitly mentioned otherwise, we shall look at second order stationary series.

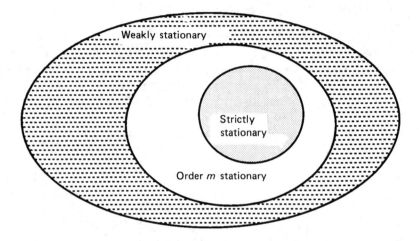

Fig. 2.2. Types of stationarity.

If $\{X_t\}$ is weakly stationary then $E[X_t] = \mu < \infty$ is independent of t, and

$$E[(X_t - \mu)(X_s - \mu)] = \gamma(t - s) < \infty \text{ depends only on } |t - s|.$$

Here the function $\gamma(t - s)$, which measures the covariance between X_t and X_s is known as the autocovariance function. The corresponding correlation $\rho(t - s)$ is known as the auto-correlation function. We give a more precise definition here since we would like to be as general as possible.

We define the *autocovariance function* $\gamma(k)$, $k = \dots -2, -1, 0, 1, 2, \dots$, as

$$\gamma(k) = E\left[(X_t - \mu)\overline{(X_{t+k} - \mu)}\right] \tag{2.1}$$

where the overbar denotes the complex conjugate. Alternatively, it will, in some circumstances, be easier to work with the equivalent expression

$$\bar{\gamma}(k) = E\left[(X_s - \mu)\overline{(X_{s-k} - \mu)}\right],$$

i.e. put $s = t + k$ in (2.1). The *autocorrelation* $\rho(k)$, $k = \dots -2, -1, 0, 1, \dots$, sequence is then defined in an analogous way to the correlation coefficient:

$$\rho(k) = \frac{\gamma(k)}{\gamma(0)}. \tag{2.2}$$

One can think of the autocorrelation as measuring the correlation between the series and a copy shifted through time by an amount k. *Notice that for complex valued random variables we multiply by the complex conjugate when we define the covariance, viz.*

$$\mathrm{cov}(UV) = E\{(U - E[U])E(\overline{V} - E[\overline{V}])\}.$$

We meet such variables in Chapter 9. As the reader has noticed, we have fallen into the most sinful ways of giving the most general definition. For real series it is quite sufficient to just drop the overbars.

The idea of concentrating on the first two moments is not unusual in statistics, and as we shall see is very fruitful in a time series context.

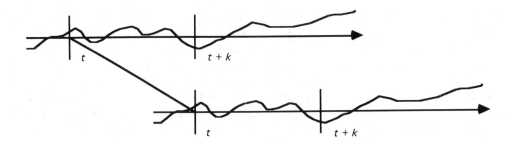

Fig. 2.3. Series and time shifted copy.

Our next step is to look a little more closely at the properties of the autocovariance and autocorrelation functions. The first point to make is that as we deal only with discrete time points to limit our subject matter our autocovariance and autocorrelations are sequences, rather than continuous functions. There is no real problem in having a continuous time index, but notice that the autocorrelation $\gamma(k)$ is now a function of the continuous parameter k. This topic is something we will only look at briefly in later chapters.

There are some rather elementary but useful properties

(1) $0 \le |\gamma(k)| \le \gamma(0)$ for all k

(2)   (a) $\gamma(k) = \gamma(-k)$ for **real** time series

      (b) $\overline{\gamma(k)} = \gamma(-k)$ for **complex** series

(3) $\gamma(0) = \mathrm{var}(X_t)$.

The first property follows from the usual correlation inequality, while the last is just a consequence of the definition of stationarity. For the second we have

$$\gamma(-k) = E\left[(X_t - \mu)\overline{(X_{t-k} - \mu)}\right] = E\left[(X_{s+k} - \mu)\overline{(X_s - \mu)}\right]$$

$$= \overline{E\left[(X_s - \mu)\overline{(X_{s+k} - \mu)}\right]} = \overline{\gamma(k)}.$$

One rather technical but vital point is that the sequence of autocovariances and auto-correlations is *positive definite*. This is a property of all covariances, and it means that for any m the $m \times m$ matrix **M** defined as

$$\mathbf{M} = \begin{bmatrix} \gamma(0) & \gamma(1) & \gamma(2) & \dots & \gamma(m-1) \\ \gamma(1) & \gamma(0) & \gamma(1) & \dots & \gamma(m-2) \\ & & \dots & & \\ & & \dots & & \\ \gamma(m-1) & \gamma(m-2) & & \dots & \gamma(0) \end{bmatrix} \qquad (2.3)$$

it has a non-zero determinant. The implications of this will become apparent in later chapters, for, in terms of the underlying mathematics, this result is of central importance since the existence of the power spectrum follows from this property. For the moment it seems more appropriate to look at some examples of stationary series.

It may also have occurred to the reader that weak stationarity and the appropriate distribution may impose strict stationarity. When the process has a multivariate normal distribution then we say that it is *Gaussian*, and in this case second order or weak stationarity implies strict stationarity. *Beware*: we need multivariate normality, not just normality of the first order marginal distributions.

2.2 SOME EXAMPLES

Example 1
Consider the series $\{X_t\}$ where

$$X_t = \varepsilon_t \quad \text{for all } t$$

and the $\{\varepsilon_t\}$ are zero mean independent identically distributed (iid) variates with common variance σ^2. Then it is clear that the series is strictly stationary since the joint distribution of the series at any set of time points is the same as at a translated set. Since the series is strictly stationary then it is also weakly stationary. This can also be shown directly since

$$\gamma(k) = E[X_t X_{t+k}] = \sigma^2 \quad k = 0$$
$$0 \quad k \neq 0. \qquad (2.4)$$

If we modified our definition to require that the X_t were merely uncorrelated, then the new series is still second order stationary but not necessarily strictly stationary. This weaker conclusion follows since the joint distributions are not specified. An example of a realization of such a process is given in Fig. 2.4. It consists of 100 simulated observations. This process, known as the *white noise process*, is an important building brick in our later studies.

Generating or simulating such a series is a fairly simple exercise; all we need is to generate a sequence of iid random variables. We have used our local computer's library routines for generating sequences of independent deviates (after we checked them). For readers who wish to write their own programs we recommend the algorithm of Wichmann & Hill (1982), the details of which are given in Chapter 3. Fig. 2.5 shows four realizations of this series plotted together.

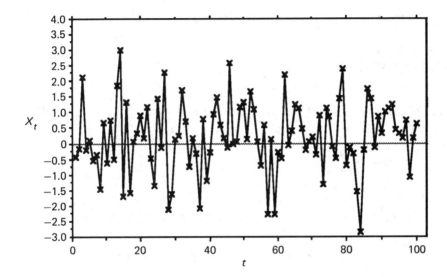

Fig. 2.4. Series (white noise).

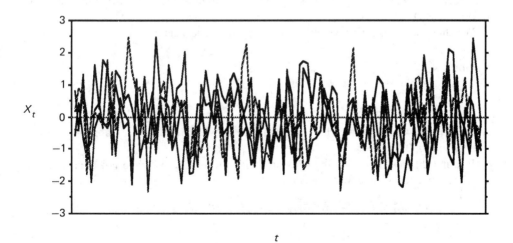

Fig. 2.5. Four realizations of a noise series.

Example 2

Suppose now that we have the series $\{X_t\}$ defined by $X_t = (-1)^t \varepsilon_t$ where the $\{\varepsilon_t\}$ are a sequence of zero mean uncorrelated random variables with constant variance σ^2. Then the autocovariance of $\{X_t\}$ is given by

$$\gamma(k) = E[X_t X_{t+k}] = E[(-1)^t \varepsilon_t (-1)^{t+k} \varepsilon_{t+k}] = (-1)^{2t+k} E[\varepsilon_t \varepsilon_{t+k}]$$

$$= \sigma^2 \quad k = 0$$

$$= 0 \quad k \neq 0.$$

In consequence this series is also weakly stationary.

Example 3

Suppose we define the series $\{X_t\}$ as

$$X_t = a\cos(\omega t + \phi)$$

where ω and a are nonstochastic constants and ϕ is a uniform random variable on the interval $[-\pi, \pi]$. Then

$$E[X_t] = \frac{a}{2\pi} \int_{-\pi}^{\pi} \cos(\omega t + \phi)\, d\phi = 0$$

while

$$(2\pi)^2 E[X_t X_{t+k}] = a \int_{-\pi}^{\pi} \cos(\omega t + \phi)\cos(\omega t + \omega k + \phi)\, d\phi$$

$$\frac{a^2}{2} \int_{-\pi}^{\pi} [\cos(2\omega t + \omega k + 2\phi) + \cos(\omega t)]\, d\phi = a^2 \pi \cos(\omega k) \quad \text{for } k \neq 0$$

$$= a^2 \pi \quad k = 0.$$

The series is thus weakly stationary and we can plot the autocorrelation function $\rho(k) = \cos(\omega k)$.

We shall meet this series, known as the harmonic series, again.

Example 4

One last example is the series $\{X_t\}$ defined as

$$X_t = \varepsilon_t + \varepsilon_{t-1}$$

where $\{\varepsilon_t\}$ is a white noise series from Example 1. We have plotted a realization of such a series in Fig. 2.6.

It is not difficult to derive the autocorrelations when $\{\varepsilon_t\}$ is white noise, an exercise we were tempted to leave for the reader.

$$\gamma(k) = E[X_t X_{t+k}] = E[\varepsilon_t \varepsilon_{t+k} + \varepsilon_t \varepsilon_{t+k-1} + \varepsilon_{t-1} \varepsilon_{t+k} + \varepsilon_{t-1} \varepsilon_{t+k-1}]$$

$$= 2\sigma^2 \quad k = 0$$

$$= -\sigma^2 \quad k = \pm 1$$

$$= 0 \quad \text{otherwise.}$$

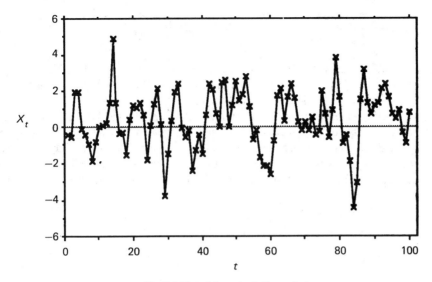

Fig. 2.6. Plot of the series in Example 4.

As is probably obvious, any series which has a trend cannot be stationary. This may not be a problem since in many cases we may be able either to eliminate the trend or to model it. This is what we attempted in Chapter 1, leaving an irregular component after trend removal which we might model as a stationary process. As an example of trend removal, suppose that we have an additive trend model of the type we looked at in Chapter 1:

$$Y_t = a + bt + X_t$$

with a and b as non-random constants, while X_t is a weakly stationary process with covariances $\{\gamma_x(k)\}$. If we difference the series we have

$$W_t = \nabla Y_t = Y_t - Y_{t-1} = b + X_t - X_{t-1}.$$

Thus we can see that

$$E[W_t] = b, \qquad \text{a constant}$$

while

$$\begin{aligned}
\gamma_w(k) = E[(W_t - b)(W_{t+k} - b)] &= E[(X_t - X_{t-1})(X_{t+k} - X_{t+k-1})] \\
&= \gamma_x(k) - \gamma_x(k-1) - \gamma_x(k+1) + \gamma_x(k) \\
&= 2\gamma_x(k) - \gamma_x(k-1) - \gamma_x(k+1) \qquad |k| > 1.
\end{aligned}$$

Some reflection should convince the reader that the differenced process is (weakly) stationary. Thus, as we see, it is not difficult to move from a stationary to a non-stationary process in some circumstances. If the series has a polynomial trend, say $P(t)$, where

$$P(t) = \sum_{j=0}^{k} p_j t^j$$

so that $Y_t = P(t) + X_t$ then it is not difficult to show (see exercise 5) that differencing k times gives ∇Y_t, which has a mean but no trend and is weakly stationary. We discuss the modelling process in greater detail in later chapters.

If we consider seasonal models it is clear that they are not weakly stationary in the sense that we use above. To handle cyclic behaviour we can attempt to model it in the same way as the simple seasonal models we looked at in Chapter 1. The 'irregular' component is then left as the stationary process. There are obviously practical details to be considered, and there is a fuller discussion of these and other problems in later chapters.

2.3 GENERATING GAUSSIAN SERIES

Suppose that we wish to simulate a stationary time series and to make life rather simpler we are content to settle for a Gaussian series. Thus our intention is to generate a fragment of a realization $\mathbf{X} = \{X_1, X_2, \ldots, X_N\}$ which has a specified autocorrelation structure, with autocorrelations $\{\gamma(k)\}$, and which can be regarded as the realization of a multivariate normal distribution. It is easy enough, by using a random number generator, to generate a value from $\mathbf{u} = \{u_1, u_2, \ldots, u_N\}$ when the u_i are independent standard normal variables so we might try to find a way of moving from the u domain to the x domain.

An obvious approach is to construct a correlation matrix $\mathbf{C} = (\gamma(|i - j|))$ for an n-dimensional normal distribution and then find the decomposition:

$$\mathbf{C} = \mathbf{L}\mathbf{L}^T$$

for lower triangular matrix $\mathbf{L}$. Since we have now what amounts to the square root of $\mathbf{C}$ we can generate our required series from transformations of white noise vectors $\mathbf{u}$ via

$$\mathbf{X} = \mathbf{L}\mathbf{u}$$

since $E[\mathbf{X}\mathbf{X}^T] = E[\mathbf{L}\mathbf{u}(\mathbf{L}\mathbf{u})^T] = E[\mathbf{L}\mathbf{u}\mathbf{u}^T\mathbf{L}^T] = \mathbf{C}$.

Finding such a lower triangular matrix is a standard process in numerical analysis; the technique is called the Cholesky decomposition, and there are many algorithms, see for example Press *et al.* (1986). This method has been used for known $\mathbf{C}$ by Granger & Joyeux (1980) and Geweke & Porter-Hudack (1983). Sadly, this procedure works poorly for empirical problems, as sampling variation in the estimated $\mathbf{C}$ causes numerical instability.

Suppose that we wish to generate a Gaussian series whose covariances are given by

$$\gamma(0) = 1 + \psi^2 \quad \gamma(1) = \psi \quad \gamma(k) = 0 \qquad k > 1,$$

a series we shall meet again. Then

$$
\mathbf{C} = \begin{pmatrix}
1+\psi^2 & \psi & 0 & 0 & 0 & \dots \\
\psi & 1+\psi^2 & \psi & 0 & 0 & \dots \\
0 & \psi & 1+\psi^2 & \psi & 0 & \dots \\
0 & 0 & \psi & 1+\psi^2 & \psi & \dots \\
& \cdot & \cdot & \cdot & \cdot & \cdot
\end{pmatrix}.
$$

Usually, we perform a numerical factorization, but in this case we note that

$$
\begin{pmatrix}
1 & 0 & 0 & 0 & 0 & \dots \\
\psi & 1 & 0 & 0 & 0 & \dots \\
0 & \psi & 1 & 0 & 0 & \dots \\
0 & 0 & \psi & 1 & 0 & \dots \\
\cdot & \cdot & \cdot & \cdot & \cdot & \cdot
\end{pmatrix}
\begin{pmatrix}
1 & \psi & 0 & 0 & 0 & \dots \\
0 & 1 & \psi & 0 & 0 & \dots \\
0 & 0 & 1 & \psi & 0 & \dots \\
0 & 0 & 0 & 1 & \psi & \dots \\
\cdot & \cdot & \cdot & \cdot & \cdot & \cdot
\end{pmatrix} = \mathbf{L}\mathbf{L}^T
$$

$$
= \begin{pmatrix}
1 & \psi & 0 & 0 & 0 & \dots \\
\psi & 1+\psi^2 & \psi & 0 & 0 & \dots \\
0 & \psi & 1+\psi^2 & \psi & 0 & \dots \\
0 & 0 & \psi & 1+\psi^2 & \psi & \dots \\
& \cdot & \cdot & \cdot & \cdot & \cdot
\end{pmatrix}.
$$

This is not quite the matrix that we wanted, but the only problem is in the end points of the diagonal. Rather than perform an exact factorization it is easier to simulate an $n+2$ tuple and discard the end points. Thus we generate $\mathbf{u}$, a standard normal vector, and our $n+2$ tuple is just $\mathbf{X} = \mathbf{L}\mathbf{u}$. There are alternative methods of factorization, such as the algorithm developed by Tunnicliffe-Wilson (1969, 1979). This fits a special type of model called a 'moving average model' of the form

$$
X_t = \varepsilon_t + \theta_1\varepsilon_{t-1} + \dots + \theta_q\varepsilon_{t-q},
$$

and it is proved to be both simple to use and rapidly convergent. It does, however, require a strictly positive definite sequence, and we have encountered some problems here when using estimated autocorrelations.

2.4 STATIONARITY AND PREDICTION AND NON-DETERMINISTIC SERIES

In Chapter 1 we said that we were interested in random or irregular series and that perfectly predictable series were of less interest; in fact we are happy to leave this to the mathematicians. To be more precise we shall choose to study those series where we are unable to predict X_{t+k} given $X_t, X_{t-1}, X_{t-2}, X_{t-3}, \dots$ without error that is the expected mean square error of prediction

$$
E\left[\left(X_{t+k} - X_{t+k|t}\right)^2\right] > 0
$$

where $X_{t+k|t}$ denotes the predictor based on values of the series up to and including time t. Such series are said to be *non-deterministic*, while series capable of perfect prediction are said to be *deterministic*. Thus, for example, the series in Example 1 is evidently non-deterministic, while the series $\{X_t\}$ defined as

$$X_t = \cos(2\pi t) \qquad \text{for all } t$$

is clearly deterministic.

Wold (1938) was able to prove that any time series can be expressed as the weighted sum $\lambda U_t + \mu V_t$ of a deterministic component U_t and a non-deterministic component V_t, although the weights may be zero in some cases. This ties in with the results of the Kolmogorov approach to prediction and time series, but from our rather more pragmatic viewpoint an important consequence is the result we summarize as a theorem.

Wold's theorem

Suppose that $\{X_t\}$ is a zero mean weakly stationary non-deterministic time series; then $\{X_t\}$ has the representation

$$X_t = \sum_0^\infty \psi_j \varepsilon_{t-j} \tag{2.5}$$

where $\{\varepsilon_t\}$ is a sequence of uncorrelated zero mean random variables having a common variance $\sigma^2 > 0$ and having

$$\sum_0^\infty \psi_j^2 < \infty.$$

More generally, if the one step mean square error of prediction is greater than 0 then $\{X_t\}$ can be written as

$$X_t = \sum_0^\infty \psi_j \varepsilon_{t-j} + V_t$$

where

(a) $\displaystyle\sum_0^\infty \psi_j^2 < \infty$ with $\psi_0 = 1$

(b) $\{\varepsilon_t\}$ is white noise with zero mean and variance σ^2

(c) $E[X_t V_s] = 0$ for all integral $t, s, s \neq t$

(d) $\{V_t\}$ is deterministic.

While the proof is complex, see Brockwell & Davis (1987), and the implications far reaching, we shall use this result immediately to reassure ourselves that models of the form $X_t = f(t) +$ random component are a reasonable class of models for time series.

2.5 THE GENERAL LINEAR REPRESENTATION

The model in (2.5) above,

$$X_t = \sum_0^\infty \psi_j \varepsilon_{t-j},$$

is known as the *general linear representation* or *general linear model*, and is an important part of the foundations of the subject; see Chapter 8 for details. Engineers often refer to this model as the *innovations* representation or the *random shocks* model.

The correlation structure of the series in (2.5) is easily obtained since

$$\gamma(k) = E[X_t X_{t+k}] = \sum_i \sum_j \psi_i \psi_j E[\varepsilon_{t-i} \varepsilon_{t+k-j}],$$

and since

$$E[\varepsilon_r \varepsilon_s] = \sigma^2 \quad r = s$$
$$= 0 \quad r \neq s$$

$$\gamma(k) = \sum_{i=0}^\infty \psi_i \psi_{i+k}, \tag{2.6}$$

so

$$\rho(k) = \frac{\displaystyle\sum_{i=0}^\infty \psi_i \psi_{i+k}}{\displaystyle\sum_{i=0}^\infty \psi_i^2}. \tag{2.7}$$

This model crops up in many places, although the form is disguised, either simply, for example,

$$X_t = \varepsilon_t - 0.7\varepsilon_{t-1},$$

or in a rather more subtle manner. Finite versions of the general linear model are known as *moving average models*, usually abbreviated to MA or MA(q) models where q is the order. These models are considered in more detail in later chapters.

2.6 PREDICTION

Given (2.5) we can also put some flesh on the concept of prediction which we have alluded to in rather vague terms. Suppose we have $X_t, X_{t-1}, X_{t-2}, \ldots$, that is knowledge of the entire past of the series at time t and we wish to predict X_{t+k} for some $k > 0$. We will choose to do so by using a predictor $X_{t+k|t}$, which is a linear combination of the known past values, viz.

$$X_{t+k|t} = \sum_{u=0}^{\infty} h_u X_{t-u},$$ (2.8)

and our aim is to minimize the minimum mean square error of prediction

$$E\left[\left(X_{t+k} - X_{t+k|t}\right)^2\right].$$ (2.9)

Now if $\{X_t\}$ is stationary and non-deterministic then it has a representation of the form (2.5):

$$X_t = \sum_0^{\infty} \psi_j \varepsilon_{t-j},$$

and so we can rewrite (2.8) in the form

$$X_{t+k|t} = \sum_{u=0}^{\infty} g_u \varepsilon_{t-u}$$ (2.10)

for some sequence $\{g_u\}$. Thus we may write

$$\begin{aligned}
X_{t+k} - X_{t+k|t} &= \sum_{u=0}^{\infty} \psi_u \varepsilon_{t+k-u} - \sum_{u=0}^{\infty} g_u \varepsilon_{t-u} \\
&= \sum_0^{k-1} \psi_u \varepsilon_{t+k-u} + \sum_k^{\infty} \psi_u \varepsilon_{t+k-u} - \sum_0^{\infty} g_u \varepsilon_{t-u} \\
&= \sum_0^{k-1} \psi_u \varepsilon_{t+k-u} + \sum_0^{\infty} (\psi_{u+k} - g_u) \varepsilon_{t-u}.
\end{aligned}$$

Now recall that the ε_j's are uncorrelated, so if we now square and take expectations the cross-terms vanish, and we have

$$E\left[\left(X_{t+k} - X_{t+k|t}\right)^2\right] = \sigma^2 \sum_0^{k-1} \psi_u^2 + \sigma^2 \sum_{u=0}^{\infty} (\psi_{u+k} - g_u)^2,$$ (2.11)

which is minimized by choosing

$$g_u = \psi_{u+k},$$

so the optimal predictor is

$$X_{t+k/t} = \sum_{u=0}^{\infty} \psi_{u+k} \varepsilon_{t-u}$$ (2.12)

and the minimum value of the mean square error is just

$$E\left[\left(X_{t+k} - X_{k+k|t}\right)^2\right] = \sigma^2 \sum_0^{k-1} \psi_u^2.$$ (2.13)

so for the case where $k = 1$, and we are considering the 'one step ahead' predictor, the value of the mean square error is σ^2, which is the variance of ε_t.

This optimal predictor requires knowledge of the model coefficients, but it can be used to predict. Thus for one model known as the autoregressive model of order 1

$$X_t - \alpha X_{t-1} = \varepsilon_t \quad \text{for } |\alpha| < 1$$

which, as we shall see in later chapters, may be written

$$X_t = \sum_{j=0}^{\infty} \alpha^j \varepsilon_{t-j}$$

so that the $\psi_u = \alpha^u$ and we find that k step predictor (2.10) has $g_u = \alpha^{u+k}$, giving

$$X_{t+k|t} = \sum_{0}^{\infty} \alpha^{u+k} \varepsilon_{t-u} = \alpha^k \sum_{0}^{\infty} \alpha^u \varepsilon_{t-u} = \alpha^k X_t.$$

This procedure can be rather complex; for example suppose that we have

$$X_t = \varepsilon_t + \beta \varepsilon_{t-1} \quad \text{for some constant } \beta < 1,$$

then the optimum one step ahead predictor is

$$X_{t+1|t} = \beta \varepsilon_t.$$

However, we do not observe the $\{\varepsilon_t\}$ series, but just the $\{X_t\}$ series! To acquire a useful predictor we need to express ε_t in terms of past and present X_t. This is not too difficult from first principles, as after some algebra

$$\varepsilon_t = -\beta X_t + \beta^2 X_{t-1} - \beta^3 X_{t-2} + \beta^4 X_{t-3} - \ldots.$$

The reader will no doubt be pleased to learn that we can and will develop a more direct approach which we shall use in later chapters. In practical situations we must estimate the model parameters, obtain the general linear representation and use (2.12); however, there is an additional source of error since we need to take into account the sampling error of the coefficient estimates.

2.7 SAMPLE ESTIMATES

All the theory and structure defined above is all very well, but when one is working with data, all is not quite so clear cut. Suppose that we have the fragment of a realization shown in Fig. 2.7. How may we use the autocorrelations etc.? The answer is to estimate the quantities of interest, and that is our next topic.

Suppose that we have a stationary process $\{X_t\}$ with a mean μ and an autocovariance sequence $\{\gamma(k)\}$ and we observe a fragment of a realization, say $\{X_1, X_2, \ldots, X_N\}$. Since the process is stationary it seems reasonable to use as an estimate

$$\hat{\mu} = \overline{X} = \frac{1}{N} \sum_{j=1}^{N} X_j. \tag{2.14}$$

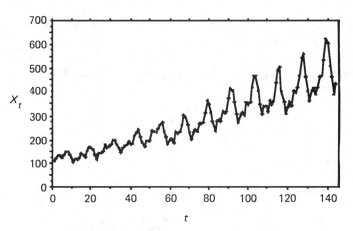

Fig. 2.7. Airline passengers (by month).

For the autocovariances the way forward is a little less clear, but it would seem reasonable to use a similar form of estimate to a covariance estimate between two samples, only here to use the original process and a copy shifted by $k = 0, 1,\ldots$. There are two standard forms of covariance estimates:

$$\hat{\gamma}(k) = \frac{1}{N - |k|} \sum_{t=1}^{N} \left(X_t - \overline{X}\right)\left(X_{t+|k|} - \overline{X}\right) \quad k = 0, \pm 1, \pm 2,\ldots, N-1, \quad (2.15)$$

which we may show as an unbiased estimate of the autocovariance sequence, and

$$\hat{\gamma}(k) = \frac{1}{N} \sum_{t=1}^{N} \left(X_t - \overline{X}\right)\left(X_{t+|k|} - \overline{X}\right) \quad k = 0, \pm 1, \pm 2,\ldots, N-1, \quad (2.16)$$

which is a biased estimate but which has other properties such as a smaller mean square error and positive definiteness. Both estimators are in current use although it is fair to say that the second (biased) variant is the more popular. We shall stick with this version for almost all of this book. The estimates of the autocorrelations are then just the autocovariance estimates divided by the zero lag autocovariance, i.e. the variance.

In common with many authors we shall denote the estimates of the autocovariances as c(k) and the autocorrelations as r(k).

It is not altogether clear why the quantities that we describe above, which are averages through time, should estimate the autocorrelations which are *ensemble* averages. In fact we can use these estimates. The analogy is rather like being at a large party; we can get an impression of the party by moving throughout the building and seeing what is happening. The alternative is to sit in one room, say the kitchen, and observe the passage of people through this room over time. If there is a degree of movement we would expect the two forms of observation to come up with the same answer. The formal method for studying the relations between the ensemble and the time averages is called ergodic theory, and is a well established subject. We shall not consider any ergodic theory but content ourselves with quoting the required results.

If the process is stationary then the estimates defined above are reasonable estimates in that they converge (in distribution) to the parameters they estimate as N tends to infinity. A sufficient condition is that

$$\gamma(k) \to 0 \quad \text{as } k \to \infty \qquad \text{and that} \quad \sum_{0}^{\infty} \gamma^2(k) < \infty. \tag{2.17}$$

Many authors have derived the moments and the sampling distributions of the autocovariances and autocorrelations, and details can be found in the references, e.g. Priestley (1981). We summarize what we feel are the most useful.

(1) $E[c(k)] \to \dfrac{|k|}{N} \gamma(k) \quad \text{as } N \to \infty \quad$ so the bias is of order $\dfrac{1}{N}$

(2) $N \operatorname{cov}\{c(h), c(k)\} \to \displaystyle\sum_{j=-\infty}^{\infty} [\gamma(j)\gamma(j+h-k) + \gamma(j-k)\gamma(j+h)]$

$$+ \sum_{j=-\infty}^{\infty} \kappa(h, -j, k-j) \quad \text{as } N \to \infty.$$

Here we assume that the series is fourth order stationary and the fourth order cumulant is defined as

$$\kappa(p, q, r) = E\{X_t X_{t+p} X_{t+q} X_{t+r}\} - \gamma(p)\,\gamma(q-r) - \gamma(r)\,\gamma(p-q). \tag{2.18}$$

For a Gaussian process the fourth order cumulants are zero, see Newton (1989), and the expressions are simplified. For our purposes it is sufficient to note that when N is large the bias in the autocovariance estimate is negligible, while for the special case where the process is just noise with zero mean and variance σ^2, we can prove the following useful results:

(a) $c(k) \sim N\left(0, \dfrac{\sigma^4}{N}\right) \quad k \neq 0$

(b) $r(k) \sim N\left(0, \dfrac{1}{N}\right)$

(c) $c(0) \sim N\left(\sigma^2, \dfrac{2\sigma^4}{N}\right). \tag{2.19}$

As an illustration of this point we finish with two plots of autocorrelation functions (Fig. 2.8, 2.9). These are of the random series plotted in Fig. 2.4, which should be uncorrelated with zero mean and unit variance and the series $\{X_t\}$ constructed from it in Example 4.

We shall now consider the problem of modelling series, given the basics developed in the first two chapters.

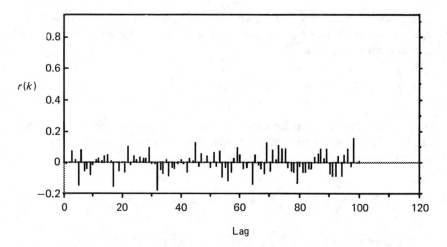

Fig. 2.8. Autocorrelations of the random series in Fig. 2.4.

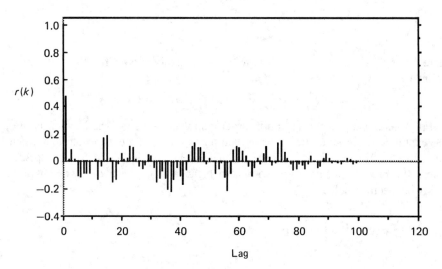

Fig. 2.9. Autocorrelations of series in Fig. 2.6.

EXERCISES

(1) Suppose that $\{X_t\}$ is defined as $X_t = 1$ with probability 0.5 and $X_t = -1$ with probability 0.5, and each X_t is independent. Then

(i)   Is the process $\{X_t\}$ stationary?

(ii)   What are the moments to order 2?

(2) If $\{\varepsilon_t\}$ is a white noise series, which of the following series are stationary?

(i) $X_t = \varepsilon_t\varepsilon_{t-1}$.
(ii) $X_t = \varepsilon_t \cos \omega t + \varepsilon_t \sin \omega t$.
(iii) $X_t = \varepsilon_t \cos \omega t + \varepsilon_{t-1} \sin \omega t$.
(iv) $X_t = (\varepsilon_t)^p$ where p is an integer exceeding 1.

(3) Suppose that $\{S_t\}$ is defined as $S_t = a + bt + X_t$ where X_t is stationary. Show that the differenced series is weakly stationary.

(4) Suppose that $\{S_t\}$ is defined as $S_t = \alpha + \beta \cos \theta t + X_t$ for some known value θ. Show that $\{S_t - S_{t-p}\}$ is stationary for a suitably chosen p.

(5) If $S_t = P(t) + X_t$ where $P(t)$ is a polynomial of order p in t and $\{X_t\}$ is second order stationary, show that $Z_t = (1 - B)^P S_t$ is second order stationary.

(6) If $\{X_t\}$ is defined as

$$X_t = \sum_{j=1}^{t} \varepsilon_j,$$

where $\{\varepsilon_t\}$ is a white noise series, show that $\{X_t\}$ is not weakly stationary.

(7) $\{X_t\}$ is defined as $X_t = \varepsilon_t + b\varepsilon_{t-1}$ where $\{\varepsilon_t\}$ is assumed to be independent normal. Find the moment generating function of X_t and hence of $\sum w_j X_j$. Hence show that $\{X_t\}$ is strictly stationary.

(8) If $\{\varepsilon_t\}$ is a white noise process, is the series defined as $e^{i\omega t}\varepsilon_t$ also white noise? Is this process stationary?

(9) Show that, given an uncorrelated time series $\{\varepsilon_t\}$ a weakly stationary time series, X_t can be constructed such that $X_t = 2X_{t+1} + \varepsilon_{t+1}$. Show also that X_t constructed as above, satisfies $X_t = 0.5X_{t-1} + e_t$ where $\{e_t\}$ is not the same as $\{\varepsilon_t\}$.

(10) Suppose $X_t = -1.7 + \varepsilon_t - 0.6\varepsilon_{t-1} + 0.3\varepsilon_{t-2}$.

(i)   Is the process stationary?
(ii)   If $X_{93} = 3.8$, would you expect X_{94} to be above or below the mean of the process?

(11) Consider the process generated by $X_t = \alpha X_{t-1} + \varepsilon_t$ where $|\alpha| > 1$. Show that this may be written as $\alpha B(\alpha^{-1}B^{-1} - 1)X_t = \varepsilon_t$ and hence that $X_t = \alpha^{-1}B^{-1}(\alpha^{-1}B^{-1} - 1)^{-1}\varepsilon_t$. Deduce that the original process can be modelled in terms of future ε_t's rather than past ones.

(12) Generate a realization of 100 observations from each of the models in Exercise 9. Compute the sample autocorrelations and compare them with the actual values.

3

Time series modelling: the first steps

You know very well that unless you're a scientist it's much more important for a theory to be shapely than for it to be true.

Christopher Hampton (British playwright)

3.1 TIME SERIES MODELS

In Chapter 1 we introduced some techniques for seasonal adjustment, trend fitting, and smoothing of a time series $X(t)$. These were all based on the notion that a suitable *model* for the data might be

$$X(t) = T(t) + S(t) + R(t) \tag{3.1}$$

where $T(t)$, $S(t)$ and $R(t)$ are the trend, seasonal, and irregular or random components respectively. We made several references to models and *modelling*, assuming that the reader was familiar with the idea of a mathematical or statistical model. As we intend to emphasize the modelling approach to time series analysis it might be helpful if we digress in order to clarify what we mean by a model.

A mathematical model is a set of mathematical equations between entities of interest. In statistics, the model is usually stochastic in that at least one relationship within the model is not exact. The nature of this uncertainty is represented by one or more random variables. As with all mathematical models there is no suggestion that a particular model holds exactly—indeed several different models may be postulated for the same data—but that an increased understanding of the behaviour of the data of interest can be gained by modelling.

A time series model aims to be a complete representation of the mechanism which may generate or account for an observed time series. It will express any observation in the series as a mathematical function of some combination of time, other variables, known values of interest, and one or more random components.

While (3.1) may be a reasonable model for many time series it will usually be more useful to model the individual components themselves in more detail. For instance, in Chapter 2, Example 1, we considered the model $X_t = \varepsilon_t$ where the $\{\varepsilon_t\}$ are a sequence of independent, identically distributed random variables with constant variance σ^2. This might be a suitable model for the irregular component $R(t)$ (as it is stationary) as would the models in Examples 2 and 3.

In time series practice, several broad classes of model have been developed—most over the last 25 years. As with novel ideas in any discipline, as each type is introduced, its originators and their disciples usually claim that this is *the* model, that it will replace all its predecessors, and that the associated methodology is the best thing since wholemeal rolls. Weighty tomes describe the new philosophy in great detail, but frequently do not place it in relation to other model types. To the novice this can often be totally confusing since few texts offer a general 'stand back' approach.

It is our aim to place these often competing philosophies into perspective by emphasizing the features common to all time series methodologies. The interested reader can always pursue more detail at a later date.

In this chapter we aim to illustrate the statistical concepts common to most types of time series model with the help of three simple models. We will not, at this stage, be concerned with properties peculiar to individual types of model.

3.2 THREE SIMPLE MODELS

(i) Model A, an autoregressive model

Suppose that our model is

$$X_t = \phi_1 X_{t-1} + \phi_2 X_{t-2} + \varepsilon_t \tag{3.2}$$

where the series $\{\varepsilon_t\}$ (also a time series) is a white noise series with zero mean and variance σ^2. Note that (3.2) has a similar form to the multiple linear regression model. The difference is that in regression the variable of interest is regressed onto a linear function of other known (explanatory) variables, whereas here X_t is expressed as a linear function of its own past values—thus the description '*auto*regressive'. As the values of X_t at the two previous times X_{t-1}, X_{t-2} are involved in the model it is said to be an *autoregressive* model of *order* two or AR(2) model.

Fig. 3.1 shows a time series generated by the model $X_t = 0.5X_{t-1} + 0.3X_{t-2} + \varepsilon_t$ with $\sigma^2 = 2$. Notice that it is smoother than a white noise series—compare Fig. 2.4, for instance.

(ii) Model B, a structural model

Suppose that $X_t = \mu_t + \varepsilon_t$ where $\{\varepsilon_t\}$ is a white noise series with zero mean and variance σ_ε^2, and that $\mu_t = \mu_{t-1} + \eta_t$ where we make a similar assumption about the series $\{\eta_t\}$ but assume that its variance is σ_η^2. In this model there is an underlying trend component μ_t which itself changes randomly over time. The behaviour of μ_t is described as a random walk, so this model is referred to as a *random walk plus noise* model. It is a special case of the *structural* models which we will see in later chapters. Fig. 3.2 shows data simulated from such a model; as one might expect, it is clear that the trend fluctuates over time.

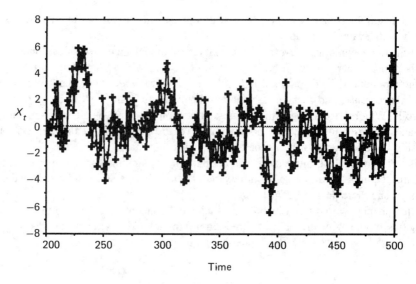

Fig. 3.1. Simulated data from the AR(2) model $X_t = 0.5X_{t-1} + 0.3X_{t-2} + \varepsilon_t$.

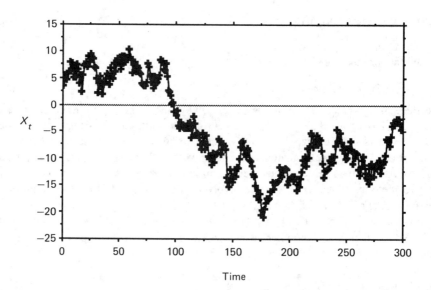

Fig. 3.2. Data simulated from a random walk plus noise model.

(iii) Model C, a trigonometric model

Suppose that we model our series by using

$$X_t = \beta \cos(2\pi f t + \phi) + \varepsilon_t$$

where the amplitude β, frequency f, and phase ϕ are parameters and ε_t is a white noise series as usual. As the deterministic part of this model is periodic this model will be appropriate only for data which are cyclic or seasonal. The frequency f will usually be suggested by the data—for instance for monthly data with an annual cycle, i.e. a period of 12 months, a frequency of $\frac{1}{12}$ could be taken. A realization of data generated from this model is shown in Fig. 3.3.

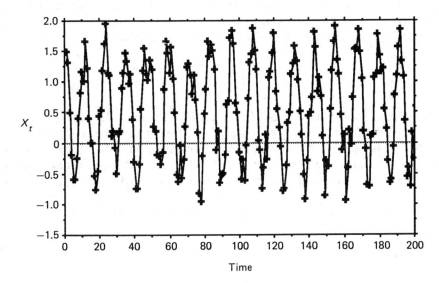

Fig. 3.3. Realization of model C, $X_t = \beta \cos(2\pi f t + \phi) + \varepsilon_t$.

3.3 ESTIMATION

Each of models A, B, and C contains at least one unknown parameter. If we are given a time series and suspect that a particular model is suitable, we need to be able to estimate these parameter(s) from the data. In common with most statistical models we would like estimators to be 'good' in the sense that they are unbiased and of small standard error or mean square error—at least for large samples.

In statistics generally we have results which help us in our attempts at estimation; for instance, the Gauss–Markov theorem gives us the multiple linear regression estimators with minimum variance—even when the observations are not normally distributed. When considering time series, however, the serial correlation between observations introduces complications, and few 'nice' results exist. The reader might care to recall the emphasis placed on independent errors in introductory (and advanced) texts.

The study of time series estimation frequently becomes bogged down in the mire of different computational routines. We would like to draw these together by pointing out their underlying commonality. Our philosophy is that in most cases all of these apparently different methodologies will produce very similar results, and that in practice in this non-ideal world a student or professional has only a limited range of software available, and will have no or very little choice of estimation routine anyway. Standard statistical inference leads us to two possible approaches.

(i) Least squares
As all our models in section 3.2 are of the form

$$X_t = M(t, \theta) + \varepsilon_t$$

where $M(t, \theta)$ is a known function of time t and θ a vector of unknown parameters, it is quite possible to calculate least squares estimates in an analogous way to fitting a regression model by minimizing the sum of squares:

$$\sum_{t=1}^{N} (X_t - M(t, \theta))^2.$$

However, bear in mind that unlike the linear regression function $M(t, \theta)$ need not necessarily be a 'nice' function of t—it may depend on other values of the time series as it does for model A, or may involve another random series as in model B. Also, if the model is not linear in the unknown parameters an analytic solution for θ may not exist, in which case a numerical optimization algorithm must be used to find the value of θ at which the minimum occurs.

To calculate the least squares estimators of model A we need to minimize

$$\sum_{t=1}^{N} (X_t - \phi_1 X_{t-1} - \phi_2 X_{t-2})^2 \qquad (3.3)$$

with respect to ϕ_1 and ϕ_2. We have already commented on the similarity of (3.2) to the multiple linear regression model. In the multiple linear regression case the derivatives of the corresponding expression to (3.3) can be equated to zero to obtain the normal equations. The solutions to these equations give analytic estimators of the regression parameters. If we knew all the values of $\{X_{t-1}\}$ and $\{X_{t-2}\}$ a similar procedure would be equally valid here, but we don't know these for $t = 1$ or $t = 2$. This can be surmounted by assuming that X_1 and X_2 are fixed, and excluding the first two terms from the sum of squares in (3.3). That is, we minimize

$$\sum_{t=3}^{N} (X_t - \phi_1 X_{t-1} - \phi_2 X_{t-2})^2 \qquad (3.4)$$

with respect to ϕ_1 and ϕ_2. This is equivalent to setting the first two 'errors' to zero.

The accompanying estimate of σ^2, the variance of ε_t, we shall take as the minimum value of (3.4) divided by the number of squared errors included in the sum less the number of parameters estimated, that is $(N-2) - 2 = N - 4$ degrees of freedom in this case.

It should be emphasized that as the explanatory variables here are not independent of X_t, such least squares estimators do not necessarily have the same optimal properties of least squares in regression, although Mann & Wald (1943) have shown that the standard results from regression are still asymptotically valid.

Least squares estimates can be obtained analytically for model C by observing that

$$\beta \cos(2\pi ft + \phi) = \beta_1 \cos(2\pi ft) + \beta_2 \sin(2\pi ft)$$

where

$$\beta = \sqrt{\beta_1^2 + \beta_2^2}, \quad \phi = \tan^{-1}\left(-\frac{\beta_1}{\beta_2}\right) \quad \beta_1 = \beta \cos\phi \quad \text{and} \quad \beta_2 = -\beta \sin\phi.$$

This enables our model to be rewritten to eliminate the 'phase' ϕ so that we now need to minimize

$$\sum_{t=1}^{N} (X_t - \beta_1 \cos(2\pi ft) - \beta_2 \sin(2\pi ft))^2$$

with respect to β_1, β_2. This again has the same format as the sum of squares in the linear regression model, but now the explanatory variables are $\cos(2\pi ft)$ and $\sin(2\pi ft)$ (which incidentally have nice orthogonality properties). As the explanatory variables are independent of X_t the usual properties of linear least squares estimators will hold and the least squares estimates of β_1 and β_2 can be calculated in the usual way (see Chapter 1, section 1.2).

(ii) Maximum likelihood estimation

The most common principle underlying an estimation procedure is maximum likelihood. Maximum likelihood estimators are attractive because under general conditions they are asymptotically unbiased and have minimum variance.

As with least squares we start with the non–time series case. Suppose that we have a sample of independent observations X_t, $t = 1, ..., N$ each with p.d.f. $f(X_t)$. Then the joint density function is

$$f(X_1, X_2, ..., X_N) = \prod_{t=1}^{N} f(X_t). \tag{3.5}$$

The likelihood function is the joint probability (3.5), but is regarded as a function of the parameter vector θ, and as such is written

$$L(\theta) = \prod_{t=1}^{N} f(X_t; \theta).$$

The maximum likelihood estimates (MLEs) are naturally found by maximizing $L(\theta)$ with respect to θ.

The problem with time series is that the observations are *not* independent, so that (3.5) is *not* applicable. If, however, we denote all observations up to and including X_t by $\mathbf{X}_t$ we can write

$$f(X_1, X_2, ..., X_N) = f(X_N | \mathbf{X}_t) \; f(X_1, X_2, ..., X_{N-1})$$

$$= f(X_N | \mathbf{X}_{N-1}) \, f(X_{N-1} | \mathbf{X}_{N-2}) \, f(X_1, X_2, ..., X_{N-2}),$$

and so on until

$$f(X_1, X_2, \ldots, X_N) = \prod_{t=1}^{N} f(X_t | \mathbf{X}_{t-1}),$$

where $f(X_t|\mathbf{X}_{t-1})$ is the conditional distribution of X_t given all observations prior to t. So the likelihood $L(\theta)$ can be written as the product of these conditional distributions. If our model enables us to write down these conditional distributions, then we are in business! Bear in mind that (unlike least squares) this will require exact knowledge of the distribution of the random terms in the model. In Chapter 4 we will examine an algorithm (the Kalman filter) which produces such conditional distributions for a general class of time series models.

We will use model A to illustrate this *decomposition* of the likelihood function. To obtain the conditional distributions for model A we will need to make some additional assumptions about the exact probability distribution of the $\{\varepsilon_t\}$ series. The usual assumption is that the uncorrelated error terms ε_t are also normally distributed. The mean of the conditional distribution $f(X_t|X_1, X_2, X_3, \ldots, X_{t-1})$ is $\phi_1 X_{t-1} + \phi_2 X_{t-2}$, and the variance of the conditional distribution is $E\{[X_t - (\phi_1 X_{t-1} + \phi_2 X_{t-2})]^2\} = E\{\varepsilon_t^2\} = \sigma^2$. It follows from the normality assumption of the ε_t's that the conditional distribution of $X_t|X_1, X_2, X_3, \ldots, X_{t-1}$ is also normal, and therefore

$$f(X_t|X_1, X_2, X_3, \ldots, X_{t-1}) = \frac{1}{\sqrt{(2\pi)}\sigma} \exp\left[\frac{-(X_t - \phi_1 X_{t-1} - \phi_2 X_{t-2})^2}{2\sigma^2}\right].$$

Problems arise for $t=1$ and $t=2$ because $f(X_1)$ and $f(X_2|X_1)$ are not known. To circumvent this, we assume that the first two observations X_1, X_2 are fixed and define the *conditional likelihood* as

$$L(\theta) = \prod_{t=3}^{N} f(X_t|X_1, X_2, \ldots, X_{t-1}).$$

The exact likelihood can be obtained by multiplying $L(\theta)$ by the joint probability density of X_1 and X_2, but if N is large it has been shown that this has only a small effect.

The conditional log-likelihood is therefore

$$\log L(\phi_1, \phi_2) = -\frac{(N-2)}{2} \log(2\pi\sigma^2) - \frac{1}{2\sigma^2} \sum_{t=3}^{N} (X_t - \phi_1 X_{t-1} - \phi_2 X_{t-2})^2.$$

If σ^2 is known, maximizing the conditional likelihood is equivalent to minimizing,

$$\sum_{t=3}^{N} (X_t - \phi_1 X_{t-1} - \phi_2 X_{t-2})^2,$$

the sum of squares (3.4) which was minimized to obtain the least squares estimators. This means that for model A the conditional MLEs are the same as the least squares estimators. We stress that this is not always the case, although least squares estimates usually give good approximations to maximum likelihood.

Returning to maximum likelihood estimates in general, if σ^2 is unknown we can obviously estimate it by using the least squares results. Alternatively, it is easily shown that the conditional maximum likelihood estimator of σ^2 is the minimum sum of squares from (3.4) divided by the number of terms included in the sum.

As is well known, under certain regularity conditions MLEs are asymptotically multivariate normally distributed with covariance matrix equal to the inverse of the asymptotic information or Hessian matrix,

$$\mathbf{H} = \frac{\partial^2 \log L(\boldsymbol{\theta})}{\partial \boldsymbol{\theta} \, \partial \boldsymbol{\theta}^{\mathrm{T}}}.$$

The i, jth element of this matrix $\mathbf{H}$ is the derivative of the log-likelihood obtained when differentiated first with respect to θ_i and then again with respect to θ_j. For models fitted to independent data, analytic second derivatives can often be found, but the time series case is more complex, and usually the derivatives have to be evaluated numerically. The diagonal elements of the inverse Hessian will give approximations to the variance of the parameter estimates and the square roots of these give standard errors for each parameter. These are traditionally shown in brackets after or below each parameter estimate.

As in linear regression, for large N, under the null hypothesis that a parameter is zero, the ratio of the parameter estimate divided by its standard error should be approximately distributed as a standard normal variable. A ratio greater than 1.96 in absolute value therefore indicates a significant parameter (at the 95% level), that is one which *should* be included in the model, *given that all the other parameters remain the same*. One way of automatically selecting a model is to carry out a 'backwards elimination' procedure. To do this we fit a large model and eliminate any superfluous parameters one by one until all the parameters are significant. At each step, the parameter corresponding to the smallest absolute non-significant ratio is zeroized and the model refitted. We have adopted backwards elimination as a model fitting procedure in this book, although other methods analogous to forward or stepwise regression can also be used.

We illustrate the results of model fitting by considering a time series of the number of reported purse snatchings in a particular area of Chicago on days 28 days apart. It has been used extensively by Harvey (see Harvey 1989, page 89). A plot of the data is shown in Fig. 3.4.

For reasons to be discussed in section 3.6, both models A and B may be appropriate for the purse data. Details of how these models are estimated appear in later chapters, but for now we quote the results.

Before fitting model A, the AR(2) model, we will subtract the estimated mean of this series, (13.9155) from each observation to give the series $\{X_t\}$. The reason for this will become apparent when we consider ARMA models in Chapter 5. The maximum likelihood estimates of the parameters are $\phi_1 = 0.307841$ (standard error 0.078087) and $\phi_2 = 0.400178$ (0.78739), and $\sigma^2 = 36.115343$, so the fitted model is

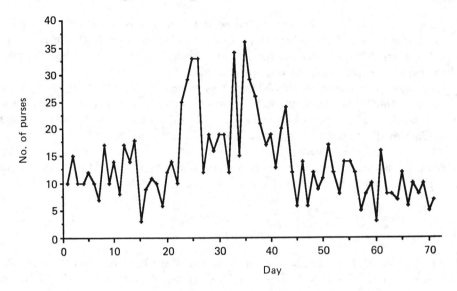

Fig. 3.4. Purse snatching in Chicago.

$$X_t = 0.0307841 X_{t-1} + 0.400178 X_{t-2} + \varepsilon_t$$

where $\text{var}(\varepsilon_t) = 36.115343$. All the parameters are clearly significantly different from zero. The maximum log-likelihood for this model is –221.6485.

Alternatively, if model B, the random walk plus noise model, is fitted to the purse series the parameter estimates are $\sigma_\varepsilon^2 = 24.783588$ (standard error 4.215) and $\sigma_\eta^2 = 5.148778$ (standard error 2.321), and the maximum log-likelihood is –227.7604.

In terms of likelihood there is little to choose between the models. More detailed study of the fits of the models to the data is required. Such examinations are discussed in later chapters.

We will use these parameter estimates and models to illustrate forecasting in the next section.

3.4 FORECASTING

Often the motivation for modelling a time series is to make forecasts. For forecasting purposes we will assume that the parameters of the fitted model are known *exactly*, although of course in practice only estimates will be available.

While it may be possible to incorporate knowledge of other time series variables into our model, and so into our forecasts, for simplicity we will assume that the only data available are past values of the series itself. To be explicit we assume that at time t we have knowledge of $X_1, X_2, \ldots, X_t$ and we wish to make forecasts of $X_{t+1}, X_{t+2}, X_{t+3}$, and so on. Methods based on such models are often called autoprojective, and can be very good. The forecast of X_{t+k} made with knowledge of the series up to and including time t is called the *k step ahead* forecast at time *t*, and we will write this as $X_{t+k|t}$. We will refer to *t* as the *origin* and *k* the *lead time* of such a forecast.

As forecasters our problem can be stated as follows. Given a model and an observed time series, how should $X_{t+k|t}$ be calculated? We would like $X_{t+k|t}$ to be a 'good' forecast in some sense—but what do we mean by 'good'? Obviously a 'good' forecast must be 'close to' the actual value in some sense, and it will be useful to consider the *k step ahead forecast error* or *prediction error* $X_{t+k} - X_{t+k|t}$. A sensible criterion would be to choose $X_{t+k|t}$ to minimize the mean square error (MSE) of this prediction error; that is,

$$\text{MSE} = E\left(X_{t+k} - X_{t+k|t}\right)^2. \tag{3.6}$$

The whole situation is analogous to parameter estimation, the difference here being that we are 'estimating' (predicting) the value of a random variable X_{t+k}, whereas for parameter estimation we are estimating a fixed parameter.

In section 2.6 we restricted ourselves to forecasts which were linear functions of the known past values of the series, and established that the linear forecasts with minimum mean square error were those with coefficients ψ_j from the general linear representation (2.5) (see (2.11) and (2.12)). This also enabled us to calculate an expression for the mean square error of such forecasts (2.13). This is all very well and is useful theoretically, but (i) in practice we do not always know the linear representation of the model and (ii) this gives only the minimum mean square *linear* predictors. We would like to be able to calculate the predictor which minimizes the mean square error (3.6).

We can expand (3.6) to give

$$\text{MSE} = E\left(X_{t+k}^2\right) - 2E\left(X_{t+k|t} \cdot X_{t+k}\right) + E\left(X_{t+k|t}\right)^2.$$

Remember, however, that at time *t*, $X_{t+k|t}$ is a known function of the data up to and including time *t*, so it is *not* a random variable. The MSE therefore becomes

$$E\left(X_{t+k}^2\right) - 2X_{t+k|t}E(X_{t+k}) + X_{t+k|t}^2,$$

which is a quadratic in $X_{t+k|t}$ and so can be minimized by differentiating with respect to $X_{t+k|t}$ and setting the derivative to 0. This gives $-2E(X_{t+k}) + 2X_{t+k|t} = 0$ so that $X_{t+k|t} = E(X_{t+k})$ minimizes the MSE. We conclude that the minimum mean square error forecast of X_{t+k} is just the conditional expectation of X_{t+k} given values of the series up to and including time *t*, that is, $X_1, X_2,..., X_t$. A byproduct of this is that our notation for the prediction $X_{t+k|t}$ also denotes the *conditional expectation* of X_{t+k} at time *t*.

The prediction error of the minimum MSE forecast is $X_{t+k} - X_{t+k|t}$ where $X_{t+k|t}$ has a *fixed* value at time *t* but X_{t+k} is a random variable. The prediction error is therefore also a random variable as we must expect. It is easy to see that at time *t* the prediction error has zero mean and variance $\{E(X_{t+k} - X_{t+k|t})^2\}$, which is the same as the MSE of our forecast.[†] For this reason the variance/MSE is often referred to as the *prediction error*

---

† Remember, we are assuming that our model and its parameters are known.

variance (PEV). Note that as it is the conditional expectation $X_{t+k|t}$ will also be the minimum variance unbiased forecast of X_{t+k} at time t.

We illustrate the conditional expectations forecast described above, using our models A, B, and C. We will consider the PEVs of our example models. We will start by taking model A, the AR(2) model (3.2), and as stated earlier we emphasize that for forecasting we must assume that this model is correct. Given

$$X_{t+1} = \phi_1 X_t + \phi_2 X_{t-1} + \varepsilon_{t+1}.$$

At time t, X_t and X_{t-1} are known, and it follows that

$$X_{t+1|t} = \phi_1 X_t + \phi_2 X_{t-1} + \varepsilon_{t+1|t}$$

where $\varepsilon_{t+1|t}$ denotes the conditional expectation of ε_{t+1} at time t, which is zero since the ε_t's are independent. The one step forecast of an AR(2) model is therefore $X_{t+1|t} = \phi_1 X_t + \phi_2 X_{t-1}$. The corresponding one step ahead prediction error is

$$X_{t+1} - X_{t+1|t} = \phi_1 X_t + \phi_2 X_{t-1} + \varepsilon_{t+1} - (\phi_1 X_t + \phi_2 X_{t-1}) = \varepsilon_{t+1},$$

so that the prediction error variance is σ^2. If we consider lead time $k = 2$ in the same way we can write

$$X_{t+2} = \phi_1 X_{t+1} + \phi_2 X_t + \varepsilon_{t+2},$$

and taking conditional expectations as before we have

$$X_{t+2|t} = \phi_1 X_{t+1|t} + \phi_2 X_t \tag{3.7}$$

as $\varepsilon_{t+2|t} = 0$. An expression for the forecast with lead time 1, $X_{t+1|t}$ has already been calculated, so $X_{t+2|t}$ can be evaluated by using this in the above expression.

We illustrate these ideas, using the model fitted to the purse data, to forecast the snatchings after the end of the sample period. As we are forecasting from the end of the fitted series and not incorporating any later data items, such forecasts are often called *extrapolative* forecasts. (We give our calculations to six decimal places so that the reader can check our results.)

We can say that $X_{72|71} = 0.307841 X_{71} + 0.400178 X_{70}$ and as the 70th and 71st observations of the original series are 5 and 7 respectively,

$$X_{72|71} = 0.307841 \, (7 - 13.9155) + 0.400178 \, (5 - 13.9155) = -5.696661.$$

Adding back the mean the predicted number of purse snatchings in period 72 is 8.218839. Similarly $X_{73|71} = 0.307841. \, (-5.696661) + 0.400178. \, (-6.9155) = -4.521097$, and the predicted number of purse snatchings for time 73 is 9.394403.

The k step ahead forecast, $k = 3, 4, 5$ etc., can be calculated from

$$X_{t+k|t} = \phi_1 X_{t+k-1|t} + \phi_2 X_{t+k-2|t} \tag{3.8}$$

in a similar manner. Notice that this forecast function takes the same form as the original AR(2) model equation. The reader may like to check that the predicted number of purses snatched for periods 74, 75, 76 are 10.244043, 10.976031, and 11.541375 respectively.

We could, of course, obtain an expression for $X_{t+2|t}$ in terms of $X_t, X_{t-1}, X_{t-2}, \ldots$, etc., by substituting for $X_{t+1|t}$ in (3.7) to give

$$X_{t+2|t} = \phi_1(\phi_1 X_t + \phi_2 X_{t-1}) + \phi_2 X_t = (\phi_1^2 + \phi_2)X_t + \phi_1\phi_2 X_{t-1}.$$

Similar expressions for $X_{t+3|t}$, $X_{t+4|t}$, and so on can be determined by substituting previously calculated forecasts in (3.8) for $k = 3, 4, 5$, etc. It will be useful when we consider the prediction error variances to observe now that these forecasts are all linear functions of known X_t's so that our minimum MSE predictors are also linear predictors.

Whilst we know that the conditional expectation minimizes the mean square forecast error, we often need to make some sort of probabilistic statement about the reliability of our forecasts. We have already seen that the one step prediction error variance of our autoregressive model is just σ^2. The PEVs for lead times greater than one are more difficult to obtain. However, we have already noted that because of the nature of the model our conditional expectation (minimum mean square error) predictor happens to be linear. There exists an equivalent general linear representation of the model (2.5), and so, as the model is stationary, our predictor is the same as the minimum mean square linear predictor (2.12) of section 2.6. An expression (2.13) for the prediction error variance of the minimum mean square error linear predictor is available in terms of the coefficients of the infinite linear representation.

In Chapter 5 we will show that the general linear representation of an AR(2) model (and in fact all AR models) is

$$X_t = \varepsilon_t + \psi_1\varepsilon_{t-1} + \psi_2\varepsilon_{t-2} + \psi_3\varepsilon_{t-3} \ldots \tag{3.9}$$

where the ε_t's are the random terms from the AR model equation and the ψ's are constant coefficients. In particular, the general linear representation of the AR(2) model fitted to the purse data is $X_t = \varepsilon_t - 0.307841\varepsilon_{t-1} + 0.4494944\varepsilon_{t-2} + \ldots$.

From (2.13) the k step ahead prediction error variance is therefore

$$\sigma^2(\psi_{k-1}^2 + \psi_{k-2}^2 + \ldots + \psi_1^2 + 1),$$

so that the one step PEV of our AR(2) model will be σ^2, the two step PEV will be

$$\sigma^2(\psi_1^2 + 1^2) = 36.115343(0.307841^2 + 1^2) = 39.537852,$$

and the three step

$$\sigma^2(\psi_2^2 + \psi_1^2 + 1^2) = 48.385012,$$

and so on. As might be expected these variances become larger as we forecast more steps ahead and the future becomes more uncertain. It is not hard to show that in the limit the PEV is just the variance of the series. Fig. 3.5 shows forecasts and 95% *prediction intervals* of $X_{t+k|t} \pm 1.96 \sqrt{\text{PEV}}$ of the purse data produced from this AR(2) model.

We now turn our attention to forecasting our other models. Forecasts of model C would clearly take the form

$$X_{t+k|t} = \beta\cos(2\pi f(t+k) + \phi) + \varepsilon_{t+k|t}.$$

and would merely be $\beta\cos(2\pi f(t+k) + \phi)$, a straightforward function of time. Again, assuming that the parameters are known exactly the prediction error is simply ε_{t+k}, so that the PEV is σ^2 for all lags. Even if estimation error were taken into account this

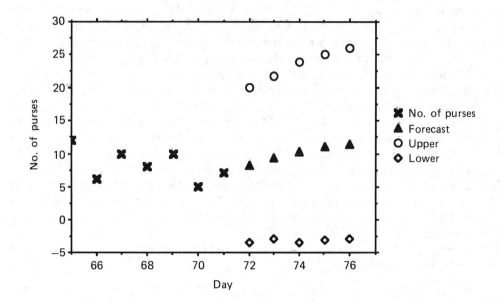

Fig. 3.5. Extrapolative forecasts and 95% prediction intervals for purse data produced by fitting
an AR(2) model.

model can be treated as a regression model, so there is no problem in estimating prediction error variances.

For model B as $X_{t+k} = \mu_t + \eta_{t+1} + \eta_{t+2} + \dots + \eta_{t+k} + \varepsilon_{t+k}$ the conditional expectation of X_{t+k} is just the current μ_t and the k step ahead error variance is $E(X_{t+k} - X_{t+k|t})^2 = k\sigma_\eta^2 + \sigma_\varepsilon^2$. Recall the $\{\eta_t\}$'s and the $\{\varepsilon_t\}$'s are independent. Note that this PEV is *not* σ_ε^2. This assumes that μ_t is known, whilst in practice we will require some method of estimating μ_t, and any error in such estimation must be taken into account. As with other complications we leave this point until Chapters 4 and 6. For interest's sake we show extrapolative forecasts and 95% prediction limits of $X_{t+k|t} \pm 1.96 \sqrt{\text{PEV}}$ for the purse data, using this model in Fig. 3.6. Note that they differ from the forecasts and predictions calculated by fitting the AR(2) model (Fig. 3.5). It is therefore vital to check the suitability of a model before forecasting. We consider this in the next section.

In all the above we have assumed that the parameters of our model are known exactly. In practice, of course, this is not true, and the model parameters will have been estimated. This means that some of the error made in forecasting will be due to estimation error rather than just to the random error in the model. We hope in all we do, however, that the estimation error is small, and it is possible to show that estimation error in the parameters does not affect prediction markedly, unless the sample size is small.

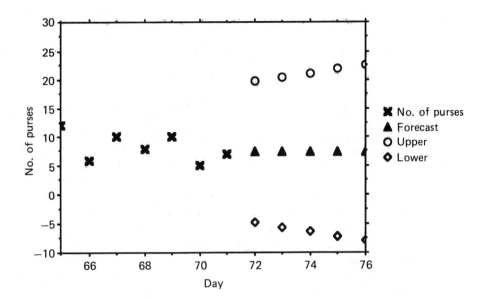

Fig. 3.6. Extrapolative forecasts of the purse data using model B (random walk plus noise).

3.5 MODEL EVALUATION

(i) Diagnostic checking

As with any statistical model, once the model is fitted we need to ascertain whether or not it is appropriate for the data. If we were fitting a linear regression model, we would expect the error terms ε_t to be independent and identically distributed if they were available. In practice of course, we can only calculate the *residuals*—the actual values less the fitted values of the data. These can then be tested to see whether or not they conform to the assumptions the model makes about ε_t.

Diagnostic checking for time series proceeds in a similar way. The residuals are usually the one step prediction errors $V_t = X_t - X_{t|t-1}$, as they have properties which can be tested. For some models (A and C here, for example) with known parameters the one step prediction error is the same as the random noise stream (ε_t here) so that the PEV is simply σ^2.

As when calculating forecasts we must be aware that the V_t's will be the theoretical forecast errors only if the parameters of the model and sometimes some past values of the data are known exactly. For large samples this is usually a reasonably safe assumption.

Many tests of residuals have been suggested, but are usually specific to a particular type of model. In general they test for

(a)   serial correlation of the residuals

(b)   normality or a common distribution of the residuals.

Once these prediction errors or residuals have been calculated it is wise to start by plotting them to spot any deviations from the model assumptions. For instance, something is amiss if the residuals get larger over time or if they exhibit any sort of cyclic behaviour. Fig. 3.7 shows a time series plot of the standardized residuals (residuals divided by their standard errors) of the AR(2) model fitted to the purse data—there are no apparent cycles or trends. Fig. 3.8 gives a histogram of these residuals—remember that if the model is appropriate we expect the standardized residuals to approximately have a standard normal distribution. The sample mean of the residuals is −0.016 and the variance 0.993, and the histogram looks reasonable, although it might be considered a little skew and one residual exceeds 3. Fig. 3.9 shows the sample autocorrelations of the residuals. The brackets show 95% confidence limits calculated using an approximate variance due to Bartlett, which is valid if the theoretical autocorrelations at lag k and above are zero, and we describe Bartlett's result in more detail in section 3.6.

As the sample autocorrelations of a white noise process have approximate variance of $1/N$ (see (2.19)) the sample autocorrelations of uncorrelated residuals should be less than about $2/\sqrt{N}$ in absolute value. All our autocorrelations satisfy this requirement so no serial correlation is indicated.

In the next chapter we will see that for the general state space model the prediction errors or residuals are produced as a 'byproduct' of the maximum likelihood estimation algorithm as are their estimated standard deviations, and that theoretically the residuals have zero mean. This means that the standardized residuals can readily be calculated. We will assume in this chapter that we have access to these standardized residuals for any model we fit.

We leave it to the reader to examine the residuals from model B fitted to the purse data.

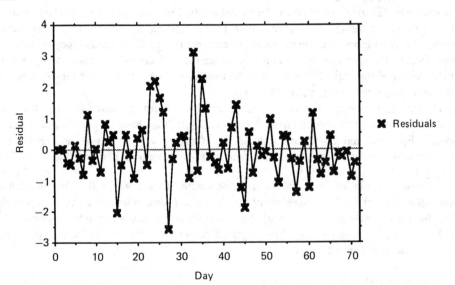

Fig. 3.7. Time series plot of the one step prediction errors from the AR(2) model fitted to the
purse data.

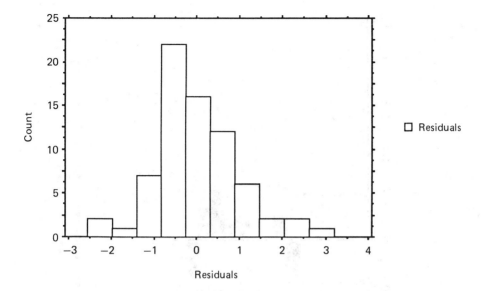

Fig. 3.8. Histogram of the residuals from AR(2) model fitted to the purse data.

A general test for serial correlation of the residuals is given by the *portmanteau test* of Box & Pierce which was later modified by Ljung & Box. The first $k(> 10)$ autocorrelations of the residuals can be tested together using the Q statistic

$$Q(k) = N^*(N^* + 2) \sum_{i=1}^{k} (N^* - i)^{-1} r_v^2(i)$$

where the $r_v^2(i)$ are the autocorrelations of the residuals and N^* is the number of observations used to calculated these. Under the null hypothesis that the residuals are independent normal, $Q(k)$ has approximately a χ^2 distribution with degrees of freedom $k + 1$ minus the number of estimated parameters in the model. For instance the $Q(12)$ statistic for the AR(2) model (model A) fitted to the purse data is calculated from the autocorrelations shown in Fig. 3.9 and is 7.86. As the model fits three parameters (ϕ_1, ϕ_2, σ^2) if the residuals are uncorrelated, we would expect Q to have a χ^2 distribution with 10 degrees of freedom. The Q statistic therefore gives us no evidence to reject the null hypothesis. Similarly $Q(20) = 16.92$ (18 degrees of freedom) also supports the hypothesis of uncorrelated residuals. Out of interest, when we fitted the random walk plus noise model (model B) we obtained $Q(12) = 13.25$ (11 degrees of freedom) and $Q(20) = 20.41$ (19 degrees of freedom), which also gave no cause for concern. The reader should not rely entirely on the portmanteau test, as it may not be a powerful test in some circumstances.

(ii) Post-sample comparison
The one step forecast errors gives us a measure of goodness of fit inside the sample period, but they don't tell us how well our model will hold up outside this period—for forecasting, for instance. To judge this it is sensible to hold back some of the most recent

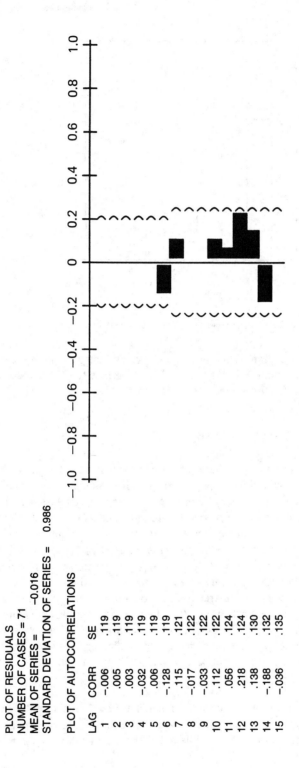

PLOT OF RESIDUALS
NUMBER OF CASES = 71
MEAN OF SERIES = -0.016
STANDARD DEVIATION OF SERIES = 0.986

PLOT OF AUTOCORRELATIONS

LAG	CORR	SE
1	-.006	.119
2	.005	.119
3	.003	.119
4	-.032	.119
5	.006	.119
6	-.128	.119
7	.115	.121
8	-.017	.122
9	-.033	.122
10	.112	.122
11	.056	.124
12	.218	.124
13	.138	.130
14	-.188	.132
15	-.036	.135

Fig. 3.9. Autocorrelations of the residuals from fitting AR(2) model to the purse data.

observations in a time series for *post-sample* comparison. Data from this *post-sample* period are *not* used to fit the model. The model can then be used to forecast into the post-sample period, and the 'actuals' will then be available to judge how well the model does. The obvious disadvantage of this is that fewer data are available for model fitting, so that the parameter estimates will be less reliable.

Some criteria must be used to gauge how well the model is doing. Suppose that the model is fitted to N observations, and that m further observations have previously been retained for post-sample comparison. The model can then be used to calculate the forecast $X_{N+1|N}$. This can be compared with X_{N+1} (known, but held back from model fitting) to give a one step ahead prediction error. The same fitted model can then be used, along with the actual X_{N+1}, to calculate the one step ahead forecast of X_{N+2} at time $N+1$, that is, to calculate $X_{N+2|N+1}$. This, in turn, can be compared with the actual X_{N+2} and an error evaluated. Continue similarly until all the post-sample data are used up, that is to $X_{N+m|N+m-1}$.

We will illustrate this approach by using the purse data and the AR(2) model once again. To correspond to other authors who have used these data we fitted the model to all 71 observations. For argument's sake, however, we will suppose that an additional 5 observations are available as a post-sample period and that these are 8, 11, 10, 9, and 6 for periods 72 to 76 respectively.

We already know that the formula for one step prediction with this model is $X_{t+1|t} = \phi_1 X_t + \phi_2 X_{t-1}$ where the X_t's are observations with their mean already subtracted. We have already calculated $X_{72|71}$. $X_{73|72} = 0.307841 X_{72} + 0.400178 X_{71} = 0.307841(8 - 13.9155) + 0.400178(7 - 13.9155) = -4.588464$, so at time 72 the predicted number of purse snatchings at time 73 is 9.327036. The one step prediction error variance is σ^2, which was previously estimated to be $\hat{\sigma}^2 = 36.115343$. The reader can check that the remaining one step forecasts are 10.650737, 11.543429, and 10.835410 respectively. We retain six decimal places, as these figures are used in later calculations. Fig. 3.10 shows the one step forecasts and 95% limits for this post-sample period.

The resultant one step forecast errors can then be squared and averaged to give a post-sample prediction mean square error. If the model is correctly specified we would expect this to be a reliable estimate of the model's prediction error variance. Another estimate of the PEV, say $\hat{\text{PEV}}$, will have been obtained from the estimation procedure, and usually is a function of N^* residuals from the model fit. If the model is correctly specified it can be shown that the ratio of these estimated variances

$$\xi(m) = \frac{\sum\limits_{N+1}^{N+m} V_t^2}{m\hat{\text{PEV}}} \tag{3.10}$$

will approximately have an F distribution with m and N^* degrees of freedom respectively. Even if this statistic is not significant, however, the model need not be good—as the prediction error variance within the sample period may have been poor.

For the purse data AR(2) model the sum of squares of the five post-sample prediction errors is 33.120384, so 6.624077 gives an estimate of the prediction error variance. The estimation procedure gave 36.115343. We have not described our estimation methods

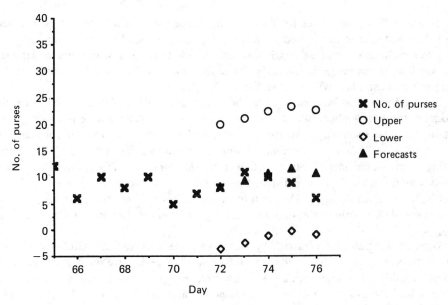

Fig. 3.10. One step post-sample predictions for the purse data, assuming model A.

yet, but this was calculated by omitting the first two residuals. The ratio is therefore 0.183414, which is clearly not significant compared to $F_{5,69}$, so gives nothing to suggest that the model is inadequate for forecasting.

Another way of evaluating the forecasting power of a model is to use the extrapolative forecasts $X_{N+1|N}, X_{N+2|N}, X_{N+3|N}, \ldots, X_{N+m|N}$. No formal test of the validity of the model is available, as the errors are not independent of each other, although the sum of squares of the errors of such forecasts can be used to compare the predictive ability of different models. The sum of squares of the extrapolative forecasts of the purse data in the post-sample period are 37.2969 for the AR(2) model and 24.7860 for the random walk plus noise model. On this criterion the random walk model is clearly favoured.

(iii) Comparing models

As more than one model can be fitted quite sensibly to a set of data, we require some means of deciding between two or more models. It is obviously desirable that the maximum likelihood is high. Care must be taken as in regression, for if we fit both a full model and the same model with some parameters set to zero (a nested model), the maximum likelihood of the nested model must be the same as or smaller than that of the full model. Before maximum likelihoods can be compared, some sort of penalty must therefore be made for the number of estimated parameters in a model. Akaike's information criterion (AIC) has been widely adopted and justified. It is usually calculated as AIC = −2 (log-likelihood) + 2 (number of parameters in model). The model with the smallest AIC is selected. This procedure amounts to subtracting a penalty of one from the maximum likelihood for each parameter estimated and then comparing. If we look at the two models fitted to the purse data, model A has 3 parameters and model B has 2, so their

respective AICs are 449.2971 and 459.5207, and on the basis of this criterion   model
A(AR(2)) is preferred.

Other comparison criteria can be used, and various justifications have been made for
each. We will not concern ourselves with these in this book.

3.6 MODEL SELECTION

So far we have pulled our example models out of a hat in an *ad hoc* fashion and have
then estimated them. We have not considered how we must choose a model in the first
place.

The models considered so far in this chapter already contain a fixed number of parameters. In fact, each of these is a special (simple) case of a broader class of model. For
instance, model A is a member of the broad class of Autoregressive–Moving–Average
(ARMA) models

$$X_t = \phi_1 X_{t-1} + \phi_2 X_{t-2} + \dots + \phi_p X_{t-p} + \varepsilon_t + \theta_1 \varepsilon_{t-1} + \dots + \theta_q \varepsilon_{t-q} \tag{3.11}$$

where the ε_t's are a white noise as usual, and the ϕ_i's and θ_j's are called the *autoregressive* and *moving average* parameters respectively. The values p and q are the 'orders' of
the model and give the number of parameters of each type. Thus, in model A, $p = 2$ and
$q = 0$, as only the terms in the past X_t's appear. It is therefore called an autoregressive
model of order 2 and written AR(2). Once p and q are *known* an estimation algorithm will
give parameter estimates for the ϕ_i's and θ_j's, and for σ_ε^2 the variance of ε_t. If an ARMA
model is appropriate the analyst must therefore supply p and q. She could try a range of
possible values in turn (time consuming and often impracticable) or hope to gain some
insight from the data. Alternatively, she could fit a model with large orders p, q and
eliminate non-significant parameters one by one using backward elimination.

Similarly model B is a special case of the basic structural model considered in Chapter
6. It has two parameters σ_ε^2 and σ_η^2. More elaborate models of the same type are
available. For example, we could elaborate by also modelling a gradual change in η_t, that
is, say that $\eta_t = \eta_{t-1} + \zeta_t$ where $\{\zeta_t\}$ is a iid random noise stream with zero mean and
variance σ_ζ^2.

In this section we consider the following. Suppose that we are given a time series,
asked to model it with a view to forecasting, but given no further hints. Where should we
start?

The first thing to do is to plot the data against time. This, along with whatever
knowledge we have of the nature of the data, should suggest whether a seasonal component is appropriate or not, and whether a trend should be included in the model.

Take Figs 1.1 to 1.4 of Chapter 1. The UK index of industrial production in Fig. 1.1
shows a clear upward trend; the annual rainfall does not appear to show either an obvious
cycle or a trend; whereas the UK primary fuel consumption is clearly seasonal. Sales of
jeans in Fig. 1.4 might have a trend and might be cyclic if not seasonal.

From then on, the way forward is less clear. Depending on whether our series displays
trend or seasonal components or both we could use exponential smoothing or moving

average techniques to smooth/forecast series. We will explain the relationship of exponential smoothing to model building in the next section. However, we would prefer to model each component explicitly.

The choice of model type is partly influenced by experience and partly by the facilities available. We show in later chapters, however, that most key classes of model are part of the same basic framework (the general state space model), so we will not dwell on such decisions here. Each model type usually offers variations to cope with combinations of trend, seasonal, and irregular components as part of the whole methodology. Some model types incorporate a facility for a trend and/or seasonal component so that an all-in-one model can be fitted to the actual data, whereas others rely on deseasonalizing or detrending first and then fitting a stationary non-seasonal model to the deseasonalized data.

Assuming that we have selected   our class of model, e.g. ARMA or structural, a plot of the data will usually indicate the presence of a trend or a seasonal component, it will not (usually) indicate model orders. With the advent of fast computing it is now practical to try every possible set of orders for a model. However, it is less time consuming if some 'hints' are gathered from the series itself. Any model implies a particular joint distribution of the random variables $X_1, X_2, \ldots, X_N$ which will have certain properties. Some such properties were defined in Chapter 2—stationarity, autocorrelation, and so on. We saw also that some of these properties—for instance the autocorrelations—can be estimated from the data. Just as it would be madness to fit a stationary model to non-stationary data, the idea of model selection is to find a model whose properties broadly 'match' those of the data.

To gain some insight into the selection process we look at some properties of our three elementary models A, B, C.

As stated above, model A is an AR(2) model. In Chapter 5 we obtain conditions on the ϕ_i's for an autoregressive model to be stationary. The autocorrelations of the model can be calculated as follows. Multiply (3.2) by X_{t-k} and take expectations to give

$$\gamma(k) = E(X_t X_{t-k}) = \phi_1 E(X_{t-1} X_{t-k}) + \phi_2 E(X_{t-2} X_{t-k}) + E(\varepsilon_t X_{t-k}).$$

From the general linear representation (3.9) and the assumption that the ε_t's are independent it is evident that the last term is 0 for $k > 0$, so

$$\gamma(k) = \phi_1 \gamma(k-1) + \phi_2 \gamma(k-2), \qquad k = 1, 2, \ldots$$

and so

$$\rho(k) = \phi_1 \rho(k-1) + \phi_2 \rho(k-2) \qquad \text{for } k > 0.$$

As $\rho(k) = \rho(-k)$ and $\rho(0) = 1$, the relation for $k = 1$ gives $\rho(1) = \phi_1 + \phi_2 \rho(1)$ and $\rho(1)$ can be expressed in terms of the parameters of the model

$$\rho(1) = \frac{\phi_1}{1 - \phi_2}.$$

By similar reasoning

$$\rho(2) = \phi_1\rho(1) + \phi_2\rho(0) = \frac{\phi_1^2}{1-\phi_2} + \phi_2,$$

and so on, while

$$\gamma(0) = \phi_1\gamma(1) + \phi_2\gamma(2) + \sigma^2.$$

An AR(2) process may exhibit a 'fading sinusoidal' autocorrelation function as shown in Fig. 3.11. Notice that the autocorrelation function of the process tends to zero in absolute values as the lag k tends to infinity. This is true of a general stationary AR(p) process although the autocorrelation function may not decay sinusoidally. We will see the reason for the sinusoidal effect in later chapters. For instance if $\phi_2 = 0$ in the AR(2) model we have an AR(1) process. The autocorrelations of an AR(1) process are easily shown to be ϕ_1^k. Fig. 3.12 shows the autocorrelation function of the AR(1) model with $\phi_1 = 0.9$; the autocorrelations decay exponentially.

In model B,

$$\nabla X_t = X_t - X_{t-1} = \mu_t - \mu_{t-1} + \varepsilon_t - \varepsilon_{t-1} = \eta_t + \varepsilon_t - \varepsilon_{t-1} \quad \text{as} \quad \mu_t = \mu_{t-1} + \eta_t.$$

It is easy to show that the autocovariance of the differences at lag 1 is $-\sigma_\varepsilon^2$ and at other lags is zero.

Model C is seasonal, as the mean at time t is a periodic function of t.

Of course the sample autocorrelations are random variables and for model selection it will often be useful to test whether the true autocorrelations are zero beyond a certain lag. An approximate result due to Bartlett (1946) says that for large samples if the autocorrelations $\rho(m)$ are zero for all lags $m > k$ then

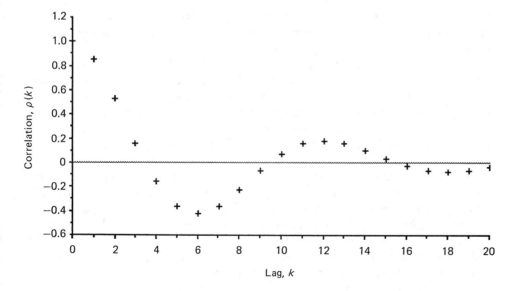

Fig. 3.11. Autocorrelation function of $X_t = 1.5X_{t-1} - 0.75X_{t-2} + \varepsilon_t$: AR(2) model.

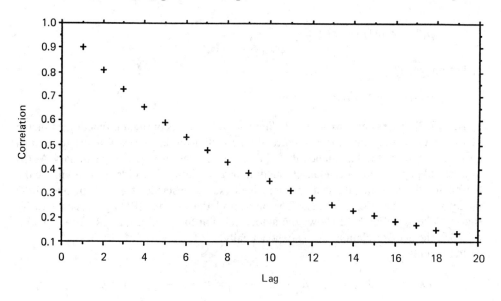

Fig. 3.12. Theoretical autocorrelation function of the AR(1) model $X_t = 0.9X_{t-1} + \varepsilon_t$.

$$\mathrm{var}\big(r(k)\big) = \frac{1}{N}\Big(1 + 2\rho(1)^2 + 2\rho(2)^2 + \ldots + \rho(k-1)^2\Big).$$

In practice the unknown autocorrelation $\rho(i)$ are approximated by the sample autocorrelations $r(i)$. Computer software often gives 95% confidence limits (assuming normality) using this variance approximation.

In section 3.3 we fitted both model A, AR(2), and B, random walk plus noise, to the purse data. Now let us look again at Fig. 3.4 and see how these models suggested themselves. There are 71 observations. As no seasonality is apparent from the data, model C will not be suitable. Some typical computer output showing the autocorrelations of the data and of the differenced data is shown in Figs 3.13 and 3.14. The brackets show limits of 1.96 standard errors about 0 for the autocorrelations as described above.

The autocorrelations of the differences are within two standard errors of zero at all but lag 1—where the autocorrelation is negative—so model B may be a reasonable model. They are not all positive or of alternating sign, so an AR(1) model is unlikely. The autocorrelation function may exhibit a fading sinusoidal pattern, so an AR(2) model (model A) might be appropriate, and in fact we give further evidence to support this in Chapter 5. Of course in practice we would hope to have a large range of models and model orders at our disposal, but from our limited choice of models A and B might be worth estimating. Both of them or only one may be suitable.

We have sought here to give only a general idea of model selection. The properties of each class of models are discussed more fully in the appropriate chapters.

PLOT OF NUMBER
NUMBER OF CASES = 71
MEAN OF SERIES = 13.915
STANDARD DEVIATION OF SERIES = 7.464

PLOT OF AUTOCORRELATIONS

LAG	CORR	SE
1	.493	.119
2	.534	.145
3	.363	.170
4	.294	.181
5	.261	.187
6	.163	.192
7	.243	.194
8	.183	.199
9	.179	.201
10	.243	.203
11	.204	.207
12	.227	.210
13	.147	.214
14	-.022	.215
15	-.023	.215

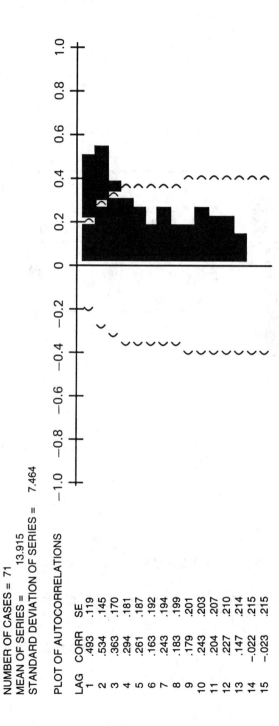

Fig. 3.13. Autocorrelation function of purse data.

PLOT OF NUMBER
NUMBER OF CASES = 70
MEAN OF SERIES = -0.043
STANDARD DEVIATION OF SERIES = 7.511

PLOT OF AUTOCORRELATIONS

LAG	CORR	SE
1	-.548	.120
2	.217	.151
3	-.106	.156
4	-0.30	.157
5	.055	.157
6	-.170	.157
7	.141	.160
8	-.062	.161
9	-.064	.162
10	.111	.162
11	-.075	.163
12	.112	.164
13	.089	.165
14	-.188	.165
15	.070	.168
16	-.030	.169
17	-.012	.169
18	.030	.169
19	.093	.169
20	-.177	.170

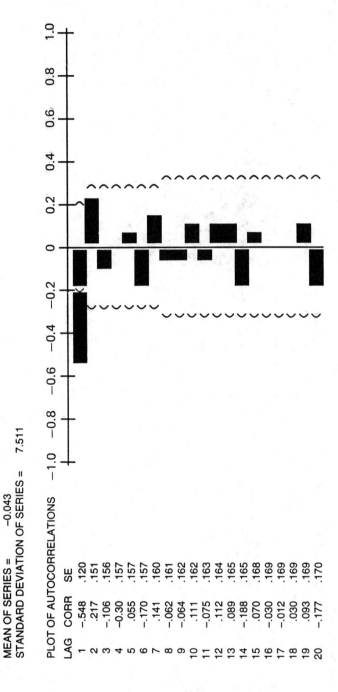

Fig. 3.14. Autocorrelations of diffferenced purse data.

3.7 IDENTIFICATION

To illustrate the idea of identification we will consider a new model $X_t = \varepsilon_t + 0.6\varepsilon_{t-1}$ where ε_t is a random white noise series with zero mean and variance σ^2 as before. It is easily shown that $\gamma(0) = 1.36\sigma^2$ and

$$\gamma(1) = E(X_t X_{t-1}) = E(\varepsilon_t + 0.6\varepsilon_{t-1})(\varepsilon_{t-1} + 0.6\varepsilon_{t-2}) = 0.6\sigma^2$$

since ε_t, ε_{t-1}, and ε_{t-2} are uncorrelated, and that

$$\gamma(2) = E(\varepsilon_t + 0.6\varepsilon_{t-1})(\varepsilon_{t-2} + 0.6\varepsilon_{t-3}) = 0.$$

In fact $\gamma(k) = 0$ for all $k > 1$. So the autovariances are zero apart from $\gamma(0)$, $\gamma(1)$.

Now consider the model $X_t = 0.6\varepsilon_t + \varepsilon_{t-1}$ with the same σ^2. This also has zero mean and autovariances $1.36\sigma^2, 0.6\sigma^2, 0, 0,\dots$. If the ε_t's are normally distributed the X_t's will also have a normal distribution and so the autocorrelation function and the mean will completely define the multivariate normal joint pdf of $f(X_1, X_2,\dots, X_N)$. This means that the models above will have the same joint pdf so that the likelihood of both models will be the same. We say the models are *likelihood equivalent*. More generally, the likelihood of the model $X_t = \theta_0\varepsilon_t + \theta_1\varepsilon_{t-1}$ will be the same as the likelihood of the model $X_t = \theta_1\varepsilon_t + \theta_0\varepsilon_{t-1}$ for any values of θ_1 and θ_2. So if $\theta_0 = \hat{\theta}_0$ and $\theta_1 = \hat{\theta}_1$ are MLEs of the model, $\theta_0 = \hat{\theta}_1$ and $\theta_1 = \hat{\theta}_0$ will also be MLEs, and more than one set of maximum likelihood estimates can be found. When this is the case we say that the model is 'not identified'.

If a model is not identified in this way, numerical maximization algorithms may have trouble converging or at best will have to work harder—even if only because more possible sets of parameter values need to be considered. This problem can usually be overcome by imposing one or more additional constraints on the parameters which ensure that only one of each set of likelihood equivalent models are considered. One such scheme here would be to stipulate that $\theta_0 > \theta_1$.

We will see later—when considering ARMA models—that there are other advantages in imposing such additional constraints.

For now it is sufficient to realize that a class of models need not be identified in this sense. Harvey uses a terminology (1989, p. 205) which distinguishes between a *model* which specifies the class of probability distribution for the process but does not define the parameter values and a *structure* which specifies particular parameter values within that distribution. A structure is then identifiable if no other structure has the same joint density function. A model is identifiable if *all* its possible structures are identifiable.

3.8 EXPONENTIAL SMOOTHING AND ALL THAT

You may have wondered about the role of exponential smoothing, deseasonalizing, and detrending discussed in Chapter 1 in modelling. These methods certainly assume a 'model' in the sense of T + S + I, and they do allow 'smoothed' forecasts to be made. However, without any further modelling detail, the distribution of the forecast error cannot be calculated.

Exponential smoothing and its like are employed on an 'if it works don't knock it' basis. The forecasts achieved make no claims of optimality, as there are no underlying assumptions other than that the series in some way has a memory. In later chapters, however, we will see that there are model structures for which the forecasts calculated using exponential smoothing are indeed optimal.

3.9 SIMULATION

A model structure completely 'explains' the random process which has produced a particular time series. We can turn this on its head, and use the model to *generate* or simulate a realization of the time series. All we need is the model and some means of producing one or more series of numbers which have the same properties as the series of random terms in the model.

Suppose that we wished to simulate a series from our model C. For any value of time (t) we can calculate the deterministic term $\beta(\cos(2\pi f t + \phi)$. To obtain X_t we require a number which is a realization of the random term ε_t. To do this we need to make some assumption about the distribution of ε_t. It is usual to assume normality.

We do not intend to go into details here about random number generators—the interested reader is referred to Knuth (1981) for details. Most computer operating systems provide an intrinsic (uniform) random number function (although some have been shown to be more 'random' than others—but that is another story). In the absence of one of these a simple routine is given in the Appendix.

A pair of independent normal variates z_1, z_2 (zero mean, unit variance) can be produced from a pair of uniform (0, 1) random variables r_1, r_2 by using what is known as the Box–Muller method.

$$z_1 = (-2 \log r_1)^{1/2} \cos(2\pi r_2)$$
$$z_2 = (-2 \log r_1)^{1/2} \sin(2\pi r_2).$$

These can be transformed into $N(\mu, \sigma^2)$ variates y_1, y_2 in the usual way, namely $y_1 = \mu + \sigma z_1$, $y_2 = \mu + \sigma z_2$. Usually $\mu = 0$ is required for random noise simulation.

To simulate models which involve past values of X_t as well as independent noise streams like ε_t care must be taken. For instance to generate an X_t from model A

$$X_t = \phi_1 X_{t-1} + \phi_2 X_{t-2} + \varepsilon_t,$$

we need to know X_{t-1} and X_{t-2}. This means that we cannot generate X_1 and X_2 but will have to set these *start-up* values arbitrarily to 'kick off' the simulation. This situation is analogous to having to make assumptions about X_1 and X_2 when calculating the least squares estimators in section 3.3. We will see in later chapters that if the model is stationary the effects of such start-up values wear off over time, that is, for the same $\{\varepsilon_t\}$ series the same X_t's will be generated for large t for any values of X_1 and X_2. If the model is non-stationary the current values of X_t are a function of X_1 and X_2 even for large t.

An analogous situation occurs if we want to simulate a mixed ARMA model, as this requires values for some past noise terms $\varepsilon_0, \varepsilon_{-1}, \varepsilon_{-2}...$, as well as for the first few

X_t's. We will see in Chapter 5 that restrictions can be placed on the parameters of an ARMA model which make future observations asymptotically (that is, for large t) independent of such start-up values. Further, these restrictions are the same as those required to calculate least squares or maximum likelihood estimates.

Similar problems arise when simulating model B. To generate X_t we need to generate values for the μ_t as well, and so we require starting values for μ_1 say. This is dealt with in Chapter 4.

To reduce the effect of start-up values it is usual to ignore the first 50 or 100 observations simulated.

Table 3.1 demonstrates the generation of data from an AR(2) model

$$X_t = 0.5X_{t-1} + 0.3X_{t-2} + \varepsilon_t,$$

where ε_t is independent normal mean 0, variance $\sigma^2 = 2$. Observations 201 to 500 are shown in Fig. 3.1. Fig. 3.15 shows the theoretical autocorrelation function and sample autocorrelation function of the simulated data. Note that as for any realization the autocorrelations of the generated data differ from the theoretical autocorrelations of the model.

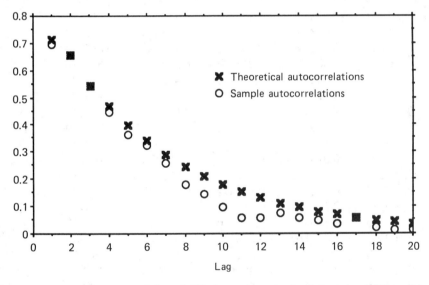

Fig. 3.15. Sample autocorrelation of 500 observations simulated from the AR(2) model $X_t = 0.5X_{t-1} + 0.3X_{t-2} + \varepsilon_t$ shown with theoretical autocorrelations.

EXERCISES

In all the following questions ε_t denotes an independent identically distributed random series with zero mean and variance σ^2.

(1) Write down the function to be minimized when calculating the least squares estimates of the ARMA model $X_t = \phi_1 X_{t-1} + \varepsilon_t + \theta_1 \varepsilon_{t-1}$.

Do you need to make any assumptions about the values of any X_t's or ε_t's?

Table 3.1. Some calculations from simulation of the AR(2) series $X_t = 0.5X_{t-1} + 0.3X_{t-2} + \varepsilon_t$, $\sigma^2 = 2$. Calculations shown for times 1–10, 101–110 and 491–500 only

t	$r_t U(0, 1)$	$z_t N(0, 1)$	σz_t	$\phi_1 X_{t-1}$	$\phi_2 X_{t-2}$	X_t
1	0.186298	1.264937	1.788891	0	0	0
2	0.128806	1.326932	1.876565	0	0	0
3	0.394813	1.243630	1.758759	0	0	1.758759
4	0.067193	0.558631	0.790024	0.879379	0	1.669403
5	0.678892	0.045451	0.064278	0.834702	0.527628	1.426607
6	0.241777	0.878932	1.242997	0.713303	0.500821	2.457121
7	0.186154	1.394755	1.972481	1.228561	0.427982	3.629024
8	0.887556	−1.190387	−1.683462	1.814512	0.737136	0.868187
9	0.725443	0.741234	1.048263	0.434093	1.088707	2.571063
10	0.938025	−0.304169	−0.430160	1.285532	0.260456	1.115828
101	0.012000	−0.238354	−0.337083	−1.273115	−0.783056	−2.393255
102	0.262769	2.964601	4.192578	−1.196627	−0.763869	2.232082
103	0.593321	−0.078046	−0.110373	1.116041	−0.717976	0.287691
104	0.262168	1.018798	1.440798	0.143846	0.669624	2.254268
105	0.867636	−0.532799	−0.753492	1.127134	0.086307	0.459950
106	0.497166	0.009487	0.013416	0.229975	0.676280	0.919672
107	0.880894	−0.503432	−0.711960	0.459836	0.137985	−0.114139
108	0.504381	−0.013860	−0.019601	−0.057070	0.275901	0.199230
109	0.111101	−1.949930	−2.757617	0.099615	−0.034242	−2.692244
110	0.440166	0.769681	1.088493	−1.346122	0.059769	−0.197859
491	0.551624	−0.010762	−0.015220	−1.688095	−0.161100	−1.864415
492	0.251570	1.090715	1.542505	−0.932208	−1.012857	−0.402560
493	0.735277	0.572977	0.810312	−0.201280	−0.559325	0.049707
494	0.880385	−0.535456	−0.757249	0.024854	−0.120768	−0.853163
495	0.009486	1.630545	2.305940	−0.426582	0.014912	1.894270
496	0.160302	2.580140	3.648869	0.947135	−0.255949	4.340055
497	0.171428	1.818592	2.571878	2.170027	0.568281	5.310186
498	0.959835	−0.468943	−0.663186	2.655093	1.302016	3.292924
499	0.153315	1.124787	1.590689	1.646962	1.593056	4.830707
500	0.848630	−1.576508	−2.229518	2.415354	0.988177	1.174012

(2) Derive an expression for the conditional MLEs of $X_t = \phi_1 X_{t-1} + \varepsilon_t$ if σ^2 is unknown.

(3) Calculate an expression for the autocovariances of the ARMA(1, 1) model in Exercise 1. HINT: multiply the model by X_{t-k} throughout and then take expectations, remembering that $E(X_t \varepsilon_{t+k}) = 0$ for $k > 0$. Consider the cases $k > 1$, $k = 0$, and $k = 1$ separately.

(4) Take the *moving average* model $X_t = \varepsilon_t + \theta_1\varepsilon_{t-1} + \theta_2\varepsilon_{t-2}$. What properties would your require of a time series for this to be a suitable model?

(5) How many times does the following model need differencing to make it stationary? What is the autocorrelation function of the stationary differences?

$$X_t = \mu_t + \varepsilon_t$$
$$\mu_t = \mu_{t-1} + \beta_t + \eta_t$$
$$\beta_t = \beta_{t-1} + \zeta_t$$

where ε_t, η_t and ζ_t are white noise disturbances with variances σ^2, σ_η^2 and σ_ζ^2 respectively. What properties would you require of a time series for this to be a suitable model?

(6) Is the structure $X_t = \phi_1 X_{t-1} + \varepsilon_t$ identifiable?

(7) Is the structure $X_t = \phi_1 X_{t-1} + \varepsilon_t + \theta_1\varepsilon_{t-1}$ identifiable?

(8) Simulate a sample from the model $X_t = 0.6X_{t-1} + \varepsilon_t$ where ε_t is normally distributed with zero mean and variance 2. Use $X_1 = 3$.

  Simulate another sample from the same model but with $X_1 = -2$, using the same noise series ε_t. Compare your results.

(9) Perform the same procedure as in Exercise 8 but for the model $X_t = 1.1X_{t-1} + \varepsilon_t$. Again, compare your results.

APPENDIX: A RANDOM NUMBER GENERATOR

The following algorithm (in Fortran) to produce a series of independently distributed uniform variates is taken directly from Wichmann & Hill (1982) and will be suitable for most simple simulation programs when an intrinsic random number generator is not available.

```
      FUNCTION RANDOM (L)
C     RETURNS A PSEUDO RANDOM NUMBER RECTANGULARLY
C     DISTRIBUTED BETWEEN 0 AND 1.
C
C     IX, IY AND IZ SHOULD BE SET TO INTEGER VALUES
C     BETWEEN 1 AND 30000 BEFORE FIRST ENTRY
C
C     INTEGER ARITHMETIC UP TO 30323 IS REQUIRED
C
C
      COMMON /RAND/IX, IY, IZ
      IX=171*MOD(IX, 177)-2*(IX/177)
      IY=172*MOD(IY, 176)-35*(IY/176)
      IZ=170*MOD(IZ, 178)-63*(IZ, 178)
C
      IF(IX.EQ.0)  IX=IX+30269
      IF(IY.EQ.0)  IY=IX+30307
      IF(IZ.LT. 0)  IX=IX+30323
C
C     IF INTEGER ARITHMETIC UP TO 5212632 IS AVAILABLE
C     THE PRECEDING 6 STATEMENTS MAY BE REPLACED BY
C     IX=MOD (171*IX, 30269)
C     IY=MOD (171*IX, 30307)
C     IZ=MOD (170*IZ, 30323)
C
C     ON SOME MACHINES, THIS MAY SLIGHTLY INCREASE
C     THE SPEED.  THE RESULTS WILL BE IDENTICAL.
      RANDOM=AMOD (FLOAT(IX)/30269.0+FLOAT(IY)/30307.0+
     *                FLOAT(IZ)/30323.0,1.0)
      RETURN
      END
```

4

The general state space model

The theory of space and time is a cultural artifact made possible by the intervention of graph paper.

Jaques Vallee, *CoEvolution Quarterly*, 18L82 Winter, 1977/78.

4.1 INTRODUCTION

In this chapter we introduce the *state space model*. This was originally devised by control engineers but has been adopted and adapted to model time series. The exact form and parametrization varies from author to author, but we use a general form which we call the general state space model (GSS).

Suppose that the observed value of a time series at time t, X_t, is a function of one or more, say d, random variables $\alpha_t^{(1)}, \ldots, \alpha_t^{(d)}$ which also occur at time t but which are *not* observed. These variables are called the *state* variables, and we can represent them by the vector $\alpha_t = (\alpha_t^{(1)}, \ldots, \alpha_t^{(d)})^{\mathrm{T}}$ which we call the *state*. Notice that the series $\{\alpha_t\}$ is a *vector* time series. Details of vector time series are beyond the scope of this book, but readers can regard α_t as a vector random variable observed at time t.

The simplest model for the relationship between X_t and the $\alpha_t^{(i)}$'s is to assume that X_t is a linear function of the $\alpha_t^{(i)}$. However, we can introduce greater flexibility by including some random fluctuation. That is, we assume that

$$X_t = h_1 \alpha_t^{(1)} + h_2 \alpha_t^{(2)} + \ldots + h_d \alpha_t^{(d)} + \varepsilon_t$$

where the h_i are constant parameters and the series $\{\varepsilon_t\}$ is an iid noise series with zero mean and variance σ_ε^2. In matrix notation we write

$$X_t = \mathbf{H}\alpha_t + \varepsilon_t \tag{4.1}$$

where $\mathbf{H}$ is a d-dimensional row vector of parameters. This equation (4.1) is known as the *measurement* or *observation* equation, and ε_t is the *measurement* noise.

To progress further we will need to introduce the concept of a *vector white noise* series. Suppose for each time t we have $\boldsymbol{\eta}_t = (\eta_t^{(1)}, \eta_t^{(2)}, \ldots \eta_t^{(n)})^\mathrm{T}$ a vector of n *independent* random variables with zero mean and covariance matrix

$$\sum = \mathrm{diag}(\sigma_1^2, \sigma_2^2, \ldots, \sigma_n^2).$$

So the second term, $\eta_t^{(2)}$, for instance, is a random variable with zero mean and a variance σ_2^2 which is uncorrelated with each of $\eta_t^{(1)}, \eta_t^{(3)}, \ldots, \eta_t^{(d)}$. To make life as simple as possible we assume that any two of these noise vectors, that is, $\boldsymbol{\eta}_t$ and $\boldsymbol{\eta}_s$ where $t \neq s$ are uncorrelated. By this we mean that for all integer t, s where $t \neq s$, $E(\boldsymbol{\eta}_t \boldsymbol{\eta}_s^\mathrm{T}) = \mathbf{0}$, where $\mathbf{0}$ is the zero matrix. The series of vectors $\{\boldsymbol{\eta}_t\}$ has analogous properties to the univariate white noise process and is therefore called a vector white noise process.

Returning to the state space model, suppose that the state variables at time t $\boldsymbol{\alpha}_t = (\alpha_t^{(1)}, \ldots, \alpha_t^{(d)})^\mathrm{T}$ are dependent on the previous states $\boldsymbol{\alpha}_{t-1}$, $\boldsymbol{\alpha}_{t-2}$, etc. A simple model for the evolution of the state vector might be

$$\boldsymbol{\alpha}_t = \boldsymbol{\phi} \boldsymbol{\alpha}_{t-1}$$

where $\boldsymbol{\phi}$ is a $d \times d$ matrix of parameters. For example, if the state dimension is 2 the model is

$$\alpha_t^{(1)} = \phi_{11} \alpha_{t-1}^{(1)} + \phi_{12} \alpha_{t-1}^{(2)} \quad \text{and} \quad \alpha_t^{(2)} = \phi_{21} \alpha_{t-1}^{(1)} + \phi_{22} \alpha_{t-1}^{(2)}$$

where

$$\boldsymbol{\phi} = \begin{pmatrix} \phi_{11} & \phi_{12} \\ \phi_{21} & \phi_{22} \end{pmatrix}.$$

As usual the model will be more flexible if we build random terms into each equation of the model. We introduce the n-dimensional vector random noise vector $\boldsymbol{\eta}_t$ as described above and include a linear function of its components in each equation of the system. For instance, for the $d = 2$ case suppose also that $n = 2$ (this need not be so) and the state noise vector $\boldsymbol{\eta_t} = (\eta_t^{(1)}, \eta_t^{(2)})^\mathrm{T}$. Then our model becomes

$$\alpha_t^{(1)} = \phi_{11} \alpha_{t-1}^{(1)} + \phi_{12} \alpha_{t-1}^{(2)} + k_{11} \eta_t^{(1)} + k_{12} \eta_t^{(2)}$$

and

$$\alpha_t^{(2)} = \phi_{21} \alpha_{t-1}^{(1)} + \phi_{22} \alpha_{t-1}^{(2)}$$

where the k_{ij} are additional parameters. This allows the random parts of each equation to be correlated with each other. Our model can then be written

$$\boldsymbol{\alpha}_t = \boldsymbol{\phi} \boldsymbol{\alpha}_{t-1} + \mathbf{K} \boldsymbol{\eta}_t \tag{4.2}$$

where $\boldsymbol{\phi}$ is a d by d matrix of parameters, and $\mathbf{K}$ is a d by n matrix of parameters. The state noise $\boldsymbol{\eta}_t$ is an n-dimensional white noise vector with covariance matrix

$$\sum = \text{diag}(\sigma_1^2, \sigma_2^2, ..., \sigma_n^2).$$

The equations (4.2) are known as the *state equations*. As ϕ describes the evolution from one state to the next it is called the *transition* matrix, and $\mathbf{K}$ is known as the *state noise coefficient* matrix for obvious reasons.

Equations (4.1) and (4.2) jointly form the general state space model. To recap, we have an observation X_t, a set of state variables $\alpha_t^{(1)}, ..., \alpha_t^{(d)}$ which are *not* observed, a zero mean random term ε_t of variance σ_ε^2 from a white noise series $\{\varepsilon_t\}$, and a vector random term $\boldsymbol{\eta}_t = (\eta_t^{(1)}, ..., \eta_t^{(n)})^T$ with covariance matrix

$$\sum = \text{diag}(\sigma_1^2, \sigma_2^2, ..., \sigma_n^2)$$

from a vector white noise series $\{\boldsymbol{\eta}_t\}$. For example, a simple state space model might be

$$X_t = (0.5 \quad 0.5)\boldsymbol{\alpha}_t + \varepsilon_t$$

and

$$\boldsymbol{\alpha}_t = \begin{pmatrix} 0.7 & 0 \\ 2 & 0.8 \end{pmatrix}\boldsymbol{\alpha}_{t-1} + \begin{pmatrix} 1 \\ 0.5 \end{pmatrix}\eta_t$$

with $\text{var}(\varepsilon_t) = 0.5$ and $\text{var}(\eta_t) = 4$. The $1 \times d$ matrix $\mathbf{H}$, $d \times d$ matrix ϕ and $d \times n$ matrix $\mathbf{K}$ all contain parameters of the model. If these parameters are unknown they must be estimated. It is important to remember that, in general, the state variables are not observed. Notice also that all the information in the past of the series $\{X_t\}$ which can influence X_t must be contained only in the state variables α_t.

In the engineering context from which this formulation came the model represents a physical system which changes over time, the difference being that the state noise variables are a set of external *deterministic* variables which act as inputs to the system as opposed to random variables. For instance, the state might be a set of coordinates representing the position of a rocket, and the observation a signal emitted by the rocket at each time point which is based on the rocket's position but obscured by measurement error.

Before we consider the properties of these models we will look at some examples. Most types of state space model postulated in the literature are special cases of (4.1), (4.2), which fix a particular subset of parameters, usually to 0 or 1. By way of illustration we introduce ARMA models and structural models as special classes of state space model. They are described in more detail in Chapters 5 and 6 respectively.

(i) Structural models
The random walk plus noise model (model B) in Chapter 3 was

$$X_t = \mu_t + \varepsilon_t, \qquad \mu_t = \mu_{t-1} + \eta_t, \qquad \text{var}(\varepsilon_t) = \sigma_\varepsilon^2.$$

This is a trivial GSS model in which the one-dimensional state α_t is merely μ_t. The ϕ matrix is now scalar unity, as are $\mathbf{K}$ and $\mathbf{H}$, and the state noise variance is merely

$$\Sigma = \sigma_\eta^2.$$

The variances σ_ε^2, σ_η^2 are the only parameters of the model which require estimation.

More complicated structural models often take the form of a measurement of the form $X_t = \mu_t + \gamma_t + \varepsilon_t$ where μ_t is the trend or level, γ_t is the seasonal component, and ε_t is the irregular component at time t. The state equations then describe the evolution of μ_t and γ_t. One possibility for these is

$$\mu_t = \mu_{t-1} + \beta_t + \eta_t,$$
$$\beta_t = \beta_{t-1} + \zeta_t,$$

and

$$\gamma_t = -\sum_{j=1}^{s-1} \gamma_{t-j} + \omega_t$$

where s is the number of seasons and η_t, ζ_t, and ω_t are mutually uncorrelated white noise disturbances with zero mean and variances σ_η^2, σ_ζ^2, and σ_ω^2 respectively. This model has been wide used by Harvey—see, for instance, Harvey & Todd (1983)—who refers to it as the basic structural model (BSM). It can be placed in GSS form where the state is $\alpha_t = (\mu_t, \beta_t, \gamma_t, \gamma_{t-1}, \ldots, \gamma_{t-s+2})$ and the state noise vector is $\eta_t = (\eta_t, \zeta_t, \omega_t)$. For instance the BSM with a period $s = 4$ has measurement equation

$$X_t = (1 \quad 0 \quad 1 \quad 0 \quad 0) \begin{pmatrix} \mu_t \\ \beta_t \\ \gamma_t \\ \gamma_{t-1} \\ \gamma_{t-2} \end{pmatrix} + \varepsilon_t$$

and state equation

$$\begin{pmatrix} \mu_t \\ \beta_t \\ \gamma_t \\ \gamma_{t-1} \\ \gamma_{t-2} \end{pmatrix} = \begin{pmatrix} 1 & 1 & 0 & 0 & 0 \\ 0 & 1 & 0 & 0 & 0 \\ 0 & 0 & -1 & -1 & -1 \\ 0 & 0 & 1 & 0 & 0 \\ 0 & 0 & 1 & 1 & 0 \end{pmatrix} \begin{pmatrix} \mu_{t-1} \\ \beta_{t-1} \\ \gamma_{t-1} \\ \gamma_{t-2} \\ \gamma_{t-3} \end{pmatrix} + \begin{pmatrix} 1 & 0 & 0 \\ 0 & 1 & 0 \\ 0 & 0 & 1 \\ 0 & 0 & 0 \\ 0 & 0 & 0 \end{pmatrix} \begin{pmatrix} \eta_t \\ \zeta_t \\ \omega_t \end{pmatrix}$$

where

$$\Sigma = \operatorname{diag}(\sigma_\eta^2, \sigma_\zeta^2, \sigma_\omega^2).$$

We can write this more succinctly as

$$X_t = (1 \quad 0 \quad 1 \quad 0 \quad 0)\alpha_t + \varepsilon_t$$

and

$$\alpha_t = \begin{pmatrix} 1 & 1 & 0 & 0 & 0 \\ 0 & 1 & 0 & 0 & 0 \\ 0 & 0 & -1 & -1 & -1 \\ 0 & 0 & 1 & 0 & 0 \\ 0 & 0 & 0 & 1 & 0 \end{pmatrix} \alpha_{t-1} + \begin{pmatrix} 1 & 0 & 0 \\ 0 & 1 & 0 \\ 0 & 0 & 1 \\ 0 & 0 & 0 \\ 0 & 0 & 0 \end{pmatrix} \begin{pmatrix} \eta_t \\ \zeta_t \\ \omega_t \end{pmatrix}$$

where

$$\Sigma = \text{diag}\left(\sigma_\eta^2, \sigma_\zeta^2, \sigma_\omega^2\right).$$

Note that the transition matrix ϕ of the BSM is in general an $s+1$ by $s+1$ matrix. Observe that it can be partitioned into blocks and that only the blocks on the diagonal contain non-zero elements. We call such a matrix a *diagonal block* matrix. In the above equations the upper 2×2 diagonal block describes the mechanism for generating the trend and the lower 3×3 block models the seasonal component. The matrix **K** is $(s+1) \times 3$ and can also be partitioned into blocks corresponding to the trend and seasonal components. Most structural models can be partitioned in this way.

The equations for the trend component μ_t are motivated as follows. If we had a deterministic linear trend this could be modelled by $\mu_t = \alpha + \beta t$, $t = 1, \ldots, N$. Equivalently we could write $\mu_t = \mu_{t-1} + \beta$ and set $\mu_0 = \alpha$. The BSM model allows greater flexibility by allowing the slope β to vary stochastically as

$$\beta_t = \beta_{t-1} + \zeta_t$$

and similarly allowing μ_t itself to change randomly in the form of

$$\mu_t = \mu_{t-1} + \beta_{t-1} + \eta_t.$$

For obvious reasons such a trend is called a *local linear trend*.

We still have not explained the form of the seasonal component γ_t of the BSM. One way of modelling the seasonal component in a regression model is to use a dummy variable for each season and require that the coefficients of these (the seasonal effects) sum to zero, as described in Chapter 1. In the notation of the model above we let $\gamma_t = \gamma_{t-s}$ so that the seasonal effect is fixed for each season, and require that

$$\gamma_t = -\sum_{j=1}^{s-1} \gamma_{t-j}.$$

The basic structural model again allows us greater flexibility by enabling the seasonal effect from one cycle to the next to evolve randomly by the inclusion of the random term ω_t of variance σ_ω^2.

Chapter 6 describes these and other structural models and their properties in more detail.

(ii) ARMA models

We encountered the general ARMA model in Chapter 3 (3.11). At first sight—since it has only one equation and one noise series—it does not seem compatible with the GSS model. However, consider the GSS model

$$X_t = (1 \quad 0 \quad 0)\alpha_t, \qquad \alpha_t = \begin{pmatrix} \phi_1 & 1 & 0 \\ \phi_2 & 0 & 1 \\ \phi_3 & 0 & 0 \end{pmatrix} \alpha_{t-1} + \begin{pmatrix} 1 \\ \theta_1 \\ \theta_2 \end{pmatrix} \eta_t$$

where η_t is a scalar white noise series of variance σ_1^2. We can write

$$\alpha_t = \left(\alpha_t^{(1)}, \alpha_t^{(2)}, \alpha_t^{(3)} \right)^{\mathrm{T}}$$

as usual so that the bottom row of the state equation is

$$\alpha_t^{(3)} = \phi_3 \alpha_{t-1}^{(1)} + \theta_2 \eta_t.$$

The second from bottom row of the state equation gives

$$\alpha_t^{(2)} = \phi_2 \alpha_{t-1}^{(1)} + \alpha_{t-1}^{(3)} + \theta_1 \eta_t,$$

but we can substitute for $\alpha_{t-1}^{(3)}$ to give

$$\alpha_t^{(2)} = \phi_2 \alpha_{t-1}^{(1)} + \phi_3 \alpha_{t-2}^{(1)} + \theta_2 \eta_{t-1} + \theta_1 \eta_t.$$

Finally, we take the first row

$$\alpha_t^{(1)} = \phi_1 \alpha_{t-1}^{(1)} + \alpha_{t-1}^{(2)} + \eta_t$$

and substitute for $\alpha_{t-1}^{(2)}$ to give

$$\alpha_t^{(1)} = \phi_1 \alpha_{t-1}^{(1)} + \phi_2 \alpha_{t-2}^{(1)} + \phi_3 \alpha_{t-3}^{(1)} + \theta_2 \eta_{t-2} + \theta_1 \eta_{t-1} + \eta_t$$

which is an ARMA model equation as in (3.11) but in the first component of the state $\alpha_t^{(1)}$ with noise term η_t. As there is no measurement noise, however, $\alpha_t^{(1)} = X_t$, so this state space model is equivalent to an ARMA (3, 2) model in X_t.

It is now clear that these seemingly disparate model types can both be considered within the GSS framework. Even model C of Chapter 3 can be represented in state space form (see Exercise 2 at the end of the present chapter). We will consider the properties and techniques peculiar to particular model types in later chapters, but for now we concern ourselves with some common features of all GSS models.

4.2 PROPERTIES OF STATE SPACE MODELS

As $\alpha_t = \phi \alpha_{t-1} + \eta_t$ we can substitute for α_{t-1} repeatedly to obtain

$$X_t = \mathbf{H}\alpha_t + \varepsilon_t = \mathbf{H}(\phi^t \alpha_0 + \phi^{t-1}\mathbf{K}\eta_1 + \ldots + \mathbf{K}\eta_t) + \varepsilon_t$$

$$= \mathbf{H}\phi^t \alpha_0 + \mathbf{H}\phi^{t-1}\mathbf{K}\eta_1 + \mathbf{H}\phi^{t-2}\mathbf{K}\eta_2 + \ldots + \mathbf{H}\mathbf{K}\eta_t + \varepsilon_t$$

or the infinite representation

$$X_t = \mathbf{HK}\boldsymbol{\eta}_t + \mathbf{H}\boldsymbol{\phi}\mathbf{K}\boldsymbol{\eta}_{t-1} + \mathbf{H}\boldsymbol{\phi}^2\mathbf{K}\boldsymbol{\eta}_{t-2} + \ldots \varepsilon_t \tag{4.3}$$

or

$$X_t = (\boldsymbol{\psi}_0 + \boldsymbol{\psi}_1 B + \ldots)\boldsymbol{\eta}_t + \varepsilon_t$$

where B is the backward shift operator.

For (weak) stationarity we require that $E(X_t)$ and the autocorrelations of $\{X_t\}$ are independent of t. To formally prove the conditions for a state space model to be stationary would require advanced results on the convergence of sums of vector random variables, so we will take an intuitive approach. Looking at (4.3), if the model is stationary we would expect X_t to be a function of recent $\boldsymbol{\eta}_t$'s only, and the influence of $\boldsymbol{\eta}_t$'s in the distant past to decay. We therefore require that the coefficient of $\boldsymbol{\eta}_{t-i}$, $\mathbf{H}\boldsymbol{\phi}^i\mathbf{K}$ decays for large i. A necessary and sufficient condition for this is that $\boldsymbol{\phi}^i -> 0$ as $i -> \infty$. We can prove this will happen if and only if all the eigenvalues of $\boldsymbol{\phi}$ are less than unity in absolute value. In fact a *necessary and sufficient condition for (weak) stationarity is that all the eigenvalues of $\boldsymbol{\phi}$ lie within the unit circle.*

If the eigenvalues of $\boldsymbol{\phi}$ lie *outside* the unit circle (4.3) will not converge, the model is non-stationary and X_t will depend more on noises from the distant past than recent noises. The magnitude of the mean will also increase with **t**, so such a model is called an *explosive* model. When the eigenvalues of $\boldsymbol{\phi}$ lie *on* the unit circle the mean will drift up or down, as time changes but will not 'explode' in this way. Most of the structural models considered in this book come into this last category, as does the class of ARMA models called integrated (ARIMA) models (see section 5.6).

Assuming a zero mean, the autocovariance of the model at lag k will be

$$\gamma(k) = E(X_t X_{t+k})$$
$$= E\{(\mathbf{HK}\boldsymbol{\eta}_t + \mathbf{H}\boldsymbol{\phi}\mathbf{K}\boldsymbol{\eta}_{t-1} + \mathbf{H}\boldsymbol{\phi}^2\mathbf{K}\boldsymbol{\eta}_{t-2} + \ldots \varepsilon_t)$$
$$(\mathbf{HK}\boldsymbol{\eta}_{t+k} + \mathbf{H}\boldsymbol{\phi}\mathbf{K}\boldsymbol{\eta}_{t+k-1} + \ldots + \mathbf{H}\boldsymbol{\phi}^k\mathbf{K}\boldsymbol{\eta}_t + \mathbf{H}\boldsymbol{\phi}^{k+1}\mathbf{K}\boldsymbol{\eta}_{t-1} + \ldots + \varepsilon_{t+k})\}$$

Taking the transpose of the expression in the second bracket and using the independence of the $\boldsymbol{\eta}_t$'s and ε_t's gives

$$\gamma(k) = \mathbf{H}\boldsymbol{\phi}^k\left(\mathbf{K}\boldsymbol{\Sigma}\mathbf{K}^\mathrm{T} + \boldsymbol{\phi}\mathbf{K}\boldsymbol{\Sigma}\mathbf{K}^\mathrm{T}\boldsymbol{\phi}^\mathrm{T} + \boldsymbol{\phi}^2\mathbf{K}\boldsymbol{\Sigma}\mathbf{K}^\mathrm{T}\boldsymbol{\phi}^{2\mathrm{T}} + \ldots\right)\mathbf{H}^\mathrm{T} \quad k > 0$$

and

$$\gamma(0) = \mathbf{H}\left(\mathbf{K}\boldsymbol{\Sigma}\mathbf{K}^\mathrm{T} + \boldsymbol{\phi}\mathbf{K}\boldsymbol{\Sigma}\mathbf{K}^\mathrm{T}\boldsymbol{\phi}^\mathrm{T} + \boldsymbol{\phi}^2\mathbf{K}\boldsymbol{\Sigma}\mathbf{K}^\mathrm{T}\boldsymbol{\phi}^{2\mathrm{T}} + \ldots\right)\mathbf{H}^\mathrm{T} + \sigma_\varepsilon^2.$$

Notice that our stationarity requirement that all the eigenvalues of $\boldsymbol{\phi}$ lie inside the unit circle will ensure convergence here as well.

To model a stationary series with non-zero mean we can obviously include a constant mean μ in the measurement equation so that it becomes

$$X_t = \mathbf{H}\boldsymbol{\alpha}_t + \mu + \varepsilon_t.$$

4.3 IDENTIFICATION

Observe that

$$X_t = \mathbf{H}^* \alpha_t^* + \varepsilon_t, \quad \alpha_t^* = \phi^* \alpha_{t-1}^* + \eta_t$$

where

$$\mathbf{H}^* = \mathbf{H}\mathbf{T}^{-1}, \quad \phi^* = \mathbf{T}\phi\mathbf{T}^{-1} \quad \text{and} \quad \mathbf{K}^* = \mathbf{T}\mathbf{K}$$

for a non-singular square matrix $\mathbf{T}$ is an equivalent system to (4.1), (4.2) in the sense that the same set of random noise 'inputs' η_t and ε_t will produce the same set of 'outputs' X_t. This amounts to saying that we can linearly transform the state into $\alpha_t^* = \mathbf{T}\alpha_t$. Such equivalence is called *input–output* equivalence in the engineering literature. Models which are equivalent in this way will have the same likelihood, so as this would allow more than one model from each input–output equivalence class the model is not identified (see section 3.7). To ensure that *exactly one* model from each input–output equivalence class is allowed a canonical form should be selected. One such form for a model with one state noise input is

$$X_t = (1 \quad 0 \quad \ldots \quad 0)\alpha_t, \quad \alpha_t = \begin{pmatrix} \phi_1 & 1 & 0 & . & 0 \\ \phi_2 & 0 & 1 & . & 0 \\ . & & . & . & . \\ \phi_{d-1} & 0 & 0 & . & 1 \\ \phi_d & 0 & 0 & 0 & 0 \end{pmatrix} \alpha_{t-1} + \begin{pmatrix} \theta_0 \\ \theta_1 \\ . \\ . \\ . \\ \theta_{d-1} \end{pmatrix} \eta_t.$$

Notice that the state space representation of the ARMA model given earlier in this chapter takes this canonical form. Other model types, as we saw with the structural model example, overcome input–output equivalence by fixing many of the parameters of the model to 1 or 0 in a systematic way.

So far we have assumed that ε_t is a zero mean white noise term with variance σ_ε^2 and that η_t is a vector white noise with variance matrix Σ. So only the second order moments of these random terms have been specified—we don't know the form of their probability distributions. To use likelihood-based estimation we need to determine the probability distributions of the random terms, and so of the series $\{X_t\}$ completely. The usual assumption is that ε_t is normally distributed and η_t has a multivariate normal distribution. *We will make this assumption in all that follows.*

The second order moments σ_ε^2 and $\text{var}(\mathbf{K}\eta_t) = \mathbf{K}\Sigma\mathbf{K}^T$ now totally determine the probabilistic structure of the state space model (4.1), (4.2).

So it follows that if $\mathbf{H}$, and ϕ and σ_ε^2 are the same for two models, and these models have the same $\mathbf{K}\Sigma\mathbf{K}^T$ the two models have the same likelihood. For example, if the first model has $\mathbf{K} = (1 \quad 0.5)^T$ and $\eta_t = (\eta_t^{(1)})$, a scalar with variance $\sigma_1^2 = 4$, and the second $\mathbf{K} = (2 \quad 1)^T$ and $\sigma_1^2 = 1$ but $\mathbf{H}$ and ϕ are the same, the two models are likelihood-equivalent. The problem is overcome if either Σ or the first n rows of $\mathbf{K}$ are set to the identity matrix. So the first of the models given above would be allowed but not the second.

It can also be shown that under these normality assumptions a system with a vector state noise η_t has an equivalent representation to a system with a scalar state noise, that is, for a stochastic canonical form we need only consider a scalar η_t. Unfortunately, however, even if Σ or K are constrained as described above, the model is still not identified in the sense of section 3.7. We will see in later chapters that two such models can still be likelihood-equivalent and that for efficient estimation further constraints must be placed on the parameters of the model.

We have seen that under the normality assumption the canonical form above with $\theta_0 = 1$ goes some way to identifying the state space model. The other parameters may be fixed or unknown, depending on the type of state space model under consideration. In the next section we consider estimation of the unknown parameters of a state space model.

4.4 EVALUATING THE LIKELIHOOD FUNCTION

As we have already seen, we can place a diverse range of models in the GSS form of (4.1), (4.2). In this and the following section we will assume that such a model holds and that some or all of the parameters H, ϕ, K, Σ and σ_ε^2 are unknown and must be estimated. Note that the states α_t change with t; they are *not* parameters of the model. The state space model lends itself particularly well to maximum likelihood estimation. In section 4.5 we will use a numerical maximization routine to find the maximum likelihood estimates, but first we need to evaluate the likelihood of a state space structure at a particular set of parameter values, that is, for particular values of $\theta = \{H, \phi, K, \Sigma, \sigma_\varepsilon^2\}$.

Firstly, we restate the assumption made in the previous section that for each t (i), ε_t is normally distributed and (ii) η_t is multivariate normally distributed. We recall from section 3.3 that the likelihood of a time series can be decomposed into the product of the conditional distributions of each X_t on its predecessors, that is

$$L(\theta) = \prod_{t=1}^{N} f\left(X_t | X_1, X_2, ..., X_{t-1}\right).$$

Equivalently we could calculate the log-likelihood

$$\log L(\theta) = \sum_{t=1}^{N} \log f\left(X_t | X_1, X_2, ..., X_{t-1}\right).$$

From (4.3) it should be clear that as each observation X_t is a linear function of normal random noises, the joint distribution of the series $\{X_t\}$ is multivariate normal. Hence, by the properties of the multivariate normal distribution, the distribution of any observation conditional on any others must also be normal. In particular, the conditional distribution of X_t given data up to and including $t - 1$, $f(X_t|X_1, X_2,..., X_{t-1})$ required for the likelihood will be normal. We will denote the mean of this distribution by

$$X_{t|t-1} = E\left(X_t | X_{t-1}, X_{t-2}, ..., X_1\right)$$

and the variance F_t. As the conditional distribution $f(X_t|X_1, X_2,..., X_{t-1})$ is normal we can write,

$$\log f\left(X_t|X_1, X_2,..., X_{t-1}\right) = -\frac{1}{2}\log 2\pi - \frac{1}{2}\log F_t - \frac{1}{2F_t}\left(X_t - X_{t|t-1}\right)^2$$

$$= -\frac{1}{2}\log 2\pi - \frac{1}{2}\log F_t - \frac{V_t^2}{2F_t},$$

where $V_t = X_t - X_{t|t-1}$ is the prediction error.

The log-likelihood of the series is therefore

$$\log L(\theta) = -\frac{N}{2}\log 2\pi - \frac{1}{2}\sum_{t=1}^{N}\log F_t - \frac{1}{2}\sum_{t=1}^{N}\frac{V_t^2}{F_t}. \tag{4.4}$$

To evaluate the likelihood we need $X_{t|t-1}$ and F_t for all $t = 1,..., N$. We can obtain these using a set of recursions called the *Kalman filter* recursions.

The Kalman filter recursions are a set of equations which are processed for a given state space model for each time $t = 1,..., N$ successively. The Kalman filter recursions were originally devised by engineers to obtain optimal estimates of the states $\{\alpha_t\}$ of a state space model. The equations at time t require the minimum mean square estimate of the previous state $\mathbf{a}_{t-1}$ and the covariance matrix of this state $\mathbf{C}_{t-1}$ and produce a minimum mean square estimate $\mathbf{a}_t$ of the current state and a corresponding covariance matrix $\mathbf{C}_t$. This state estimate is of less direct interest to us than to the engineers. For us the attraction is that $X_{t|t-1}$ and F_t, which we need for the likelihood, (4.4) are produced as byproducts of the equations at time t.

We give an outline derivation of the Kalman filter recursions. Suppose that we are currently at time $t - 1$, so that we have observed $X_1, X_2,..., X_{t-1}$; we do *not* know any of the states $\alpha_1, \alpha_2,..., \alpha_{t-1}$. Suppose, however, for the moment that we have an estimator $\mathbf{a}_{t-1}$ of the state α_{t-1} which is the minimum mean square error estimator (MMSE) or equivalently the conditional expectation of α_{t-1} given observations $X_1, X_2,..., X_{t-1}$. Suppose also that $\mathbf{C}_{t-1}$ is the corresponding $d \times d$ covariance matrix of estimation error, that is

$$\mathbf{C}_{t-1} = E\left\{(\alpha_{t-1} - \mathbf{a}_{t-1})(\alpha_{t-1} - \mathbf{a}_{t-1})^{\mathrm{T}}\right\}.$$

Of course, $\mathbf{C}_{t-1}$ will be a positive semi-definite matrix, as it is a covariance matrix.

(i) The Kalman filter prediction equations

It will be useful to introduce the notation $\mathbf{a}_{t|t-1}$ for the conditional expectation of the state α_t at time $t - 1$, that is, given observations up to and including time $t - 1$ and $\mathbf{C}_{t|t-1}$ for the corresponding covariance matrix. We know from (4.2) that $\alpha_t = \phi\alpha_{t-1} + \mathbf{K}\eta_t$ so

$$\mathbf{a}_{t|t-1} = E\left(\alpha_t|X_1 X_2,..., X_{t-1}\right) = \phi\mathbf{a}_{t-1} \tag{4.5}$$

as the expected value of η_t is zero. The variance of this conditional estimator of the state is

$$\mathbf{C}_{t|t-1} = E\left\{(\boldsymbol{\alpha}_t - \mathbf{a}_{t|t-1})(\boldsymbol{\alpha}_t - \mathbf{a}_{t|t-1})^{\mathrm{T}}\right\}.$$

However,

$$\boldsymbol{\alpha}_t - \mathbf{a}_{t|t-1} = \boldsymbol{\phi}\boldsymbol{\alpha}_{t-1} + \mathbf{K}\boldsymbol{\eta}_t - \boldsymbol{\phi}\mathbf{a}_t = \boldsymbol{\phi}(\boldsymbol{\alpha}_{t-1} - \mathbf{a}_{t-1}) + \mathbf{K}\boldsymbol{\eta}_t$$

and we have assumed that we know the covariance matrix of the state estimate

$$\mathbf{C}_{t-1} = E\left\{(\boldsymbol{\alpha}_{t-1} - \mathbf{a}_{t-1})(\boldsymbol{\alpha}_{t-1} - \mathbf{a}_{t-1})^{\mathrm{T}}\right\}.$$

The variance of the state estimate $\boldsymbol{\alpha}_t$ at time $t-1$ is therefore

$$\mathbf{C}_{t|t-1} = \boldsymbol{\phi}\mathbf{C}_{t-1}\boldsymbol{\phi}^{\mathrm{T}} = \mathbf{K}\boldsymbol{\Sigma}\mathbf{K}^{\mathrm{T}}. \tag{4.6}$$

As $X_t = \mathbf{H}\boldsymbol{\alpha}_t + \varepsilon_t$ and the mean of ε_t is zero, $X_{t|t-1} = \mathbf{H}\mathbf{a}_{t|t-1} = \mathbf{H}\boldsymbol{\phi}\mathbf{a}_{t-1}$. Now, recall from section 3.4 that $X_{t|t-1}$ is the optimal one step predictor of X_t at time $t-1$ as well as the conditional expectation of X_t at time $t-1$. The variance of the conditional distribution of X_t at time $t-1$ which we require for the likelihood is $F_t = E\{(X_t - X_{t|t-1})^2\}$ and will therefore also be the one step prediction error variance. The one step prediction error is

$$V_t = X_t - X_{t|t-1} = X_t - \mathbf{H}\mathbf{a}_{t|t-1} \tag{4.7}$$

so it follows that the one step PEV is

$$F_t = E\left\{\left(X_t - \mathbf{H}\mathbf{a}_{t|t-1}\right)^2\right\} = E\left\{\left(\mathbf{H}(\boldsymbol{\alpha}_t - \mathbf{a}_{t|t-1}) + \varepsilon_t\right)^2\right\}.$$

However, as ε_t is by assumption independent of $\mathbf{H}(\boldsymbol{\alpha}_t - \mathbf{a}_{t|t-1})$ we can write

$$F_t = \mathbf{H}\mathbf{C}_{t|t-1}\mathbf{H}^{\mathrm{T}} + \sigma_\varepsilon^2. \tag{4.8}$$

To recap, so far we have assumed that we have the mean and covariance matrix $\mathbf{a}_{t-1}$ and $\mathbf{C}_{t-1}$ of the estimator of $\boldsymbol{\alpha}_{t-1}$ at time $t-1$ and have developed equations (4.5) and (4.6) for the state estimate $\mathbf{a}_{t|t-1}$ and its variance $\mathbf{C}_{t|t-1}$. These are known as the *prediction equations* of the Kalman filter. We have also obtained expression (4.7) for the prediction error V_t and (4.8) for the variance F_t of the conditional distribution of X_t given $X_1, \ldots, X_{t-1}$. It is these values which we require for the log-likelihood (4.4).

(ii) The Kalman filter updating equations
This is all very well but the prediction equations relied on the assumption that the estimate $\mathbf{a}_{t-1}$ and its covariance matrix $\mathbf{C}_{t-1}$ were known. The Kalman filter *updating equations* enable $\mathbf{a}_t$ and $\mathbf{C}_t$ to be calculated as soon as the latest observation X_t becomes available, assuming that the prediction equations for time t as described in (i) above have already been calculated. Our derivation of these will again be intuitive and involves multiple linear regression models with correlated error terms. It is not essential that the time series analyst understands the derivation of the equations completely, and if these are difficult we suggest skimming through the next few paragraphs and rejoining us after (4.13). On the other hand, if the reader requires more rigour, the original paper by Kalman (1960) or Jazwinski (1970) give full details.

When the observation X_t becomes available we can construct a linear model

$$\begin{pmatrix} \mathbf{a}_{t|t-1} \\ X_t \end{pmatrix} = \begin{pmatrix} \mathbf{I} \\ \mathbf{H} \end{pmatrix} \alpha_t + \begin{pmatrix} \mathbf{a}_{t|t-1} - \alpha_t \\ \varepsilon_t \end{pmatrix} \tag{4.9}$$

We can think of (4.9) as a particular multiple linear regression model $\mathbf{Y} = \mathbf{X}\beta + \epsilon$ where $\mathbf{Y}$ is the vector of dependent variables, $\mathbf{X}$ contains the independent variables and β is a vector of unknown coefficients. The vector ϵ contains random error terms which may be correlated, and so we assume that the covariance matrix of ϵ is $\mathbf{W}$. The Gauss–Markov theorem states that the minimum mean square linear estimator of β is

$$\hat{\beta} = (\mathbf{X}^T \mathbf{W}^{-1} \mathbf{X})^{-1} \mathbf{X}^T \mathbf{W}^{-1} \mathbf{Y}.$$

The variance covariance matrix of $\hat{\beta}$ is $(\mathbf{X}^T \mathbf{W}^{-1} \mathbf{X})^{-1}$. We can apply this to (4.9) in order to estimate α_t and calculate its covariance matrix $\mathbf{C}_t$. We set

$$\mathbf{X} = \begin{pmatrix} \mathbf{I} \\ \mathbf{H} \end{pmatrix}, \quad \mathbf{Y} = \begin{pmatrix} \mathbf{a}_{t|t-1} \\ X_t \end{pmatrix}, \quad \text{and} \quad \epsilon = \begin{pmatrix} \mathbf{a}_{t|t-1} - \alpha_t \\ \varepsilon_t \end{pmatrix}$$

so

$$\mathbf{W} = \begin{pmatrix} \mathbf{C}_{t|t-1} & 0 \\ 0 & \sigma_\varepsilon^2 \end{pmatrix}.$$

The MMSE estimate of α_t is therefore

$$\mathbf{a}_t = \left\{ (\mathbf{I} \quad \mathbf{H}^T) \begin{pmatrix} \mathbf{C}_{t|t-1} & 0 \\ 0 & \sigma_\varepsilon^2 \end{pmatrix}^{-1} \begin{pmatrix} \mathbf{I} \\ \mathbf{H} \end{pmatrix} \right\}^{-1} (\mathbf{I} \quad \mathbf{H}^T) \begin{pmatrix} \mathbf{C}_{t|t-1} & 0 \\ 0 & \sigma_\varepsilon^2 \end{pmatrix}^{-1} \begin{pmatrix} \mathbf{a}_{t|t-1} \\ X_t \end{pmatrix}$$

$$= \mathbf{C}_t \left[\mathbf{C}_{t|t-1}^{-1} \mathbf{a}_{t|t-1} + \mathbf{H}^T X_t / \sigma_\varepsilon^2 \right] \tag{4.10}$$

where $\mathbf{C}_t$ is the variance of $\mathbf{a}_t$ which is

$$\mathbf{C}_t = \left[\mathbf{C}_{t|t-1}^{-1} + \mathbf{H}^T \mathbf{H} / \sigma_\varepsilon^2 \right]^{-1}. \tag{4.11}$$

This matrix inversion is nasty and it can be shown (using a well known matrix inversion lemma) that if $\mathbf{A}$ is $n \times n$, $\mathbf{B}$ is $n \times m$ and $\mathbf{C}$ is $m \times m$ then

$$(\mathbf{A} + \mathbf{B}\mathbf{C}\mathbf{B}^T)^{-1} = \mathbf{A}^{-1} - \mathbf{A}^{-1}\mathbf{B}(\mathbf{C}^{-1} + \mathbf{B}^T \mathbf{A}^{-1} \mathbf{B})^{-1} \mathbf{B}^T \mathbf{A}^{-1}.$$

Setting

$$\mathbf{A} = \mathbf{C}_{t|t-1}^{-1}, \quad \mathbf{B} = \mathbf{H}^T \quad \text{and} \quad \mathbf{C} = 1/\sigma_\varepsilon^2$$

gives, from (4.11),

$$\mathbf{C}_t = \mathbf{C}_{t|t-1} - \mathbf{C}_{t|t-1} \mathbf{H}^T \mathbf{H} \mathbf{C}_{t|t-1} / F_t, \tag{4.12}$$

as F_t is a scalar. This form has the advantage of avoiding any matrix inversions. Substituting (4.12) into (4.10) and rearranging gives the more convenient form

$$\mathbf{a}_t = \mathbf{a}_{t|t-1} + \mathbf{C}_{t|t-1}\mathbf{H}^{\mathrm{T}}(X_t - \mathbf{H}\mathbf{a}_{t|t-1})/F_t. \tag{4.13}$$

So, given $\mathbf{a}_{t-1}$, $\mathbf{C}_{t-1}$ and the latest data item X_t and having calculated the prediction equations we can calculate $\mathbf{a}_t$ and $\mathbf{C}_t$ from (4.12) and (4.13). Equations (4.7), (4.12) and (4.13) are known as the *updating equations*.

Notice that as $V_t = X_t - \mathbf{H}\mathbf{a}_{t|t-1}$, (4.13) shows that the state estimate $\mathbf{a}_t$ is the one step prediction of the state adjusted by a weighted prediction error V_t. In effect $\mathbf{a}_{t|t-1}$ is being corrected by an amount which depends on the magnitude and sign of the prediction error. The weight $(\mathbf{C}_{t|t-1}\mathbf{H})/F_t$ is frequently called the *Kalman gain*.

The *prediction* equations (4.5) and (4.6) followed by the *updating equations* (4.8), (4.12) and (4.13) are collectively known as the *Kalman filter* recursions. At each iteration we also calculate the prediction error $V_t = X_t - \mathbf{H}\mathbf{a}_{t|t-1}$ (4.7) as it is required for the log-likelihood. For ease of reference we repeat all these equations.

The prediction equations:

$$\mathbf{a}_{t|t-1} = \boldsymbol{\phi}\mathbf{a}_{t-1} \tag{4.5}$$

$$\mathbf{C}_{t|t-1} = \boldsymbol{\phi}\mathbf{C}_{t-1}\boldsymbol{\phi}^{\mathrm{T}} + \mathbf{K}\boldsymbol{\Sigma}\mathbf{K}^{\mathrm{T}} \tag{4.6}$$

The updating equations:

$$F_t = \mathbf{H}\mathbf{C}_{t|t-1}\mathbf{H}^{\mathrm{T}} + \sigma_\varepsilon^2 \tag{4.8}$$

$$\mathbf{C}_t = \mathbf{C}_{t|t-1} - \mathbf{C}_{t|t-1}\mathbf{H}^{\mathrm{T}}\mathbf{H}\mathbf{C}_{t|t-1}/F_t \tag{4.12}$$

$$\mathbf{a}_t = \mathbf{a}_{t|t-1} + \mathbf{C}_{t|t-1}\mathbf{H}^{\mathrm{T}}(X_t - \mathbf{H}\mathbf{a}_{t|t-1})/F_t \tag{4.13}$$

and required for the log-likelihood:

$$V_t = X_t - \mathbf{H}\mathbf{a}_{t|t-1} \tag{4.7}$$

In practice we start the recursions at $t = 1$. This requires the estimator of the state at $t = 0$, $\mathbf{a}_0$ and the corresponding error covariance matrix $\mathbf{C}_0$, and we discuss the choice of these later in this section. Given $\mathbf{a}_0$, $\mathbf{C}_0$, the prediction equations are used to calculate $\mathbf{a}_{1|0}$, $\mathbf{C}_{1|0}$ and F_1. Once X_1 becomes available, the prediction error V_1 and the updating equations can be processed to give $\mathbf{a}_1$ and $\mathbf{C}_1$. As we wish to evaluate the log-likelihood (4.4) it is sensible to accumulate

$$\sum \log F_t \quad \text{and} \quad \sum \frac{V_t^2}{F_t}$$

as you go along. This completes iteration 1, and the cycle repeats itself. The second iteration produces $\mathbf{a}_{2|1}$, $\mathbf{C}_{2|1}$, F_2 and then when X_2 becomes available V_2, $\mathbf{a}_2$ and $\mathbf{C}_2$. Again the cumulative sum of $\log F_t$ and of V_t^2/F_t can be calculated. The data are processed one at a time in this way for $t = 1, \ldots, N$ until the

$$\sum_{t=1}^{N} \log F_t \quad \text{and} \quad \sum_{t=1}^{N} \frac{V_t^2}{F_t}$$

have been calculated. These can be inserted into (4.4) to evaluate the log-likelihood of the data at these parameter values.

The reader will have noticed that our derivation of the updating equations requires that $\sigma_\varepsilon^2 = \text{var}(\varepsilon_t) > 0$ whereas, the state space model (for instance the ARMA model) may have zero measurement noise. It has been shown, however, that the updating equations are still valid even if $\varepsilon_t = 0$, so this need not worry us unduly.

We should note here that the Kalman filter recursions are still valid if the random terms in the state space model are merely white noise and not necessarily normally distributed. In this case, however, the state estimators calculated will be minimum mean square *linear* estimators as opposed to minimum mean square error estimators.

(iii) Steady state

After a number of iterations of the filter most state space models quite rapidly converge to a *steady state*. By this we mean that all the covariance matrices of the Kalman filter, that is, C_t, $C_{t|t-1}$ and F_t, converge to fixed values. When this happens, computing time can be saved by omitting equations (4.6), (4.8) and (4.12). The Kalman gain will also reach a fixed value. We will see later that the steady state prediction error variance F_t has particular significance.

In practice we check at every iteration whether the filter has converged to a steady state or not. One way of doing this is to calculate the sum of the absolute values of the elements in the lower triangle (including diagonal) of $C_{t|t-1} - C_{t-1|t-2}$ but any sensible criteria—the sum of squares of the elements for instance—could be used. If this is smaller than an arbitrary value—we usually use 0.0001 or 0.000001—then we assume that a steady state has been reached by time t. As it is possible for consecutive prediction error variances F_{t-1} and F_t to be the same when the system is not in steady state we do *not* recommend monitoring these quantities.

The ideas described above can be illustrated simply using the random walk plus noise model (model B from Chapter 3) and the purse data. As established in section 4.1 the state is one dimensional, and $H = 1$, $\phi = 1$ and $K = 1$ are fixed for this type of model. The 'free' parameters are therefore σ_ε^2 and σ_η^2. We quoted the MLEs of these in section 3.3, but now we will consider evaluation of the log-likelihood using the Kalman filter recursions at the particular parameter values $\sigma_\varepsilon^2 = 20$ and $\sigma_\eta^2 = 5$. The recursions start at $a_0 = 0$, $C_0 = 100\,000$. We assume that a steady state has been reached when our criterion is less than 0.000001. Output from the first few iterations is shown in Table 4.1. Notice that the steady state criterion is met at $t = 20$, although by iteration 19 the filter has converged to a steady state, and that the other covariances F_t and C_t are also in a steady state by then. The steady state covariances $C_{t|t-1}$, C_t, and F_t would take the same values for any data set, as they are functions of the model structure and the start-up parameters a_0, C_0 only. Notice that the first prediction is suspiciously large and therefore we ignore both it (see (iv)) and the corresponding prediction error variance in the calculation of likelihood and use $N - 1$ instead of N in the log-likelihood (4.4). If we continue for the remainder of the 71 observations we obtain

Table 4.1. Kalman filter iterations for random walk plus noise model with $\sigma_\varepsilon^2 = 20$ and $\sigma_\eta^2 = 5$, start-up values $a_0 = 0$, $C_0 = 100000$.

t	$a_{t|t-1}$	X_t	V_t	$C_{t|t-1}$	F_t	C_t	a_t
0						100000	0
1	0	10	10	100005	100025	19.996	0
2	9.998	15	5.002	24.996001	44.99601	11.1103	12.9776692
3	12.77692	10	−2.276692	16.110321	36.110321	8.9228	11.537894
4	11.537894	10	−1.537894	13.922835	33.922835	8.2085	10.906701
5	10.906701	12	1.093299	13.208533	33.208533	7.9549	11.341555
6	11.341555	10	−1.341555	12.954903	32.954903	7.8622	10.814177
7	10.814177	7	−3.814177	12.862201	32.862201	7.828	9.321315
8	9.321315	17	7.678685	12.827961	32.827961	7.8153	12.321863
9	12.321863	10	−2.321863	12.815265	32.815265	7.8106	11.415112
10	11.415112	14	2.584888	12.810551	32.810551	7.8088	12.424355
11	12.424355	8	−4.424355	12.808800	32.808800	7.8081	10.697054
12	10.697054	17	6.302946	12.808149	32.808149	7.8079	13.157695
13	13.157695	14	0.842305	12.807907	32.807907	7.8078	13.486523
14	13.486523	18	4.513477	12.807817	32.807817	7.8078	15.248536
15	15.248536	3	−12.248536	12.807784	32.807784	7.8078	10.466847
16	10.466847	9	−1.466847	12.807771	32.807771	7.8078	9.894207
17	9.894207	11	1.105793	12.807767	32.807767	7.8078	10.325896
18	10.325896	10	−0.325896	12.807765	32.807765	7.8078	10.198670
19	10.198670	6	−4.198670	12.807764	32.807764	7.8078	8.559559
20	8.559559	12	3.440441	12.807764	32.807764	7.8078	9.902666
21	9.902666	14	4.097334	12.807764	32.807764	7.8078	11.502217
22	11.502217	10	−1.502217	12.807764	32.807764	7.8078	10.915769
23	10.915759	25	14.084231	12.807764	32.807764	7.8078	16.414087
24	16.414087	29	12.585913	12.807764	32.807764	7.8078	21.327479
25	21.327479	33	11.672521	12.807764	32.807764	7.8078	25.884294
...	etc.	...	...	...	...	...	...

$$\sum_{t=2}^{71} \log F_t = 244.811063 \quad \text{and} \quad \sum_{t=2}^{71} \frac{V_t^2}{F_t} = 83.226038,$$

giving a log-likelihood of -228.344249.

(iv) Start-up values

Again the astute reader will be wondering how we 'kick off' the Kalman filter recursions, that is—how do we know a_0 and C_0? It can be shown that for models which reach a steady state the state estimates for large t are unaffected by the choice of values for a_0 and C_0—even if the model is non-stationary. This means that only the contribution to the likelihood of the first few observations differs for different values of a_0 or C_0 so that for large data sets the effect of these first few observations will be negligible and the MLEs will be asymptotically unaffected by the starting states.

To illustrate this, Table 4.2 shows some of the Kalman filter iterations for the same model and the same data as Table 4.1 but with the starting values a_0 and C_0 changed. As before, the iterations tend to a steady state. The early iterations differ from Table 4.1 but later iterations converge to those of Table 4.1 and by iteration 23 all the quantities shown are identical—even $a_{t|t-1}$, which as we will see later implies that in spite of the different starting values predictions from the model would agree. As the residuals and prediction error variances differ for the first 22 iterations the log-likelihood is sensitive to the start-up values and is slightly different at -228.339088 for these starting values. With a long series the hope is that the effect of start-up values on the log-likelihood is small.

If the model is non-stationary and in the absence of any prior information on the initial state, a_0 can be set to zero and C_0 to M times the identity matrix where M is a very large number—for instance 10 000 or 100 000. This large covariance matrix indicates that little or nothing is known of the initial state. In effect we are using the first few observations to estimate the starting values, so again the first few prediction errors and variances should be omitted from the likelihood function. This is rather like setting a vague prior in Bayesian inference. As it seems reasonable to use the first d observations to estimate the d-dimensional state, we will ignore the first d terms in the likelihood so that the summations in (4.4) are for $t = d + 1, \ldots, N$ only and N is replaced by $N - d$ to give

$$\log L(\boldsymbol{\theta}) = -\frac{N-d}{2} \log 2\pi - \frac{1}{2} \sum_{t=d+1}^{N} \log F_t - \frac{1}{2} \sum_{t=d+1}^{N} \frac{V_t^2}{F_t}. \tag{4.14}$$

When the model is stationary then a_0 and C_0 can be set to the unconditional mean and covariance matrix of α_t. As the transition equation is

$$\boldsymbol{\alpha}_t = \boldsymbol{\phi}\boldsymbol{\alpha}_{t-1} + \mathbf{K}\boldsymbol{\eta}_t, \quad \mathbf{C}_0 = \boldsymbol{\phi}\mathbf{C}_0\boldsymbol{\phi}^{\mathrm{T}} + \mathbf{K}\boldsymbol{\Sigma}\mathbf{K}^{\mathrm{T}}$$

and in theory this can be solved for C_0 to give the starting values—see Gardner, Harvey & Phillips (1980).

Of course the random walk model is a particularly simple state space model, as the state has dimension 1. The first few iterations of fitting an AR(2) model with parameters $\phi_1 = 0.5$, $\phi_2 = 0.3$ and $\sigma^2 = 36$ to the (mean subtracted) purse data are shown in Table

Table 4.2. Kalman filter iterations for some random walk model and data as Table 4.1 but with different C_0 and a_0.

t	$a_{t\|t-1}$	X_t	V_t	$C_{t\|t-1}$	F_t	C_t	a_t
0						1000	10
1	10	10	0	1005	1025	19.6098	10
2	10	15	5.0	24.609756	44.609756	11.0334	12.758338
3	12.758337	10	−2.758338	16.033352	36.033352	8.8992	11.530992
4	11.530992	10	−1.530992	13.899173	33.899173	8.2003	10.903262
5	10.903262	12	1.096738	13.200302	33.200302	7.9519	11.339320
6	11.339320	10	−1.339320	12.951917	32.951917	7.8611	10.812894
7	10.812894	7	−3.812894	12.861101	32.861101	7.8276	9.320612
8	9.320612	17	7.679388	12.827553	32.827553	7.8151	12.321377
9	12.321377	10	−2.321377	12.815114	82.815114	7.8105	11.414822
10	11.414822	14	2.585178	12.810495	32.810495	7.8088	12.424176
⋮							
18	10.325890	10	−0.325890	12.807765	32.807765	7.8078	10.198666
19	10.198666	6	−4.1986666	12.807764	32.807764	7.8078	8.559557
20	8.559557	12	3.440443	12.807764	32.807764	7.8078	9.902665
21	9.902665	14	4.097335	12.807764	32.807764	7.8078	11.502216
22	11.502216	10	−1.502216	12.807764	32.807764	7.8078	10.915769
23	10.915759	25	14.084231	12.807764	32.807764	7.8078	16.414087
24	16.414087	29	12.585913	12.807764	32.807764	7.8078	21.327479
25	21.327479	33	11.672521	12.807764	32.807764	7.8078	25.884294

4.3. This model progresses very quickly to steady state, and the steady state prediction error variance is exactly equal to σ^2. We will see later that this is a feature of some ARMA models.

4.5 MAXIMIZING THE LIKELIHOOD FUNCTION

In the previous section we described how to evaluate the likelihood for a particular state space model and parameter set. Usually, some of the parameters of the GSS model are fixed to 0 or 1, whereas the others are unknown. The likelihood is obviously a function of the parameters (known and unknown) in the model. To obtain the maximum likelihood estimates the likelihood function must be maximized with respect to the *unknown* parameters.

When you use statistical software to fit a time series model it is not always clear how the model is estimated. For ARMA model estimation software manuals usually describe some variant of least squares or cite Box–Jenkins methods. For instance, MINITAB uses least squares, SYSTAT cites Box–Jenkins whereas STAMP uses exact maximum likelihood. To the uninitiated there appear to be several competing estimation methods. It is crucial to remember, however, that these are all variants or approximations to maximum

Table 4.3. First few Kalman iterations of an ARMA model placed in state space form with parameters $\phi_1 = 0.5$, $\phi_2 = 0.3$ and $\sigma^2 = 36$.

t	$a_{t|t-1}$	X_t	V_t	$C_{t|t-1}$		F_t	C_t		a_t
0							100000	0	0
							0	100000	0
1	0	−3.9155	−3.9155	125036	0	125036	0	0	−3.9155
				0	0		0	7200.5183	−0.469725
2	−2.427425	1.0845	3.511975	7236.5183	0	7236.518251	0	0	1.0845
				0	0		0	0	−1.17465
3	−0.6324	−3.9155	−3.2831	36	0	36	0	0	−3.9155
				0	0		0	0	0.32535
4	−1.6324	−3.9155	−2.2831	36	0	36	0	0	−3.9155
				0	0		0	0	−1.17465
5	−3.1324	−1.9155	1.2169	36	0	36	0	0	−1.9155
				0	0		0	0	−1.17465

likelihood and that for most purposes you will obtain broadly similar estimates whichever procedure you use.

Our recommendation is to use whatever software is available to you. We give some estimation results obtained from various software in Chapters 5 and 6. If you don't have access to any time series programs or if it is important that you obtain exact maximum likelihood estimates, this section and section 4.4 supply all the information required to write a likelihood evaluation program, maximize the likelihood and obtain numerical estimates of the standard errors by using library subroutines. As this is a practical book we emphasize that these estimation results will be sensitive to your choice of starting values, the rule for the steady state, whether the concentrated likelihood is used, the choice of numerical optimization parameters and the machine constants used by your computer. The cost of a maximum likelihood program may not be worth the extra accuracy.

(i) The maximization algorithm

Most mathematical subroutine libraries include a numerical optimization procedure. We used E04JBF from the NAG library. For this routine the user must supply the function to be maximized and an initial set of parameter values and supply some parameters which control the optimization algorithm. Readers reduced to writing their own maximization code may find *Numerical Recipes* (Press *et al.*, 1986), a useful guide to optimization or Nash (1979). It is not as difficult as one might suppose!

For state space estimation the user must supply a subroutine that evaluates the likelihood at a particular set of parameter values as described in section 4.4. Ideally the initial values of the parameters should be a good guess of the MLEs to minimize computing time and to avoid convergence to a purely local minimum. (Tips on good initial values for ARMA models and structural models are discussed in Chapters 5 and 6 respectively.) Analytic derivatives are not easily available for the likelihood of the state space model so derivatives must be calculated numerically. A crucial control parameter is the differencing interval or step length for these numerical derivatives. We usually take 10^{-6} or, if this gives problems, 10^{-4}. For efficiency, where possible the set of possible parameter values should be constrained so that the model is uniquely identified as described in section 3.7. Most optimization routines have this facility.

Fig. 4.1 shows some output obtained during estimation of the random walk plus noise model fitted to the purse data using a numerical optimization routine. The initial values used are those of the likelihood evaluation in Table 4.1 as are the starting values $\mathbf{a}_0$ and $\mathbf{C}_0$, i.e. $\sigma_\varepsilon^2 = 20$, $\sigma_\eta^2 = 5$. The differencing intervals are 0.000001. As the NAG optimization routine used is a minimization, the function to be minimized is $-2*$log-likelihood.

We have shown results from every fifth iteration and the final iteration of the minimization algorithm. Using the NAG terminology the iteration number is 'niter', the number of function evaluations (several of these are made to ascertain the gradient at each iteration point) is given by 'nf', and 'norm' indicates the square root of the sum of squares of the derivatives of the objective function with respect to the parameters.

(ii) Concentrating out a parameter

The MLEs and maximum likelihood cited in Chapter 3 differ slightly from those shown

```
a0  0.0000000000000000E+0                              initial state estimate
c0  100000.0000000000                                  initial state covariance
istart      2                      first observation to be included in likelihood
totabs  1.0000000000000000E-06                         criterion for steady state


INITIAL LOG LIK -228.3442492526178                     initial log-likelihood
  ******* FUNCTION VALUE IS 456.6884985052357          -2 log-likelihood
    PARAMETERS  DERIVATIVES
    20.0000000000000000   -0.53988775
     5.0000000000000000   -0.48562302
niter 0 nf 0 norm   0.726160                            'NAG' output


******* FUNCTION VALUE IS  455.5210999262439
PARAMETERS  DERIVATIVES
    24.7817980824491793   -0.00000078         estimates after 5 iterations
     5.1508010762739194   -0.00000106                   of maximization
niter 5 nf 47 norm    0.000001


*******FUNCTION VALUE IS  455.5210999262395
PARAMETERS DERIVATIVES                          estimates after 6 iterations
    24.7818070195309366   -0.00000004                   of maximization
     5.1508030271128578    0.00000000
niter 6 nf 54 norm    0.000000


*********RESULT************
e04jbf fail is   0                            successful exit from NAG routine
MAXIMUM LOG LIKELIHOOD IS -227.760550
steady state reached by    21 iterations
AIC is   915.0421998524789
 PARAMETER              S.ERROR  RATIO
   24.7818073645058967  4.393342  5.640765 maximum likelihood estimates
    5.1508030402947058  2.488801  2.069592
PREDiction error variance is 38.945084889928270        final prediction error
                                                                    variance
```

Fig. 4.1. Output from numerical optimization routine showing convergence of parameter estimates to maximum likelihood estimates for random walk plus noise model fitted to purse data.

in Fig. 4.1 because they were obtained using the same starting values but assuming that all variances in the model are in fact multiplied by a scaling factor. This is a 'dodge' favoured by Harvey, and is to be recommended. One parameter in the model is 'concentrated out', hence reducing by one the number of parameters to be estimated. This is done by selecting one of the noise variances in the model e.g. $\sigma_\varepsilon^2, \sigma_\eta^2, \sigma_\zeta^2$ or σ_ω^2 for structural models or σ^2 for ARMA models (there is no choice) as the scaling variance. When there is a choice it is safest to choose the noise variance which is likely to be the largest, as problems can be encountered if the scaling variance is near zero. We will call this variance σ^{*2}. All the other variance parameters in the model now represent the true noise variances *divided by* σ^{*2}. Suppose, for example that σ_ε^2 is taken as the scaling variance in the basic structural model, i.e. $\sigma^{*2} = \sigma_\varepsilon^2 = $ variance (ε_t). The model is still parameterized using

$$\Sigma = \mathrm{diag}(\sigma_\eta^2, \sigma_\zeta^2, \sigma_\omega^2)$$

as before but the σ^2 parameters are now interpreted as the corresponding variances scaled by σ^{*2}, i.e.

$$\sigma_\eta^2 = (\text{variance } \eta_t)\big/\sigma_\varepsilon^2, \quad \sigma_\zeta^2 = (\text{variance } \zeta_t)\big/\sigma_\varepsilon^2$$

and

$$\sigma_\omega^2 = (\text{variance } \omega_t)\big/\sigma_\varepsilon^2.$$

The scaling variance must now be fixed to 1.

For a particular model structure the Kalman filter iterations can be calculated in exactly the same way as for the unconcentrated case. When the Kalman recursions are calculated using the scaled variances the resultant matrics $\mathbf{C}_t$, $\mathbf{C}_{t|t-1}$, $\mathbf{F}_t$ will also be scaled by σ^{*2}, that is, $\mathbf{C}_t = $ (covariance matrix of $\mathbf{a}_t)/\sigma^{*2}$ and so on. That is, now the covariance matrix of $\mathbf{a}_0$ is $\sigma^{*2}\mathbf{C}_0$, of $\mathbf{a}_t$ is $\sigma^{*2}\mathbf{C}_t$, and the prediction error variance at time t is now $\sigma^{*2}F_t$. Table 4.4 shows the first few Kalman iterations of the random walk model fitted to the purse data where $\sigma^{*2} = \sigma_\varepsilon^2$. As σ_ε^2 is the scaling parameter the initial value of σ_ε^2 must be set to 1, and we have used $\sigma_\eta^2 = 0.1$.

Writing down the log-likelihood (4.14) in terms of these newly defined parameters gives

$$\log L(\boldsymbol{\theta}) = -\frac{N-d}{2}\log 2\pi - \frac{N-d}{2}\log \sigma^{*2} - \frac{1}{2}\sum_{t=d+1}^{N}\log F_t$$

$$-\frac{1}{2\sigma^{*2}}\sum_{t=d+1}^{N}\frac{v_t^2}{F_t}. \tag{4.15}$$

The advantage of this is that we can maximize (4.15) with respect to σ^{*2} by setting the derivative to zero and solving to give

$$\sigma^{*2} = \frac{1}{N-d}\sum_{t=d+1}^{N}\frac{v_t^2}{F_t}.$$

(Try this; it's not difficult!) If we substitute for σ^{*2} in (4.15) we obtain the *concentrated* likelihood function

Table 4.4. Kalman filter iterations for random walk plus noise with σ_ε^2, as scaling parameter and $\sigma_\eta^2 = 0.1$ fitted to purse data.

t	$a_{t|t-1}$	X_t	V_t	$C_{t|t-1}$	F_t	C_t	C_t
0						100000	0
1	0	10	10	100000.1	100001.1	1	9.9999
2	9.9999	15	5.0001	1.099990	2.09999	0.5238	12.618989
3	12.618989	10	−2.618989	0.623807	1.623807	0.3842	11.612869
4	11.612869	10	−1.612869	0.484163	1.484163	0.3262	11.086719
5	11.086719	12	0.913281	0.426220	1.426220	0.2988	11.359649
⋮	⋮	⋮	⋮	⋮	⋮	⋮	⋮
21	10.042726	14	3.957274	0.370158	1.370158	0.2702	11.111813
22	11.111813	10	−1.111813	0.370157	1.370157	0.2702	10.811449
23	10.811449	25	14.188551	0.370157	1.370157	0.2702	14.644579
24	14.644579	29	14.355421	0.370157	1.370157	0.2702	18.522790
25	18.522790	33	14.477210	0.370157	1.370157	0.2702	22.433903
	etc.						

$$\log L(\boldsymbol{\theta}) = -\frac{N-d}{2}(\log 2\pi + 1) - \frac{1}{2}\sum \log F_t - \frac{N-d}{2}\log \sigma^{*2},$$

which needs to be maximized with respect to the parameters other than σ^{*2}, that is, with respect to one fewer parameter than before.

For the example in Table 4.4, by the 71st iteration

$$\sum_{t=2}^{71} \log F_t = 22.805470 \quad \text{and} \quad \sum_{t=2}^{71} \frac{V_t^2}{F_t} = 2006.628222.$$

The maximum likelihood estimate of σ^{*2} at these parameter values is therefore $\sigma^{*2} = 28.666117$, which can be used in (4.15) to calculate that the log-likelihood at these parameter values is −228.2.

Fig. 4.2 shows the maximum likelihood estimation of the random walk model of Table 4.4. The MLEs fitted to the purse data using the concentrated likelihood starting at the parameter values differ slightly from those of the unconcentrated estimation because the starting value $C_0 = 100\,000$, whilst numerically the same needs to be multiplied by the scaling factor (itself a function of the parameter estimates) to give the covariance matrix of $\mathbf{a}_0$ when using the concentrated algorithm. The starting value variances for the unscaled and scaled methods are therefore different and result in different MLEs although these will be the same asymptotically. Notice that as σ_ε^2 is the scaling variance, variance(η_t) = $0.2078483857411718 \times \sigma_\varepsilon^2$.

Another example (Fig. 4.3) shows the (exact likelihood) estimation results from fitting an AR(2) model to the purse data. The initial values are the same as the parameters used in Table 4.3. Software packages give the following results.

---

a0 0.0000000000000000E+00   *initial state estimate*
c0 100000.00000000000   *initial state covariance*

totabs 1.0000000000000000E-06   *criterion for steady state*
INITIAL LOG LIK -228.1784964498997

ESTIMATION

******* FUNCTION VALUE IS 456.3569928997994
PARAMETERS DERIVATIVES   *initial parameter estimate*
   0.1000000000000000 -22.64844002
niter 0 nf 0 norm   22.648440

******* FUNCTION VALUE IS 455.5209849391062
PARAMETERS DERIVATIVES
   0.2078483857411718 -0.00000126
niter 4 nf 21 norm   0.000001

******* FUNCTION VALUE IS 455.5209849391062
PARAMETERS DERIVATIVES
   0.2078483857411718 -0.00000126
niter 4 nf 23 norm   0.000001

********************** RESULTS *******************
MAXIMUM LOG LIKELIHOOD IS -227.7604924695531
steady state reached by   17 iterations
AIC is   459.5209849391062
variance used to scale   24.78168000595917
   PARAMETER   S.ERROR T RATIO
   24.7816900059591658   4.212549   5.882826
    5.1508342636767422   2.322683   2.217622
PREDiction error variance is   38.94499527142553

FINAL STATE VECTOR 7.386587277495729   *final state estimate a_{71}*

Fig. 4.2. Output from numerical optimization routine as in Fig. 4.1 but now using concentrated
likelihood from initial point in Table 4.4.

Software	ϕ_1	ϕ_2	σ^2
MINITAB	0.3050	0.4036	36.86
	(0.1113)	(0.1125)	
SYSAT	0.305	0.403	36.91
	0.112	0.113	
Exact likelihood	0.3078	0.4002	36.1153

```
INITIAL LOG LIK   -223.1316654555017
ESTIMATION
******* FUNCTION VALUE IS   446.2633309110034
PARAMETERS   DERIVATIVES
    0.5000000000000000   29.64503548          initial AR parameters and
    0.3000000000000000   -1.10070605          corresponding derivatives
niter   0 nf 0 norm   29.665463


******* FUNCTION VALUE IS   443.2970655887218
PARAMETERS   DERIVATIVES
    0.3078411968533823   0.00000014
    0.4001778391900951   0.00000260
niter   5 nf 36 norm   0.000003


******* FUNCTION VALUE IS   443.2970655887218
PARAMETERS   DERIVATIVES
    0.3078411968533823   0.00000014
    0.4001778391900951   0.00000260
niter   6 nf 38 norm   0.000003


******* FUNCTION VALUE IS   443.2970655887218
PARAMETERS   DERIVATIVES
    0.3078411968533823   0.00000014
    0.4001778391900951   0.00000260
niter   6 nf 52 norm   0.000003


********************** RESULTS *******************
MAXIMUM LOG LIKELIHOOD IS   -221.6485327943609
steady state reached by   4 iterations
AIC is   449.2970654
variance used to scale   36.11534329165023
    PARAMETER              S.ERROR   RATIO
    0.3078411968533823   0.078087   3.942280
    0.4001778391900951   0.078739   5.082353
   36.1153432916502286   4.347772   8.306633
PREDiction error variance is   36.11534329165023
FINAL STATE VECTOR      -6.915500000000000   -3.567785525299293
```

Fig. 4.3. Maximum likelihood estimation of AR(2) model fitted to purse data.

(iii) Standard errors

Standard errors for the maximum likelihood estimates may be calculated using a numerical derivative routine (for instance E04XAF from the NAG library) to obtain the inverse of the Hessian matrix (see section 3.3). We should point out, however, that such numerical derivatives are not very reliable and depend on the differencing intervals chosen. We and others have frequently encountered failures in such routines.

If the data are very extensive the objective function may appear to be flat and the Hessian routine may fail. If a failure is encountered it is therefore worth scaling such data. An equivalent model for the scaled data has the same $\mathbf{H}$, ϕ and $\mathbf{K}$ matrices, but all the variance parameters will be scaled by the square of the scaling factor. The state estimates will be scaled in the same way as the data.

In spite of Hessian failures we have obtained broadly similar standard errors to those published elsewhere which have not affected the significance or otherwise of the parameters. More accurate methods are available to estimate the Hessian for specific models but these are much more complicated and sometimes rely on frequency domain methods.

The asymptotic normality of the MLEs is conditional on a set of regularity conditions. If these do not hold, the calculation of standard errors becomes more complicated; for instance, when the true value of a variance parameter in the state space model is zero, as it lies on the boundary of the parameter space. In this case the distribution of the estimate may be related to the normal distribution—for instance with a density function that looks like half a normal distribution with a probability of a half at zero. Harvey goes into more detail (Harvey 1989, page 210 onwards).

(iv) The EM algorithm

While considering parameter estimation we shall briefly mention an algorithm called the EM algorithm which has been adapted to maximize the likelihood for time series models and is advocated, for example, by Shumway (1988). The main disadvantage from our viewpoint is that whilst the algorithm is based on a state space form, the ϕ and $\mathbf{K\Sigma K}^{\mathrm{T}}$ matrices have no particular structure. Also, the EM algorithm is less efficient than using a numerical optimization algorithm and it converges to a *local* rather than a global optimum and so may be sensitive to the choice of initial values. However, if no other software or numerical optimization routine is available the EM algorithm can be implemented relatively easily. Harvey (1989, page 188) considers the EM algorithm for his structural models.

(v) Smoothed estimators

These give estimates of the states based on the whole series as opposed to the $\mathbf{a}_t$'s, which are based on the series up to time t only and so are useful to estimate the components (trend seasonal etc.) of a structural model.

When the usual Kalman recursions have been run the final state estimate $\mathbf{a}_N$ and associated error variance $\mathbf{C}_N$ are, of course, the conditional expectation of α_N and its covariance given all N observations. The Kalman *smoothing* or backward recursions start with $\mathbf{a}_N$ and $\mathbf{C}_N$, and are processed for $t = N - 1,\dots, 1$. For each t the conditional expectation estimator of α_t given all N observations $\mathbf{a}_{t|N}$ and its covariance $\mathbf{C}_{t|N}$ are calculated. The equations, which we shall not derive, are

$$\mathbf{a}_{t|N} = \mathbf{a}_t + \mathbf{C}_t^* \left(\mathbf{a}_{t+1|N} - \phi \mathbf{a}_t \right) \tag{4.16}$$

$$\mathbf{C}_{t|N} = \mathbf{C}_t + \mathbf{C}_t^* \left(\mathbf{C}_{t+1|N} - \mathbf{C}_{t+1|t} \right) \mathbf{C}_t^{*\mathrm{T}} \tag{4.17}$$

where

$$\mathbf{C}_t^* = \mathbf{C}_t \boldsymbol{\phi}^T \mathbf{C}_{t+1|t}^{-1}$$

for $t = N - 1, N - 2,\ldots, 1$. They require $\mathbf{C}_t$ and $\mathbf{a}_t$ for $t = 1,\ldots, N$ from the forward recursions so these must have been stored previously. Of course, as the smoothed estimators of $\boldsymbol{\alpha}_t$ are based on all the observations and not just those up to time t, $\mathbf{C}_{t|N}$ will be smaller than $\mathbf{C}_t$ in the sense that $\mathbf{C}_t - \mathbf{C}_{t|N}$ will be positive semidefinite.

By way of illustration, consider again the random walk plus noise model fitted to the purse data. As the state of this model comprises the trend term μ_t only the smoothing equations calculate an estimate of the trend at each time period given the whole series. The purse data can then be decomposed into a trend component and an irregular component. Fig. 4.4 shows the estimated trend and actual purse data.

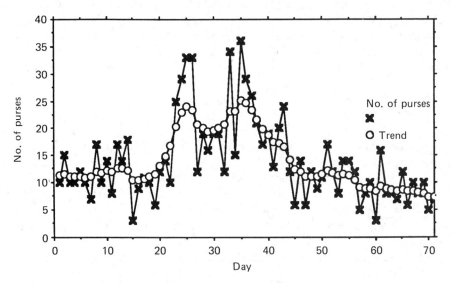

Fig. 4.4. Trend component of purse data calculated by smoothing the state estimate of the random walk plus noise model.

4.6 PREDICTION

In Chapter 3 we calculated forecasts and prediction error variances for some simple models, and saw that this can be fiddly. Forecasting procedures can be simplified greatly, however, by placing time series models into the general state space model. As before, when forecasting we must assume that the parameter values of the GSS model (4.1), (4.2) are known exactly, so our prediction error variances do not include an element for estimation error.

In section 4.5 we showed that for a model in state space form the conditional expectation of the one step predictor $X_{t|t-1}$ and its variance are produced as byproducts of the Kalman filter. The state space model also lends itself nicely to the calculation of predictors and their variances more than one step ahead.

At time t the Kalman filter will give $\mathbf{a}_t$, the MMSE of α_t based on the observations up to X_t inclusive. We already know that the one step predictor of the state is $\alpha_{t+1|t} = \phi\mathbf{a}_t$ and of X_{t+1} is $X_{t+1|t} = \mathbf{H}\phi\mathbf{a}_t$. To predict $k > 1$ steps ahead we proceed as follows.

We can easily write

$$
\begin{aligned}
\alpha_{t+k} &= \phi\alpha_{t+k-1} + \eta_{t+k} \\
&= \phi(\phi\alpha_{t+k-2} + \eta_{t+k-1}) + \eta_{t+k} \\
&= \phi^2\alpha_{t+k-2} + \phi\eta_{t+k-1} + \eta_{t+k} \\
&= \phi^3\alpha_{t+k-3} + \phi^2\eta_{t+k-2} + \phi\eta_{t+k-1} + \eta_{t+k},
\end{aligned}
$$

and so on until

$$
\alpha_{t+k} = \phi^k\alpha_t + \phi^{k-1}\eta_{t+1} + \ldots + \phi\eta_{t+k-1} + \eta_{t+k}.
$$

Taking conditional expectations gives the convenient form

$$
E\left(\alpha_{t+k|t}\right) = \phi^k\mathbf{a}_t.
$$

The conditional expectations forecast of X_{t+k} at time t is therefore simply

$$
X_{t+k|t} = \mathbf{H}\phi^k\mathbf{a}_t.
$$

Notice that the current state estimate $\mathbf{a}_t$ captures all the information about the past required to predict future X_t's and so the forecast takes into account any uncertainty associated with the starting value X_0.

The variance of the k step forecast errors will be

$$
\begin{aligned}
E\left(X_{t+k} - X_{t+k|t}\right)^2 &= E(\mathbf{H}\phi^k\alpha_t + \mathbf{H}\phi^{k-1}\eta_{t+1} + \mathbf{H}\phi^{k-2}\eta_{t+2} + \ldots + \mathbf{H}\phi\eta_{t+k-1} \\
&\qquad\qquad + \mathbf{H}\eta_{t+k} + \varepsilon_{t+k} - \mathbf{H}\phi^k\mathbf{a}_t)^2 \\
&= E\left(\mathbf{H}\phi^k(\alpha_t - \mathbf{a}_t) + \mathbf{H}\sum_{i=1}^{k}\phi^{k-i}\mathbf{K}\eta_{t+i} + \varepsilon_{t-k}\right)^2
\end{aligned}
$$

but as the terms in the expectation are mutually independent by assumption, the k step prediction error variance is

$$
\mathbf{H}\left\{\phi^k\mathbf{C}_t(\phi^k)^{\mathrm{T}} + \sum_{i=1}^{k}\phi^{k-i}\mathbf{K}\Sigma\mathbf{K}^{\mathrm{T}}\phi^{k-i}\right\}\mathbf{H}^{\mathrm{T}} + \sigma_\varepsilon^2. \tag{4.18}
$$

Equation (4.18) assumes that $\mathbf{C}_t$, Σ and σ_ε^2 are actual variances that have *not* been scaled by σ^{*2}. If they have been scaled by σ^{*2}, (4.18) needs to be multiplied by σ^{*2} to represent the k step PEV.

By noting again that for the AR(2) model (model A) the first state $\alpha_t^{(1)} = K_t$ and from the transition equation that the second state $\alpha_t^{(2)} = \phi_2\alpha_{t-1}^{(1)} = \phi_2 X_{t-1}$ it is easy to check that $X_{t+1|t} = \mathbf{H}\boldsymbol{\phi}\mathbf{a}_t$ and $X_{t+2|t} = \mathbf{H}\boldsymbol{\phi}^2\mathbf{a}_t$ give the expressions for the one and two step predictions of the AR(2) model obtained in section 3.4. Numerically, the final state estimate $\mathbf{a}_{71}$ at the MLEs is $(-6.9155, -3.567786)^\mathrm{T}$ (see Fig. 4.3) and the reader can confirm that premultiplying this by

$$(1 \quad 0)\begin{pmatrix} 0.30784 & 1 \\ 0.400178 & 0 \end{pmatrix}$$

gives the one step predictor. The two step predictor is calculated as

$$(1 \quad 0)\begin{pmatrix} 0.30784 & 1 \\ 0.400178 & 0 \end{pmatrix}^2\begin{pmatrix} -6.9155 \\ -3.567786 \end{pmatrix},$$

and so on.

The beauty of using the state space form for prediction is that MMSE estimates of the state have already been produced as a byproduct of the estimation procedure. For example, in Chapter 3 we saw that the k step predictor of the random walk plus noise model (model B) is μ_t for all k, but without state space methods we could not ascertain the value of μ_t directly from the data. When the model is placed into GSS form, however, the state comprises μ_t only, and the prediction $X_{t+k|t} = \mathbf{H}\boldsymbol{\phi}^k\mathbf{a}_t$ uses the latest available estimate of μ_t.

For instance, for the random walk model fitted to the purse data the final state estimate from the maximum likelihood model is $a_{71} = 7.386587$ (see Fig. 4.2) so the latest estimate of $\mu_{71} = 7.386587$. From (4.18) the k step prediction error variances for this example are $C_{t+k}\sigma_\eta^2 + \sigma_\varepsilon^2$, whereas the PEV calculated in Chapter 3 was merely $k\sigma_\eta^2 + \sigma_\varepsilon^2$. This is because the term involving $\mathbf{C}_t$ in (4.18) presents the error in estimating the state (μ_t here) whereas in Chapter 3 our calculations assumed that μ_t was known. The steady state C_t for this model is 9.0125, giving a one step prediction error variance of 38.9450, two step of 44.0958, and so on.

For the AR(2) model, however, the steady state C_t and so C_{71} is just a matrix of zeroes because, as stated earlier, the state α_t of the AR(2) model is an exact function of the observations. There is therefore no contribution to the error variance due to the uncertainty of the state estimators, and the PEVs will be the same as those in Chapter 3. It is left to the reader to check this.

In many models, if the sample is large enough and if the parameters obey certain restrictions, the components of the forecast functions can be estimated exactly without recourse to the state space representation or the Kalman filter. When this does not happen we say that there is a finite sample prediction *problem*. It is an advantage of the Kalman filter that it can handle such cases.

4.7 MODEL SELECTION, COMPARISON, AND EVALUATION

(i) Model selection and comparison

As described in Chapter 3, we would ideally like to select a particular GSS model type because it has properties which match those of the data. Such selection methods specific to ARMA and structural models are considered in Chapters 5 and 6 respectively. In practice, however, there is frequently no obvious model, and the sample properties may be misleading, especially for small samples. A general method of finding a suitable model is to use a backwards elimination procedure in an analogous way to its use in multiple linear regression.

In backwards elimination the modeller starts by fitting a large order state space model—for instance order 4 or 5. If any of the parameter estimates are too small to be significantly different from zero (so that the ratio of parameter estimate divided by standard error is less than, say, 2 in absolute value) then the modeller sets the least significant parameter (the one with the lowest non-significant ratio) to zero and refits the model. Of course, the standard error and resultant ratio apply to each parameter in the presence of the other parameters so only one parameter should be eliminated at once. We continue until all the parameters remaining are significant and this model is chosen.

At each stage of the backwards elimination we could calculate AIC = –2 log-likelihood + number of parameters as described in section 3.5. As the inclusion of insignificant parameters is not likely to improve the log-likelihood we would hope that the minimum AIC model would be the same as the final model obtained using the backwards elimination procedure, although this need not necessarily be the case.

AIC can, of course, be used to compare disparate model types as well, although care should be taken that the AICs are based on likelihoods which use the *same number* of residuals. For instance, the random walk plus noise model has state dimension 1 so the residual from the first observation was omitted from the likelihood, whereas estimation of the AR(2) model omits the first two residuals, and so the likelihoods cannot be compared using the AICs. To remedy this it is best to omit the same number of residuals from the likelihood when making such comparisons—usually a number corresponding to the highest state dimension of the models under consideration.

We illustrate backwards elimination and AIC comparison by fitting an ARMA model to our old friend the purse data. We already know from studying the autocorrelations and partial autocorrelations that an AR(2) model is likely, but in the absence of such information we could start by fitting a large order ARMA and proceed with backwards elimination. Here, we start with a state space model of dimension 3, an ARMA(3, 2) model as shown in section 4.1(ii). After fitting the full ARMA(3, 2) the least significant parameter is ϕ_3, so this is zeroized and an ARMA(2, 2) model is fitted. The least significant parameter of this is θ_2, so this is eliminated and an ARMA(2, 1) model is fitted, and so on. The maximum log-likelihood, AIC and prediction error variance for the succession of fitted models, each with one fewer non-zero parameters, are shown in Table 4.5 until all the parameters in the model are significant. As expected, the log-likelihood and prediction error variances are little affected by the elimination of non-significant parameters, and the AIC reduces steadily at each step. For interest—to show that it is not an appropriate model—we have included the same statistics for the AR(1) model. At the (erroneous) elimination of the (significant) ϕ_2 parameter the log-likelihood reduces, AIC increases, and the PEV is greatly inflated.

Table 4.5. Illustration of the backwards elimination procedure fitting and ARMA model to the purse data, including results from an AR(1) model fit for comparison.

Step	Model	Maximum log-likelihood	AIC	Prediction error variance
1	ARMA(3, 2)	−218.766	449.533	36.458992
2	ARMA(2, 2)	−218.789	447.578	36.490394
3	ARMA(2, 1)	−218.820	445.640	36.525374
4	AR(2)	−218.834	443.667	36.539880
	AR(1)	−224.537	453.074	43.213203

(ii) Diagnostics

Even when a model is suggested using AIC or backwards elimination it may still be inappropriate for the data and diagnostic checks must be made as described in section 3.5. When the state space model is properly specified the residuals V_t should have a normal distribution with zero mean and variance F_t. It is easiest to work with the standardized residuals

$$\tilde{V}_t = V_t / \sqrt{F_t}.$$

When the parameters of the model are known exactly the standardized residuals are $N(0, 1)$ (standard normal) distributed and if parameters are estimated they should be *approximately* $N(0, 1)$. Similarly, it can be shown that when the parameters are known the residuals will be independent whereas they will be *approximately* independent if the parameters are estimated. As stated in Chapter 3, the portmanteau test statistic for the first k autocorrelations is

$$Q(k) = N^*(N^* + 2) \sum_{i=1}^{k} (N^* - i)^{-1} r_v^2(i)$$

where $r_v^2(i)$ is the sample autocorrelation at lag i of the standardized residuals and where $N^* = N - d$ is now the number of observations less the state dimension assuming that the first d observations are not included in the likelihood function. Harvey (1989, p. 259) conjectures that under the null hypothesis that the residuals are uncorrelated $Q(k)$ should have a χ^2 distribution with $k - n^*$ degrees of freedom where n^* is one less than the number of estimated state space parameters.

(iii) Post-sample prediction

If the model is correct the sum of squares of the standardized prediction errors in the sample period will have a χ^2_{N-d} distribution. Similarly, the corresponding sum of squares of m standardized post-sample one step prediction errors will be χ^2_m. If the model is correct the ratio of these will have an F distribution with m and $N-d$ degrees of freedom respectively, i.e.

$$\xi(m) = \frac{\displaystyle\sum_{t=N+1}^{N+m} \tilde{V}_t^2 \big/ m}{\displaystyle\sum_{t=d+1}^{N} \tilde{V}_t^2 \big/ (N-d)}.$$

Notice that the denominator is also the estimate of the concentrated out (scaling) variance σ^{*2} described in section 4.4. If N is large we can expect to have reached a steady state during the sample period so that we can write $F_t \sim F$ for $t = N+1, \ldots, N+m$ where F is the steady state value of F_t

$$\xi(m) = \frac{\displaystyle\sum_{t=N+1}^{N+m} V_t^2}{mF\sigma^{*2}}. \tag{4.19}$$

We now note that $\sigma^{*2}F$ is the steady state prediction error variance so that (4.19) corresponds to our statistic $\xi(m)$ in (3.10). As explained in Chapter 3, it is important to remember that even if this statistic is not significant we may not have a good model, as the prediction errors in the sample period may be large.

4.8 SIMULATION OF STATE SPACE MODELS

As in section 3.9 the state space model (4.1), (4.2) can be simulated as long as the random noise series $\{\varepsilon_t\}$ and $\{\eta_t\}$ are available. To start the simulation a value for α_0 is required. We have already seen that

$$X_t = \mathbf{H}\boldsymbol{\phi}^t\boldsymbol{\alpha}_0 + \mathbf{H}\mathbf{K}\boldsymbol{\eta}_t + \mathbf{H}\boldsymbol{\phi}\mathbf{K}\boldsymbol{\eta}_{t-1} + \mathbf{H}\boldsymbol{\phi}^2\mathbf{K}\boldsymbol{\eta}_{t-2} + \ldots + \mathbf{H}\boldsymbol{\phi}^{t-1}\mathbf{K}\boldsymbol{\eta}_1 + \varepsilon_t$$

and that stationary series (when the eigenvalues of $\boldsymbol{\phi}$ are less than 1 in absolute value) are asymptotically independent of $\boldsymbol{\alpha}_0$. It is therefore reasonable to ignore the first 50 or 100 observations generated by such a model. If the eigenvalues of $\boldsymbol{\phi}$ lie on or outside the unit circle the effect of $\boldsymbol{\alpha}_0$ and noises in the infinite past remains or increases respectively through time. Figs 4.5 and 4.6 each show two series generated using the same model noise stream but with different starting values $\boldsymbol{\alpha}_0$. Fig. 4.5 shows realizations of a stationary model and Fig. 4.6 of a non-stationary model.

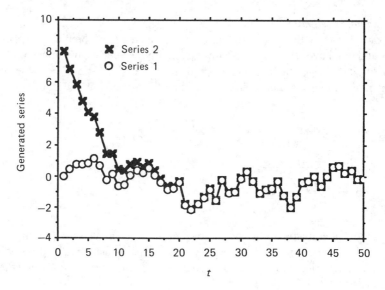

Fig. 4.5. Two realizations of the stationary AR(1) model in state space form $X_t = \alpha_t$, $\alpha_t = 0.8\alpha_{t-1} + \eta_t$ where $\sigma_\eta^2 = 0.25$ generated from the same noise stream $\{\eta_t\}$. Series 1 starts with $\alpha_0 = 10$, whereas series 2 has $\alpha_0 = 0$. Owing to the stationarity the series converge early.

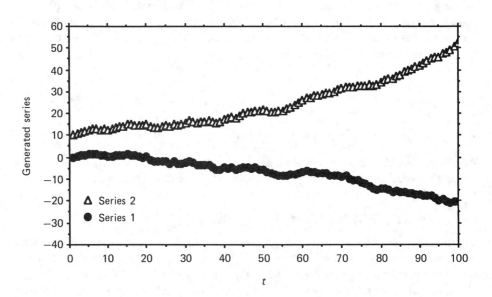

Fig. 4.6. Two realizations of the non-stationary AR(1) model in state space form $X_t = \alpha_t$, $\alpha_t = 1.02\alpha_{t-1} + \eta_t$ where $\sigma_\eta^2 = 0.25$ generated from the same noise stream $\{\eta_t\}$. Series 1 starts with $\alpha_0 = 0$, whereas series 2 has $\alpha_0 = 10$. The series do not converge.

EXERCISES

(1)   The distance of a missile from base can be measured, but is subject to error. The distance covered follows a first order difference equation for successive time periods and increases by β_t per unit time. However, β_t fluctuates as a random walk. Write down a state space model for this system.

(2)   Show that the model C in Chapter 3 can be represented by a GSS model. Hint: use $\cos(2\pi f t + \phi) = \cos(2\pi f (t-1) + \phi)\cos(2\pi f) - \sin(2\pi f)\sin(2\pi f (t-1) + \phi)$.

(3)   Place the model $\Delta X_t = 0.5X_{t-1} + 0.3X_{t-2} + \varepsilon_t + 0.1\varepsilon_{t-1}$ in state space form. How can you tell from the state space representation that the model is non-stationary?

(4)   Show that the model

$$X_t = (1 \quad 0)\alpha_t + \varepsilon_t \quad \alpha_t = \begin{pmatrix} 1 & 0.2 \\ 0.1 & 0 \end{pmatrix}\alpha_{t-1} + \begin{pmatrix} 1 \\ 0.2 \end{pmatrix}\eta_t$$

is equivalent to the model

$$X_t = (1 \quad -2)\alpha_t + \varepsilon_t \quad \alpha_t = \begin{pmatrix} 1.2 & -2.2 \\ 0.1 & -0.2 \end{pmatrix}\alpha_{t-1} + \begin{pmatrix} 1.4 \\ 0.2 \end{pmatrix}\eta_t.$$

(5)   Show that the Kalman filter recursions for $X_t = \mu_t + \varepsilon_t$, $\mu_t = \mu_{t-1} + \eta_t$ where var $\varepsilon_t = \sigma_\varepsilon^2$, var $\eta_t = \sigma_\eta^2$ simplifying to $\alpha_{t|t-1} = (I - G)\alpha_{t-1|t-2} + GX_t$, where G is the Kalman gain. Find the corresponding equation for $C_{t|t-1}$ in terms of $C_{t-1|t-2}$. Show that starting the recursion, setting $C_{1|0}$ to a very large number is equivalent to setting $a_1 = X_1$, $C_1 = \sigma_\varepsilon^2$.

(6)   Fit a random walk model to the 60 observations from a paper machine shown (row-wise) below and use this to forecast the next four time periods. Use diagnostic checking to ascertain whether this is a suitable model for the data or not.

33.5	34	33.5	33.8	33.5	33
33	33.5	33.5	33.3	33.3	33.5
33	32.5	32.5	32.8	32.8	32.5
32.5	32.2	32.5	32.5	32.5	32.3
32	32.5	32.5	32.5	34	33.3
33	32.5	32.5	32.5	32.8	32.8
32.8	32.2	32.7	33	33	33
32.5	32	32	31.8	31.8	31.8
32.5	32.7	32.7	32	32	32.6
32.4	32.4	32.5	32.5	32.5	32.5

(7) Consider the ARMA(1, 1) model $X_t = 0.6X_{t-1} + 0.4\varepsilon_{t-1} + \varepsilon_t$. Use the state space representation to calculate expressions for the 1 and 2 step predictors and their error variances once in steady state given that at time t the state estimate covariance matrix $\mathbf{C}_t$

takes the form $\begin{pmatrix} 0 & 0 \\ 0 & c \end{pmatrix}$.

(8) Fit an AR(2) model to the paper data in Exercise 6. If necessary reduce the number of parameters using backward elimination. Compare the AIC of your final model with the random walk plus noise model fitted in Exercise 6 taking care to include the same number of observations in the likelihood. Compare the estimation results from a software package with your exact estimation results and comment.

(9) Fit a random walk plus noise model to the first 70 observations of the jeans data (as shown in Fig. 1.4) given below (row-wise) and use this to forecast the remaining two observations. Examine the residuals and use diagnostic checking to comment on the fit of the model. It may be helpful to scale the data—say by 100—as the magnitude of the raw data is large.

1998	1968	1937	1827	2027	2286	2484	2266	2107	1690
1808	1927	1924	1959	1889	1819	1824	1979	1919	1845
1801	1799	1952	1956	1969	2044	2100	2103	2110	2375
2030	1744	1699	1591	1770	1950	2149	2200	2294	2146
2241	2369	2251	2126	2000	1759	1947	2135	2319	2352
2476	2296	2400	3126	2304	2190	2121	2032	2161	2289
2137	2130	2154	1831	1899	2117	2266	2176	2089	1817
2162	2267								

(10) Use state space methods to fit an AR(1) model to the jeans data as above. Contrast your results with those of the random walk plus noise model. Fit an AR(2) model in the same way. Use whatever statistical software you have available to estimate the model using ARMA methods. Do these results differ greatly from the state space results?

(11) Use a state space representation to simulate 50 observations from (i) an AR(1) model with parameter $\phi_1 = 0.7$, (ii) an AR(1) model with parameter 1.01, and (iii) a random walk with noise model. Choose arbitrary starting values, but in each case say whether your simulation is sensitive to these. Repeat with changed starting values to confirm your answers.

5

ARMA (Box–Jenkins) models

Time present and time past
Are both perhaps present in time future
And time future contained in time past.

T.S. Eliot, Burnt Norton, Part 1.

5.1 INTRODUCTION

We met the autoregressive-moving average or ARMA(p, q) model in passing in Chapter 3, section 3.6, and placed an ARMA(3, 2) model into the general state space form in section 4.1. In this chapter we will make a more detailed study of ARMA models.

To recap, the general ARMA model of autoregressive order p and moving average order q is

$$X_t = \phi_1 X_{t-1} + \dots + \phi_p X_{t-p} + \varepsilon_t + \theta_1 \varepsilon_{t-1} + \dots + \theta_q \varepsilon_{t-q} \tag{5.1}$$

where the $\{\varepsilon_t\}$ are i.i.d. with zero mean and variance σ^2. If all the θ_i's are zero we say that we have an *autoregressive* or AR model, whereas if the ϕ_i's are all zero we have a *moving average* or MA model. The MA model is a finite version of the general linear representation considered in section 2.5.

A methodology for ARMA models was developed largely by Box & Jenkins (1970), and so the models are often called Box–Jenkins models. This was before state space methods had been devised for time series, so they are based on the ARMA difference equation (5.1).

As ARMA models can be represented in state space form we already have the means (described in Chapter 4) of obtaining some properties, estimating, forecasting and simulating ARMA models. In practice, however, many students will not have access to state space software or the time to write it, and will of necessity have to use 'conventional' 'Box–Jenkins' methods and software. In this chapter we will both consider ARMA models as state space models *and* describe the Box–Jenkins ARMA methodology. Studying the two approaches in parallel in this way should greatly increase our understanding of the model.

It will sometimes be useful to represent the ARMA model using the backward operator B and write (5.1) as

$$(1 - \phi_1 B - \phi_2 B^2 ... - \phi_p B^p) X_t = (1 + \phi_1 B + ... + \phi_q B^q) \varepsilon_t.$$

For obvious reasons we will refer to the polynomial on the left hand side of this equation
as the AR polynomial and the polynomial on the right hand side as the MA polynomial.

The ARMA model can be placed in GSS form of state dimension $d = \max(p, q + 1)$ as
follows:

$$X_t = (1 \quad 0 \quad ... \quad 0) \alpha_t \tag{5.2a}$$

$$\alpha_t = \begin{pmatrix} \phi_1 & 1 & 0 & 0 & 0 \\ \phi_2 & 0 & 1 & 0 & 0 \\ \vdots & \vdots & \vdots & \vdots & 1 \\ \phi_d & 0 & . & 0 & 0 \end{pmatrix} \alpha_{t-1} + \begin{pmatrix} 1 \\ \theta_1 \\ \theta_2 \\ \vdots \\ \theta_{d-1} \end{pmatrix} \eta_t \tag{5.2b}$$

where $\phi_i = 0$ for any $i > p$ and $\theta_j = 0$ for any $j > q$ and $\{\eta_t\}$ is a scalar white noise
sequence of zero mean and variance σ^2. Notice that this is the canonical state space form
given in section 4.3 with no measurement noise.

To show that (5.2) is indeed a representation of an ARMA model we proceed as
described in section 4.1 for the ARMA(3, 2) model. Writing the state vector as

$$\alpha_t = \left(\alpha_t^{(1)}, \alpha_t^{(2)}, ..., \alpha_t^{(d)} \right)^{\mathrm{T}}$$

the bottom row of the state equation is

$$\alpha_t^{(d)} = \phi_d \alpha_{t-1}^{(1)} + \phi_{d-1} \eta_t$$

and the second from bottom row gives

$$\alpha_t^{(d-1)} = \phi_{d-1} \alpha_{t-1}^{(1)} + \alpha_{t-1}^{(d)} + \phi_{d-2} \eta_t.$$

Substituting for $\alpha_{t-1}^{(d)}$ using the bottom row equation gives

$$\alpha_t^{(d-1)} = \phi_{d-1} \alpha_{t-1}^{(1)} + \phi_d \alpha_{t-2}^{(1)} + \phi_{d-1} \eta_{t-1} + \phi_{d-2} \eta_t$$

which expresses $\alpha_t^{(d-1)}$ in terms of the first state elements. We proceed similarly with the
third from bottom row of the transition equation but substituting for $\alpha_{t-1}^{(d-1)}$ using the
expression just obtained from the second from last row to obtain an expression for
$\alpha_t^{(d-2)}$ in terms of $\alpha_{t-1}^{(1)}$, $\alpha_{t-2}^{(1)}$, $\alpha_{t-3}^{(1)}$. We continue working up the transition equations in
this way until from the top equation, we obtain

$$\alpha_t^{(1)} = \phi_1 \alpha_{t-1}^{(1)} + \phi_2 \alpha_{t-2}^{(1)} + ... + \phi_d \alpha_{t-d} + \eta_t + \theta_1 \eta_{t-1} + ... + \theta_{d-1} \eta_{t-(d-1)}.$$

Note that this is our ARMA equation (5.1) but with $\alpha_t^{(1)}$ in place of X_t. However, as there is not measurement noise in the state space representation (5.2), X_t is exactly equal to the 'top' state $\alpha_t^{(1)}$, and the state space representation is equivalent to the ARMA model.

There are other ways of placing ARMA models in state space form, but these are all input–output (see section 4.3) equivalent to (5.2).

5.2 STATIONARITY

We will start by considering conditions for the AR(1) model

$$X_t = \phi X_{t-1} + \varepsilon_t \tag{5.3}$$

to be stationary. A short cut is to say that in state space form (4.1), (4.2) the transition matrix ϕ is merely the scalar ϕ, so $|\phi| < 1$ is the condition for stationarity. However, as we wish to establish the stationarity conditions of more complex models we will consider other methods as well.

If we substitute for X_{t-1} in (5.3) to give $X_t = \phi(\phi X_{t-2} + \varepsilon_{t-1}) + \varepsilon_t$ and then substitute for X_{t-2} and so on, we obtain

$$X_t = \phi^t X_0 + \varepsilon_t + \phi\varepsilon_{t-1} + \ldots + \phi^{t-1}\varepsilon_1. \tag{5.4}$$

Continuing to substitute for the X_ts in this way gives

$$X_t = \varepsilon_t + \phi\varepsilon_{t-1} + \ldots + \phi^{t-1}\varepsilon_1 + \phi^t\varepsilon_0 + \phi^{t+1}\varepsilon_{-1} + \phi^{t+2}\varepsilon_{-2} + \ldots$$

and, if we assume an infinite past,

$$X_t = \sum_{j=0}^{\infty} \phi^j \varepsilon_{t-j}. \tag{5.5}$$

This is the *infinite moving average* representation of the AR(1) model. When the model is stationary it is none other than the general linear representation (2.5) of the AR(1) model.

It is clear from (5.5) that the variance of X_t is

$$\sigma^2 \sum_{j=0}^{\infty} \phi^{2j}$$

(compare with section 2.5), and so for this to be finite the infinite sum must converge, that is, $|\phi| < 1$. This will also ensure that for large t, X_t is independent of X_0 (see (5.4)) and will therefore have a constant mean.

To consider the conditions for ARMA models of greater order to be stationary it will help to regard the model as a difference equation in X_t and consider its solution. The first appendix to this chapter outlines the solution method for such linear difference equations.

To find the general solution of the AR(1) model we first solve the homogeneous equation $X_t - \phi X_{t-1} = 0$ to give the complementary function $X_t = k\phi^t$ where k is an unknown constant.

The infinite MA representation (5.5) which we obtained by repeated substitution for X_t is a particular solution to this equation. An alternative way of calculating this particular solution which is practical for more general ARMA models is to assume that it is of form

$$X_t = \psi_0 \varepsilon_t + \psi_1 \varepsilon_{t-1} + \psi_2 \varepsilon_{t-2} + \ldots = (1 + \psi_1 B + \psi_2 B^2 + \ldots)\varepsilon_t = \psi(B)\varepsilon_t$$

and to find the ψ coefficients. As the AR(1) model is $(1 - \phi B)X_t = \varepsilon_t$, substituting for X_t gives $(1 - \phi B)\psi(B)\varepsilon_t = \varepsilon_t$. Equating the coefficients of B on the left and right hand sides of this equation gives $(1 - \phi B)(\psi_0 + \psi_1 B + \ldots) = 1$ so that

$$\psi_0 = 1,$$
$$\psi_1 - \phi\psi_0 = 0,$$

so

$$\psi_1 = \phi, \quad \text{and} \quad \psi_2 - \phi\psi_1 = 0,$$

giving

$$\psi_2 = \phi^2$$

and so on, which agrees with (5.5).

The general solution of the original AR(1) difference equation is therefore the sum of the complementary function and the particular solution

$$X_t = k\phi^t + \sum_{j=0}^{\infty} \phi^j \varepsilon_{t-j}. \tag{5.6}$$

When $|\phi| < 1$ the complementary function tends to zero for large t, so only the second term of (5.6), the particular solution, remains and the mean of X_t is independent of t. In addition the variance of the remaining term of (5.6) converges for $|\phi| < 1$, so the model is weakly stationary.

The value of the constant k in the general solution can be determined from the initial conditions. For instance, if $X_0 = 0$, (5.6) gives

$$k = -\sum_{j=0}^{\infty} \phi^j \varepsilon_{-j}$$

and the general solution is

$$X_t = -\sum_{j=0}^{\infty} \phi^{t+j} \varepsilon_{-j} + \sum_{j=0}^{\infty} \phi^j \varepsilon_{t-j} = \sum_{j=0}^{t-1} \phi^j \varepsilon_{t-j},$$

which is (5.4) with $X_0 = 0$.

Note that we could also have obtained (5.5) by writing $X_t = (1 - \phi B)^{-1}\varepsilon_t$ and expanding $(1 - \phi B)^{-1}$ as an infinite expansion $(1 - \phi B)^{-1} = 1 + \phi B + \phi^2 B^2 + \ldots$ to give

$$X_t = (1 + \phi B + \phi^2 B^3 + \phi^3 B^3 + \ldots)\varepsilon_t.$$

We can apply the same reasoning to the stationarity of the AR(2) model

$$X_t = \phi_1 X_{t-1} + \phi_2 X_{t-2} + \varepsilon_t.$$

The solution to the homogeneous difference equation $X_t - \phi_1 X_{t-1} - \phi_2 X_{t-2} = 0$ depends on the roots r_1, r_2 of the equation $\phi(z) = 1 - \phi_1 z - \phi_2 z^2 = 0$ (see Appendix 5.1) which we shall assume are distinct although they may be complex. The complementary function is of the form $X_t = k_1(1/r_1)^t + k_2(1/r_2)^t$ where k_1 and k_2 are arbitrary constants which are fixed by the starting values. The particular solution is the infinite MA representation $X_t = \phi^{-1}(B)\varepsilon_t = \psi(B)\varepsilon_t$. From the model $\phi(B)X_t = \varepsilon_t$ the coefficients ψ_i are such that $\phi(B)\psi(B)\varepsilon_t = \varepsilon_t$, so $\phi(B)\psi(B) = 1$ and it follows that $\psi_0 = 1$, $\psi_1 = \phi_1$, $\psi_2 = \phi_2 + \phi_1^2$, and so on. The general solution to the AR difference equation (assuming unique roots) is therefore

$$k_1\left(\frac{1}{r_1}\right)^t + k_2\left(\frac{1}{r_2}\right)^t + \sum_{j=0}^{\infty} \psi_j \varepsilon_{t-j}.$$

For the model to have a constant mean, the complementary function must decay for large t, so we require $|1/r_1| < 1$ and $|1/r_2| < 1$. It is not immediately obvious from the above what conditions are required for ϕ_1 and ϕ_2 to ensure that the variance of the particular solution converges. The AR polynomial, however, takes the form

$$\phi(B) = \left(1 - \frac{1}{r_1}B\right)\left(1 - \frac{1}{r_2}B\right),$$

where r_1, r_2 are its roots. A particular solution is $X_t = \psi(B)\varepsilon_t = \phi^{-1}(B)\varepsilon_t$, so using partial fractions we can write

$$\phi^{-1}(B) = \left(\frac{a}{\left(1 - \frac{1}{r_1}B\right)} + \frac{b}{\left(1 - \frac{1}{r_2}B\right)}\right),$$

where a and b are constants. Each of the terms in $\phi^{-1}(B)$ can be expanded—for instance, the first is

$$a\left(1 + \frac{1}{r_1}B + \left(\frac{1}{r_1}B\right)^2 + \left(\frac{1}{r_1}B\right)^3 + \dots\right),$$

so if the variance of $\psi(B)\varepsilon_t = \phi^{-1}(B)\varepsilon_t$ is to converge we require that

$$\frac{1}{|r_1|} < 1 \quad \text{and} \quad \frac{1}{|r_2|} < 1.$$

Hence the condition for an AR(2) model to be stationary is that both the roots r_1 and r_2 of the AR polynomial are of modulus greater than 1.

Similar logic can be applied to the general AR(p) model. Assuming that the roots of the corresponding AR polynomial $\phi(z) = 1 - z\phi_1 - \ldots - \phi_p z^p$ are distinct and denoting these $r_1, r_2, \ldots, r_p$ the complementary function (see Appendix 5.1) is

$$ k_1 \left(\frac{1}{r_1}\right)^m + k_2 \left(\frac{1}{r_2}\right)^m + \ldots + k_p \left(\frac{1}{r_p}\right)^m $$

where $k_1, k_2, \ldots, k_p$ are constants which depend on p starting values—for instance, $X_1, X_2, \ldots, X_p$. If the roots all lie outside the unit circle the complementary function will decay to zero for large t and the model will be stationary.

So, in general, an *AR(p) model is stationary if and only if the roots of the AR polynomial $\phi(z) = 1 - z\phi_1 - \ldots - \phi_p z^p$ all lie outside the unit circle*. It is fairly easy to show that the eigenvalues of ϕ in (5.2) are the same as the reciprocals of the roots of the AR polynomial, so that as might be expected, the condition on the roots of the AR polynomial is identical to the condition on the eigenvalues of the transition matrix in the equivalent state space representation.

(ii) ARMA stationarity

Perhaps the easiest way to deduce conditions for ARMA stationarity is to observe that the stationarity of a state space model is unaffected by the parameter values in the state noise coefficient matrix $\mathbf{K}$ and depends only on the eigenvalues of ϕ. As ϕ contains the AR coefficients of an ARMA model, the stationarity or otherwise is unaffected by the MA coefficients. So like the AR model an ARMA model is stationary if the roots of the AR polynomial all lie outside the unit circle.

We could have established this without recourse to state space models by noticing that the homogeneous equation of the ARMA difference equation (5.1) is exactly the same as that of the corresponding AR equation. An ARMA equation therefore has the same complementary function as the corresponding AR(p) model and so the same restriction on the roots of the AR polynomial for stationarity. In a similar way as for the AR(1) and AR(2) models considered already, an ARMA model has an infinite MA representation which is a particular solution of the ARMA difference equation.

(iii) Stationarity of a moving average model
As the MA model

$$ X_t = \varepsilon_t + \theta_1 \varepsilon_{t-1} + \ldots + \theta_q \varepsilon_{t-q} \tag{5.7} $$

has a finite number of terms it is obvious that it has zero mean and finite variance and is therefore (weakly) stationary, for any finite values of the θ_j.

A stationary series need not have a zero mean. An ARMA model with mean μ can be written

$$ (X_t - \mu) = \phi_1 (X_{t-1} - \mu) + \ldots + \phi_p (X_{t-p} - \mu) + \varepsilon_t $$

or alternatively $X_t = C + \phi_1 X_{t-1} + \ldots$ where $C = \mu - \phi_1 \mu - \phi_2 \mu - \ldots \phi_p \mu$. The observation equation of the corresponding state space model is

$$X_t = (1 \ 0 \ \ldots \ 0)\alpha_t + \mu + \varepsilon_t$$

so the stationarity condition on the ϕ_i's will remain the same as for the zero mean case.

For most of the ARMA models fitted in this book we have either assumed that a zero mean model is appropriate or have estimated the mean μ by the series mean and subtracted the mean from the data before fitting a zero mean model.

5.3 INVERTIBILITY AND IDENTIFICATION

In this section we define a characteristic of some ARMA models called *invertibility*. We will see that invertibility is necessary to identify an ARMA model and that it has repercussions for least squares estimation. To understand and justify the conditions for an ARMA model to be invertible we must first understand what is mean by the *infinite AR representation* of an ARMA model. This is an analogous representation to the infinite moving average process which we have already encountered for AR(1) and AR(2) models (5.5). So we start by considering the infinite MA representation of an ARMA model.

(i) The infinite MA and infinite AR representations of an ARMA model
We can obtain an infinite MA representation

$$X_t = \sum_{j=0}^{\infty} \psi_j \varepsilon_{t-j} \quad \text{or} \quad X_t = \psi(B)\varepsilon_t$$

for the ARMA model (5.1) by repeated substitution for the X_t's. For instance, for the ARMA(1, 1) model we have

$$\begin{aligned}
X_t &= \phi X_{t-1} + \varepsilon_t + \theta \varepsilon_{t-1} \\
&= \phi(\phi X_{t-2} + \varepsilon_{t-1} + \theta \varepsilon_{t-2}) + \varepsilon_t + \theta \varepsilon_{t-1} \\
&= \phi^2 X_{t-2} + \varepsilon_t + (\theta + \phi)\varepsilon_{t-1} + \theta \varepsilon_{t-2} \\
&= \phi^2(\phi X_{t-3} + \varepsilon_{t-2} + \theta \varepsilon_{t-3}) + \varepsilon_t + (\theta + \phi)\varepsilon_{t-1} + \theta \varepsilon_{t-2}
\end{aligned}$$

and so on. It is often easier to obtain the ψ's by substituting $X_t = \psi(B)\varepsilon_t$ into the ARMA model equation $\phi(B)X_t = \theta(B)\varepsilon_t$ to give $\phi(B)\psi(B)\varepsilon_t = \theta(B)\varepsilon_t$ and equating the coefficients on the left and right hand sides. For the ARMA(1, 1) case we must equate the coefficients of the right and left sides of $(1 - \phi B)\psi(B) = 1 + \theta B$. From the constant term $\psi_0 = 1$, the coefficient of B gives $-\phi + \psi_1 = \theta$, so $\psi_1 = \theta + \phi$; equating the coefficients of B^2 gives $-\phi\psi_1 + \psi_2 = 0$, so $\psi_2 = \phi\psi_1 = \phi(\theta + \phi)$, and so on, to give

$$\varepsilon_t = X_t - (\phi + \theta)X_{t-1} + \theta(\phi + \theta)X_{t-2} - \theta^2(\phi + \theta)X_{t-3} + \text{etc.} \ \ldots$$

An alternative way of obtaining the ψ coefficients is to invert the AR polynomial and expand. For example, for the ARMA(1, 1) model again we write

$$\varepsilon_t = (1 - \phi B)^{-1}(1 + \theta B) = (1 + \phi B + \phi^2 B^2 + \ldots)(1 + \theta B).$$

When the AR polynomial has order greater than 1 (as for the AR(2) polynomial in section 5.2), we require

$$X_t = (1 - \phi B - \phi_2 B^2 - \ldots - \phi_p B^p)^{-1}(1 + \theta B)\varepsilon_t,$$

and inversion of the AR polynomial is more complicated. In this case we need to factorize the polynomial as

$$\phi(B) = \left(1 - \frac{1}{r_1}B\right)\left(1 - \frac{1}{r_2}B\right)\ldots\left(1 - \frac{1}{r_p}B\right)$$

and use partial fractions to write

$$\phi^{-1}(B) = \left(\frac{a_1}{\left(1 - \frac{1}{r_1}B\right)} + \frac{a_2}{\left(1 - \frac{1}{r_2}B\right)} + \ldots + \frac{a_p}{\left(1 - \frac{1}{r_p}B\right)}\right)$$

where the a_is are constants and expand each term as

$$\left(1 + \frac{1}{r_1}B + \left(\frac{1}{r_1}B\right)^2 + \ldots\right)$$

to obtain the polynomial of the MA only representation.

As we saw for the AR(1) model in section 5.2 the coefficients of the infinite MA representation converge to zero if and only if the model is stationary and the MA representation gives the particular solution of the ARMA difference equation in X_t (5.1). The general solution is the sum of the complementary function and the particular solution, but the complementary function must decay to zero if the model is stationary.

The ARMA model also has an infinite AR representation

$$\varepsilon_t = \sum_{j=0}^{\infty} \pi_j X_{t-j},$$

that is,

$$\varepsilon_t = X_t + \pi_1 X_{t-1} + \pi_2 X_{t-2} + \ldots$$

where the π_i's are constant coefficients. To see this, substitute in the ARMA model equation (5.1) for past values of ε_t repeatedly. For instance, in the ARMA(1, 1) case the ARMA equation gives

$$\begin{aligned}
\varepsilon_t &= X_t - \phi X_{t-1} - \theta \varepsilon_{t-1} \\
&= X_t - \phi X_{t-1} - \theta(X_{t-1} - \phi X_{t-2} - \theta \varepsilon_{t-2} - \ldots \\
&= X_t - (\phi + \theta)X_{t-1} + \theta(\phi + \theta)X_{t-2} - \theta^2(\phi + \theta)X_{t-3} \ldots \\
&\qquad + (-\theta)^{k-1}(\phi + \theta)X_{t-k} + \ldots \text{ etc.}
\end{aligned}$$

The coefficients π_j can be calculated in similar ways to those of the infinite MA representation. One possibility is to substitute $\varepsilon_t = \pi(B)X_t$ into the ARMA equation $\phi(B)X_t = \theta(B)\varepsilon_t$ to give $\phi(B)X_t = \theta(B)\pi(B)X_t$ and equate the coefficients of powers of B. For the ARMA(1, 1) case we have $(1 - \phi B) = (1 + \theta B)\pi(B)$ so $\pi_0 = 1$, $\pi_1 = -(\theta + \phi)$, $\pi_2 = \theta\pi_1$, $\pi_3 = -\theta\pi_2$, and so on. We could also write $\varepsilon_t = \theta^{-1}(B)\phi(B)X_t$ and expanding giving

$$\varepsilon_t = (1 - \theta B + \theta^2 B^2 \ldots)(1 - \phi B).$$

A useful consequence of the MA representation of any ARMA model is that the random term ε_t and any previously occurring observations X_{t-k} are independent. This follows, as the MA representation of X_{t-k} is $X_{t-k} = \varepsilon_{t-k} + \psi_1\varepsilon_{t-k-1} + \psi_2\varepsilon_{t-k-2}$ etc., so X_{t-k} is a linear function of $\varepsilon_{t-k}, \varepsilon_{t-k-1}, \ldots$ etc. but not of ε_t. As the ε_t's are independent by assumption, ε_t must therefore be independent of $\varepsilon_{t-k}, \varepsilon_{t-k-1}, \ldots$ etc. and so of X_{t-k}. This is true for any $k > 0$ and for any stationary ARMA model. We make use of this result in the next section.

(ii) Invertibility

The infinite AR representation

$$\varepsilon_t = \sum_{j=0}^{\infty} \pi_j X_{t-j}$$

expresses the current ε_t in terms of the current and past X_t's only. Evaluation of this ε_t is going to be important for forecasting and least squares estimation. However, we do not know an infinite number of past X_t's, and so we would like the π_j weights in the AR representation to decay as we go further back in time. Indeed this is essential if we are to perform computations. (Compare again with the MA representation.) For instance, the infinite AR representation of the MA(1) model

$$X_t = (1 + \theta B)\varepsilon_t = \varepsilon_t + \theta\varepsilon_{t-1}$$

is

$$\varepsilon_t = (1 + \theta B)^{-1} X_t = (1 - \theta B + \theta^2 B^2 - \theta^3 B^3 + \ldots)X_t$$

It is obvious that if $|\theta| \geq 1$ the weights increase as we go back in time, or if $|\theta| = 1$ they remain the same and we need data from the infinite past to calculate ε_t. When $|\theta| < 1$ the weights will decay to zero and our estimate of ε_t will converge. For the general ARMA model we have already seen that the weights of the MA only representation $X_t = \psi(B)\varepsilon_t$ decay if and only if all the roots of the polynomial $\phi(B)$ lie outside the circle. Now we have the analogous situation $\varepsilon_t = \pi(B)X_t$ and to *ensure* that the weights π decay we must introduce the condition that all the roots of $\theta(B)$ the MA polynomial lie outside the unit circle. This is known as the *invertibility* condition. It is the same condition on $\theta(B)$ as the stationarity condition on the AR polynomial $\phi(B)$.

(iii) Identification

As in sections 3.7 and 4.3 we assume that ε_t is independent normally distributed with zero mean in what follows. In section 3.7 we saw that the MA(1) models

$$X_t = \theta_0 \varepsilon_t + \theta \varepsilon_{t-1} \quad \text{and} \quad X_t = \theta_1 \varepsilon_t + \theta_0 \varepsilon_{t-1}$$

are not identified in the sense that they have identical autocorrelations and so are likelihood equivalent. To avoid this we constrained the parameters of the model to one from each pair of likelihood equivalent models by requiring that $|\theta| < 1$. This is the same as the condition required above for the infinite AR representation of the MA(1) model to converge. This is *not* a coincidence. In general, for any MA model there are two or more MA models of the same order q which have the same autocovariances and so are likelihood equivalent. If we stipulate that we will only consider models which satisfy the invertibility condition then this will restrict to one and only one model from each likelihood equivalence class and will so identify the model.

It can be shown that two ARMA models (5.1) are likelihood equivalent if (a) they have the same AR parameters ϕ_i and (b) the autovariances of the moving average part of the model $\varepsilon_t + \theta_1 \varepsilon_{t-1} + \ldots + \theta_q \varepsilon_{t-q}$ are the same for all lags. So constraining the ARMA(p, q) model's MA coefficients to be invertible identifies the model.

For instance

$$X_t = 0.9 X_{t-1} + \varepsilon_t + \theta \varepsilon_{t-1} \qquad \mathrm{var}(\varepsilon_t) = \sigma^2$$

is likelihood equivalent to

$$X_t = 0.9 X_{t-1} + \theta \varepsilon_t + \varepsilon_{t-1}$$

also with $\mathrm{var}(\varepsilon_t) = \sigma^2$ as the MA parts of the model are equivalent.

Another obvious occurrence of likelihood equivalent ARMA models is when the MA polynomial and the AR polynomial of an ARMA model have a common factor (and so a common root). A common factor can be 'cancelled' out so that the same model can be represented by another model with smaller orders p and q. For example, the ARMA(2, 1) model $(1 - 0.5B - 0.24B^2)X_t = (1 + 0.3B)\varepsilon_t$ has common factor $(1 + 0.3B)$ and so is the same as $(1 - 0.8B)X_t = (1 + 0.3B)\varepsilon_t$ which has smaller orders. If a model has common factors like this it will not be identifiable, and so computational problems associated with over parameterization may arise.

5.4 PROPERTIES OF STATIONARY ARMA MODELS

As described in Chapter 3, a range of properties of models can be matched with sample properties to select an appropriate model. For stationary ARMA models the autocorrelation function and the partial autocorrelation function are particularly useful.

(i) The autocorrelation function
The autocorrelation function of the AR(1) model $X_t = \phi X_{t-1} + \varepsilon_t$ can be obtained directly by multiplying the model equation by X_{t-k} where $k > 0$ and taking expectations to give

$$E(X_t X_{t-k}) = \phi E(X_{t-1} X_{t-k}) + E(\varepsilon_t X_{t-k}).$$

If the process is stationary it will have zero mean and so

$$E(X_t X_{t-k}) = \gamma(k),$$
$$E(X_{t-1} X_{t-k}) = \gamma(k-1)$$

and from section 5.3

$$E(\varepsilon_t X_{t-k}) = 0.$$

This gives $\gamma(k) = \phi\gamma(k-1)$ for all $k > 0$. We can divide through by the variance $\gamma(0)$ to obtain the same equation in the autocorrelations, that is, $\rho(k) = \phi\rho(k-1)$. As $\rho(0) = 1$, this gives $\rho(1) = \phi$, $\rho(2) = \phi\rho(1) = \phi^2$, and so on, so that the autocorrelation at lag k of an AR(1) model is $\rho(k) = \phi^k$. A plot of the autocorrelation function of the AR(1) model with $\phi = 0.9$ was given in Fig. 3.12. If the coefficient is negative the autocorrelations are of alternating sign as shown in Fig. 5.1.

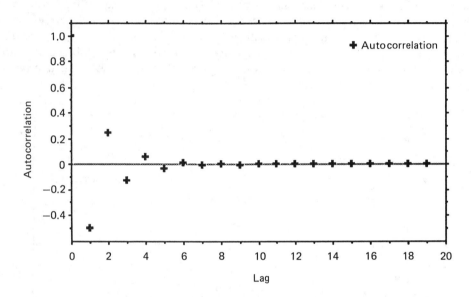

Fig. 5.1. Theoretical autocorrelation function of the AR(1) model $X_t = -0.5X_{t-1} + \varepsilon_t$.

The form of the autocorrelation function of a general ARMA(p, q) model can be derived in a similar manner. Take the ARMA model (5.1) and multiply both sides by X_{t-m} where $m > q$, giving

$$X_t X_{t-m} = \phi_1 X_{t-1} X_{t-m} + \ldots + \phi_p X_{t-p} X_{t-m} + \varepsilon_t X_{t-m}$$
$$+ \theta_1 \varepsilon_{t-1} X_{t-m} + \ldots + \theta_q \varepsilon_{t-q} X_{t-m}.$$

As the noise ε_t is independent of any observations prior to time t the expectation of the terms involving the ε_t's are zero if $t - q > t - m$, that is, if $m > q$ so taking expectations throughout gives a recurrence relation for the autocovariances $\gamma(k)$,

$$\gamma(m) = \phi_1 \gamma(m-1) + \ldots + \phi_p \gamma(m-p) \qquad m > q. \qquad (5.8)$$

It is often easier to work in terms of the autocorrelations

$$\rho(m) = \phi_1 \rho(m-1) + \ldots + \phi_p \rho(m-p) \qquad m > q. \qquad (5.9)$$

Notice that this difference equation is the same as the corresponding AR equation except that here we have no random ε_t terms, so it is the same as the homogeneous AR equation (see Appendix 5.1). The general solution of (5.9) is therefore the same as the complementary function of the solution for X_t. Assuming that the roots of the AR polynomial are distinct and denoting these $r_1, r_2, \ldots, r_p$, the complementary function is

$$\rho(m) = k_1 \left(\frac{1}{r_1}\right)^m + k_2 \left(\frac{1}{r_2}\right)^m + \ldots + k_p \left(\frac{1}{r_p}\right)^m$$

where $k_1, k_2, \ldots, k_p$ are constants which depend on starting values, e.g. $\rho(0), \ldots, \rho(p-1)$. If the roots are all real, $\rho(m)$ will decay exponentially to zero at a rate which depends on the largest root. This supports our calculations for the AR(1) model $X_t = \phi X_{t-1} + \varepsilon_t$, as the AR polynomial is $(1 - \phi z)$ which has a single root $1/\phi$. If we take an ARMA model with two real roots, for instance $X_t = 0.5X_{t-1} + 0.3X_{t-2} + \varepsilon_t + 0.5\varepsilon_{t-1}$, the autocorrelation function will decay exponentially as shown in Fig. 5.2.

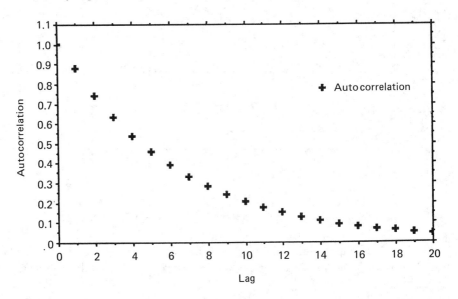

Fig. 5.2. Autocorrelation function of the ARMA(2, 1) model $X_t = 0.5X_{t-1} + 0.3X_{t-2} + \varepsilon_t + 0.5\varepsilon_{t-1}$. This model has two real roots and so does not exhibit a sinusoidal autocorrelation structure.

If a pair of roots of (5.9) are complex, say $r_i = re^{i\theta}$, $r_{i+1} = re^{-i\theta}$, the complementary function becomes $r^m \{C_1 \cos(m\theta) + C_2 \sin(m\theta)\}$ where the constants C_1 and C_2 may be complex and in consequence $\rho(m)$ will contain a sinusoidal term.

Since $|r| < 1$ the correlations decay exponentially. For example take the AR(2) model $X_t = 1.5X_{t-1} - 0.75X_{t-2} + \varepsilon_t$. The reader can verify that the corresponding AR polynomial has complex roots

$$\left(1 \pm i/\sqrt{3}\right) \quad \text{or} \quad \sqrt{4/3}\, e^{\pm i\pi/6},$$

which of course lie *outside* the unit circle, confirming that the model is stationary. The autocorrelation function

$$\gamma(m) = C_1 e^{\frac{\pi m i}{6}} + C_2 e^{-\frac{\pi m i}{6}}$$

takes the form of a decaying sine wave, as shown in Fig. 3.11. The autocorrelation function of an ARMA model with the same AR polynomial also exhibits the fading sinusoidal pattern (see Fig. 5.3), with peaks and troughs at lags which are multiples of 6.

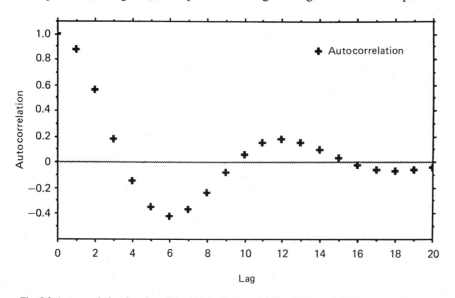

Fig. 5.3. Autocorrelation function of the ARMA(2, 1) model $X_t = 1.5X_{t-1} - 0.75X_{t-2} + \varepsilon_t + 0.5\varepsilon_{t-1}$. The AR polynomial has two imaginary roots, so the autocorrelation function exhibits a sinusoidal pattern.

The autocovariances of an MA model of order q are

$$\gamma(k) = E\left\{(\varepsilon_t + \theta_1\varepsilon_{t-1} + \dots \theta_q\varepsilon_{t-q})(\varepsilon_{t-k} + \theta_1\varepsilon_{t-k-1} + \dots + \theta_q\varepsilon_{t-k-q})\right\}$$

$$= \theta_k + \sum_{i=1}^{q-k} \theta_i\theta_{i+k}$$

as $E(\varepsilon_i\varepsilon_j) = 0$ for $i \neq j$. In particular, *the autocovariances are zero* for lags greater than q (see Fig. 5.4). This should in theory make MA models easy to spot from the sample autocorrelations.

(ii) The partial autocorrelation function
If ϕ_k is the coefficient of X_{t-k} in an AR(k) model it is the *partial autocorrelation coefficient* between X_t and X_{t-k} when the intermediate values $X_{t-1},\dots,X_{t-k+1}$ are considered fixed. If the true AR order is really p then ϕ_k will be zero for $k > p$ so that the partial autocorrelations of an AR model exhibit similar properties to the autocorrelations of an

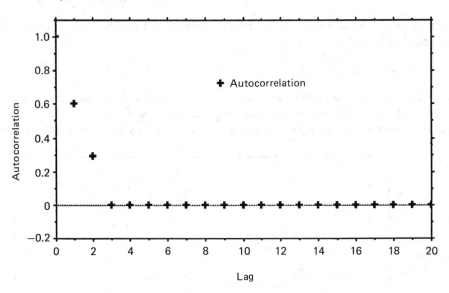

Fig. 5.4. Theoretical autocorrelation function of the MA(2) model $X_t = \varepsilon_t + 0.7\varepsilon_{t-1} + 0.5\varepsilon_{t-2}$. Note that the autocorrelations are zero for all lags greater than 2.

MA model. The partial autocorrelations can be estimated by fitting an AR(k) model to the data. The Yule–Walker estimates described in section 5.5 are frequently used for this, as they are easy to calculate. The *estimated* final AR coefficient $\hat{\phi}_{kk}$ obtained from this fit is the sample partial autocorrelation at lag k. Fitting successively larger order models gives the partial autocorrelations. Many older texts use computational devices to avoid this process, see Box & Jenkins (1970) or Appendix 5.2. As the sample partial autocorrelations are estimates of the true partial autocorrelations they will be small for $k > p$, the true AR order. Some sample partial autocorrelation functions are shown in section 5.7 and are used to aid model selection.

5.5 ESTIMATION

As an ARMA model can be placed in state space form the exact maximum likelihood estimates can be obtained by using the state space estimation methods described in Chapter 4. While exact likelihood methods are, in general, to be preferred, most commercial statistical software uses some variant of least squares, as least squares is quicker to calculate and has the advantage that analytic derivatives are available for the maximization.

In section 3.3 we showed that the conditional maximum likelihood estimates of the AR(2) model (with known σ^2) are also the least squares estimators. Similarly, for AR(p) models (with known σ^2) we can regard the first p observations as fixed, so that maximizing the conditional likelihood function is equivalent to minimizing the sum of squares

$$\sum_{t=p+1}^{N}(X_t - \phi_1 X_{t-1}\ldots - \phi_p X_{t-p})^2,$$

and we have a similar situation to least squares estimation in linear regression. The one step prediction of X_t at time $t-1$ for this model is

$$X_{t|t-1} = \phi_1 X_{t-1} + \phi_2 X_{t-2} + \ldots + \phi_p X_{t-p}$$

so that the one step prediction error $X_t - X_{t|t-1}$ is merely ε_t and we are minimizing the sum of the squared prediction errors

$$\sum \varepsilon^2.$$

More generally, consider least squares estimation of the ARMA(p, q) model. Take for instance, the ARMA(1, 1) model $X_t = \phi X_{t-1} + \varepsilon_t + \theta\varepsilon_{t-1}$. The conditional expectation of X_t at time $t-1$ is $X_{t|t-1} = \phi X_{t-1} + \theta\varepsilon_{t-1}$, as the conditional expectation of ε_t at time t is $\varepsilon_{t|t-1} = 0$. The one step prediction error is therefore $X_t - X_{t|t-1} = \varepsilon_t$, and for least squares we would again like to minimize $\sum \varepsilon^2$. To calculate these errors

$$\varepsilon_t = X_t - \phi X_{t-1} - \theta\varepsilon_{t-1}$$

we require the previous prediction error ε_{t-1}. As our first observation is X_1, we can start by calculating ε_2, but we still need a value for ε_1. One possibility is to arbitrarily set $\varepsilon_1 = 0$. Given the arbitrary ε_1, ε_2 can be calculated, and this can be used to calculate ε_3, and so on. The expression

$$\sum \varepsilon^2 = \sum_{t=2}^{N}(X_t - \phi_1 X_{t-1} - \theta_1\varepsilon_{t-1})^2$$

can be then minimized numerically to obtain the least squares estimates.

To investigate the error incurred in assigning an arbitrary value to ε_1 in this way we take the expression for ε_t and substitute in for ε_{t-1} and then ε_{t-2}, and so on to give

$$\begin{aligned}
\varepsilon_t &= X_t - X_{t|t-1} = X_t - \phi X_{t-1} - \theta\varepsilon_{t-1}\\
&= X_t - \phi X_{t-1} - \theta(X_{t-1} - \phi X_{t-2} - \theta\varepsilon_{t-2})\\
&= \ldots\\
&= X_t - (\phi + \theta)X_{t-1} + \theta(\phi + \theta)X_{t-2} - \theta^2(\phi + \theta)X_{t-3}\ldots\\
&\qquad - (-\theta)^{t-3}(\phi + \theta)X_2 - (-\theta)^{t-2}\phi X_1 + (-\theta)^{t-1}\varepsilon_1.
\end{aligned}$$

If we continued indefinitely we would obtain the infinite autoregressive representation described in section 5.3, but we stop here, as we are only interested in the effect of ε_1. From the above expression it is apparent that if $|\theta| < 1$ the coefficient of ε_1 decays exponentially as t becomes larger and the effect of any error made in arbitrarily setting ε_1 will also diminish. However, if $|\theta| \geq 1$ the influence of ε_1 will remain the same or increase and the effect of any such error will be compounded. This means that for the ARMA(1, 1) model it is only sensible to estimate the ε_t's in this way, when $|\theta| < 1$. Notice that this is none other than the invertibility requirement of section 5.3.

The situation is similar for the ARMA(p, q) model. $N - p$ prediction errors can be calculated using

$$\varepsilon_t = X_t - \phi_1 X_{t-1} - \dots - \phi_p X_{t-p} - \theta_1 \varepsilon_{t-1} - \dots - \theta_q \varepsilon_{t-q}$$

for $t = p + 1, \dots, N$ where we arbitrarily set $\varepsilon_p = \dots = \varepsilon_{p+1-q} = 0$. Again, we can show that the influence of these starting values wears off for large N if and only if the model is invertible. Alternatively, least squares can be based on all the prediction errors, that is, $t = 1, \dots, N$, but $X_0, X_{-1}, \dots, X_{1-p}$ and $\varepsilon_0, \varepsilon_1, \dots, \varepsilon_{1-q}$ must be set arbitrarily, so the model must be both stationary and invertible.

As we have seen, unconditional least squares is an approximation of maximum likelihood. Box and Jenkins improved this approximation by developing an unconditional least squares technique which does not rely on arbitrary starting values. We refer the reader to Box & Jenkins (1970) for details, but we will briefly outline the idea. They use the observed series and ARMA model equation (assumed stationary) to 'forecast' periods before the start of the sample data, that is, X_0, X_{-1}, X_{-2}, and so on, which they called *backcasting*. Backcasting continues until the backcasts converge to the model mean, say at time $t = -Q + 1$. Assuming that noises prior to $t = -Q$ are zero, these backcasts are then used with the model equation to calculate pre-series noises $\varepsilon_{-Q+1}, \dots, \varepsilon_{-2}, \varepsilon_{-1}, \varepsilon_0$. Box and Jenkins show that an approximation to exact likelihood is given if

$$\sum_{t=-Q+1}^{N} \varepsilon^2$$

is the sum of squared errors to be minimized. However, the sum of squares used to estimate σ^2 is still

$$\sum_{t=1}^{N} \varepsilon^2,$$

which is divided by $N - p - q - 1$ if a constant term or mean is fitted, and $N - p - q$ otherwise. Most least squares software uses this unconditional least squares approach, although not many backcast. The process must be stationary and invertible, and even then if there are roots near the unit circle then the backcasting may have to go back a very long way before the backcasts converge to the mean, and the software may return an error message 'back forecasts not dying out rapidly' or similar.

Fig. 5.5 shows output from the estimation of an AR(2) model fitted to the purse data using MINITAB. MINITAB fits an ARMA model with a constant term as default. As you can see, the results are broadly similar to the maximum likelihood estimates $\phi_1 = 0.307841$, $\phi_2 = 0.400178$ and $\sigma^2 = 36.115343$ from Fig. 4.3. Even the diagnostic checking parameter Q(12) is similar to the Q(12) = 7.86 reported in section 3.5 for the state space estimation.

We have already seen that least squares estimation requires an ARMA model to be both stationary and invertible otherwise the estimation depends on X_t's and ε_t's from the

```
MTB > arima 2 0 0 cl

Estimates at each iteration
Iteration    SSE      Parameters
    0      3258.80   0.100   0.100   11.212
    1      2699.55   0.202   0.250    7.628
    2      2508.92   0.300   0.395    4.189
    3      2507.97   0.305   0.403    3.940
    4      2507.96   0.305   0.404    3.920
    5      2507.96   0.305   0.404    3.918
Relative change in each estimate less than 0.0010


Final Estimates of Parameters
Type        Estimate   St.Dev.   t-ratio
AR 1        0.3050     0.1113    2.74
AR 2        0.4036     0.1125    3.59
Constant    3.9179     0.7239    5.41
Mean        13.442     2.483


No. of obs.:  71
Residuals:   SS = 2506.43          (backforecasts excluded)
             MS = 36.86  DF = 68


Modified Box-Pierce chisquare statistic
Lag          12        24        36        48
Chisquare   7.9(DF=10) 22.4(DF=22) 31.6(DF=34) 36.3(DF=46)
```

Fig. 5.5. MINITAB output fitting AR(2) model to purse data.

infinite past. When calculating likelihood state space methods the infinite past is represented by the starting values a_0 and C_0 (section 4.4), and the Kalman recursions take into account the uncertainty represented by these starting values. We stated (section 4.4(iii)) that for large N the Kalman filter recursions are independent of a_0 and C_0. This means that we do *not* have to demand that an ARMA model is stationary and invertible when state space estimation methods are used.

When using state space methods for estimation we will again assume that the noises are normally distributed. If nothing is known about the past of the series, the Kalman filter iterations can be started by setting $a_0 = 0$ and C_0 to a large diagonal matrix as described in section 4.4. We have done this for all the model fits reported in this book. If the model is known to be stationary, starting values for the initial state and covariance matrix can be obtained by setting $a_0 = 0$ and C_0 to the solution of $C_0 = \phi C_0 \phi^T + KK^T \sigma^2$, which reduces to a set of linear equations. For instance, take the MA(1) model with parameter θ and noise variance σ^2. It is easily shown that the solution is

$$C_0 = \sigma^2 \begin{pmatrix} \theta^2 + 1 & \theta \\ \theta & \theta^2 \end{pmatrix}.$$

This could also be evaluated directly by observing that

$$\alpha_t = \begin{pmatrix} X_t \\ \theta_1 \varepsilon_t \end{pmatrix}.$$

Gardner, Harvey, & Phillips (1980) give an algorithm for solving these equations which can be used for more complex cases.

Estimation of the AR(p) model is particularly quick when using state space methods, as the model reaches a steady state after the pth iteration. A glance at the iterations of Table 4.3 confirms this for a particular AR(2) model.

The parameter estimates of the ARMA model should be broadly similar whether exact likelihood or a variant on least squares is used. Notice, however, that if σ^2 is the scaling variance of the state space model (see section 4.5) the denominator of its estimator is $N - d$, the number of residuals used in the likelihood, where d is usually the state dimension. The denominator of the estimator of σ^2 when least squares is used is $N - p - q$ (or $N - p - q - 1$ if a constant term is fitted). This difference is analogous to the estimation of the variance of a simple random sample. When likelihood is used the denominator is N, whereas an unbiased estimator has denominator $N - 1$. A comparison of the estimation of an AR(2) model to the purse using MINITAB, exact likelihood and SYSTAT (without backcasting) is shown in Table 5.1.

Table 5.1. Comparison between parameter estimates obtained when fitting an AR(2) model to the purse data using various estimation methods

Parameter	Exact likelihood	MINITAB	Systat (default uses no backcasting)
ϕ_1	0.307841	0.3050	0.305
ϕ_2	0.400178	0.4036	0.403
σ^2	36.115343	36.86	Sum of square errors/68 = 36.91176

All iterative numerical estimation methods can have accelerated convergence by the use of good initial values for the estimators. A popular way to obtain these for stationary ARMA models is to use the sample autocorrelations as follows.

Equation (5.9) for $m = q + 1, \ldots, q + p$ gives a set of p equations in the p unknown AR parameters $\phi_1, \phi_2, \ldots, \phi_p$. The coefficients in these equations are the autocorrelations $\rho(k)$, which are unknown. We can, however, use the sample autocorrelations $r(k)$ in place of the $\rho(k)$ and then solve the system of equations for the AR parameters.

If we consider the AR(p) case, the system of equations (5.9) for $m = 1, 2, \ldots, p$ become

$$\rho(1) = \phi_1\rho(0) + \phi_2\rho(1) + \phi_3\rho(2) + \phi_4\rho(3) + \ldots + \phi_p\rho(p-1)$$
$$\rho(2) = \phi_1\rho(1) + \phi_2\rho(0) + \phi_3\rho(1) + \phi_4\rho(2) + \ldots + \phi_p\rho(p-2)$$
$$\vdots \qquad\qquad\qquad\qquad\qquad \vdots$$
$$\rho(m) = \phi_1\rho(m-1) + \phi_2\rho(m-2) + \phi_3\rho(m-3) + \phi_4\rho(m-4) + \ldots + \phi_p\rho(m-p),$$

which can be written as the matrix system

$$\begin{pmatrix} 1 & \rho(1) & \rho(2) & \cdots & \cdots & \rho(p-1) \\ \rho(1) & 1 & \rho(1) & \rho(2) & \cdots & \rho(p-2) \\ \rho(2) & \rho(1) & 1 & \rho(1) & \cdots & \rho(p-3) \\ \vdots & \vdots & \vdots & \vdots & \cdots & \vdots \\ \rho(p-1) & \rho(p-2) & \rho(p-3) & & \cdots & 1 \end{pmatrix} \begin{pmatrix} \phi_1 \\ \phi_2 \\ \vdots \\ \phi_p \end{pmatrix} = \begin{pmatrix} \rho(1) \\ \rho(2) \\ \vdots \\ \rho(p) \end{pmatrix}. \qquad (5.10)$$

The equations in (5.10) are known as the *Yule–Walker equations*. The matrix in the system has a particular structure (called a Toeplitz matrix) which can be exploited to solve for the ϕ's efficiently. One method is that of the Durbin–Levinson recursions, which we describe in Appendix 5.2. The resulting *Yule–Walker estimates* can be shown to be an approximation to the least squares estimators, although appreciable differences can occur if the AR polynomial has roots near the unit circle. As the Yule–Walker estimates are quicker to calculate than the least squares or maximum likelihood estimates, the Yule–Walker estimate of ϕ_p is frequently used as an estimated pth partial autocorrelation coefficient.

For example, take the AR(1) model. The single equation is $\rho(1) = \phi_1\rho(0)$, so $\phi_1 = \rho(1)$, so the parameter estimator is $\hat{\phi}_1 = r(1)$, the first sample autocorrelation coefficient. For the AR(2) model we have two Yule–Walker equations $\rho(1) = \phi_1\rho(0) + \phi_2\rho(-1)$, $\rho_2 = \phi_1\rho(1) + \phi_2\rho(0)$. Remembering that $\rho(k) = \rho(-k)$ these can be solved to give

$$\hat{\phi}_1 = \frac{\rho(1)\,(1-\rho(2))}{1-\rho^2(1)},$$

$$\hat{\phi}_2 = \frac{\rho(2) - \rho^2(1)}{1-\rho^2(1)}.$$

For the purse data used extensively in Chapters 3 and 4 the sample autocorrelations at lags 1 and 2 are 0.493 and 0.534 respectively (see Fig. 3.13), giving Yule–Walker estimates of 0.303504 and 0.384372. These are encouragingly close to the MLEs calculated in Fig. 4.3. The estimation (shown in Fig. 5.6) is quicker than starting from the arbitrary initial values in Fig. 4.3.

```
INITIAL LOG LIK  -221.6663656969950
ESTIMATION
******* FUNCTION VALUE IS  443.3327313939900
PARAMETERS   DERIVATIVES
    0.3035040000000000   -2.58589956
    0.3843720000000000   -3.80224442
niter  0  nf  0  norm  4.598254


******* FUNCTION VALUE IS  443.2970655887218
PARAMETERS   DERIVATIVES
    0.3078412082901417   0.00000137
    0.4001778285428662   0.00000153
niter  4  nf  32  norm  0.000002


******* FUNCTION VALUE IS  4432970655887218
PARAMETERS   DERIVATIVES
    0.3078412082901417   0.00000137
    0.4001778285428662   0.00000153
niter  4  nf  46  norm  0.000002


********************* RESULTS *******************


MAXIMUM LOG LIKELIHOOD IS  -221.6485327943609
steady state reached by   4 iterations
AIC is   449.2970655887212
variance used to scale   36.11534329164984
      PARAMETER            S.ERROR  T RATIO
    0.3078412082901417    0.078087  3.942280
    0.4001778285428662    0.078739  5.082353
   36.1153432916498396    4.347888  8.306410
PREDiction error variance is   36.11534329164984
FINAL STATE VECTOR   -6.915500000000000   -3.567785430373924
```

Fig. 5.6. Maximum likelihood estimation of AR(2) model fitted to the purse data starting from Yule–Walker estimates of parameters.

It is possible to obtain a full set of parameter estimates from the Yule–Walker equations by noting that if we multiply the AR equation by X_t and take expectations remembering that $E(X_t \varepsilon_t) = \sigma^2$ we obtain the additional equation

$$\gamma(0) = \phi_1 \gamma(1) + \phi_2 \gamma(2) + \phi_3 \gamma(3) + \phi_4 \gamma(4) + \ldots + \phi_p \gamma(p) + \sigma^2.$$

If the sample covariances and Yule–Walker estimates are used instead of the corresponding γ's and ϕ's in this equation we can calculate an estimate of σ^2.

5.6 NON-STATIONARY MODELS

It is obviously possible to write down ARMA models which violate the stationarity condition, for instance $X_t = 1.1X_{t-1} + \varepsilon_t$. Most ARMA software uses least squares estimation which requires stationarity and invertibility, and so cannot estimate models with roots on or inside the unit circle.

To allow ARMA techniques to handle non-stationary data, a special class of non-stationary model has been devised. Recall that if our time series is $\{X_t\}$ then $\{W_t\}$, where $W_t = \nabla X_t = X_t - X_{t-1}$, is the *differenced* series. We could continue and difference again to obtain $\nabla^2 X_t = (1 - B)^2 = (X_t - X_{t-1}) - (X_{t-1} - X_{t-2})$, and so on. The idea is to difference a non-stationary series one or more times until the resulting series W_t is stationary, and then fit a stationary, zero mean ARMA model to $\{W_t\}$. If a better fit can be obtained by fitting an ARMA model with a non-zero mean to the W_t series, we can write $(W_t - \mu)$ in place of W_t, although the mean of a differenced series can usually be taken as zero, which renders this unnecessary.

If we have to difference once, the model can be written $\phi(B)(1 - B)X_t = \theta(B)\varepsilon_t$. If we need to difference twice before the series becomes stationary our model becomes $\phi(B)(1 - B)^2 X_t = \theta(B)\varepsilon_t$. In general, a model which, when differenced d times, gives a stationary ARMA(p, q) model is called an autoregressive *integrated* moving-average or ARIMA(p, d, q) model. The order d stands for the degree of differencing.

As $\phi(B)(1 - B)^d$ is still a polynomial in B it is evident that the ARIMA model is just a special case of a non-stationary ARMA model where d roots of the AR polynomial are constrained to equal unity. In effect, the ARIMA model constrains one or more factors of the AR polynomial to be $(1 - B)$.

While the theoretical autocorrelations for a non-stationary series are not defined, the sample autocorrelations of any time series can always be calculated in the usual way. If a series has high autocorrelations $r(k)$ for large k which do not tend to zero this is a strong indication that the series is non-stationary, and if ARIMA models (as opposed to fitting a non-stationary ARMA model using state space methods) are to be used, the data should be differenced.

To illustrate these ideas we will consider a daily time series of temperature readings over a one year period due to Piggot (1980) which have already been deseasonalized. Fig. 5.7 shows a plot of the raw data. The level of the data appears to change over time or drift, and so the series does not appear to be stationary. In addition, the sample autocorrelations are large at high lags (Fig. 5.8).

This suggests that it may be a good idea to difference the data. The differenced data is shown in Fig. 5.9 and now looks to have a constant (zero) mean. The autocorrelations of the differenced data (Fig. 5.10) clearly decay for large lags, indicating that the differenced series is stationary, and are small for lags greater than 4. We will see in section 5.7 that this suggests that an MA(4) model may be appropriate.

We fitted the MA(4) model to the first 359 differenced data points using a standard least squares package. (The final six observations we held back for post-sample comparison.) The fitted model was

$$W_t = \varepsilon_t + 0.0722\varepsilon_{t-1} - 0.3085\varepsilon_{t-2} - 0.1312\varepsilon_{t-3} - 0.2022\varepsilon_{t-4}$$

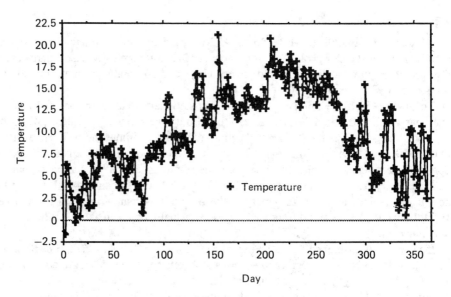

Fig. 5.7. Time series of daily undifferenced temperature data (already deseasonalized) over a one
year period.

with $\sigma^2 = 2.464$, so the fitted ARIMA model is therefore

$$\nabla X_t = \varepsilon_t + 0.0722\varepsilon_{t-1} - 0.3085\varepsilon_{t-2} - 0.1312\varepsilon_{t-3} - 0.2022\varepsilon_{t-4}.$$

Out of interest we also fitted an MA(4) model to the 359 differenced observations
using state space methods to obtain

$$W_t = \varepsilon_t + 0.07735\varepsilon_{t-1} - 0.299655\varepsilon_{t-2} - 0.117933\varepsilon_{t-3} - 0.185456\varepsilon_{t-4}$$

where $\sigma^2 = 2.380365$ (which is also the prediction error variance). The state order was 5,
so the first 5 residuals were omitted from the likelihood function. This gave a maximum
likelihood of 655.972416 and an AIC of 1321.944834.

Differencing techniques were developed before the advent of fast computing and the
Kalman filter algorithm for likelihood, when it was difficult to estimate non-stationary
ARMA models. If state space software is available (and unless the series is short) an
alternative modelling procedure is to fit a non-stationary ARMA state space model directly to the original data. As this does not constrain any roots of the AR polynomial to
be unity, it has the advantage of allowing a broader class of model than ARIMA models
and therefore may possibly give a closer model fit. Conversely, the autocorrelation function and partial autocorrelations cannot be used for model selection, and a procedure like
backwards elimination must be used to alight on a suitable model.

For example, we use state space methods to fit an ARMA(5, 4) model to the first 360
observations of the temperature data, that is, a state space ARMA model with state
dimension 5. Several parameters were not significant, so we performed a backwards
elimination procedure until only ϕ_1, ϕ_4, θ_2, θ_3 and θ_4 remained and were all significantly

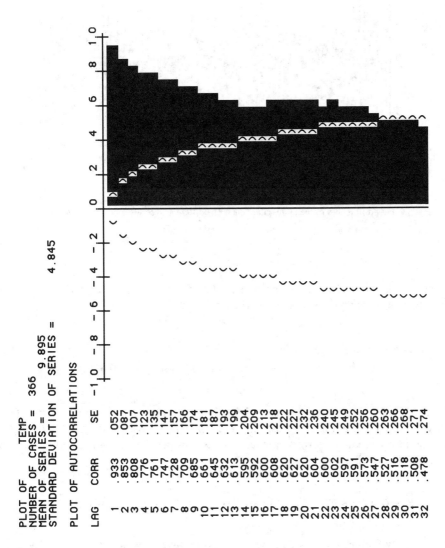

```
PLOT OF        TEMP
NUMBER OF CASES =    366
MEAN OF SERIES =       9.895
STANDARD DEVIATION OF SERIES =      4.845

PLOT OF AUTOCORRELATIONS

LAG   CORR    SE
  1   .933   .052
  2   .853   .087
  3   .808   .107
  4   .776   .123
  5   .761   .135
  6   .747   .147
  7   .728   .157
  8   .709   .166
  9   .685   .174
 10   .661   .181
 11   .645   .187
 12   .632   .193
 13   .613   .199
 14   .595   .204
 15   .592   .209
 16   .600   .213
 17   .608   .218
 18   .620   .222
 19   .627   .227
 20   .620   .232
 21   .604   .236
 22   .600   .240
 23   .602   .245
 24   .597   .249
 25   .591   .252
 26   .573   .256
 27   .547   .260
 28   .527   .263
 29   .516   .266
 30   .518   .268
 31   .508   .271
 32   .478   .274
```

Fig. 5.8 Autocorrelations of the daily temperature series. These are non-zero even at large lags, suggesting that the series is not stationary.

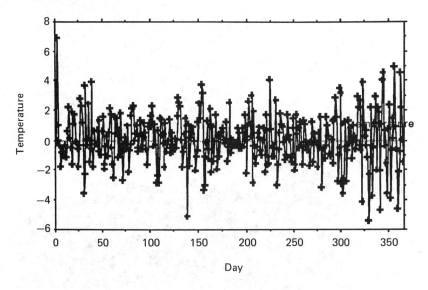

Fig. 5.9. First differences of the temperature data. The differenced series appears to be stationary.

non-zero (although a Hessian error was signalled for the final three parameters so the significance of these could be doubted). The final model was

$$X_t = 1.086392 X_{t-1} - 0.087262 X_{t-4} + \varepsilon_t$$
$$- 0.388547 \varepsilon_{t-2} - 0.172580 \varepsilon_{t-3} - 0.161700 \varepsilon_{t-4}$$

with an AIC of 1325.096916 and $\sigma^2 = 2.361517$. We continued to zeroize some of the other parameters to explore the possibilities of smaller models, but only obtained higher AICs and larger prediction error variances. As ϕ_1 was persistently non-zero we fitted an ARMA (1, 4) model as well. The estimated model was

$$X_t = 0.997799 X_{t-1} + \varepsilon_t + 0.080507 \varepsilon_{t-1} - 0.294715 \varepsilon_{t-2} - 0.112532 \varepsilon_{t-3}$$

and the AIC was almost as low as the model chosen by backward elimination. The form of this non-stationary model is the same as the model obtained fitting an MA(4) model to first differences only, but now the first AR parameter is not constrained to be 1. The AIC of the differenced model cannot be compared, as fitting a state order 5 to differenced data effectively omits the residual from the first 6 data items from the likelihood but the new model has a smaller PEV (2.373412). Table 5.2 shows the AICs and maximum log-likelihoods of all models fitted using state space methods.

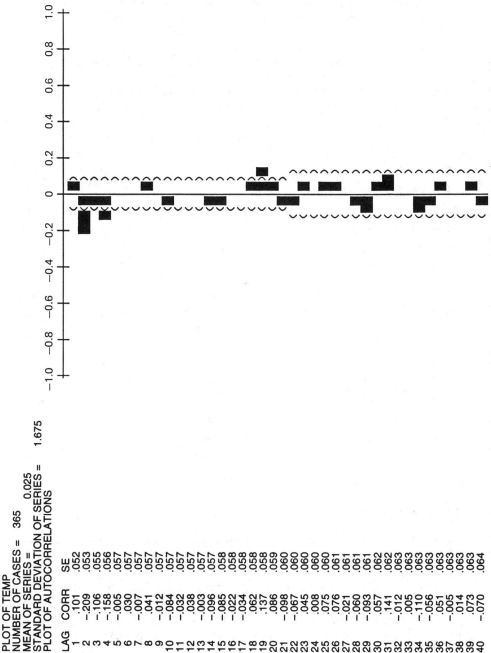

PLOT OF TEMP
NUMBER OF CASES = 365
MEAN OF SERIES = 0.025
STANDARD DEVIATION OF SERIES = 1.675
PLOT OF AUTOCORRELATIONS

LAG	CORR	SE
1	.101	.052
2	-.209	.053
3	-.106	.055
4	-.158	.056
5	-.005	.057
6	.030	.057
7	-.007	.057
8	.041	.057
9	-.012	.057
10	-.084	.057
11	-.032	.057
12	.038	.057
13	-.003	.057
14	-.096	.057
15	-.085	.058
16	-.022	.058
17	-.034	.058
18	.062	.058
19	.137	.058
20	.086	.059
21	-.098	.060
22	-.067	.060
23	.045	.060
24	.008	.060
25	.075	.060
26	.076	.061
27	-.021	.061
28	-.060	.061
29	-.093	.061
30	.057	.062
31	.141	.062
32	-.012	.063
33	.005	.063
34	-.110	.063
35	-.056	.063
36	.051	.063
37	-.005	.063
38	.014	.063
39	.073	.063
40	-.070	.064

Fig. 5.10. Autocorrelations of the differenced temperature data. These are only significantly different from zero at lags 2 and 4.

Table 5.2. Comparison of exact likelihood fits to raw temperature data. *$Q(20) = 23.04$ (16 d.o.f.), so just acceptable. Models with AIC marked ** have significant Q statistics, and as such are probably inappropriate, as they have autocorrelated residuals.

Backwards elimination for temperature data (undifferenced)				
Model	Zeroized parameters	Least-significant parameter (non-significant unless stated)	Maximum likelihood	AIC
ARMA(5, 4)	—	ϕ_5	−656.431074	1332.86
ARMA(4, 4)	—	ϕ_2	−656.431244	1330.86
ARMA(4, 4)	ϕ_2	θ_1	−656.445753	1328.90
ARMA(4, 4)	$\phi_2\,\theta_1$	ϕ_3	−656.515389	1327.03
ARMA(4, 4)	$\phi_2\,\theta_1\,\phi_3$	All significant	−656.548458	1325.10
Other models				
ARMA(4, 3)	$\phi_2\,\theta_1\,\phi_3$	All significant but ϕ_4 least significant	−660.771196	1331.54*
ARMA(1, 3)	θ_1	θ_3	−663.098026	1334.20**
ARMA(1, 2)	θ_1	All significant	−663.691498	1333.38**
ARMA(4, 3)	$\phi_2\,\theta_1\,\phi_3\,\theta_2$	θ_3	−673.779259	1355.56**
ARMA(4, 0)	$\phi_2\,\phi_3$	All significant	−673.926288	1353.85**
ARMA(1, 4)	—	All significant	−657.296770	1326.59

5.7 MODEL SELECTION

As shown in section 5.6, Table 5.2 when state space estimation software is available, a stationary or non-stationary ARMA model can be fitted directly to the data. The non-zero parameters can be chosen by a procedure such as backward elimination, and the modeller can look at the AIC and prediction error variance of each of the fitted models as a further guide.

When using commercial software to fit ARIMA models, the analyst must first difference the data until it is stationary. As demonstrated for the temperature series in section 5.6, a time series plot will usually show up any change in level, and if the sample autocorrelations do not decay for large lags then the series is clearly *not* stationary and must be differenced.

Once the differenced series is stationary the analyst needs to supply the ARMA orders p, q. Note that a complete backwards elimination procedure cannot be followed, as the software does not usually allow the user to zeroize particular parameters. Historically, the ARMA modelling literature has placed great emphasis on the study of the sample autocorrelation and partial autocorrelation functions as an aid to selecting the model orders (see, for instance, Box–Jenkins (1970)). This is a skilled task, however, and because of the large standard errors often encountered for the sample autocorrelations and partial autocorrelations does not always yield helpful results. With modern fast computing it has become less important, as it is quite practical to fit every set of ARMA orders p, q up to a certain level and study the significance or otherwise of the parameters and compare prediction error variances. It is still natural, however, to look at the stationary observed time series for any obvious clues about the model orders.

We suggest the following rules of thumb:

	Autocorrelations	**Partial autocorrelations**
MA(q)	non-zero at lags 1 to q only	tails off—no pattern
AR(p)	tails off—damped exponential or damped sine wave, depending on roots of AR polynomial	non-zero at lags 1 to p only
ARMA(p, q)	irregular pattern at lags 1 to q then tails off as damped exponential and/or damped sine wave	tails off—no pattern

To test whether the autocorrelations are zero we can use Bartlett's result as described in 3.6.

The corresponding result for the variance of the sample partial autocorrelations is that

$$\text{var}(\hat{\phi}_{kk}) = \frac{1}{N}$$

for $k > m$, where the first m partial autocorrelations only are assumed to be non-zero.

To illustrate ARMA model selection we consider the purse data. From the autocorrelation function (Fig. 3.13) the autocorrelations are small for large lags, so the series is probably stationary and the sample autocorrelations at lags 1 and 2, and maybe at lag 3, are non-zero. The partial autocorrelation function of the series is shown in Fig. 5.11. The PACFs at the first two lags are clearly significant, and those at higher lags are close to zero, suggesting an AR(2) model.

When fitting the temperature data in section 5.6 we fitted an MA(4) model to the differences. The partial autocorrelation function of the differences is shown in Fig. 5.12. The PACs are small after lag 4, suggesting that an AR(4) model may also be appropriate.

The selection of an ARMA model which contains both autoregressive and moving average terms is less straightforward, and the autocorrelations and PACs do not usually point unambiguously towards a particular model. To illustrate the selection of a mixed

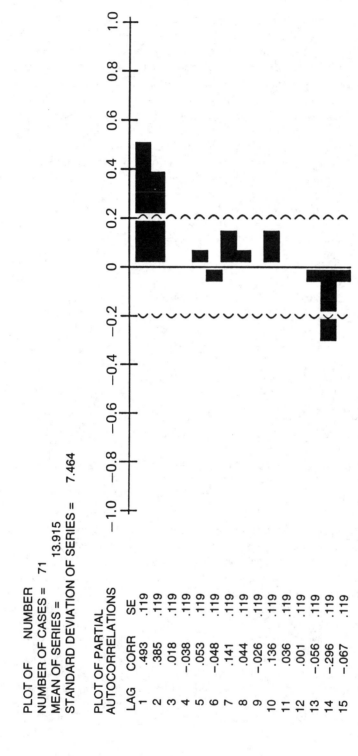

PLOT OF   NUMBER
NUMBER OF CASES =   71
MEAN OF SERIES =   13.915
STANDARD DEVIATION OF SERIES =   7.464

PLOT OF PARTIAL
AUTOCORRELATIONS

LAG	CORR	SE
1	.493	.119
2	.385	.119
3	.018	.119
4	−.038	.119
5	.053	.119
6	−.048	.119
7	.141	.119
8	.044	.119
9	−.026	.119
10	.136	.119
11	.036	.119
12	.001	.119
13	−.056	.119
14	−.296	.119
15	−.067	.119

Fig. 5.11. Partial autocorrelation function of the purse data.

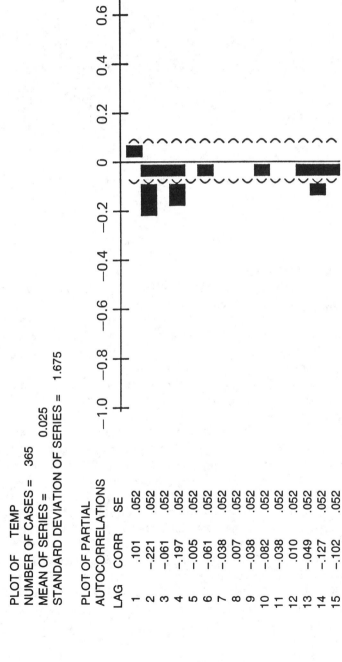

PLOT OF   TEMP
NUMBER OF CASES =   365
MEAN OF SERIES =   0.025
STANDARD DEVIATION OF SERIES =   1.675

PLOT OF PARTIAL
AUTOCORRELATIONS

LAG	CORR	SE
1	.101	.052
2	-.221	.052
3	-.061	.052
4	-.197	.052
5	-.005	.052
6	-.061	.052
7	-.038	.052
8	.007	.052
9	-.038	.052
10	-.082	.052
11	-.038	.052
12	.010	.052
13	-.049	.052
14	-.127	.052
15	-.102	.052

Fig. 5.12. Partial autocorrelation function of the differenced temperature data.

model we have generated 200 observations from an ARMA(1, 2) model, which are shown in Fig. 5.13.

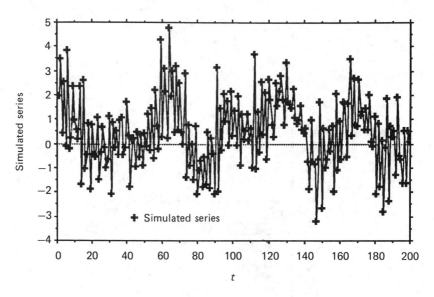

Fig. 5.13. Simulated data set from an ARMA(1, 2) model.

The sample autocorrelation function and partial autocorrelations are shown in Fig. 5.14. The autocorrelations are significant up to lag 7 and do not seem to decay rapidly, so a moving average process is not indicated. Further, the partial autocorrelations are non-zero at some large lags, so an autoregressive process is unlikely. We could notice that the first autocorrelation is very small and that the autocorrelations exhibit a fading sinusoidal pattern from the second onwards, that is, that the difference equation for the autocorrelations (5.9) holds for $m > 1$ only, indicating an MA order of 1 and an AR order of at least 2 (as there are imaginary roots of the AR polynomial). This happens to be true for our generated series, but in general it is too much to ask that the sample autocorrelations conform to the expected theoretical pattern to such an extent.

To fit an ARMA model these data we would probably proceed by fitting models with a variety of orders, studying the significance of the parameter estimates and comparing the prediction error variances. For instance an ARMA(3, 3) model fitted using MINITAB gave ϕ_1 and ϕ_3 non-significant (PEV = 1.004). Fitting an ARMA (2, 3) gave ϕ_1 non-significant, PEV = 1.004 (that is, no increase) and satisfactory Q statistics. ARMA(2, 2) gave ϕ_2 not significant and PEV = 1.004, whereas ARMA(1, 2) gave a 'convergence criterion not met after 25 iterations' message, but all parameters significant and PEV = 1.003. The fitted model was $X_t = 0.8782X_{t-1} + \varepsilon_t - 1.4020\varepsilon_{t-1} + 0.9039\varepsilon_{t-2}$ with $Q(12) = 6.3$ (9 d.o.f.) and $Q(24) = 26.4$ (21 d.o.f.), which seems acceptable, although a histogram and autocorrelation function of the residuals should be plotted to ensure that they are normal and independent (see section 5.9). ARMA(1, 1) gave a vastly increased PEV of 1.902, as might be expected, and huge highly significant Q's, $Q(12) = 74.2$

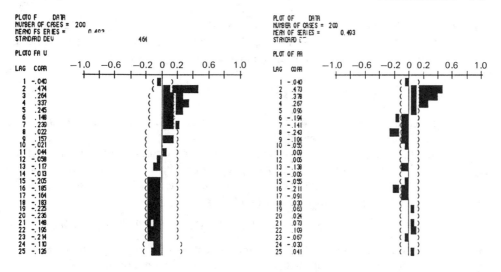

Fig. 5.14. Sample autocorrelations and partial autocorrelations of the simulated series of Fig. 5.13.

(10 d.o.f.), $Q(24) = 98$ (22 d.o.f.). So the ARMA (1, 2) model (the generating model) seems to be indicated most strongly.

For interest we used state space software, and a backwards elimination process yielded an ARMA(3, 3) model with $\theta_2 = 0$. Omitting the first 4 residuals from the likelihood we obtained an AIC of 567.84 and a final PEV of 0.967390, although steady state was not reached. Fitting an ARMA(1, 2) model using exact likelihood and still omitting the first 4 residuals gave an AIC of 567.31, so in this case backwards elimination did not give the minimum AIC model, although the AICs are of a similar magnitude. The fitted model was $X_t = 0.900641X_{t-1} + \varepsilon_t - 1.514709\varepsilon_{t-1} + 1.000000\varepsilon_{t-2}$. The generating model was $X_t = 0.9X_{t-1} + \varepsilon_t - 1.3995\varepsilon_{t-1} + 0.9645\varepsilon_{t-2}$, which has an AR root of 0.9 and so is nearly non-stationary and MA polynomial roots $0.7255 \pm 0.7145i$, which have modulus 1.018 and are barely invertible. This accounts for the discrepancy between the least squares and maximum likelihood estimates, as the estimation will depend heavily on starting values.

We should also take the opportunity of stating that when the ARMA model is placed in state space form there is a technique called canonical correlations analysis, which can be used to select the orders of stationary ARMA models and which can be extended to include stationary models with roots on the unit circle. We have no space to describe this procedure here, but see Akaike (1976) for stationary data and Swift (1990) or Tsay (1989) for data with roots on the unit circle. An advantage of canonical correlations analysis is that some initial parameter estimates are produced as a byproduct. For non-state space correlations there are several other quantities which have been used for identification of models. These include inverse autocorrelations and inverse partial auto-correlations.

Of course, as with all types of model, more than one ARMA model may be suitable for a given series. As any mixed ARMA model also has an infinite MA and infinite AR representation the hope is that a mixed ARMA model with low orders can be used instead of a large order AR only or MA only model. This is known as the principle of parsimony. A criterion like AIC which penalizes the likelihood for the number of parameters in the model attempts to choose the most parsimonious model.

5.8 FORECASTING ARMA MODELS

In this section, as in sections 3.4 and 4.6, we will assume for forecasting purposes that the parameters of a fitted model are known exactly.

When the ARMA model has been estimated in state space form, forecasting is exactly as described in section 4.6, that is the k step ahead predictor of a general state space model is $\mathbf{H}\phi^k\mathbf{a}_t$. For example, the final state estimate of the model fitted to the temperature series by backwards elimination in section 5.6. is

$$a_{360} = (5.37000000, -1.88910447, 0.53770241, -0.25678617, 0.67872287).$$

We will leave it to the reader to check the forecasts shown in Fig. 5.15, using the state space form. Note that RPEV indicates the square root of the prediction error variance.

EXTRAPOLATIVE K step predictions

NO.	ACTUAL	FORECAST	PEV	RPEV
361	3.23000000	3.94481817	2.36151753	1.53672298
362	2.41000000	4.82331956	5.14869059	2.26907263
363	6.98000000	4.98322746	6.62886119	2.57465749
364	9.19000000	5.62386247	7.74509607	2.78300127
365	9.20000000	5.76548419	8.33064000	2.88628481
366	7.73000000	5.84268110	8.80073349	2.96660302

EXTRAPOLATIVE SUM OF SQUARED ERRORS   38.39738523172825

ONE STEP PREDICTS

NO.	ACTUAL	FORECAST	VARIANCE	RMSE
361	3.23000000	3.94481817	2.36151753	1.53672298
362	2.41000000	4.04674713	2.36151753	1.53672298
363	6.98000000	2.63915810	2.36151753	1.53672298
364	9.19000000	8.55245652	2.36151753	1.53672298
365	9.20000000	8.41351716	2.36151753	1.53672298
366	7.73000000	9.05230344	2.36151753	1.53672298

MEAN OF POST SAMPLE SQD ERRORS = 1.750732853449894

POST SAMPLE PREDICTIVE TEST (CHOW) STATISTIC
1.750731750889017   should be F   6   355

Fig. 5.15. Forecasting output from the state space estimation of temperature data.

When state space methods are not available the ARMA equation can be used directly to make forecasts. We forecast an AR(2) model in section 3.4 without recourse to state space methods but ARMA forecasting is, in general, complicated by the inclusion of the MA terms.

Take for instance the ARMA(1, 1) model. As described in section 5.5 (when we considered least squares estimation) the conditional expectation one step predictor of X_{t+1} at time t is $X_{t+1|t} = \phi X_t + \theta \varepsilon_t$. The one step prediction error is therefore unsurprisingly

$$X_{t+1} - X_{t+1|t} = \phi X_t + \theta \varepsilon_t + \varepsilon_{t+1} - (\phi X_t + \theta \varepsilon_t) = \varepsilon_{t+1}.$$

To calculate these for $t = 2, \ldots, N$ we need to set $\varepsilon_1 = 0$. As demonstrated in section 5.5, to obtain reliable estimates of the ε_t for the predictions we require $|\theta| < 1$. Two step forecasts can be calculated using

$$X_{t+2|t} = \phi X_{t+1|t} + \varepsilon_{t+2|t} + \theta \varepsilon_{t+1|t} = \phi X_{t+1|t}$$

and so on, where $\varepsilon_{t+2|t}$ and $\varepsilon_{t+1|t}$ are both zero as the ε_t's are independent by assumption.

For the general ARMA(p, q) model the one step forecast is

$$X_{t+1|t} = \phi_1 X_t + \phi_2 X_{t-1} + \ldots + \phi_p X_{t-p} + \theta_1 \varepsilon_t + \theta_2 \varepsilon_{t-1} + \ldots + \theta_q \varepsilon_{t-q+1}$$

where the $\varepsilon_t, \varepsilon_{t-1}, \ldots$ etc. are the one step prediction errors $X_t - X_{t|t-1}$, $X_{t-1} - X_{t-1|t-2}$ etc. We described briefly how to calculate these in section 5.5, as they are required for least squares estimation. We start by calculating $X_{t+1|t}$ for $t = p$. This requires values for $\varepsilon_p, \varepsilon_{p-1}, \ldots \varepsilon_{p+1-q}$, so we set these starting values arbitrarily, and set for

$$\varepsilon_p = \varepsilon_{p-1} = \ldots = \varepsilon_{p+1-q} = 0$$

for instance. We can then calculate $\varepsilon_{p+1} = X_{p+1} - X_{p+1|p}$ and use the new ε_{p+1} to obtain $X_{p+2|p+1}$, and so on for $t = p + 2, \ldots, N$. When the model is not invertible, the forecasts will still depend on the assumptions made about the starting values—even for large t, and we say that there is a *finite sample prediction* problem. As for least squares we can improve on the use of arbitrary starting values by backcasting as described in section 5.5.

This use of the residuals for forecasting is demonstrated in Fig. 5.16 by extracts of MINITAB output from the MA(4) model fit (with no constant term) to the differenced temperature data of Fig. 5.9. The fitted values (one step predictions $X_{t|t-1}$) and residuals can readily be obtained from MINITAB. Notice that X_1 does not exist, as the X's are differences of the temperature series $\{T_t\}$, that is, $X_2 = T_2 - T_1$, and so on.

As the fitted model is

$$X_t = \varepsilon_t + 0.0722 \varepsilon_{t-1} - 0.3085 \varepsilon_{t-2} - 0.1312 \varepsilon_{t-3} - 0.2022 \varepsilon_{t-4}$$

with $\sigma^2 = 2.464$ the one step forecast at time 360 is

$$X_{361|360} = \varepsilon_{361|360} + 0.722 \varepsilon_{360|360} - 0.3085 \varepsilon_{359|360}$$
$$- 0.1312 \varepsilon_{358|360} - 0.2022 \varepsilon_{357|360}.$$

Forecasts from period 360

Period	Forecast	95 Per cent Limits	
		Lower	Upper
361	−1.46001	−4.53757	1.61755
362	1.05601	−2.02957	4.14159
363	0.37433	−2.85403	3.60268
364	0.81684	−2.43668	4.07036
365	0.00000	−3.31247	3.31247

t	dif. temp X_t	resid $\hat{\varepsilon}_t$	fitted $X_{t\|t-1}$
2	−0.13	−0.25331	0.12331
3	6.82	5.89620	0.92380
4	1.03	0.14890	0.88110
5	−0.02	1.33162	−1.35162
6	−0.35	0.32225	−0.67225
⋮	⋮	⋮	⋮
350	−3.62	−3.11658	−0.50342
351	0.72	1.40920	−0.68920
352	2.37	1.40028	0.96972
353	−3.97	−4.08811	0.11811
354	−0.75	−0.46776	−0.28224
355	1.53	0.77119	0.75881
356	0.12	−0.33341	0.45341
357	4.94	4.31418	0.62582
358	0.85	0.44209	0.40791
359	−0.64	0.77119	−1.41119
360	−4.62	−4.04060	−0.57940

Fig. 5.16 MINITAB output, showing the residuals and fitted values and forecasts of the final 6 differenced periods of the temperature data.

The expected value of ε_{361} is clearly zero at time 360, so the first term on the right hand side is zero. The other $\varepsilon_{361-k|360}$ times are equivalent to ε_{360}, ε_{359}, ε_{358} and ε_{357} respectively and are estimated by the appropriate one step prediction errors. So

$$X_{361|360} = 0.0722(-4.04060) - 0.3085(0.77119) - 0.1312(0.44209)$$

$$- 0.2022(4.31418)$$

$$= -1.46.$$

(Parameter values and residuals are rounded, so our manually calculated result is slightly less accurate than MINITAB.)

In general the k step forecast is

$$X_{t+k|t} = \phi_1 X_{t+k-1|t} + \ldots + \phi_p X_{t+k-p|t} + \varepsilon_{t+k|k} + \theta_1 \varepsilon_{t+k-1|t} + \ldots + \theta_q \varepsilon_{t+k-q|t}$$

where we have

$m > 0$	$m \leq 0$
$X_{t+m|t}$ is m step forecast	$X_{t+m|t} = X_{t+m}$
$\varepsilon_{t+m|t}$ is zero	$\varepsilon_{t+m|t} = \varepsilon_{t+m}$

When $k > q$ the expected value of all the noise terms is zero and the forecast function becomes

$$X_{t+k|t} = \phi_1 X_{t+k-1|t} + \ldots + \phi_p X_{t+k-p|t}$$

so that it only depends on the autoregressive part of the model. Forecasts for $k > q$ will therefore be determined by the solution of the AR difference equation and display the same characteristics as the autocorrelation function (see (5.9) and following in section 5.4). Continuing the temperature example, the two step forecast

$$X_{362|360} = \varepsilon_{362|360} + 0.0722\varepsilon_{361|360} - 0.3085\varepsilon_{360|360}$$
$$- 0.1312\varepsilon_{359|360} - 0.2022\varepsilon_{358|360}$$
$$= 0 + 0 - 0.3085(-4.04060) - 0.1312(0.77119) - 0.2022(0.44209)$$
$$= 1.06.$$

As this is an MA(q) process, when we forecast more than $q = 4$ steps ahead, the forecast ε's are all zero and the forecast equals the constant term (equivalent to the mean for an MA process)—in this case 0.

If state space methods are used for the ARMA(1, 1) model it becomes

$$X_t = (1 \quad 0)\alpha_t, \quad \alpha_t = \begin{pmatrix} \phi & 1 \\ 0 & 0 \end{pmatrix} \alpha_{t-1} + \begin{pmatrix} 1 \\ \theta \end{pmatrix} \eta_t$$

where η_t equates with ε_t of the ARMA model. The second element of the state estimator $\mathbf{a}_t$ will be the finite sample estimator of $\theta\varepsilon_t$; call this $\theta\hat{\varepsilon}_t$. The one step predictor $X_{t+1|t}$ is therefore $\mathbf{H}\phi = \phi X_t + \theta\hat{\varepsilon}_t$. The two step predictor is $\mathbf{H}\phi^2\mathbf{a}_t = \phi^2 X_t + \phi\theta\hat{\varepsilon}_t$, and so on. Notice that the state space model can provide convergent estimates of ε_t even if the corresponding ARMA model is not invertible (see Harvey 1981b).

As an ARIMA model is a special case of a non-stationary ARMA model it can be treated in exactly the same way to make forecasts. For instance, the ARIMA(0, 1, 4) model fitted to the temperature data can be forecast using the difference equation

$$X_t = X_{t-1} + \varepsilon_t + \theta_1\varepsilon_{t-1} + \theta_2\varepsilon_{t-2} + \theta_3\varepsilon_{t-3} + \theta_4\varepsilon_{t-4}.$$

Equivalently, it is often easier to make forecasts of the differenced (stationary) series and then work backwards to calculate the forecasts of the original series implied. For instance, if we denote the undifferenced temperature series by T_t we can use the relation

$$T_{t+1} - T_t = X_{t+1} \quad \text{or} \quad T_{t+1} = T_t + X_{t+1}$$

to calculate that $T_{t+1|t} = T_t + X_{t+1|t}$. The two step predictor is calculated from

$$T_{t+2} = T_{t+1} + X_{t+2} = T_t + X_{t+1} + X_{t+2},$$

so that

$$T_{t+2|t} = T_t + X_{t+2|t} + X_{t+1|t}.$$

The forecasts continue in this way, so that the k step forecast of the original series is the sum of the 1 to k step forecasts of the differenced series. For the temperature data

$$T_{361|360} = T_{360} + X_{361|360},$$

$$T_{362|360} = T_{360} + X_{361|360} + X_{362|360},$$

and so on. As the 360th temperature is 5.37, this gives forecasts of 3.9099, 4.9660, 5.34033 for 1–3 steps ahead and 6.15717 for all subsequent lags.

We have not yet considered the calculation of variances for the predictions from the ARMA equation. To do so we need to consider the MA only representation of the ARMA model

$$X_{t+k} = \varepsilon_{t+k} + \psi_1\varepsilon_{t+k-1} + \ldots + \psi_{k-1}\varepsilon_{t+1} + \psi_k\varepsilon_t + \psi_{k+1}\varepsilon_{t-1} + \ldots. \qquad (5.11)$$

We saw how to obtain such a representation in section 5.3. As the ε_t's are independent by assumption the k step forecast can be expressed as

$$X_{t+k|t} = \psi_k\varepsilon_t + \psi_{k+1}\varepsilon_{t-1} + \ldots.$$

The prediction error will therefore be the first k terms of (5.11), and the prediction error variance will be $\sigma^2(1 + \psi_1^2 + \ldots + \psi_{k-1}^2)$.

This is fine, but it assumes that we have exact knowledge of the ε_t's. We have seen before that estimates of the ε_t's depend on arbitrary starting values and that the effect of these starting values will only decay for large t if the model is invertible. So PEVs calculated in this way are valid for invertible models and large t only.

If the model is stationary, the weights ψ_i decrease and

$$\sum_{i}^{\infty} \psi_i^2$$

will converge to $\text{var}(X_t)$, so for large k, the k step prediction error variance is the variance of the series. For non-stationary models the prediction error variance will increase indefinitely as the forecast lag increases.

Continuing with our temperature example, the ARIMA model

$$X_t = X_{t-1} + \varepsilon_t + 0.0722\varepsilon_{t-1} - 0.3085\varepsilon_{t-2} - 0.1312\varepsilon_{t-3} - 0.2022\varepsilon_{t-4}$$

has infinite MA representation

$$X_t = \varepsilon_t + 1.0722\varepsilon_{t-1} + 0.7637\varepsilon_{t-2} + 0.6325\varepsilon_{t-3}$$
$$+ 0.4303\varepsilon_{t-4} + 0.4303\varepsilon_{t-5} + \text{etc.}$$

The one step prediction error variance is therefore $\sigma^2 = 2.464$, two step $(1 + 1.0722^2)$ $\sigma^2 = 5.2966$, three step $(1 + 1.0722^2 + 0.7637^2)\, \sigma^2 = 6.7337$, and so on. Most computer software will calculate the predictions and prediction error variances of an ARIMA model automatically from the original undifferenced data. MINITAB output for the temperature series is shown in Fig. 5.17. (Again we have given model parameters to only 4 d.p. whereas software will work to as many decimal places as possible, so our calculations will differ slightly from computer output.) Note that although the prediction errors for the undifferenced series are the sums of the prediction errors of the differenced series these errors are not independent and the k step prediction error variance of the undifferenced series is not the sum of the prediction error variances of the differenced series.

Forecasts from period 360

Period	Forecast	95 Percent Limits	
		Lower	Upper
361	3.9100	0.8324	6.9876
362	4.9660	0.4537	9.4783
363	5.3403	0.2526	10.4281
364	6.1572	0.7098	11.6046
365	6.1572	0.5511	11.7633
366	6.1572	0.3967	11.9176

Fig. 5.17. Forecasts of temperature data using ARIMA(0, 1, 4) model fitted to raw data.

We should point out the following link between the one step prediction error variance of an ARMA model σ^2 and the corresponding PEV of an ARMA model in state space form. The one step prediction error variance of a state space model is F_t, which incorporates any uncertainty about the past of a state space model via the starting values $\mathbf{a}_0$ and $\mathbf{C}_0$. For large t, F_t tends to a steady state prediction error variance F. The one step PEV of an invertible ARMA model is σ^2 for large t, when the effect of starting values has worn off. If this invertible model is placed in state space form, the steady state F will be equal to σ^2. Although we cannot calculate the one step variance of a non-invertible ARMA model directly from the ARMA difference equation we *can* place it in state space form and run the Kalman recursions. The interesting fact is that when we do this the steady state PEV F will be the same as σ^2 of the likelihood equivalent invertible model.

5.9 MODEL EVALUATION

The usual diagnostic checks (see sections 3.5 and 4.7) can be performed on ARMA models. When state space methods are used for estimation, the residuals are the one step prediction errors V_t from the Kalman filter recursions, which can be standardized by dividing by the corresponding prediction error variance F_t. Alternatively, we have seen that the residuals ε_t of an ARMA model can be calculated from the ARMA equation if

and only if the model is invertible. They can be standardized by dividing by the estimate
of σ^2. These two sets of residuals will differ slightly at the start of a series owing to the
assumptions made about starting values, but by the time the filter recursions reach steady
state they should agree.

It is always sensible to plot a histogram of the standardized residuals to see whether
they are approximately normally distributed and to plot the autocorrelations of the
residuals to check that they are small for all lags. A MINITAB plot of the autocorrelations
and histogram of the standardized residuals from the ARMA(1, 2) model fitted to the
simulated data in section 5.7 and from the (inappropriate) ARMA(1, 1) model fitted to
the same data are shown in Figs 5.18 and 5.19.

The $Q(k)$ or portmanteau statistic can be calculated from the residuals as usual and so
will have $k - (p + q)$ degrees of freedom if the residuals are not autocorrelated. The
number of residuals included in the calculation of $Q(k)$ should be $N^* = N - d$ if least
squares methods have been used (where d is the degree of differencing) and $N^* = N - d$
where d is now the state dimension if the model has been estimated using state space
methods. The portmanteau statistics for the model fits to the simulated data bear out Figs
5.18 and 5.19. The ARMA(2, 1) fit to the simulated data gave $Q(12) = 6.3$ (9 d.o.f.) and
$Q(24) = 26.4$ (21 d.o.f.), so no suggestion of autocorrelated residuals whereas the
ARMA(1, 1) model gave $Q(12) = 74.2$ (10 d.o.f.) and $Q(24) = 98.4$ (22 d.o.f.), clearly
pointing to an unsuitable model.

ACF of C3

1	−0.007		X
2	0.058		XX
3	−0.073		XXX
4	0.033		XX
5	0.027		XX
6	0.000		X
7	0.074		XXX
8	−0.095		XXX
9	0.0.45		XX
10	−0.046		XX
11	0.030		XX
12	−0.011		X
13	0.017		X
14	0.092		XXX
15	−0.106		XXXX
16	−0.115		XXXX
17	−0.063		XXX
18	−0.071		XXX
19	−0.155		XXXXX

MTB > histo c3

Histogram of C3 N= 200

Midpoint	Count	
−2.5	2	**
−2.0	7	*******
−1.5	13	*************
−1.0	27	***************************
−0.5	33	*********************************
0.0	37	*************************************
0.5	37	*************************************
1.0	29	*****************************
1.5	6	******
2.0	7	*******
2.5	1	*
3.0	1	*

Fig. 5.18. The autocorrelation function of the residuals of the ARMA(1, 2) model fitted to the
simulated data. There is no evidence of autocorrelation and the histogram looks normal with zero
mean with standard deviation 1.

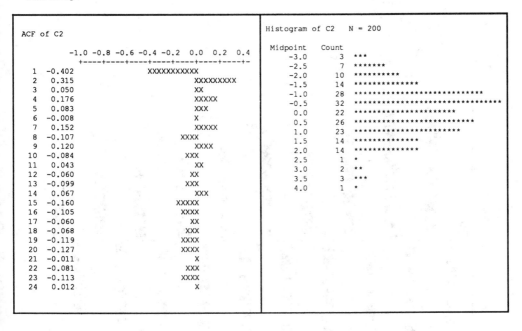

```
ACF of C2                                    Histogram of C2    N = 200

            -1.0 -0.8 -0.6 -0.4 -0.2  0.0  0.2  0.4    Midpoint   Count
            +----+----+----+----+----+----+----+-         -3.0       3   ***
  1  -0.402              XXXXXXXXXXX                        -2.5       7   *******
  2   0.315                         XXXXXXXXX               -2.0      10   **********
  3   0.050                         XX                      -1.5      14   **************
  4   0.176                         XXXXX                   -1.0      28   ****************************
  5   0.083                         XXX                     -0.5      32   ********************************
  6  -0.008                        X                         0.0      22   **********************
  7   0.152                         XXXXX                    0.5      26   **************************
  8  -0.107                     XXXX                         1.0      23   ***********************
  9   0.120                         XXXX                     1.5      14   **************
 10  -0.084                      XXX                         2.0      14   **************
 11   0.043                        XX                        2.5       1   *
 12  -0.060                       XX                         3.0       2   **
 13  -0.099                      XXX                         3.5       3   ***
 14   0.067                        XXX                       4.0       1   *
 15  -0.160                    XXXXX
 16  -0.105                     XXXX
 17  -0.060                       XX
 18  -0.068                      XXX
 19  -0.119                     XXXX
 20  -0.127                     XXXX
 21  -0.011                       X
 22  -0.081                      XXX
 23  -0.113                     XXXX
 24   0.012                        X
```

Fig. 5.19. Autocorrelations and histogram of standardized residuals from *inappropriate* ARMA(1, 1) fit to simulated data. The residuals appear to be autocorrelated and there are several (3 or more) standard deviations away from a zero mean.

5.10 SEASONAL ARMA MODELS

If we are given a time series which is clearly seasonal, the fuel data of Fig. 1.3 for instance, we could deseasonalize it as described in Chapter 1 and then fit a stationary ARMA model to the deseasonalized data. This may well work, particularly if the seasonal effects are deterministic, but it is often unrealistic. Another possibility is to build a model which incorporates the seasonality directly and fit this to the original data. In this section we extend ARMA techniques to seasonal ARMA models.

Consider again the quarterly fuel data of Fig. 1.3. Fuel consumption for the first (winter) quarter tends to be high and for the third (summer) quarter is low, so the data are clearly seasonal. When data are seasonal, an observation in one season is likely to be highly correlated with the adjacent years' observations in the same season so that the series exhibits high autocorrelations at lags which are a multiple of the length of the cycle. For instance, the autocorrelation function of the fuel series is shown in Fig. 5.20 and clearly has high correlations at lags 4, 8, 12, etc. A negative autocorrelation between data from opposite seasons—at lags 2, 6, 10, etc.—is also apparent. We would like an ARMA model which models such correlations between the same season in successive years.

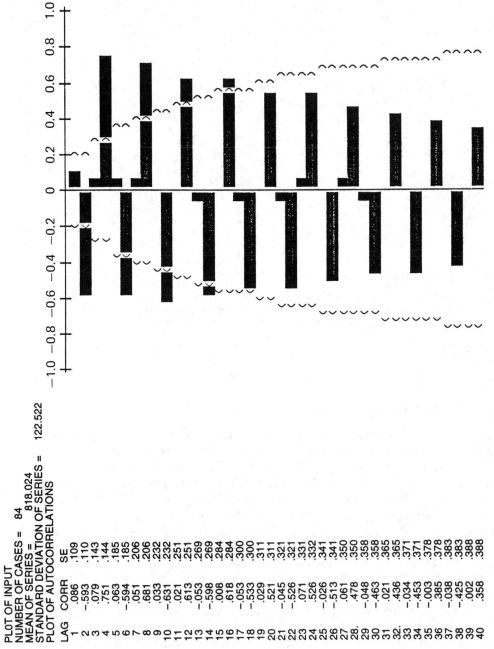

PLOT OF INPUT
NUMBER OF CASES = 84
MEAN OF SERIES = 818.024
STANDARD DEVIATION OF SERIES = 122.522
PLOT OF AUTOCORRELATIONS

LAG	CORR	SE
1	.086	.109
2	-.593	.110
3	.079	.143
4	.751	.144
5	.063	.185
6	-.594	.185
7	.051	.206
8	.681	.206
9	.033	.232
10	-.631	.232
11	.021	.251
12	.613	.251
13	-.053	.269
14	-.598	.269
15	.008	.284
16	.618	.284
17	-.053	.300
18	-.533	.300
19	.029	.311
20	.521	.311
21	-.045	.321
22	-.526	.321
23	.071	.331
24	.526	.332
25	-.026	.341
26	-.513	.341
27	.061	.350
28.	.478	.350
29	-.048	.358
30	-.463	.358
31	.021	.365
32.	.436	.365
33	-.034	.371
34	-.453	.371
35	-.003	.378
36	.385	.378
37	-.038	.383
38	-.425	.383
39	.002	.388
40	.358	.388

Fig. 5.20. Autocorrelations of the quarterly fuel series.

A simple model of period s is the *seasonal* AR(1) model

$$X_t = \phi X_{t-s} + \varepsilon_t. \tag{5.12}$$

This has autocorrelations of ϕ^k at lag ks where $k = 1, 2, 3, \ldots$ which decay exponentially as k becomes larger and a zero correlation at all lags that are not a multiple of the period s. Another simple model is the seasonal MA(1) model $X_t = \varepsilon_t + \theta \varepsilon_{t-s}$, which has zero autocorrelation at all lags except at lag s. Notice that these autocorrelation properties parallel those of the corresponding non-seasonal models. We could generalize these seasonal models to those of the form

$$\phi^*(B^s)X_t = \theta^*(B^s)u_t, \tag{5.13}$$

that is, in terms of B_s only, in which case the autocorrelation function would be non-zero at multiples of s only.

In practice, however, we usually wish to model the autocorrelations between neighbouring observations as well as those between the same season in successive years, and so we want to allow terms in the intervening lags to appear. A model which does this is $X_t + \phi_1 X_{t-1} + \phi_s X_{t-s} + \varepsilon_t$. Alternatively, we could allow the noise term u_t in (5.13) to be autocorrelated and allow it to follow an ARMA model $\phi(B)u_t = \theta(B)\varepsilon_t$.

Multiplying (5.13) all through by $\phi(B)$ gives

$$\phi(B)\phi^*(B^s)X_t = \phi(B)\theta^*(B^s)u_t = \theta(B)\theta^*(B^s)\varepsilon_t,$$

and so the general *multiplicative* seasonal ARMA model can be written

$$\phi(B)\phi^*(B^s)X_t = \theta(B)\theta^*(B^s)\varepsilon_t. \tag{5.14}$$

Notice that (5.14) is merely an ARMA model in which both the AR and MA polynomials factorize into a seasonal polynomial in B^s and a non-seasonal polynomial in B. For instance, if the noise term in (5.13) followed an ARMA(1, 1) process then the model would be

$$(1 - \phi B)(1 - \phi^* B^s)X_t = (1 + \theta B)\varepsilon_t.$$

For quarterly data this multiplies out to become

$$(1 + \phi\phi^* B^5 - \phi B - \phi^* B^4)X_t = \varepsilon_t + \theta\varepsilon_{t-1}$$

or

$$X_t - \phi X_{t-1} - \phi^* X_{t-4} + \phi\phi^* X_{t-5} = \varepsilon_t + \theta\varepsilon_{t-1},$$

which is an ARMA($s + 1$, 1) model in which some parameter values are fixed to zero and others are related to each other. In general, the order of the seasonal AR polynomial $\phi^*(B^s)$ is denoted by P and the order of $\theta^*(B^s)$ by Q (so the maximum AR order of (5.14) is $Ps + p$ and the corresponding MA order is $Qs + q$).

For model selection, as for non-seasonal models, the autocorrelation functions of the data must be 'matched' to the theoretical autocorrelation function of a seasonal model. We therefore need to know something of the autocorrelation structure of these seasonal models. A multiplicative autoregressive process $\phi(B)\phi^*(B^s)X_t = \varepsilon_t$ of orders p, P will have autocorrelations which decay according to the difference equation $\phi(B)\phi^*(B^s)\rho(m) = 0$ (see section 5.4) and partial autocorrelations which are zero for lags greater than $p + sP$. The multiplicative moving average process $X_t = \theta(B)\theta^*(B^s)\varepsilon_t$ of orders q, Q will have zero autocorrelations for lags which are more than q from multiples of s, that is, for $q < k < s - q$, $s + q < k < 2s - q$, $2s + q < k < 3s - q$, etc. and for lags which are greater than the total moving average order $Qs + q$. For mixed multiplicative ARMA models the autocorrelation functions become even more complex than for ordinary ARMA models, and we do not have room to go into details here.

In practice one will often encounter seasonal data for which the autocorrelation between the same season in different years does *not* appear to diminish as the years become further apart. The autocorrelations of the fuel series, for instance (Fig. 5.20), do not decay very quickly. For such series it will often help if we seasonally difference the data. That is, we difference the data by taking the differences between the same season in consecutive years to give

$$W_t = \nabla_s X_t = (1 - B^s)X_t = X_t - X_{t-s}.$$

Our hope is then that the differenced series can be modelled by a multiplicative ARMA model (5.14). Fig. 5.21 shows the autocorrelations of the seasonal differences of the fuel data. The reason why seasonal differencing may work is described towards the end of this section.

The autocorrelations of the seasonal differences in Fig. 5.21 become very small at large lags, so no further differencing seems necessary, and we can fit a multiplicative seasonal ARMA model (5.14) to the differences. For this example, the only non-zero autocorrelation is at lag 4, suggesting that a seasonal MA(1) may be appropriate. Using exact likelihood, fitting an MA model with only θ_4 non-zero to the seasonal differences gives $\theta_4 = 0.717056$ and $\sigma^2 = 4798.75903$ with a maximum likelihood of -425.510964 and AIC of 855.021928. Alternatively, a full MA (4) model fitted to the differenced data gives a prediction error variance of 4076.168398, a maximum likelihood of -420.513293 and an AIC of 851.026586. Only the third MA parameter θ_3 is non-significant. The first 5 residuals (corresponding to the state dimension) from the seasonally differenced data were omitted from the likelihood, so these results are based on only 75 observations. For comparison, the BSM was also fitted (see Chapter 6) and gave a PEV of 3999.903. The MA(4) model is therefore quite competitive. The likelihood and AIC of the BSM are not directly comparable, as they are based on differing numbers of observations.

We can enlarge our class of models further by allowing ordinary differencing as well as seasonal differencing. If a seasonal series is seasonally differenced D times and satisfies an ARIMA(p, d, q)X(P, Q) model we say that the full model is an ARMA(p, d, q)X(P, D, Q) model. This gives a broad class of models to use on seasonal series. Packages such as MINITAB will fit these models directly to a time series when supplied with all the orders p, d, q, P, D, Q and the period of the series.

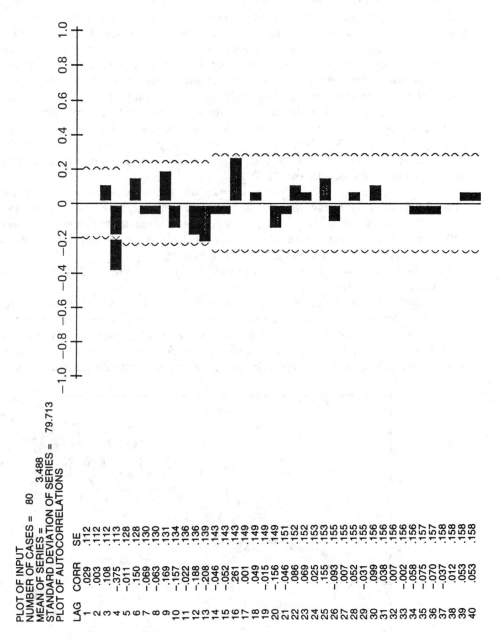

PLOT OF INPUT
NUMBER OF CASES =   80
MEAN OF SERIES =   3.488
STANDARD DEVIATION OF SERIES =   79.713
PLOT OF AUTOCORRELATIONS

LAG	CORR	SE
1	.029	.112
2	.003	.112
3	.108	.112
4	−.375	.113
5	−.011	.128
6	.150	.128
7	−.069	.130
8	−.063	.130
9	.169	.131
10	−.157	.134
11	−.022	.136
12	−.188	.136
13	−.208	.139
14	−.046	.143
15	−.052	.143
16	.261	.143
17	.001	.149
18	.049	.149
19	−.015	.149
20	−.156	.149
21	−.046	.151
22	.086	.152
23	.069	.152
24	.025	.153
25	.155	.153
26	−.093	.155
27	.007	.155
28	.052	.155
29	−.031	.155
30	.099	.156
31	.038	.156
32	.007	.156
33	−.002	.156
34	−.058	.156
35	−.075	.157
36	−.070	.157
37	−.037	.158
38	.012	.158
39	.053	.158
40	.053	.158

Fig. 5.21. Autocorrelations of the seasonal differences of the fuel series.

A classic series that is often used as an example of seasonal modelling techniques is the series of the logarithms of the monthly number of airline passenger miles from 1949 to 1960 inclusive, used by Box & Jenkins (1970). A plot of these data is shown in Fig. 5.22. It is clearly seasonal in nature and there appears to be an upward trend, so the series is non-stationary. The trend masks the seasonal pattern of the autocorrelations (Fig. 5.23) and the autocorrelations do not fade quickly, so we take ordinary differences of the data. The autocorrelations of the differenced data (Fig. 5.24) are clearly seasonal in nature and suggest seasonal differencing. The autocorrelations of the seasonally *and* ordinarily differenced data are shown in Fig. 5.25. Only the autocorrelations at lags 1, 3 or 12 are significantly different to zero, although the autocorrelation at lag 3 is barely significant. In the interests of parsimony we fitted a seasonal MA model of orders $Q = 1$, $q = 1$ although $Q = 1$, $q = 3$ might be suggested. We used MINITAB to fit the $(0, 1, 1) \times (0, 1, 1)$ model and obtained $\theta = 0.3958$ and $\theta^* = 0.6136$ with the square root of the prediction error variance equal to 0.001333.

In general, to select a suitable model for data which may be seasonal we study the autocorrelations of (i) the raw series (ii) the seasonally differenced series, (iii) the ordinarily differenced series, and if neither (ii) nor (iii) looks adequate for fitting a stationary ARMA model we (iv) both seasonally difference and ordinarily difference the series. It may be necessary to difference either way more than once.

Once fitted, we can perform diagnostic checks and forecast seasonal AR(I)MAs in exactly the same way as any other ARIMA model.

We might well argue that as the multiplicative seasonal model (5.14) is a special case of a large order ARMA model we might as well just fit a large dimension state space model to the data. The disadvantage of this is, however, that the dimension required for the state must be $\max(Ps + p, Qs + q + 1)$, so that even for low orders p, P, q, Q estimation will take a long time and large matrices will be involved with the resultant risks of

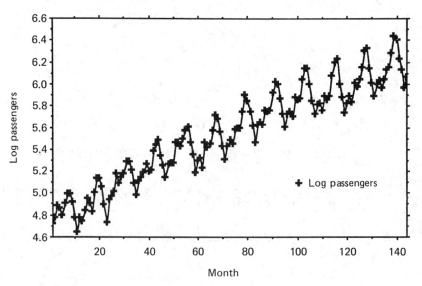

Fig. 5.22. Time series plot of logs of monthly airline passenger series 1949–1960 inclusive.

PLOT OF NUMBER
NUMBER OF CASES = 144
MEAN OF SERIES = 5.542
STANDARD DEVIATION OF SERIES = 0.440
PLOT OF AUTOCORRELATIONS

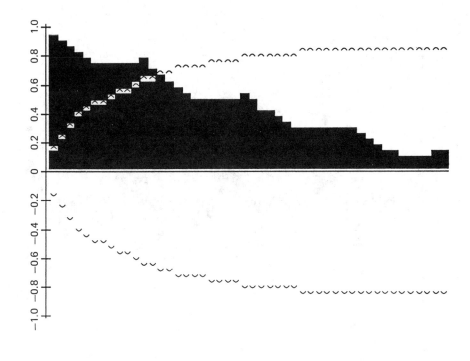

LAG	CORR	SE
1	.954	.083
2	.899	.140
3	.851	.175
4	.808	.202
5	.779	.223
6	.756	.242
7	.738	.257
8	.727	.272
9	.734	.285
10	.744	.298
11	.758	.310
12	.762	.323
13	.717	.335
14	.663	.346
15	.618	.354
16	.576	.362
17	.544	.368
18	.519	.374
19	.501	.379
20	.490	.383
21	.498	.388
22	.506	.392
23	.517	.397
24	.520	.401
25	.484	.406
26	.437	.410
27	.400	.413
28	.364	.416
29	.337	.418
30	.315	.420
31	.297	.421
32	.289	.423
33	.295	.424
34	.305	.426
35	.315	.427
36	.319	4.29
37	.286	.430
38	.245	.432
39	.211	.433
40	.175	.433
41	.146	.434
42	.125	.434
43	.106	.435
44	.099	.435
45	.104	.435
46	.111	.435
47	.120	.435
48	.125	.436

Fig. 5.23. Autocorrelations of the air passenger series. The seasonality is masked by the trend, so non-seasonal differencing is clearly required.

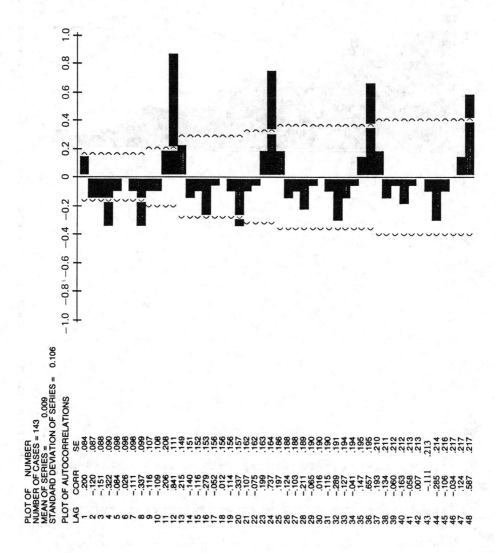

PLOT OF   NUMBER
NUMBER OF CASES = 143
MEAN OF SERIES =   0.009
STANDARD DEVIATION OF SERIES =   0.106

PLOT OF AUTOCORRELATIONS

LAG	CORR	SE
1	.200	.084
2	−.120	.087
3	−.151	.088
4	−.322	.090
5	−.084	.098
6	.026	.098
7	−.111	.098
8	−.337	.099
9	−.116	.107
10	−.109	.108
11	.206	.108
12	.841	.111
13	.215	.149
14	−.140	.151
15	−.116	.152
16	−.279	.153
17	−.052	.156
18	.012	.156
19	−.114	.156
20	−.337	.157
21	−.107	.162
22	−.075	.162
23	.199	.163
24	.737	.164
25	.197	.186
26	−.124	.188
27	−.103	.188
28	−.211	.189
29	−.065	.190
30	.016	.190
31	−.115	.190
32	−.289	.191
33	−.127	.194
34	−.041	.194
35	.147	.195
36	.657	.195
37	.193	.210
38	−.134	.211
39	−.060	.212
40	−.163	.212
41	−.058	.213
42	.007	.213
43	−.111	.213
44	−.285	.214
45	−.106	.216
46	−.034	.217
47	.124	.217
48	.587	.217

Fig. 5.24. Autocorrelations of the differenced airline series. Data a multiple of 12 lags apart are clearly highly correlated, so seasonal differencing is suggested.

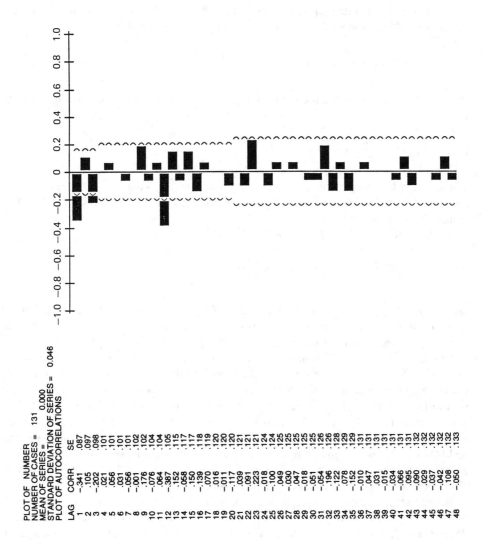

Fig. 5.25. The autocorrelations of the airline series after both ordinary and seasonal differencing. There are significant autocorrelations at lags 1, 3 and 12, but the seasonal pattern has disappeared, and the autocorrelations decay at large lags.

rounding error on matrix multiplication. We feel, therefore, that for seasonal models it is best either to stick to ARMA techniques, differencing the model until a seasonal ARMA is suggested, and using least squares software, or to use a structural seasonal model as described in Chapter 6.

We have not yet explained why seasonal differencing can eliminate seasonal patterns which do not decay further apart in time. Notice, however, that the seasonal differencing operator $1 - B^s$ has roots which all lie on the unit circle and are of form

$$e^{2\pi ji/s} \quad j = 0, 1, \ldots, s-1$$

The complementary function corresponding to this operator therefore contains terms of form

$$k_1 \sin\left(\frac{2\pi jt}{s}\right) + k_2 \cos\left(\frac{2\pi jt}{s}\right)$$

where k_1 and k_2 are constants and $j = 0, 1, \ldots, [s/2]$ where [ ] denotes the integer part of, i.e. $[s/2]$. Models which have period s are therefore likely to include such terms and so include $1 - B^s$ as a factor.

It may be that not all the factors of $1 - B^s$, that is,

$$(1 - B e^{-2\pi ji/s}) \quad j = 0, \pm 1, \ldots, \pm\left[\frac{s}{2}\right],$$

are required, that is, that terms at some of these frequencies dominate the complementary function. In this case an operator formed from the product of some of the factors may help to eliminate a cycle of period s. For instance, two factors of $1 - B^s$ are $1 - B e^{2\pi i/s}$ and $1 - B e^{-2\pi i/s}$, so for a 12 month cycle $(1 - \sqrt{3} B + B^2)X_t$ could be used. Notice that its roots are $e^{\pm 2\pi i/12}$, so that the corresponding terms of the complementary function for X_t involve $\cos(\pi t/6)$ and $\sin(\pi t/6)$. As another example, the fuel data are quarterly, so the appropriate factor of $(1 - B^4)$ corresponding to frequencies of $\pm 2\pi i/4$ is $1 + B^2$. The autocorrelations of $X_t + X_{t-2}$ are shown in Fig. 5.26. In this case the seasonality has disappeared and we can fit a non-seasonal ARMA directly. The autocorrelations suggest an MA(4) model, which gives a final prediction error variance of 4013.883 ($\sigma^2 = 3913.24$ as steady state was not reached), which again is comparable with the PEV of the seasonally differenced model or the basic structural model.

In general an operator of this type may not eliminate the seasonal pattern of the data. It has the advantage, however, that it has a lower polynomial order than the seasonal differencing factor $1 - B^s$ and so may enable state space software to be used more easily.

We conclude this section with a note of caution that the multiplicative seasonal models described in this chapter are not suitable for all forms of seasonal behaviour. As they are all ARMA models, their complementary functions comprise sinusoidal or decaying exponential terms. Sales of Easter eggs, for instance, are seasonal but occur at a single peak at Easter—they do not build up gradually to the peak and then gradually down again.

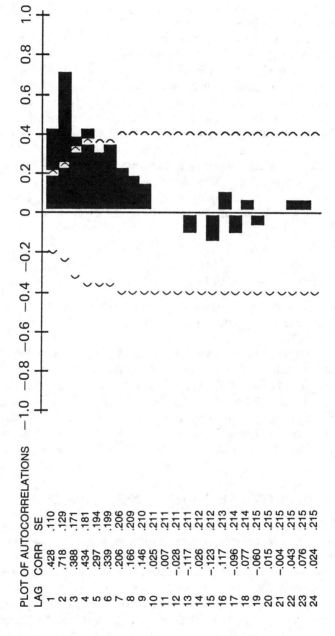

PLOT OF   INPUT
NUMBER OF CASES =   82
MEAN OF SERIES =   1638.183
STANDARD DEVIATION OF SERIES =   109.225

PLOT OF AUTOCORRELATIONS -1.0 -0.8 -0.6 -0.4 -0.2 0 0.2 0.4 0.6 0.8 1.0

LAG	CORR	SE
1	.428	.110
2	.718	.129
3	.388	.171
4	.434	.181
5	.297	.194
6	.339	.199
7	.206	.206
8	.166	.209
9	.146	.210
10	.025	.211
11	.007	.211
12	-.028	.211
13	-.117	.211
14	.026	.212
15	-.123	.212
16	.117	.213
17	-.096	.214
18	.077	.214
19	-.060	.215
20	.015	.215
21	-.004	.215
22	.043	.215
23	.076	.215
24	.024	.215

Fig. 5.26. Autocorrelations of $(1 + B^2)X_t$ for fuel series.

5.11 EXPONENTIAL SMOOTHING AND ARMA MODELS

From section 1.4 we recall that exponential smoothing merely provides a mechanism for calculating a 'smoothed' forecast as a predictor. It does not assume a model other than that the observed data are the sum of an irregular component plus a possible trend plus a possible seasonal component.

It can be shown, however (see Granger & Newbold, 1986, page 172), that the exponential smoothing forecasts are the conditional expectations forecasts for particular ARIMA models. When the first differences of a series are generated by an MA(1) model, however, that is the series is generated by an ARIMA(0, 1, 1) model with coefficient θ, the forecasts given by simple exponential smoothing ((1.13) and (1.14)) with smoothing parameter $\alpha = 1 + \theta$ are the conditional expectation forecasts. Notice that if the model is invertible the smoothing parameter will lie between 0 and 1 as required. Similarly, exponential smoothing for a series with a trend (1.17), (1.18) and (1.19) is optimal for an ARIMA(0, 2, 2) model with parameters θ_1 and θ_2 if $A = 1 - \theta_2$ and $C = 1 + \theta_1 + \theta_2$. The seasonal exponential smoothing equations (1.20), (1.21) are optimal for a seasonally differenced and twice ordinarily differenced ARMA model of dimension $s + 2$ where some of the coefficients are zero and the others are functions of the three smoothing parameters.

5.12 SIMULATION OF ARMA MODELS

A series X_1, X_2, etc. can be simulated from an ARMA model either by placing the model in state space form and proceeding as in section 4.8 or directly from the ARMA equation as in section 3.9.

If state space methods are used, the series depends on α_0 unless the model is stationary, but the model need not be invertible. If the ARMA model is used directly, p past observations and q noises $X_0, X_1, \ldots, X_{1-p}$ and $\varepsilon_0, \varepsilon_1, \ldots, \varepsilon_{1-q}$ are required. It is therefore sensible to ignore the first 50 or 100 observations generated to reduce the effect of these start-up values. As with least squares based estimation techniques, the model must be invertible or else the generated data will be dependent on the start-up noises, even for large t, and must be stationary or else the generated data will depend on start-up X_t's.

APPENDIX 5.1 ON LINEAR DIFFERENCE EQUATIONS

The ARMA (p, q) model $\phi(B)X_t = \theta(B)\varepsilon_t$ is a linear difference equation between $X_t, X_{t-1}, \ldots, X_{t-p}$. It is like an algebraic difference equation except that the right-hand side contains the random terms $\varepsilon_t, \ldots, \varepsilon_{t-q}$, and so the principles of solution remain the same. For details the reader is referred to Stephenson (1973, p. 493) for instance.

The *general solution* of a difference equation is the sum of a *complementary function* $C(t)$ and a *particular solution* $P(t)$. The complementary function is the complete solution $Z_t = C(t)$ of the homogeneous difference equation, that is of the original equation but with the right hand side set to zero. The particular solution is any solution to the original difference equation.

First consider the homogeneous ARMA equation $\phi(B)X_t = 0$, that is,

$$X_t - \phi_1 X_{t-1} - \phi_2 X_{t-2} \ldots - \phi_p X_{t-p} = 0,$$

and note that any function $k \cdot r^t$ where k is a constant will be a solution if r is such that $kr^t - k\phi_1 r^{t-1} \ldots - k\phi r^{t-p} = 0$ or equivalently if

$$kr^t\left(1 - \phi_1\left(\frac{1}{r}\right)^1 \ldots - \phi_{p-1}\left(\frac{1}{r}\right)^{p-1}\right) = kr^t\phi\left(\frac{1}{r}\right) = 0.$$

So for kr^t to be a solution, either $r = 0$, which is a trivial solution, or r is any solution to $\phi(1/r) = 0$. So $X_t = kr^t$ will be a solution to the homogeneous difference equation if r is the reciprocal of a root of the polynomial $\phi(B)$.

If the roots of the AR polynomial $\phi(B)$ are distinct and are $r_1, r_2, \ldots, r_p$, $X_t = k(1/r_i)^t$ is a solution to the homogeneous difference equation for any $i = 1, \ldots, p$. It can be shown that any linear function of such solutions is also a solution of the homogeneous equation so that the complementary function is of form

$$k_1\left(\frac{1}{r_1}\right)^t + k_2\left(\frac{1}{r_2}\right)^t + \ldots + k_p\left(\frac{1}{r_p}\right)^t$$

where $k_1, \ldots, k_p$ are constants. The constants will be determined later by the starting values $X_1, \ldots, X_p$. If the AR polynomial has d equal roots r_0, the part of the complementary function corresponding to this root is $(k_0 + k_1 t + \ldots + k_{d-1}t^{d-1})r_0^t$.

The particular solution to the difference equation is any solution to the original difference equation, that is, any expression for X_t for which $\phi(B)X_t = \theta(B)\varepsilon_t$ holds. As explained in the text, one such solution for the ARMA equation can be found by inverting the AR polynomial to give $X_t = \phi^{-1}(B)\phi(B)\varepsilon_t$. The coefficients of $\phi^{-1}(B)$ will increase in magnitude as the power of B increases unless all the roots of $\phi(B)$ are on or outside the unit circle. In this case each term of the complementary function will tend to zero as $t \to \infty$, and the general solution will asymptotically comprise the particular solution only.

APPENDIX 5.2 THE DURBIN–LEVINSON RECURSION

We are concerned with an efficient solution method for the Yule–Walker equations (5.10), that is, for

$$\begin{pmatrix} 1 & \rho_1 & \rho_2 & \cdot & \cdots & \rho_{p-1} \\ \rho_1 & 1 & \rho_1 & \rho_2 & \cdots & \rho_{p-2} \\ \rho_2 & \rho_1 & 1 & \rho_1 & \cdots & \rho_{p-3} \\ \vdots & \vdots & \vdots & \vdots & \cdots & \vdots \\ \rho_{p-1} & \rho_{p-2} & \rho_{p-3} & \cdot & \cdots & 1 \end{pmatrix}\begin{pmatrix} \phi_1 \\ \phi_2 \\ \phi_3 \\ \vdots \\ \phi_p \end{pmatrix} = \begin{pmatrix} \rho_1 \\ \rho_2 \\ \vdots \\ \rho_p \end{pmatrix} \quad \text{say} \quad \mathbf{R}_p\phi_p = \rho_p. \quad \text{(A.1)}$$

Note we use ρ_k in place of $\rho(k)$ in the matrix for ease of representation. We will use the structure of the matrix $\mathbf{R}_p$ to devise a recursive method for solving these equations, which is commonly known as the Durbin–Levinson recursion. We view it with a little scepticism since there are some problems with numerical stability in some marginal cases.

Suppose at step k that we are interested in the corresponding k-dimensional system

$$
\begin{pmatrix}
1 & \rho_1 & \rho_2 & \cdot & \cdots & \rho_{k-1} \\
\rho_1 & 1 & \rho_1 & \rho_2 & \cdots & \rho_{k-2} \\
\rho_2 & \rho_1 & 1 & \rho_1 & \cdots & \rho_{k-3} \\
\vdots & \vdots & \vdots & \vdots & \cdots & \vdots \\
\rho_{k-1} & \rho_{k-2} & \rho_{k-3} & \cdot & \cdots & 1
\end{pmatrix}
\begin{pmatrix}
\phi_{1,k} \\ \phi_{2,k} \\ \vdots \\ \phi_{k,k}
\end{pmatrix}
=
\begin{pmatrix}
\rho_1 \\ \rho_2 \\ \vdots \\ \rho_k
\end{pmatrix}
\quad \text{or} \quad \mathbf{R}_k \boldsymbol{\phi}_k = \boldsymbol{\rho}_k. \quad (A.2)
$$

Notice that the values of the coefficients ϕ now depend on k, necessitating a second subscript k.

Omitting the final equation, (A.2) may also be written

$$
\begin{pmatrix}
1 & \rho_1 & \rho_2 & \cdot & \cdots & \rho_{k-2} \\
\rho_1 & 1 & \rho_1 & \rho_2 & \cdots & \rho_{k-3} \\
\rho_2 & \rho_1 & 1 & \rho_1 & \cdots & \rho_{k-4} \\
\vdots & \vdots & \vdots & \vdots & \cdots & \vdots \\
\rho_{k-2} & \rho_{k-3} & \rho_{k-4} & \cdot & \cdots & 1
\end{pmatrix}
\begin{pmatrix}
\phi_{1,k} \\ \phi_{2,k} \\ \vdots \\ \phi_{k-1,k}
\end{pmatrix}
=
\begin{pmatrix}
\rho_1 \\ \rho_2 \\ \vdots \\ \rho_{k-1}
\end{pmatrix}
- \phi_{k,k}
\begin{pmatrix}
\rho_{k-1} \\ \rho_{k-2} \\ \vdots \\ \rho_1
\end{pmatrix}. \quad (A.3)
$$

We will assume that at the previous $(k-1)$th step, however, we have already solved the equations (A.4), which are just (A.2) with k replaced by $k-1$

$$
\begin{pmatrix}
1 & \rho_1 & \rho_2 & \cdot & \cdots & \rho_{k-2} \\
\rho_1 & 1 & \rho_1 & \rho_2 & \cdots & \rho_{k-3} \\
\rho_2 & \rho_1 & 1 & \rho_1 & \cdots & \rho_{k-4} \\
\vdots & \vdots & \vdots & \vdots & \cdots & \vdots \\
\rho_{k-2} & \rho_{k-3} & \rho_{k-4} & \cdot & \cdots & 1
\end{pmatrix}
\begin{pmatrix}
\phi_{1,k-1} \\ \phi_{2,k-1} \\ \vdots \\ \phi_{k-1,k-1}
\end{pmatrix}
=
\begin{pmatrix}
\rho_1 \\ \rho_2 \\ \vdots \\ \rho_{k-1}
\end{pmatrix}. \quad (A.4)
$$

Reversing these equations and ϕs gives

$$
\begin{pmatrix}
1 & \rho_1 & \rho_2 & \cdot & \cdots & \rho_{k-2} \\
\rho_1 & 1 & \rho_1 & \rho_2 & \cdots & \rho_{k-3} \\
\rho_2 & \rho_1 & 1 & \rho_1 & \cdots & \rho_{k-4} \\
\vdots & \vdots & \vdots & \vdots & \cdots & \vdots \\
\rho_{k-2} & \rho_{k-3} & \rho_{k-4} & \cdot & \cdots & 1
\end{pmatrix}
\begin{pmatrix}
\phi_{k-1,k-1} \\ \phi_{k-2,k-1} \\ \vdots \\ \phi_{1,k-1}
\end{pmatrix}
=
\begin{pmatrix}
\rho_{k-1} \\ \rho_{k-2} \\ \vdots \\ \rho_1
\end{pmatrix}. \quad (A.5)
$$

So using (A.4) and (A.5) to substitute for the ρ vectors in (A.3) we obtain

$$\mathbf{R}_{k-1}\begin{pmatrix}\phi_{1,k}\\\phi_{2,k}\\\vdots\\\phi_{k-1,k}\end{pmatrix}=\mathbf{R}_{k-1}\begin{pmatrix}\phi_{1,k-1}\\\phi_{2,k-2}\\\vdots\\\phi_{k-1,k-1}\end{pmatrix}-\phi_{k,k}\mathbf{R}_{k-1}\begin{pmatrix}\phi_{k-1,k-1}\\\phi_{k-2,k-1}\\\vdots\\\phi_{1,k-1}\end{pmatrix}.$$

Since $\mathbf{R}_{k-1}$ is a covariance matrix it is non-singular (at least in all our examples) so we can premultiply by $\mathbf{R}_{k-1}^{-1}$ and obtain the following set of equations expressing the $\phi_{i,k}$s in terms of the $\phi_{i,k-1}$s and $\phi_{k,k}$.

$$\phi_{1,k}=\phi_{1,k-1}-\phi_{k,k}\phi_{k-1,k-1}$$
$$\phi_{2,k}=\phi_{2,k-1}-\phi_{k,k}\phi_{k-2,k-1}$$
$$\phi_{3,k}=\phi_{3,k-1}-\phi_{k,k}\phi_{k-3,k-1}\;.$$
$$\vdots\qquad\qquad\vdots$$
$$\phi_{k-1,k}=\phi_{k-1,k-1}-\phi_{k,k}\phi_{1,k-1}$$

(A.6)

By assumption the $\phi_{i,k-1}$s have already been calculated from the $(k-1)$th step, so the problem here is $\phi_{k,k}$. The last equation, in (A.2), hitherto unused, can be written

$$\rho_{k-1}\phi_{1,k}+\rho_{k-2}\phi_{2,k}+\rho_{k-3}\phi_{3,k}+\dots+\rho_1\phi_{k-1,k}+\phi_{k,k}=\rho_k,\tag{A.7}$$

which enables us to express $\phi_{k,k}$ in terms of the $\phi_{i,k-1}$s. So by using (A.6) to substitute for $\phi_{1,k},\dots,\phi_{k-1,k}$ into (A.7) we can obtain the following expression for $\phi_{k,k}$ in terms of the $\phi_{i,k-1}$s.

$$\phi_{k,k}=\frac{\rho_k-\rho_{k-1}\phi_{1,k-1}-\rho_{k-2}\phi_{2,k-1}-\rho_{k-3}\phi_{3,k-1}-\dots-\rho_1\phi_{k-1,k-1}}{1-\rho_{k-1}\phi_{k-1,k-1}-\rho_{k-2}\phi_{k-2,k-1}-\rho_{k-3}\phi_{k-3,k-1}-\dots-\rho_1\phi_{1,k-1}}.$$

We can thus start the recursions by solving the Yule–Walker equations (A.2) in the trivial case $k=1$ to give $\phi_{1,1}=\rho_1$. We then use the Durbin–Levinson recursion (A.8) and (A.6) to solve the equations for $k=2$, that is,

$$\phi_{2,2}=\frac{\rho_2-\rho_1^2}{1-\rho_1^2},\qquad\phi_{1,2}=\frac{\rho_1(1-\rho_2)}{1-\rho_1^2}.$$

We continue for $k=3,4,\dots$, etc. until the desired set of parameter estimates $\phi_{1,p},\phi_{2,p},\dots,\phi_{p,p}$ at $k=p$ is obtained.

An additional advantage to computational efficiency in using these recursions is that successive $\phi_{k,k}$ i.e. $\phi_{1,1}$, $\phi_{2,2}$, etc. are calculated as byproducts which are estimates of the partial autocorrelation coefficients.

EXERCISES

(1) Derive the infinite moving average representation of the model

$$X_t=0.8X_{t-1}+\varepsilon_t+0.6\varepsilon_{t-1}$$

(i) by substituting for the X_ts repeatedly, (ii) by equating the coefficients of the right and left sides of $\phi(B)\psi(B) = \theta(B)$.

(2) Place the following ARMA models in state space form and use the resultant transition matrix to determine whether the models are stationary.

(a) $X_t = 1.1X_{t-1} - 0.2X_{t-2} + \varepsilon_t + 0.7\varepsilon_{t-2}$.
(b) $X_t = X_{t-1} - 0.5X_{t-2} + \varepsilon_t + 0.5\varepsilon_{t-1} + 0.5\varepsilon_{t-2}$.

(3) Write down the AR polynomials of the models in Exercise 2 and use these to confirm whether the models are stationary or not.

(4) Obtain a recurrence relation for the autocorrelations of the AR(2) model

$$X_t = 1.1X_{t-1} - 0.2X_{t-2} + \varepsilon_t.$$

Use this to derive the first few autocorrelations of this model.

(5) In what way is your answer to Exercise 4 complicated if we consider the model

$$X_t = 1.1X_{t-1} - 0.2X_{t-2} + \varepsilon_t + 0.7\varepsilon_{t-2}$$

instead? Can you find the autocorrelations now? What broad pattern would you expect the autocorrelations from lag 3 onwards to exhibit?

(6) Are the models in Exercise 2 invertible or not?

(7) Write down a non-invertible model which is likelihood equivalent to the model $X_t = 0.8X_{t-1} + \varepsilon_t + 0.7\varepsilon_{t-2}$, $\sigma^2 = 1$.

(8) Suppose the time series of 100 observations shown below (row-wise) is to be modelled by an zero mean ARMA(2, 1) process. Use the sample autocorrelations also given below to obtain initial parameter estimates for the AR parameters using the Yule–Walker equations

−1.65397	−2.94938	0.16499	0.47396	−0.79008
−2.54085	−2.46678	−0.77959	−1.04345	0.24371
1.25169	0.49568	1.49995	−0.23664	0.94384
2.79835	0.93958	0.30017	1.79522	2.88293
1.59422	0.99002	0.89841	0.48943	0.61158
−0.15267	0.15257	0.26473	−0.15529	−2.55356
−1.00386	−0.10373	1.18787	0.31655	0.61706
2.48234	2.68420	3.86833	3.33036	1.43160
1.09665	1.78618	1.16852	0.52370	−0.99661
−0.48522	−0.04248	0.05940	−0.43211	−1.84942
−0.42835	0.01058	0.08137	0.52170	0.75583
0.74779	1.80308	0.92047	0.69618	0.73773

−0.48607	0.50085	0.45561	−1.30686	0.05791
−0.59740	−0.12147	1.00563	2.74059	1.99772
1.76788	2.48478	1.51527	2.18778	0.71951
−0.75725	−2.14201	−2.18562	−1.30595	−2.65251
−2.20865	−2.32251	−4.00028	−3.27990	−3.87995
−2.77109	−1.00302	0.84689	1.09189	2.87641
3.32726	3.61183	2.79021	1.97606	2.54480
1.85056	−0.45210	0.15516	−0.16210	0.05684

Sample autocorrelations

lag	0	1	2	3	4	5	6	7	8
	1	0.783	0.578	0.449	0.295	0.134	−0.085	−0.255	−0.356

(9) Estimate the above model by using state space software if you have it, but otherwise any time series software you have available. If possible use the Yule–Walker estimates obtained in Exercise 8 as the initial parameter values for the AR parameters. Note the Q statistics. Produce a time series plot, a histogram, and an autocorrelation plot of the residuals from your model. Comment on the suitability of this model for the data.

(10) What would you expect the steady state prediction error variance of the ARMA model $X_t = 0.8X_{t-1} + \varepsilon_t + 0.7\varepsilon_{t-2}$, $\sigma^2 = 1$ to be? Confirm this by running the Kalman filter recursions for this model for any data set.

(11) The data below show deseasonalized and scaled demand for gas for 149 consecutive days (row-wise). Plot the data and, differencing where appropriate, suggest one or more possible ARIMA model(s). Fit these models and comment on their suitability.

841.501	835.288	820.249	763.963	777.217	785.317
798.734	809.701	827.209	829.268	834.852	839.622
854.327	842.752	829.743	831.931	829.709	831.831
835.523	813.486	819.981	808.430	799.068	797.999
793.818	811.035	843.759	818.893	787.717	764.786
791.767	818.247	798.051	793.045	804.921	777.941
779.928	782.367	737.333	728.884	738.915	740.785
738.921	740.318	739.321	718.208	730.961	725.424
735.258	746.130	756.334	743.441	730.140	742.604
766.314	776.193	782.728	787.875	767.961	729.551
717.989	739.770	764.164	763.246	775.753	758.068
744.239	747.311	743.470	764.006	752.399	745.996
756.305	767.397	780.168	790.749	792.311	818.275
845.758	831.367	815.898	783.840	794.949	766.569
742.918	727.865	732.120	725.304	738.581	733.184
728.053	715.158	717.518	697.294	674.404	640.900
638.250	661.389	687.220	710.450	691.551	667.954

636.465	626.952	617.103	608.462	604.006	617.438
617.235	640.152	699.147	682.697	678.535	670.594
665.616	656.665	667.992	670.284	678.714	687.313
699.692	684.698	668.367	662.518	652.961	662.865
690.180	693.398	686.870	628.442	620.254	600.461
578.283	565.385	560.285	567.427	557.727	560.022
558.557	554.816	580.442	585.247	594.526	590.592
582.179	579.103	569.899	550.195	569.055	

(12) Fit an order 4 state space ARMA model (which may be non-stationary) directly to the data in Exercise 11 and use backwards elimination to select the final model. You will need this model for the later questions. Does AIC bear out your choice of model? Be careful to base the maximum likelihood used to calculate AIC on the same number of residuals each time.

(13) The autocorrelation function of (i) 100 observations of raw data, (ii) the differenced data, (iii) second differences, and the partial autocorrelation function of the second difference is shown below. What model(s) would you suggest for the data?

Autocorrelations of raw data

```
        -1.0 -0.8 -0.6 -0.4 -0.2  0.0  0.2  0.4  0.6  0.8  1.0
         +----+----+----+----+----+----+----+----+----+----+
 1   0.997                         XXXXXXXXXXXXXXXXXXXXXXXXXX
 2   0.995                         XXXXXXXXXXXXXXXXXXXXXXXXXX
 3   0.991                         XXXXXXXXXXXXXXXXXXXXXXXXXX
 4   0.988                         XXXXXXXXXXXXXXXXXXXXXXXXXX
 5   0.984                         XXXXXXXXXXXXXXXXXXXXXXXXXX
 6   0.980                         XXXXXXXXXXXXXXXXXXXXXXXXXX
 7   0.976                         XXXXXXXXXXXXXXXXXXXXXXXXX
 8   0.972                         XXXXXXXXXXXXXXXXXXXXXXXXX
 9   0.967                         XXXXXXXXXXXXXXXXXXXXXXXXX
10   0.962                         XXXXXXXXXXXXXXXXXXXXXXXXX
11   0.956                         XXXXXXXXXXXXXXXXXXXXXXXXX
12   0.951                         XXXXXXXXXXXXXXXXXXXXXXXXX
13   0.945                         XXXXXXXXXXXXXXXXXXXXXXXXX
14   0.939                         XXXXXXXXXXXXXXXXXXXXXXXX
15   0.932                         XXXXXXXXXXXXXXXXXXXXXXXX
16   0.925                         XXXXXXXXXXXXXXXXXXXXXXXX
17   0.919                         XXXXXXXXXXXXXXXXXXXXXXXX
18   0.911                         XXXXXXXXXXXXXXXXXXXXXXXX
19   0.904                         XXXXXXXXXXXXXXXXXXXXXXXX
20   0.896                         XXXXXXXXXXXXXXXXXXXXXXX
21   0.888                         XXXXXXXXXXXXXXXXXXXXXXX
22   0.880                         XXXXXXXXXXXXXXXXXXXXXXX
23   0.872                         XXXXXXXXXXXXXXXXXXXXXXX
24   0.863                         XXXXXXXXXXXXXXXXXXXXXXX
25   0.854                         XXXXXXXXXXXXXXXXXXXXXX
26   0.845                         XXXXXXXXXXXXXXXXXXXXXX
27   0.836                         XXXXXXXXXXXXXXXXXXXXXX
```

Autocorrelations of differenced data

```
        -1.0 -0.8 -0.6 -0.4 -0.2  0.0  0.2  0.4  0.6  0.8  1.0
        +----+----+----+----+----+----+----+----+----+----+
  1    0.994                             XXXXXXXXXXXXXXXXXXXXXXXXX
  2    0.986                             XXXXXXXXXXXXXXXXXXXXXXXXX
  3    0.976                             XXXXXXXXXXXXXXXXXXXXXXXXX
  4    0.964                             XXXXXXXXXXXXXXXXXXXXXXXXX
  5    0.951                             XXXXXXXXXXXXXXXXXXXXXXXXX
  6    0.937                             XXXXXXXXXXXXXXXXXXXXXXXX
  7    0.922                             XXXXXXXXXXXXXXXXXXXXXXXX
  8    0.906                             XXXXXXXXXXXXXXXXXXXXXXXX
  9    0.889                             XXXXXXXXXXXXXXXXXXXXXXX
 10    0.872                             XXXXXXXXXXXXXXXXXXXXXXX
 11    0.854                             XXXXXXXXXXXXXXXXXXXXXX
 12    0.837                             XXXXXXXXXXXXXXXXXXXXXX
 13    0.819                             XXXXXXXXXXXXXXXXXXXXX
 14    0.802                             XXXXXXXXXXXXXXXXXXXXX
 15    0.786                             XXXXXXXXXXXXXXXXXXXXX
 16    0.769                             XXXXXXXXXXXXXXXXXXXX
 17    0.753                             XXXXXXXXXXXXXXXXXXXX
 18    0.737                             XXXXXXXXXXXXXXXXXXX
 19    0.721                             XXXXXXXXXXXXXXXXXXX
 20    0.705                             XXXXXXXXXXXXXXXXXXX
 21    0.689                             XXXXXXXXXXXXXXXXXX
 22    0.673                             XXXXXXXXXXXXXXXXXX
 23    0.658                             XXXXXXXXXXXXXXXXX
 24    0.644                             XXXXXXXXXXXXXXXXX
 25    0.630                             XXXXXXXXXXXXXXXXX
 26    0.616                             XXXXXXXXXXXXXXXX
 27    0.602                             XXXXXXXXXXXXXXXX
```

Autocorrelations of twice differenced data

```
        -1.0 -0.8 -0.6 -0.4 -0.2  0.0  0.2  0.4  0.6  0.8  1.0
        +----+----+----+----+----+----+----+----+----+----+
  1    0.738                             XXXXXXXXXXXXXXXXXXX
  2    0.504                             XXXXXXXXXXXXX
  3    0.434                             XXXXXXXXXXX
  4    0.342                             XXXXXXXXX
  5    0.256                             XXXXXX
  6    0.188                             XXXXX
  7    0.133                             XXXX
  8    0.086                             XXX
  9    0.062                             XXX
 10    0.035                             XX
 11   -0.023                           XX
 12   -0.045                           XX
 13    0.001                            X
 14    0.011                            X
```

Autocorrelations of twice differenced data (continued)

```
15    0.024                              XX
16    0.020                              XX
17    0.020                              XX
18    0.038                              XX
19    0.032                              XX
20    0.050                              XX
21    0.019                              X
22   -0.057                              XX
23   -0.060                              XX
24   -0.033                              XX
25   -0.034                              XX
26   -0.006                              X
27    0.016                              X
```

Partial autocorrelations of twice differenced data

```
           -1.0 -0.8 -0.6 -0.4 -0.2  0.0  0.2  0.4  0.6  0.8  1.0
           +----+----+----+----+----+----+----+----+----+----+
  1   0.738                              XXXXXXXXXXXXXXXXXXX
  2  -0.088                           XXX
  3   0.209                              XXXXXX
  4  -0.092                           XXX
  5   0.033                              XX
  6  -0.048                            XX
  7   0.001                              X
  8  -0.027                            XX
  9   0.023                              XX
 10  -0.033                            XX
 11  -0.074                           XXX
 12   0.021                              XX
 13   0.096                              XXX
 14  -0.029                            XX
 15   0.070                              XXX
 16  -0.068                           XXX
 17   0.043                              XX
 18   0.004                              X
 19  -0.019                            X
 20   0.067                              XXX
 21  -0.117                          XXXX
 22  -0.093                           XXX
 23   0.042                              XX
 24   0.031                              XX
 25   0.016                              X
 26   0.074                              XXX
 27  -0.006                            X
```

(14)   Forecast the next 5 differences from your model fit in Exercise 11 using ARMA software and calculate the associated prediction error variances. The actual values are 574.697, 566.543, 600.732, 591.226, 577.936 for days 150 to 154 respectively. Calculate the mean square error of these predictions.

(15)   Use the state space model fitted in Exercise 12 to forecast the next 5 observations of the gas demand data, and using the actual values 574.697, 566.543, 600.732, 591.226, 577.936 for days 150 to 154 respectively. Calculate the mean square error of these predictions. Compare your results with those obtained using the differenced model in Exercise 14.

16)   Calculate the one step forecasts for the next five observations of the gas demand series using (a) the state space model and (b) the ARMA model already fitted (you will probably have to calculate these by hand using the last few computer-produced residuals). Calculate the post-sample prediction statistic in both cases. Do these indicate that the models are adequate?

(17)   Derive expressions for forecasting the invertible and stationary ARMA(1, 1) model $X_t = 0.7X_{t-1} + \varepsilon_t + 0.5\varepsilon_{t-1} + 0.2\varepsilon_{t-2}$ with noise variance σ^2 one, two, three, and four steps ahead. Use the infinite MA representation to calculate the corresponding prediction error variances as a function of σ^2.

(18)   The following data show daily takings (in £) at a student coffee shop (open week-days only) over a 26 week period. Fit a (multiplicative if necessary) seasonal ARMA model and examine the residuals to ascertain whether the model fit is adequate. Use the fitted model to forecast the next week's takings.

766.68	769.38	804.04	775.49	800.46	740.74	763.39
821.60	774.26	800.39	724.89	742.07	835.46	760.40
804.88	707.05	734.71	851.76	745.20	813.43	696.24
727.34	871.28	728.23	843.67	707.61	736.30	871.07
719.83	855.38	731.39	758.70	882.87	723.75	865.81
727.05	771.43	900.35	740.82	884.56	728.89	785.80
913.83	751.15	899.73	749.43	796.33	939.24	779.47
900.32	744.57	803.18	946.96	810.51	895.31	746.97
797.79	953.33	834.62	895.53	736.31	793.03	949.40
864.81	893.63	714.64	799.38	942.35	893.10	916.10
693.61	813.07	923.32	905.33	930.63	664.90	819.65
926.82	893.94	915.18	649.11	824.15	925.18	879.99
901.22	645.62	823.66	929.84	861.09	900.85	640.34
816.19	931.76	866.39	907.30	652.80	806.10	938.36
870.24	920.13	657.42	797.60	954.18	888.52	921.54
675.67	787.71	977.65	894.64	911.74	689.06	771.46
1005.98	899.20	904.83	677.17	762.43	1032.05	907.68
883.10	672.21	740.08	1059.30	915.06	852.87	659.23
731.17	1090.70	923.22	836.76			

(19)   Suggest a low order factor which might deseasonalize the data in Exercise 18.

(20)   Generate 200 observations from (i) an MA(3) model and examine whether the sample autocorrelation function truncates after lag 3 and the partial autocorrelations exhibit no particular pattern, and (ii) an AR(3) process and examine whether the PACs are close to zero after lag 3 and the autocorrelations decay sinusoidally or exponentially.

6

Structural state space models

Nothing troubles me more than time and space; yet nothing troubles me less, as I never think about them.

Charles Lamb (1775–1834) (English essayist and critic).

6.1 INTRODUCTION

Structural time series models are a class of time series models in which the observations are modelled as a sum of clearly separate components . Although they cannot be observed directly, these components are meaningful, as they represent, for instance, the trend or seasonality of a series. For example, in Chapters 3 and 4 we met the *basic structural model* in which the observation is the sum of a trend, a seasonal component, and an irregular component. We also met the *random walk plus noise* model, which is the simplest non-trivial structural model. The development of these models is largely due to Harvey (1989), who describes most of the work. An associated software package STAMP (Structural Time Series Analyser, Modeller and Predictor) is available from the London School of Economics. All these models can be placed in the general state space form (4.1), (4.2).

As the observed value is the sum of one or more unobserved components the state vector can be partitioned so that each group of states corresponds to a component. For example, in the 4-season basic structural model

$$X_t = (1 \quad 0 \quad 1 \quad 0 \quad 0) \begin{pmatrix} \mu_t \\ \beta_t \\ \gamma_t \\ \gamma_{t-1} \\ \gamma_{t-2} \end{pmatrix} + \varepsilon_t$$

$$\begin{pmatrix} \mu_t \\ \beta_t \\ \gamma_t \\ \gamma_{t-1} \\ \gamma_{t-2} \end{pmatrix} = \begin{pmatrix} 1 & 1 & 0 & 0 & 0 \\ 0 & 1 & 0 & 0 & 0 \\ 0 & 0 & -1 & -1 & -1 \\ 0 & 0 & 1 & 0 & 0 \\ 0 & 0 & 0 & 1 & 0 \end{pmatrix} \begin{pmatrix} \mu_{t-1} \\ \beta_{t-1} \\ \gamma_{t-1} \\ \gamma_{t-2} \\ \gamma_{t-3} \end{pmatrix} + \begin{pmatrix} \eta_t \\ \zeta_t \\ \omega_t \\ 0 \\ 0 \end{pmatrix},$$

where $\text{var}(\varepsilon_t) = \sigma_\varepsilon^2$, $\text{var}(\eta_t) = \sigma_\eta^2$, $\text{var}(\zeta_t) = \sigma_\zeta^2$, and $\text{var}(\omega_t) = \sigma_\omega^2$, and the noises are mutually uncorrelated, the first two states represent the trend, and the final 3 states the seasonal component. As can be seen in (6.1), all the parameter matrices in the structural model's matrix representation, namely ϕ, $\mathbf{K}$ and Σ will have a block diagonal structure in which each block corresponds to a component.

Just as an ARMA model can be placed in state space form or be represented by a single ARMA equation, it is sometimes useful to place these structural models into a single equation form. For example, consider the random walk plus noise model. The state space equations are

$$X_t = \mu_t + \varepsilon_t \tag{6.2}$$

$$\mu_t = \mu_{t-1} + \eta_t \tag{6.3}$$

so μ_t, the level of the series, is the only component. To place the model in a single equation form we note from (6.3) that $\nabla \mu_t = \eta_t$ (where ∇ is the difference operator $1 - B$ as usual) and allow ourselves to write

$$\mu_t = \nabla^{-1} \eta_t.$$

The observed value X_t can now be written in terms of the random terms

$$X_t = \frac{\eta_t}{\nabla} + \varepsilon_t.$$

6.2 SOME FURTHER STRUCTURAL MODELS

(i) Modelling trend

If the trend component of a structural model is not generated by a random walk as in (6.3) the next degree of complexity for the trend is to introduce another state β_t and allow state equations $\mu_t = \mu_{t-1} + \beta_{t-1} + \eta_t$ and $\beta_t = \beta_{t-1} + \zeta_t$, where the η_t and ζ_t are uncorrelated white noise sequences of zero mean and variances σ_η^2 and σ_ζ^2 respectively. This is a stochastic version of a deterministic linear trend $\mu_t = \alpha + \beta t$ and is therefore known as the local linear trend model. To see this, notice that for the deterministic model $\mu_t = \mu_{t-1} + \beta$, so that allowing the level μ_t to vary stochastically gives $\mu_t = \mu_{t-1} + \beta + \eta_t$, and allowing the slope β to vary stochastically gives $\beta_t = \beta_{t-1} + \zeta_t$. When placed in state space form the observation equation of the local linear trend model is $X_t = (1 \ 0)\alpha_t + \varepsilon_t$ and state equation becomes

$$\boldsymbol{\alpha}_t = \begin{pmatrix} \mu_t \\ \beta_t \end{pmatrix} = \begin{pmatrix} 1 & 1 \\ 0 & 1 \end{pmatrix} \begin{pmatrix} \mu_{t-1} \\ b_{t-1} \end{pmatrix} + \begin{pmatrix} \eta_t \\ \zeta_t \end{pmatrix}.$$

The conditional expectation forecasts from such a model will be

$$X_{t+k|t} = \hat{\mu}_t + k\hat{\beta}_t$$

where $\hat{\mu}_t$ and $\hat{\beta}_t$ are the state estimators at time t.

If $\sigma_\zeta^2 = 0$, β becomes a constant and the model becomes a random walk with 'drift' $\mu_t = \mu_{t-1} + \beta + \eta_t$, and if $\beta = 0$ we are back to the simple random walk plus noise model. The single equation form of the local linear trend model is

$$X_t = \frac{\eta_t}{\nabla} + \frac{\zeta_{t-1}}{\nabla^2} + \varepsilon_t$$

as $\nabla \beta_{t-1} = \zeta_{t-1}$.

The notion of the local linear trend model extends to higher order trend models. A local quadratic trend can be modelled by introducing another component, say δ, and letting the state equations become

$$\mu_t = \mu_{t-1} + \beta_{t-1} + \eta_t + \delta_{t-1}, \quad \beta_t = \beta_{t-1} + \delta_{t-1} + \zeta_t, \quad \delta_t = \delta_{t-1} + \xi_t$$

where ξ_t is another random disturbance term, that is,

$$\boldsymbol{\alpha}_t = \begin{pmatrix} \mu_t \\ \beta_t \\ \delta_t \end{pmatrix} = \begin{pmatrix} 1 & 1 & 1 \\ 0 & 1 & 1 \\ 0 & 0 & 1 \end{pmatrix} \begin{pmatrix} \mu_{t-1} \\ \beta_{t-1} \\ \delta_{t-1} \end{pmatrix} + \begin{pmatrix} \eta_t \\ \zeta_t \\ \xi_t \end{pmatrix}.$$

If σ_η^2, σ_ζ^2, and σ_ξ^2 are all zero, the trend becomes a global quadratic. This extends to a dth order polynomial which has a triangular transition matrix with 1's on and above the diagonal and zeros elsewhere. In general, a deterministic global trend is just a special case of a local trend.

Another possible variant for the trend is to introduce a damping factor ρ into the slope equations such that

$$\beta_t = \rho \beta_{t-1} + \zeta_t \qquad 0 \le \rho \le 1.$$

(ii) The basic structural model

As we saw in Chapter 4 the BSM comprises a local linear trend component μ_t and a seasonal component γ_t, so that the observation equation is $X_t = \mu_t + \gamma_t + \varepsilon_t$.

The diagonal block of the transition matrix corresponding to the trend is therefore

$$\begin{pmatrix} 1 & 1 \\ 0 & 1 \end{pmatrix}.$$

The seasonal component γ_t encountered in Chapter 4 took the *dummy variable* form

$$\gamma_t = -\sum_{j=1}^{s-1} \gamma_{t-j} + \omega_t$$

where ω_t is a random noise disturbance. If σ_ω^2 is zero we have a deterministic seasonal model. The diagonal block of ϕ corresponding to the seasonal component is therefore

$$\begin{pmatrix} -1 & -1 & -1 \\ 1 & 0 & 0 \\ 0 & 1 & 0 \end{pmatrix}.$$

The single equation form of the seasonal component is clearly $\omega_t/S(B)$ where $S(B)$ is the polynomial $S(B) = 1 + B + B^2 + \ldots + B^{s-1}$. The single equation form of the basic structural model is therefore

$$X_t = \frac{\eta_t}{\nabla} + \frac{\zeta_{t-1}}{\nabla^2} + \frac{\omega_t}{S(B)} + \varepsilon_t.$$

Alternative forms of seasonal component may be used within the BSM or any other structural model. For example, a single cosine wave $\gamma_t = A\cos(ft - \theta)$ gives a cycle of frequency f, amplitude A, and phase θ. Equivalently, this can be written

$$\gamma_t = \alpha\cos ft + \beta\sin ft$$

where $(\alpha^2 + \beta^2)^{1/2} = A$ and $\tan^{-1}(\beta/\alpha) = \theta$. A recursion enabling γ_t to be calculated from γ_{t-1} is

$$\begin{pmatrix} \gamma_t \\ \gamma_t^* \end{pmatrix} = \begin{pmatrix} \cos f & \sin f \\ -\sin f & \cos f \end{pmatrix} \begin{pmatrix} \gamma_{t-1} \\ \gamma_{t-1}^* \end{pmatrix}$$

where $\gamma_0 = \alpha$ and $\gamma_0^* = \beta$ where γ_t^* is merely part of the mechanism to generate γ_t. We can see by expressing (6.4) in terms of $f(t-1)$ and f by expanding each term. A stochastic version of this introduces two white noise disturbances ω_t and ω_t^* to give

$$\begin{pmatrix} \gamma_t \\ \gamma_t^* \end{pmatrix} = \begin{pmatrix} \cos f & \sin f \\ -\sin f & \cos f \end{pmatrix} \begin{pmatrix} \gamma_{t-1} \\ \gamma_{t-1}^* \end{pmatrix} + \begin{pmatrix} \omega_t \\ \omega_t^* \end{pmatrix}. \tag{6.4}$$

For convenience it is usual to assume that these two disturbances have the same variance and are uncorrelated with each other.

In practice a trigonometric seasonal pattern is usually modelled as the sum

$$\gamma_t = \sum_{j=1}^{\left[\frac{s}{2}\right]} \gamma_{jt}$$

of a set of such trigonometric terms $\gamma_{jt} = \alpha_j \cos f_j t + \beta_j \sin f_j t$ at frequencies

$$f_j = \frac{2\pi j}{s}, \qquad j = 1, ..., \left[\frac{s}{2}\right],$$

where $[x]$ denotes the integer part of x. In a similar manner as in the dummy variable formulation we constrain the sum of these seasonal components over the whole seasonal cycle to be 0, that is,

$$\sum_{j=1}^{\left[\frac{s}{2}\right]} \gamma_{jt} = 0.$$

If ordinary least squares were used to fit this model with $\cos f_j t$ and $\sin f_j t$ being taken as explanatory or exogenous variables and α_j, β_j the parameters to be estimated we would get an equivalent function and fit to using a dummy variable for each season.

Each γ_{jt} can be made to evolve randomly over time by including 2 states for each frequency f_j as in (6.4):

$$\begin{pmatrix} \gamma_{jt} \\ \gamma_{jt}^* \end{pmatrix} = \begin{pmatrix} \cos f_j & \sin f_j \\ -\sin f_j & \cos f_j \end{pmatrix} \begin{pmatrix} \gamma_{jt-1} \\ \gamma_{jt-1}^* \end{pmatrix} + \begin{pmatrix} \omega_{jt} \\ \omega_{jt}^* \end{pmatrix}.$$

Each seasonal disturbance ω_{jt} and ω_{jt}^* could have a separate variance, but in practice the number of parameters can be greatly reduced without affecting the fit of the model very much if all these variances are assumed to be equal, that is, $\mathrm{var}(\omega_{jt}) = \mathrm{var}(\omega_{jt}^*) = \sigma_\omega^2$ for all j.

When s is even, the $j = s/2$ component becomes $f_j = \pi$ and $\gamma_{jt} = -\gamma_{jt-1}$, so α_{jt}^* is not required for frequency $j = s/2$. For example, if $s = 4$ the basic structural model with trigonometric seasonal component is

$$X_t = (1 \ \ 0 \ \ 1 \ \ 0 \ \ 1)\alpha_t + \varepsilon_t$$

$$\alpha_t = \begin{pmatrix} \mu_t \\ \beta_t \\ \gamma_{1t} \\ \gamma_{1t}^* \\ \gamma_{2t} \end{pmatrix} = \begin{pmatrix} 1 & 1 & 0 & 0 & 0 \\ 0 & 1 & 0 & 0 & 0 \\ 0 & 0 & 0 & 1 & 0 \\ 0 & 0 & -1 & 0 & 0 \\ 0 & 0 & 0 & 0 & -1 \end{pmatrix} \begin{pmatrix} \mu_{t-1} \\ \beta_{t-1} \\ \gamma_{1t-1} \\ \gamma_{1t-1}^* \\ \gamma_{2t-1} \end{pmatrix} + \begin{pmatrix} \eta_t \\ \zeta_t \\ \omega_{1t} \\ \omega_{1t}^* \\ \omega_{2t} \end{pmatrix}$$

where variance ω_{1t} = variance ω_{1t}^* = variance $\omega_{2t} = \sigma_\omega^2$.

The hope in using such a seasonal representation particularly for large s is that fewer than $s - 1$ seasonal effects may be required.

We fitted basic structural models with dummy and trigonometric seasonal components respectively to the fuel data of Fig. 1.3. (ARMA models were fitted in section 5.10.) The dummy seasonal component model gave $\sigma_\omega^2 = 2746.143005$, $\sigma_\eta^2 = 204.488625$, $\sigma_\zeta^2 = 0$,

$\sigma_\omega^2 = 15.499734$ with prediction error variance 3999.303500. The maximum likelihood was -443.1868. The trigonometric model gave $\sigma_\varepsilon^2 = 2746.401471$, $\sigma_\eta^2 = 204.425090$, $\sigma_\zeta^2 = 0$, $\sigma_\omega^2 = 3.826747$ with prediction error variance 3997.081824 and maximum likelihood -443.7945. As you can see, the choice of seasonal component does not greatly affect the log-likelihood, of the parameter estimates corresponding to the non-seasonal components for this example.

(iii) Other components
It may often be natural to include an autoregressive mechanism either as another unobserved component $X_t = \mu_t + v_t$ where $v_t = \phi_1 v_{t-1} + \phi_2 v_{t-2} + \ldots + \phi_p v_{t-p} + \varepsilon_t$ or by including lagged values of X_t, $X_t = \phi_1 X_{t-1} + \phi_2 X_{t-2} + \ldots + \phi_p X_{t-p} + \mu_t + \varepsilon_t$.

6.3 PROPERTIES OF STRUCTURAL MODELS

All the structural models considered above are non-stationary; for instance, consider the eigenvalues of the ϕ matrix of the local linear trend model, so that we cannot talk about the autocorrelation structure of these models. We can, however, usually relate the single equation form to a stationary process. For instance, multiplying the single equation of the observed local linear trend model by ∇^2 gives

$$\nabla^2 X_t = \nabla \eta_t + \zeta_{t-1} + \nabla^2 \varepsilon_t = \eta_t - \eta_{t-1} = \zeta_{t-1} + \varepsilon_t - 2\varepsilon_{t-1} + \varepsilon_{t-2},$$

which is clearly (weakly) stationary, so the second differences of the local linear trend model are stationary.

For the BSM with dummy seasonal component (6.1) we multiply the single equation representation by ∇ and $1 - B^s$, and note that

$$1 - B^s = (1 - B)(1 + B + B^2 + \ldots + B^{s-1}),$$

so

$$\nabla(1 - B^s)X_t = (1 - B^s)\eta_t + S(B)\zeta_{t-1} + \nabla^2 \omega_t + \nabla(1 - B^s)\varepsilon_t,$$

which is stationary. The trigonometric seasonal component can be treated similarly, but is rather more complicated; see Harvey (1989, p. 54) for details.

Once the stationary form of the structural model is obtained its autocorrelation function can usually be easily calculated. For instance, the second differences of the local linear trend give

$$\nabla^2 X_t = \eta_t - \eta_{t-1} + \zeta_{t-1} + \varepsilon_t - 2\varepsilon_{t-1} + \varepsilon_{t-2},$$

$E(\nabla^2 X_t) = 0$, so

$$\gamma(0) = E\{(\nabla^2 X_t)^2\} = 2\sigma_\eta^2 + \sigma_\zeta^2 + 6\sigma_\varepsilon^2$$

as the random terms are mutually uncorrelated. The first theoretical autocovariance of these differences is

$$\gamma(1) = E(\eta_t - \eta_{t-1} + \zeta_{t-1} + \varepsilon_t - 2\varepsilon_{t-1} + \varepsilon_{t-2})$$
$$(\eta_{t-1} - \eta_{t-2} + \zeta_{t-2} + \varepsilon_{t-1} - 2\varepsilon_{t-2} + \varepsilon_{t-3})$$
$$= -\sigma_\eta^2 - 4\sigma_\varepsilon^2.$$

Similarly, $\gamma(2) = \sigma_\varepsilon^2$ and $\gamma(k) = 0$, $k > 2$. As all the variance parameters are positive this means that $-0.667 \le \rho(1) \le 0$ and $0 \le \rho(2) \le 0.167$ for this model, which is restrictive. Nevertheless, similar constraints apply to ARMA models. For instance, the MA(1) model must satisfy $|\rho(1)| \le \frac{1}{2}$.

Similarly, the first differences of a random walk plus noise model have $\gamma(0) = \sigma_\eta^2 + 2\sigma_\varepsilon^2$, $\gamma(1) = -\sigma_\varepsilon^2$, and $\gamma(k) = 0$, $k \ge 2$, so there is a restriction that $-0.5 \le \rho(1) \le 0$.

If all the variance parameters of the model are strictly positive the autocorrelations of $\nabla(1 - B^s)X_t$ for the BSM with dummy variable seasonal component can be shown to be zero for lags greater than $s + 1$, $\rho(s) \le 0$, $\rho(s + 1) \ge 0$ and $\rho(k) \ge 0$ for $k = 2,\ldots, s - 2$. The BSM with trigonometric seasonality has a more complicated autocorrelation structure but allows more flexibility especially if the variances of the seasonal disturbance terms are allowed to differ.

These properties emphasize the *dis*advantage that structural models place considerable restrictions on the pattern of autocorrelations which can be modelled. A key advantage, however, is that complex models can be fitted with very few parameters. ARMA models, by contrast, can model many more 'shapes' of autocorrelation functions, but require many more parameters to do this.

Harvey (1989, page 206 onwards) shows that most of the common structural models are identifiable. He does this by expressing each state space model as the sum of several ARIMA models with roots on the unit circle, and uses known results for identifying these models.

6.4 ESTIMATION

As structural models are easily placed in state space form they can be estimated by using the Kalman filter and state space techniques. Of course, the use of likelihood will require the usual assumption that the noises are normally distributed. In most structural models the parameters of the $\mathbf{H}$ and ϕ (observation and transition) matrices are fixed, the $\mathbf{K}$ matrix is usually fixed to 0's and 1's, and the state noise covariance matrix Σ is zero apart from the structural variances $\sigma_\eta^2, \sigma_\omega^2$ etc. in some diagonal elements.

As with seasonal ARMA models the order of the state can become cumbersome for state space estimation, but we have modelled monthly data with an annual cycle quite easily and successfully. Estimation will be more efficient if one parameter is concentrated out of the likelihood—usually by setting $\sigma^{*2} = \sigma_\eta^2$ or $\sigma^{*2} = \sigma_\varepsilon^2$. If σ^{*2} is set to a parameter which is zero or close to zero, the scaled variances will be large, and numerical problems will result. To be safe, as advised in Chapter 4, it is best to set σ^{*2} to the variance likely to be the largest—often σ_η^2.

Initial values for the parameters of a linear local trend model or random walk can be obtained by equating expressions for the first few theoretical autocorrelations to the corresponding sample autocorrelations and solving—to provide a sort of moment estimator. In practice, however, this rarely beneficial as there are so few parameters anyway and setting the initial parameter estimates of σ_ε^2 to 0.01 and the others to 0.1 has usually given reasonable results.

To start off the Kalman filter recursions for estimation, the starting values can be set arbitrarily. The estimation results cited in this book have taken $\mathbf{a}_0 = 0$ and $\mathbf{C}_0 = 100\,000$ when using the concentrated likelihood—that is the variance of the initial state estimate is taken as $100\,000\,\sigma^{*2}\mathbf{I}$. Fig. 6.1 shows our estimation output for the basic structural model (dummy seasonals) fitted to the fuel series, taking $\sigma^{*2} = \sigma_\varepsilon^2$.

Alternatively, starting values can be calculated by realizing that some of the state components (those representing the seasonal component) are stationary and some are not. We can assume that non-stationary elements have initial variance matrix $M\mathbf{I}$ where M is a large positive number, whilst the remaining non-stationary elements have the mean and covariance matrix of the unconditional distribution.

When σ_η^2 or σ_ω^2 is zero the corresponding component of the state is deterministic. When there are deterministic components the Kalman filter recursions need not reach a steady state, although the recursions are still valid. In practice, we have followed Harvey and STAMP and have set a variance parameter to zero if its estimated value is below 10^{-6}.

A byproduct of the state space estimation is obviously an up to date estimate $\mathbf{a}_t$ of the state vector. For instance, the final ($t = 84$) state estimate of the fuel data fit shown in Fig. 6.1 is

$$
\mathbf{a}_t = \begin{pmatrix} \mu_t \\ \beta_t \\ \gamma_t \\ \gamma_{t-1} \\ \gamma_{t-2} \end{pmatrix} = \begin{pmatrix} 829.52 \\ 1.031 \\ 64.96 \\ -120.28 \\ -72.79 \end{pmatrix}.
$$

We can interpret this as estimated tread component of 829.52, estimated slope 1.031, estimated 4th quarter (the quarter corresponding to $t = 84$) component 64.96, estimated 3rd quarter component -120.28, and estimated second quarter component -72.79. The seasonal components must total zero, so the first seasonal component must be 128.11.

If the original data were logged before model fitting (not the case here), that is if the original series was $\{Y_t\}$ and $X_t = \log Y_t = \mu_t + \gamma_t + \varepsilon_t$ for the BSM, so that $Y_t = e^{\mu_t + \gamma_t + \varepsilon_t}$, the model is a multiplicative seasonal model with multiplicative trend e^{μ_t} and seasonal effect e^{γ_t} at time t. Chapter 10 explains why it is sometimes helpful to take logs of the data in this way.

```
a0 0000000000000000000000000000E+00
C0 100000.000000000000000000

INITIAL LOG LIK -457.3444888026366
******* FUNCTION VALUE IS    914.6889776052731
PARAMETERS     DERIVATIVES
        0.1000000000000000         2.20032984
        0.1000000000000000        90.55184706
        0.1000000000000000        31.95671403
niter    0 nf    0  norm    96.050560

******* FUNCTION VALUE IS    900.2987358398071
PARAMETERS     DERIVATIVES
        0.0000000000000000       -65.56229654
        0.0012809199516384-383140.39556240
        0.1259432219307745 383325.13718294
niter    5 nf  110  norm 541972.991493

******* FUNCTION VALUE IS    900.2947374805012
PARAMETERS     DERIVATIVES
        0.0000610351562500       -65.56229654
        0.0012809199516384-382066.05875006
        0.1259432219307745        50.63289684
niter   10 nf  227  norm 541972.995459

******* FUNCTION VALUE IS    900.2947374805012
PARAMETERS     DERIVATIVES
        0.0000610351562500       -65.56229654
        0.0012809199516384-382066.05875006
        0.1259432219307745        50.63289684
niter   14 nf  315  norm 541972.995459

******* FUNCTION VALUE IS    895.9372320613632
PARAMETERS     DERIVATIVES
        0.0421319423168262       -53.06970912
        0.0000571286637498         2.21251537
        0.1156305618670136        55.46936645
niter   15 nf  381  norm    76.799348

******* FUNCTION VALUE IS    887.6376204470241
PARAMETERS     DERIVATIVES
        0.0744635715904501        -0.00025345
        0.0000000000000000      1683.23208356
        0.0056441977476053         0.00055423
niter   20 nf  446  norm     0.000609

******* FUNCTION VALUE IS    887.6376204469675
PARAMETERS     DERIVATIVES
        0.0744639389706074         0.00000295
        0.0000000000000000      1683.26448029
        0.0056441831392853         0.00010273
niter   21 nf  463  norm     0.000103

******************** RESULTS  *******************
e04jbf fail is          0
MAXIMUM LOG LIKELIHOOD IS   -443.8188102234837
AIC is     895.6376204469675
        PARAMETER            S.ERROR       Z RATIO
  2746.1430047205747655 se zero suggest scale data
   204.4886251080733679 se zero suggest scale data
     0.0000000000000000                  0.000000
    15.4997340453100134 se zero suggest scale data
PREDiction error variance is    3999.303499826818
FINAL STATE VECTOR  829.5166043129962        1.031062491692277
64.95507138666150    -120.2798452223312    -72.78998846195472
```

Fig. 6.1. Estimation output of BSM fitted to fuel data. Data were later scaled to obtain standard errors of parameter estimates.

The smoothing equations (4.16), (4.17) can be implemented to calculate smoothed values of the trend, slope, and seasonal components for every time period. Fig. 6.2 shows a plot of these for the fuel data.

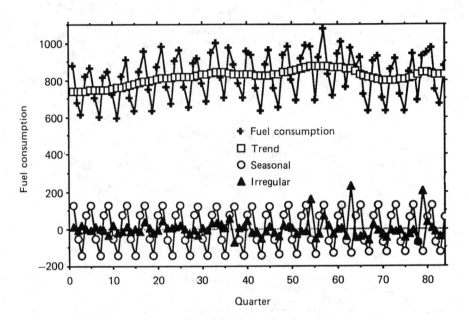

Fig. 6.2. Decomposition of fuel series using smoothed estimates from basic structural model with dummy seasonal components.

6.5 DIAGNOSTIC CHECKING AND PREDICTION

Diagnostic checking proceeds in the way described for the state space model (section 4.7). The number of parameters is now the number of unknown variances, so under the hypothesis of independent residuals, $Q(k)$ will have a χ^2 distribution with $k - n^*$ degrees of freedom, where n^* is one less than the total number of non-zero unknown parameters, that is, the number of non-zero variance parameters other than σ^{*2}. For the industrial production data, we obtain $Q(10) = 9.44$ for 8 d.o.f. and $Q(20) = 24.73$ for 18 d.o.f. for instance, which is satisfactory. The fuel data fitted to the dummy seasonal BSM gave $Q(10) = 6.84$ for 7 d.o.f. and $Q(20) = 20.52$ for 17 d.o.f., again giving no indication of model inadequacy.

The post-sample statistic $\xi(m)$ should still be $F(m, N - d)$ if the model is correct, where d is the state dimension. Forecasting the remaining 13 observations of the industrial data gave $\xi(13) = 0.27279$ which should be $F(13, 198)$ under the null hypothesis, and so is again not significant.

The k-step forecast function for a structural model is $X_{t+k|t} = \mathbf{H}\boldsymbol{\phi}^k\mathbf{a}_t$, as usual. If the model can be broken down into components, this is merely the sum of the forecast functions for each component. Forecasts and prediction limits for the fuel data are shown in Fig. 6.3, and extrapolative and one step forecasts for the industrial production data in Fig. 6.4, which also shows the actual results for comparison.

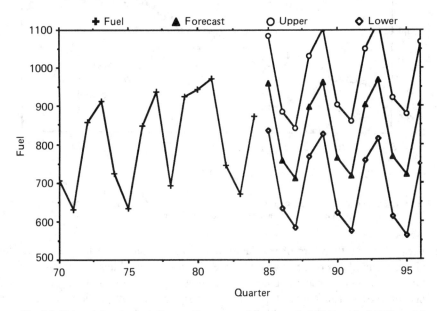

Fig. 6.3. Extrapolative forecasts for next three years of the quarterly fuel data calculated by using the basic structural model (dummy seasonal component). Upper and lower 95% prediction limits are also shown.

6.6 MODEL SELECTION

The hope, when using structural models, is that the data themselves suggest a model. For instance, a quarterly BSM might be appropriate for the fuel data of Fig. 1.3, as it shows a trend and a seasonal pattern, to which we fitted a seasonal ARMA model in section 5.11.

As for ARMA models it is sensible to check that the sample autocorrelations of suitably differenced data resemble the autocorrelations of a postulated model. For instance, the autocorrelations of the first and second differences of the logs of the industrial production index data of Fig. 1.1 are shown in Figs. 6.5 and 6.6. The plot of the data suggests a local linear trend model. The second differences have a large negative correlation at lag 1 which is compatible with either a random walk plus noise model or a local linear trend model. A local linear trend model fitted to the first 200 observations gave $\sigma_\varepsilon^2 = 0.00185669$, $\sigma_\eta^2 = 0.000951502$, $\sigma_\zeta^2 = 0.00000184265$, and a prediction error variance of 0.00390794. Notice that Fig. 6.5 suggests that the first differences are stationary. This is probably because σ_ζ^2 may be zero in which case β is constant, and the first

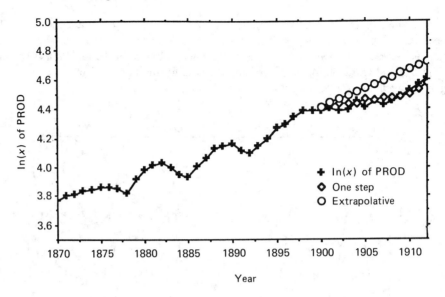

Fig. 6.4. Extrapolative and one step forecasts from threshold 1899 of the log of the industrial
production series obtained from the local linear trend model.

differences of μ_t and therefore of the data are stationary, that is, the model is a random
walk with drift model. For comparison if we fit an ordinary linear regression model
against time we obtain an estimated σ of 0.3045 (the local liner trend model gave 0.0625)
and slope of 0.0196 (our final slope was 0.0256), or for a regression on linear and
quadratic time an estimated σ of 0.1277.

If we consider the autocorrelation function of the differences of the temperature data
(Fig. 5.10) lags 2 and 4 have significantly non-zero autocorrelations, and these are both
negative. This does not correspond to the expected pattern for a local linear trend model,
and if we try to fit a local linear trend to the temperature data we find that we obtain huge
Q statistics, that is, the residuals are highly correlated, so the model is inappropriate.

The autocorrelations of the airline passenger data when seasonally and ordinarily
differenced were shown in Fig. 5.25. The negative autocorrelations at lags 1 and 12,
make the BSM a candidate model although the barely significant autocorrelation at lag 3
does not conform. The reader is asked to fit the BSM to the airline data in Exercise 6 at
the end of this chapter.

6.7 CONNECTIONS: ARMA MODELS, STRUCTURAL MODELS, AND
EXPONENTIAL SMOOTHING

Consider the random walk plus noise model (6.2), (6.3). The variance of ∇X_t is
$\sigma_\eta^2 + 2\sigma_\varepsilon^2$, autocovariance at lag one is $-\sigma_\varepsilon^2$, and at all other lags is zero. An MA (1)
model with parameter θ has variance $\sigma^2(1 + \theta^2)$ and covariance lag one of $\theta\sigma^2$. So, for

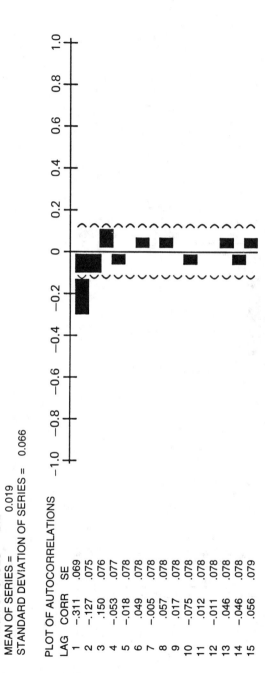

PLOT OF INDEX
NUMBER OF CASES = 212
MEAN OF SERIES = 0.019
STANDARD DEVIATION OF SERIES = 0.066

PLOT OF AUTOCORRELATIONS

LAG	CORR	SE
1	-.311	.069
2	-.127	.075
3	.150	.076
4	-.053	.077
5	-.018	.078
6	.049	.078
7	-.005	.078
8	.057	.078
9	.017	.078
10	-.075	.078
11	.012	.078
12	-.011	.078
13	.046	.078
14	-.046	.078
15	.056	.079

Fig. 6.5. Autocorrelations of differenced index data.

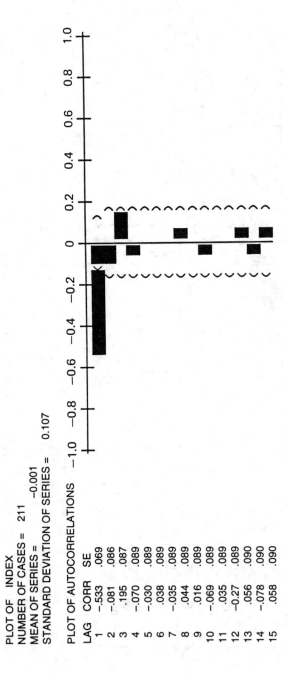

PLOT OF INDEX
NUMBER OF CASES = 211
MEAN OF SERIES = -0.001
STANDARD DEVIATION OF SERIES = 0.107

PLOT OF AUTOCORRELATIONS

LAG	CORR	SE
1	-.533	.069
2	-.081	.086
3	.195	.087
4	-.070	.089
5	-.030	.089
6	.038	.089
7	-.035	.089
8	.044	.089
9	.016	.089
10	-.069	.089
11	.035	.089
12	-.27	.089
13	.056	.090
14	-.078	.090
15	.058	.090

Fig. 6.6 Autocorrelations of twice differenced index data.

the first differences of a random walk model and an MA(1) model to be equivalent (assuming normal noises) we require $\sigma_\eta^2 + 2\sigma_\varepsilon^2 = \sigma^2(1 + \theta^2)$ and $-\sigma_\varepsilon^2 = \theta\sigma^2$ or $\sigma^2 = -\sigma_\varepsilon^2/\theta$. For convenience we divide the first equation all through by σ_ε^2, let $q = \sigma_\eta^2/\sigma_\varepsilon^2$, and rearrange to give $q + 2 = \sigma^2(1 + \theta^2)/\sigma_\varepsilon^2$ and $\theta^2 + \theta(q + 2) + 1 = 0$, so $2\theta = -(q + 2) \pm \sqrt{(q^2 + 4q)}$. The corresponding invertible MA(1) model is therefore $\theta = [-(q + 2) + \sqrt{(q^2 + 4q)}]/2$. As q is the ratio of two non-negative values, one can easily show that this model is such that $-1 \leq \theta \leq 0$. The structural random walk plus noise model is therefore equivalent to an ARIMA(0, 1, 1) model with a non-positive parameter θ.

In general, if a structural model is equivalent to an ARIMA model, there will be an implied restriction on the ARIMA parameters. For instance, second differences of the local linear trend model give an MA(2) process with severe restrictions on the MA parameters. If $\sigma_\zeta^2 = 0$, the model is non-invertible.

As we have stated before, the BSM is such that $\nabla(1 - B^s)X_t$ has zero autocorrelation at lags greater than $s + 1$, so $\nabla(1 - B^s)X_t$ is MA($s + 1$) for this model. In fact when σ_ω^2 and σ_ζ^2 are close to zero, the autocorrelations of the seasonally and ordinarily differenced BSM (with dummy seasonals) are similar to those of a seasonal ARMA(0, 1, 1) (0, 1, 1) model $\nabla(1 - B^s)X_t = (1 + \theta B)(1 + \theta_s B^s)$. Further, the model is equivalent to this seasonal ARMA model with $\theta_s = -1$ when σ_ω^2 and σ_ζ^2 of the BSM are exactly equal to zero. This may be the case for short series, as a change in the slope or seasonal pattern may not be apparent.

We have already stated (section 5.11) that simple exponential smoothing is optimal for an ARIMA(0, 1, 1) model, so that we can now deduce that it must be optimal for a random walk with noise model. Similar logical steps make it possible to deduce that exponential smoothing with a trend will provide optimal forecasts for the local linear trend model.

The relationship between these structural models and exponential smoothing can also be obtained by looking at the Kalman filter recursions in steady state. For instance, the steady state recursions for the random walk plus noise model boil down to $a_t = (1 - \lambda)a_{t-1} + \lambda X_t$, where $\lambda = [q + \sqrt{(q^2 + 4q)}]/[2 + q + \sqrt{(q^2 + 4q)}]$ and where $\sigma_\eta^2/\sigma_\varepsilon^2$ as above. Similarly, the steady state recursions for the linear trend model are none other than the exponential smoothing recursions for series with a trend.

6.8 BAYESIAN TIME SERIES MODELS[†]

A class of models has been developed which appears to resemble the general state space model and structural models, but which relies on Bayesian ideas for its interpretation. We will mention these models briefly in the context of their relationship with the models detailed in this book, but we refer the reader to West & Harrison (1989) for a comprehensive exposition. We have necessarily assumed a familiarity with the Bayesian ideas of prior and posterior distributions.

[†] This section is difficult, and may be omitted.

The models are based on the dynamic linear model (6.5), (6.6). To coincide with the notation in common use for this type of model, our observed series is now Y_t and the state vector is now $\boldsymbol{\theta}_t$.

$$Y_t = \mathbf{F}_t^T \boldsymbol{\theta}_t + v_t \qquad v_t \sim N(0, V_t) \tag{6.5}$$

$$\boldsymbol{\theta}_t = \mathbf{G}_t \boldsymbol{\theta}_{t-1} + w_t \qquad w_t \sim N(0, \mathbf{W}_t). \tag{6.6}$$

The state comprises components for trend and seasonal terms with corresponding observation vector $\mathbf{F}_t$ and diagonal block transition matrix $\mathbf{G}_t$. At first sight this resembles a time varying version of the structural models discussed in this chapter. Here, however, the state $\boldsymbol{\theta}_t$ is regarded as a vector of parameters for the observation equation which evolve over time.

At time $t - 1$ when observations up to and including Y_{t-1} are available, a distribution for $\boldsymbol{\theta}_{t-1}$ is assumed to be known and parametrized by a point estimator (usually the mean) and a covariance matrix for this point estimator. The state equation can be used in conjunction with the distribution of $\boldsymbol{\theta}_{t-1}$ to obtain a prior distribution for $\boldsymbol{\theta}_t$, again parametrized by a point estimator and its variance matrix. When the next observation Y_t becomes available it is incorporated with the prior distribution in the usual Bayesian way to give a posterior distribution for $\boldsymbol{\theta}_t$. The whole process can be repeated to obtain a posterior distribution for $\boldsymbol{\theta}_{t+1}$, and so on.

It is now well known that under some distributional assumptions the recurrence relations which calculate the posterior point estimator (usually the mean) and variance of $\boldsymbol{\theta}_t$ from those of $\boldsymbol{\theta}_{t-1}$ are linear and are the same as the Kalman filter equations which relate successive state estimates $\mathbf{a}_t$, $\mathbf{a}_{t-1}$ of the general state space model (4.1), (4.2). Of course, the variances V_t and $\mathbf{W}_t$ are required for this. In early work using this model (for instance, Harrison & Stevens 1976), $V_t = V$ and $W_t = \mathbf{W}$ were constant through time, and were fixed by the forecaster. However, difficulties were encountered in gauging these sensibly, and in later models $V_t = V$ is assumed to be time invariant and to have an assumed prior distribution with point estimator S_{t-1}, while the distribution of w_t conditional on $V = S_{t-1}$ is assumed to be $N(0, \mathbf{W}_t)$. With certain assumptions about the prior distribution for V, successive values of S_t can be generated by more linear recursions as each Y_t becomes available. $\mathbf{W}_t$ is set at each t using a discounting method which also amounts to a linear equation.

The crucial difference between these Bayesian models and the general state space model is that instead of having to estimate the parameters of the model, successive estimates of the variance parameter matrices are obtained by Bayesian methods. Likelihood or approximate likelihood techniques are *not* used. Recursions can be obtained for forecasting these models.

6.9 STRUCTURAL MODELS—PART OF THE ANALYST'S TOOLKIT

The immediately apparent advantage of structural models is that their form is suggested by the data, and that they can be decomposed into easily interpretable components. In addition, the models have few parameters, are relatively easily estimated, and component estimates for each time period can be obtained via the smoothing equations. Conversely, structural models pose considerable restrictions on the autocorrelation structure which a given time series may not conform to, and a suitable structural model may not be available.

Structural models are particularly useful for large/seasonal models when the number of parameters would become unwieldy if an ARMA model was used, and identification would be difficult. We advocate including structural models in our time series toolkit and going equipped with both these and ARMA models.

EXERCISES

(1) Write down the state space model for a BSM with a trigonometric seasonal component for monthly data which exhibits an *annual* cycle.

(2) Write down the single equation form of a BSM with (i) a local linear trend and a monthly (dummy) seasonal component, and (ii) a local quadratic trend and a monthly (dummy) seasonal component.

(3) The autocorrelations of the first differences and second differences of a time series of 300 observations are shown below. Suggest a suitable structural model for these data and obtain some initial parameter estimates.

Autocorrelations of differenced data	Autocorrelations of twice differenced data

(4) Fit a local linear trend model to the first 360 observations of the temperature data, eliminating any non-significant parameters. Perform diagnostic checks on the final estimated model(s) to ascertain the suitability of the model for the data.

(5) Fit a quarterly BSM with (i) dummy seasonal components and (ii) trigonometric seasonal components to the death rate data given in Chapter 1, Exercise 2. Eliminate non-significant parameters by using backwards elimination. Look at the diagnostic statistics, AIC, and prediction errors to suggest one or more appropriate model(s) for these data. Forecast a year ahead by using these models.

(6) Fit a BSM with dummy seasonals to the logs of the monthly airline data of Fig. 5.22. Confirm that the parameter estimates are $\sigma_\varepsilon^2 = 0.000014$, $\sigma_\eta^2 = 0.000817$, $\sigma_\zeta^2 = 0$, $\sigma_\omega^2 = 0.000083$. Estimate the multiplicative seasonal components for the final year.

(7) Use the single equation form to confirm that if $\sigma_\zeta^2 = 0$ and $\sigma_\omega^2 = 0$ for the dummy seasonal, local linear trend BSM that the model is equivalent to a multiplicative seasonal ARMA(0, 1, 1) (0, 1, 1) model as stated in section 6.7. [Hint: difference both sides of the equation so that the right hand side is the same as that of the ARMA model, and note that $(1 - B^s) = \nabla S(B)$.]

7

The frequency domain

I'm picking up good vibrations.

B. Wilson

7.1 INTRODUCTION

So far we have viewed time series in terms of models involving time functions or correlations, often known as the *time domain* view. An alternative approach is to study time series in the frequency domain, that is, in terms of repetitive cycles. Such a view is entirely natural in some disciplines but not in others; indeed it can be a little odd, and in consequence we start this section with a gentle introduction to frequency ideas.

When we examine a time series we can often see the effects of trends and of periodic oscillations; a good example is the record of passenger miles flown per month given in Fig. 7.1, or the famous series of annual sunspot numbers given in Fig. 7.2. Both series

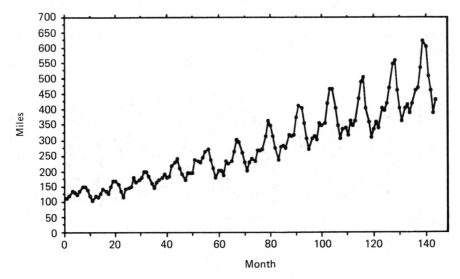

Fig. 7.1. Number of passenger miles flown.

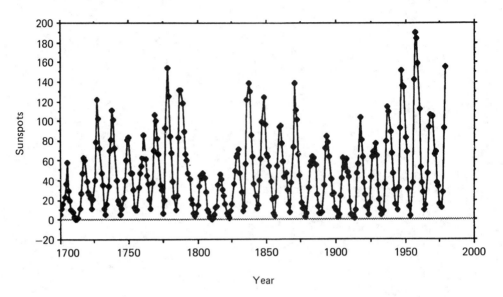

Fig. 7.2. Annual sunspot numbers.

appear to exhibit cyclic behaviour, as we see a repeating pattern. If we overplot the monthly values for successive years of the airline data, as in Fig. 7.3, we can see that the pattern of repetition is indeed consistent. This periodic behaviour is characteristic of many series, and the idea of cyclic behaviour and the associated periodicity is an important one, as it gives us a way of defining some regularity between points in a series.

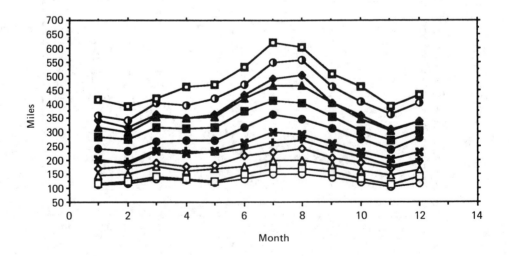

Fig. 7.3. Overplot of airline data: monthly values over years.

7.2 SOME DEFINITIONS

To be quite clear in our later discussions we begin with some definitions. We shall say
that the function $g(t)$ is *periodic* with *period T* if and only if T is the smallest number such
that

$$g(t) = g(t + kT) \quad k = \ldots, -2, -1, 0, 1, 2, \ldots.$$

This is a formal way of saying that there is a repetitive pattern and that the pattern repeats
over blocks of length T. Thus, for example, the function $f(x) = \{x\}$, where $\{x\}$ denotes
$x - \lfloor x \rfloor$ is periodic, with period 1, giving a plot of the form given in Fig. 7.4. Note $\lfloor x \rfloor$,
the 'floor' of x, in the largest integer less than or equal to x.

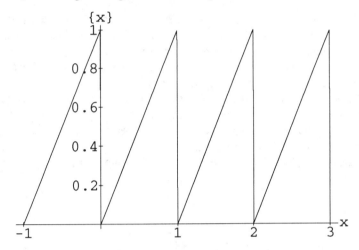

Fig. 7.4. Plot of fractional part of x.

The *inverse* of the period T is the *frequency* $f = 1/T$, which measures the 'speed of
oscillation' of the function. If we specify a standard time interval L, the frequency is then
just the number of repetitions of the function g in that time, that is, the number of
intervals of length T which can be slotted into L. The frequency f is usually measured in
cycles per unit time, for example, *cycles per second* (known as hertz). Perhaps an analogy
will help here.

Suppose we have a circle of radius T rolling along a line. Then the period is the length,
T, (Fig. 7.5) the circle rolls along the line in one revolution. The number of rotations to
move between zero and L is f, the frequency, and is just L/T. If we take L to be the unit of

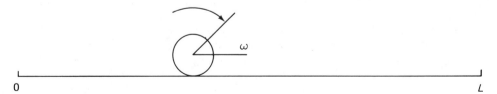

Fig. 7.5. Circle rolling along a line.

time, then the frequency is just $f = 1/T$. As is evident, the number of revolutions in a unit time interval can be measured in cycles (or revolutions) per unit time, or as the rate of rotation ω, the *angular velocity*.

Conventionally, we do not measure this angular velocity in degrees per unit time but in *radians per unit time*. Recall that if we do calculus then we *must* use radians. Since 2π radians make up one complete cycle, the angular frequency ω radians per unit time can be translated into f cycles per unit time via

$$\omega = 2\pi f \quad \text{or} \quad f = \frac{\omega}{2\pi},$$

and we talk of (angular) frequencies in *radians per unit time*. The period is then $2\pi/\omega$. It is also rather convenient, as we shall see, to introduce the rather bizarre idea of negative frequency. The idea is quite simple, as may be seen in Fig. 7.6. An angle can be in a clockwise or anticlockwise direction. If we regard going clockwise as negative, then the angle in the diagram can be written as ϕ radians or $-\theta$ radians. It follows that we can think of a range of frequencies from 0 to 2π or equivalently from $-\pi$ to π. When we use complex numbers the appeal of negative frequencies will be more apparent, as will our preference for thinking of the range of frequencies as being from $-\pi$ to π.

As the next chapters depend heavily on Fourier ideas we shall digress and develop the necessary ideas. Readers with a background in this area may wish to skip the next section.

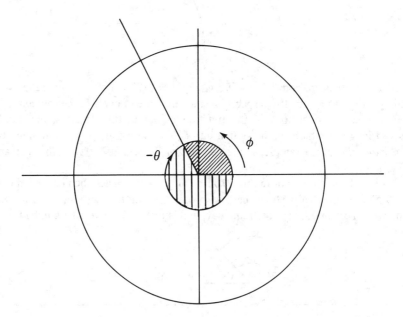

Fig. 7.6. 'Negative' frequency.

7.3 CYCLES, WAVES, AND FOURIER ANALYSIS

Consider the function $g(t) = A \cos(\omega t + \phi)$ defined over real values of t. Then A is the *amplitude* of the function, ω is the *angular frequency* measured in radians/unit time, while ϕ is the *phase* or *phase lag* also measured in radians. Fig. 7.7 is a plot of the function $2 \cos(3t + 5)$. Here we have an amplitude of 2, a phase of 5 and an angular frequency of 3 radians per unit time. The frequency is then just $3/(2\pi) = 0.4775$ hertz and period is thus $2\pi/3 = 2.0944$. The phase is 5 radians.

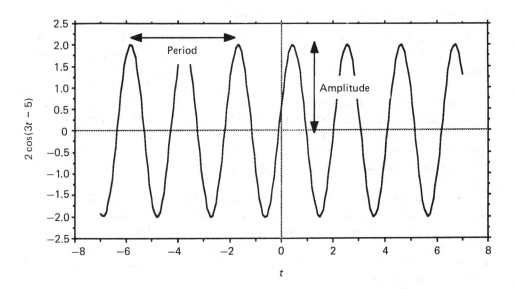

Fig. 7.7. The function: $2 \cos(3t - 5)$.

As a further illustration, suppose that time is measured in months. The harmonic terms $\cos \omega t$ and $\sin \omega t$ have periods $2\pi/\omega$, and represent variations which recur every $2\pi/\omega$ months. Thus $\cos 2\pi t/6$ has period 6 and represents values which recur every 6 months.

The cosine example above is a little different from the time series we have dealt with up to now, as it is continuous rather than discrete. This may not be an unreasonable assumption; there are many situations in which one might naturally think of a response over all time values. Thus a voltage or amplitude of a sound might be recorded as having a value for all t. Indeed, if the record is made on a chart recorder the response has the appearance of a continuous trace. In practice if we need to do any computations then we must sample the continuous record to obtain a set of numerical values, and we move from a continuous record to a discrete one. Thus a geologist recording the pressure waves in the Earth's crust following a seismic event must digitize the record in order to perform some analysis. One could go further and argue that given the constraints of our recording apparatus, only discrete sequences of observations are possible. We duck the philosophy, and shall spend almost all our time on *sequences* of observations.

There are differences between the continuous and discrete cases, as you would expect. For example, a discrete time sinusoid is periodic only if its frequency in cycles per unit time is a rational number! This can be seen as follows: since the cosine function is periodic, $\cos[2\pi f(t+T)+\phi]=\cos(2\pi ft+\phi)$, which is true only if $2\pi fT$ is an integer multiple of 2π. This means that $2\pi fT=2n\pi$ for some integer n. In consequence, $f=n/T$ is a rational number. As we have seen, this has practical implications in regression, and in choosing our sampling interval when sampling a continuous record.

7.4 DISCRETE AND CONTINUOUS SERIES: ALIASING

In the discussion at the beginning of the chapter we have used continuous functions as examples, while in the modelling we were concerned only with series recorded at discrete points in time. So far as time series are concerned, either point of view may be valid. It may be useful to think of $X(t)$ as being a response in time t, where t is continuous, or, alternatively, to regard X_t as a *sequence* of values at discrete time points. In engineering parlance this is the distinction between analogue and digital recordings. In our view there are compelling reasons for regarding time series as discrete. No matter what the recording apparatus, in the end we can only make measurements at discrete, if very close, intervals. If there is to be any analysis, then the continuous record must be sampled to give discrete numbers for analysis.

We have assumed that the discrete series that we have studied have been in some sense natural, but it is quite conceivable that a discrete series has been obtained from a continuous one by sampling. The resulting digitized or quantized trace naturally contains less information, and it is this point we now investigate further. What is more likely is that a record has been obtained from a discrete record by sampling, but we look at the analogue to digital case here.

Suppose we have a continuous record that we sample at time intervals of Δt to give a discrete record, thus

$$X_n = X(n\Delta t) \qquad n = 0,1,2,\ldots.$$

If the discrete record is all we have then we *cannot* distinguish between a sinusoid of period $2\Delta t$ (dotted line in Fig. 7.8) and those of smaller periods (solid line in Fig. 7.8). This maximum frequency $f_n = 1/(2\Delta t)$ cycles per unit time, or $\omega_n = \pi/\Delta t$, that we can observe is called the *Nyquist* or *folding frequency*. All higher frequencies are confounded with lower frequencies, and we are unable to separate them. For a sample series, we can only observe frequencies in the interval $[-\pi/\Delta t, \pi/\Delta t]$, or in hertz $[-\frac{1}{2}, \frac{1}{2}]$; all higher frequencies will be superimposed on frequencies in this interval. A frequency ω_0 in this band will have contributions from its *aliases* ω_k, where $\omega_k = \omega_0 \pm 2\pi k/\Delta t$, $k = 1, 2, 3,\ldots$. This can be seen from Fig. 7.8, or analytically, since if we have a frequency $\omega_k > 0$ greater than $\pi/\Delta t$ then at time $s = m\Delta t$ we have

$$\cos(s\omega_k) = \cos(m\Delta t\omega_0 + 2\pi mk) = \cos(m\Delta t\omega_0) = \cos(s\omega_0),$$

and the high frequency effect is mixed in or aliased with a lower frequency effect. One can think of this as a folding of the frequency range of the continuous signal.

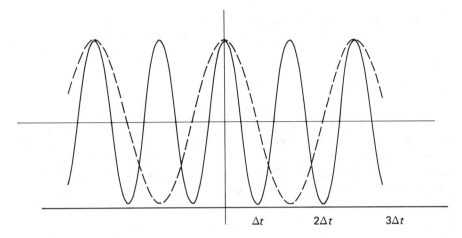

Fig. 7.8. Superimposition of frequencies.

The moral is that one must choose the sampling frequency so that the contribution of higher frequencies above the Nyquist, to the frequencies of the effects of interest is negligible. Otherwise we will lose information about high frequencies. High frequencies will also distort lower frequencies of interest if we do not choose a short enough interval Δt. There are many examples of this aliasing effect.

Example 1
Suppose that we measure the sea level at a coastal spot once a week or every 7 days. This gives a Nyquist frequency of

$$\frac{1}{2 \times 7} = \frac{1}{14}.$$

If, however, we assume a tidal effect with a period of 1 day, this will not be observable since its effect will be mixed with a lower frequency effect in the sample signal. In radian measure, the tidal frequency is $2\pi/7$, while the Nyquist frequency is $\pi/7$. The tidal effects will thus appear as an effect at frequency 0 since $2\pi/7 = 0 + 2\pi/7$. This should be obvious, since if we measure the sea level once a week we cannot deduce anything about a daily tidal effect; the only effect there is on the mean level, which is the zero frequency effect.

Example 2 (from Granger)
Suppose we measure economic data on a monthly basis (every four weeks), and there is a strong weekly cycle. Allowing for the unequal number of days per month, the weekly cycle corresponds to a frequency of 4.348 per month. This weekly effect has an alias at 0.348 cycles since

$$4.348 = 0.348 + 16 \times \tfrac{1}{4}.$$

Thus our monthly measurements contain a distortion at frequency 0.348 or $\frac{1}{0.348} = 2.87$ cycles caused by the weekly cycle. Note, we use the non-radian version

$$f_k = f_0 \pm \frac{k}{\Delta t} \qquad k = 1, 2, \ldots .$$

Example 3 (The last case for cineastes)
Devotees of western films will have noticed the very graphic aliasing effect seen in the rotation of the stagecoach wheels. These will appear normally and then rotate backwards as the stagecoach gathers speed. Since movie film is shot at 24 frames per second, there is an aliasing effect, the observed rotational speed being an alias of the real angular rotation once it exceeds the Nyquist frequency of $\pi/(1/24) = 24\pi$ radians/sec.

7.5 FOURIER ANALYSIS—THE FOURIER SERIES

For continuous functions we have a rich and powerful technique called Fourier analysis. Since we deal with discrete data we shall find it sufficient to work with Fourier series. If this were not so, we would be forced to consider the more general Fourier transform. We defer discussion of the general transform to the Appendix 7.1 since this is somewhat peripheral to our main development. Interested readers will find another insight to aliasing in this appendix, which enables us to study oscillatory behaviour and which is based on the orthogonality of the sine and cosine functions.

We begin with the 'orthogonality' results.

$$\int_{-\pi}^{\pi} \cos(\omega t) \, d\omega = \int_{-\pi}^{\pi} \sin(\omega t) \, d\omega = 0 \qquad t \neq 0$$

$$\int_{-\pi}^{\pi} \cos(s\omega)\sin(t\omega) \, d\omega = 0 \qquad \text{for all integers } s, t$$

$$\int_{-\pi}^{\pi} \sin(s\omega)\sin(t\omega) \, d\omega = \begin{array}{l} \pi \quad \text{if } s = t \neq 0 \\ 0 \quad \text{otherwise} \end{array} \qquad s, t \text{ integers}$$

$$\int_{-\pi}^{\pi} \cos(s\omega)\cos(t\omega) \, d\omega = \begin{cases} 2\pi & \text{if } s = t = 0 \\ \pi & \text{if } s = t \neq 0 \\ 0 & \text{otherwise.} \end{cases}$$

These results enable us to represent arbitrary functions as sums of sines and cosine terms where the coefficients are (simply) obtained using the orthogonal properties of the sines and cosines as given above.

Suppose we have a *periodic* function $f(x)$ which we define on an interval $[-R, R]$. The *Fourier series* $S(x)$ is a representation of $f(x)$ as a linear combination of cosine and sine functions, say

$$S(x) = \frac{1}{2}a_0 + \sum_{j=1}^{\infty} a_j \cos\left(\frac{j\pi x}{R}\right) + \sum_{j=1}^{\infty} b_j \sin\left(\frac{j\pi x}{R}\right). \tag{7.1}$$

From our orthogonality relations above, the coefficients, known as the Fourier cosine and sine coefficients, can be obtained as

$$a_j = \frac{1}{R}\int_{-R}^{R} f(x)\cos\frac{j\pi x}{R}\,dx \quad \text{and} \quad b_j = \frac{1}{R}\int_{-R}^{R} f(x)\sin\left(\frac{j\pi x}{R}\right)dx \tag{7.2}$$

while the constant is

$$a_0 = \frac{1}{R}\int_{-R}^{R} f(x)\,dx.$$

Quite often we are only interested in $f(x)$ in the range $(-R, R)$, but we should bear in mind that we have supposed that $f(x)$ is periodic or has been extended into a periodic form. After all, the sum

$$S(x) = \frac{1}{2}a_0 + \sum_{j=1}^{\infty} a_j \cos\left(\frac{j\pi x}{R}\right) + \sum_{j=1}^{\infty} b_j \sin\left(\frac{j\pi x}{R}\right) \tag{7.3}$$

will be periodic with period $(-R, R)$. For simplicity it is often rather nicer to work with a function on $(-\pi, \pi)$, in which case

$$S(x) = \frac{1}{2}a_0 + \sum_{j=1}^{\infty} a_j \cos(jx) + \sum_{j=1}^{\infty} b_j \sin(jx), \qquad f(x) = S(x)$$

with

$$a_j = \frac{1}{\pi}\int_{-\pi}^{\pi} f(x)\cos(jx)\,dx \quad \text{and} \quad b_j = \frac{1}{\pi}\int_{-\pi}^{\pi} f(x)\sin(jx)\,dx$$

while the constant is

$$a_0 = \frac{1}{\pi}\int_{-\pi}^{\pi} f(x)\,dx.$$

The case of a 'half' range $[0, R]$ or $[-R, 0]$ is a little more complex, but there is no real problem since we need only extend the definition into the other interval. So we define $F(x) = f(x),\ 0 < x < R$, and $F(x) = f(x),\ -R < x < 0$, or $F(x) = f(x),\ 0 < x < R$, and $F(x) = -f(x),\ -R < x < 0$.

This means that we can end up with a series for $F(x)$, and a cosine or sine representation for $f(x)$, as we wish. See Exercise 7.3.

Example 4

Suppose that we have the function

$$f(x) = -1 \quad -\pi < x < 0$$
$$ 1 \quad 0 < x < \pi.$$

Then

$$a_0 = \frac{1}{\pi}\left\{ -\int_{-\pi}^{0} dx + \int_{0}^{\pi} dx \right\} = 0$$

and

$$a_j = \frac{1}{\pi}\left\{ -\int_{-\pi}^{0} \cos(jx)\, dx + \int_{0}^{\pi} \cos(jx)\, dx \right\} = 0$$

while

$$b_j = \frac{1}{\pi}\left\{ -\int_{-\pi}^{0} \sin(jx)\, dx + \int_{0}^{\pi} \sin(jx)\, dx \right\}$$

$$= \frac{2}{\pi}\int_{0}^{\pi} \sin(jx)\, dx = -\frac{2}{\pi j}\{\cos j\pi - 1\}$$

$$= \frac{2}{\pi j}\{1 - (-1)^j\}.$$

Hence,

$$f(x) = \frac{4}{\pi}\left\{ \sin x + \frac{\sin 3x}{3} + \frac{\sin 5x}{5} + \frac{\sin 7x}{7} + \dots \right\}.$$

Example 5

$$f(x) = x^2 \quad -\pi < x < \pi.$$

In this case,

$$b_j = \frac{1}{\pi}\int_{-\pi}^{\pi} x^2 \sin jx\, dx = 0$$

while

$$a_j = \frac{1}{\pi}\int_{-\pi}^{\pi} x^2 \sin jx\, dx = 4\frac{(-1)^j}{j^2} \qquad a_0 = \frac{1}{\pi}\int_{-\pi}^{\pi} x^2\, dx = \frac{2\pi^2}{3}$$

and so

$$f(x) = \frac{\pi^2}{3} + \sum_{j=1}^{\infty} 4\frac{(-1)^j}{j^2}\cos(jx).$$

In evaluating these coefficients we make extensive use of the symmetry or otherwise of the coefficients.

There are some obvious questions we might ask; for example, is $S(x)$ always convergent and does it converge to f? By and large, provided that the function $f(x)$ is not too eccentric, we have no problems, and (7.1) is true. A more accurate statement is as follows.

If $f(x)$ is periodic of period X on $[0, X]$, and at least one of the following is true, the Fourier series exists, and $S(x)$ converges to $f(x)$.

(i) f is piecewise monotonic on $[0, X]$
(ii) f has a finite number of minima and maxima and discontinuities on $[0, X]$
(iii) f is of bounded variation on $[0, X]$
(iv) f is piecewise smooth on $[0, X]$.

At each point of continuity, $S(x)$ will equal $f(x)$, and at a jump point

$$S(x) = \tfrac{1}{2}\left\{ f(x^+) + f(x^-) \right\},$$

splitting the difference. Term by term integration is no problem in that if we integrate $S(x)$ term by term, the resulting series is the integral of $f(x)$. Differentiation term by term is more difficult. Suppose that $f(x)$ has jumps, and we need to be a little more wary. Details may be found in Champeney (1987).

A truncated Fourier series is obviously not going to match a function exactly, and at discontinuities the truncated expression always overshoots the mark very slightly, a phenomenon known as Gibbs phenomenon. This is illustrated in Fig. 7.9, which displays the function $f(x)$ in Example 4 and three terms of the Fourier series. The reader will recall that the Fourier series split the difference at jumps in the function. This may be seen above as well as the overshoot at the discontinuities.

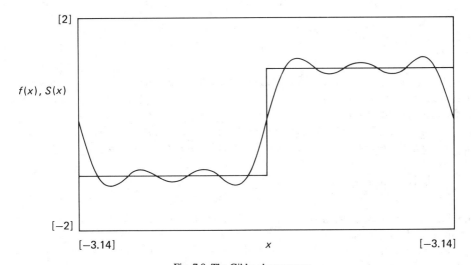

Fig. 7.9. The Gibbs phenomenon.

As may be evident to the reader, life is always simpler in the complex plain, and we can rewrite the Fourier series in complex form. Thus

$$f(x) = \sum_{-\infty}^{\infty} c_j e^{i\pi jx/R} \tag{7.4}$$

where

$$c_j = \frac{1}{2R} \int_{-R}^{R} f(x) e^{i\pi jx/R} \, dx.$$

This follows since

$$\int_{-\pi}^{\pi} e^{i\omega jx} \, d\omega = 0 \quad \text{for all } j \neq 0.$$

We shall often use the complex notation for simplicity, but that is not its only attraction.

Example 6

Suppose we define a function as a sequence of rectangles on $-2 < x \leq 2$

$$f(x) = \begin{cases} 1 & |x| < 1 \\ 0 & \text{otherwise.} \end{cases}$$

Then

$$c_j = \frac{1}{4} \int_{-2}^{2} f(x) e^{-i\pi jx/2} \, dx = \frac{1}{\pi j} \sin(\pi j/2),$$

giving

$$f(x) = \sum_{-\infty}^{\infty} \frac{\sin(j\pi) \, e^{ijx\pi/2}}{j\pi}.$$

The plot of the modulus of the complex coefficients c_j against frequency is called the *amplitude spectrum* of the function, and a plot of the *phase angle* or argument of the coefficient against frequency is known as the *phase spectrum* of the function. Since we have a sequence of discrete frequencies in the series, the plots are a sequence of lines giving rise to the expression *line spectrum*. Thus for our example above

$$|c_j| = \frac{1}{j\pi} |\sin(\pi j/2)|$$

and the phase is always zero since the coefficients are real in this case. The amplitude spectrum is shown in Fig. 7.10.

We leave Fourier series with one last and very useful, result, which is often known as Parseval's theorem.

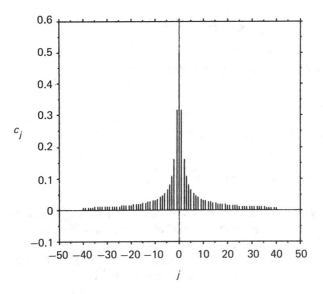

Fig. 7.10. Discrete spectrum.

Parseval's theorem

Suppose that $f(x)$ and $g(x)$ are periodic on $(-R, R)$ and have Fourier series, say

$$f(x) = \frac{1}{2}a_0 + \sum_{j=1}^{\infty} a_j \cos\left(\frac{j\pi x}{R}\right) + \sum_{j=1}^{\infty} b_j \sin\left(\frac{j\pi x}{R}\right)$$

$$g(x) = \frac{1}{2}A_0 + \sum_{j=1}^{\infty} A_j \cos\left(\frac{j\pi x}{R}\right) + \sum_{j=1}^{\infty} B_j \sin\left(\frac{j\pi x}{R}\right).$$

Then

$$\frac{1}{R}\int_{-R}^{R} f(x)g(x)\,dx = \frac{1}{2}a_0 A_0 + \sum_{1}^{\infty}(a_j A_j - b_j B_j). \tag{7.5}$$

In the complex case, say

$$f(x) = \sum_{-\infty}^{\infty} c_j\, e^{ij\pi x/R},$$

while

$$g(x) = \sum_{-\infty}^{\infty} C_j\, e^{ij\pi x/R},$$

then

$$\frac{1}{R}\int_{-R}^{R} f(x)\overline{g}(x)\,\mathrm{d}x = \sum_{-\infty}^{\infty} c_j\overline{C}_j.$$

A related important expression is the *convolution* of f and g:

$$\int_{-R}^{R} f(x)\overline{g}(y-x)\,\mathrm{d}x.$$

We have the simple expression

$$\int_{-R}^{R} f(x)\overline{g}(y-x)\,\mathrm{d}x = \sum_{-\infty}^{\infty} c_j\overline{C}_j\,\mathrm{e}^{\mathrm{i}\pi y j/R}. \tag{7.6}$$

The convolution will come into its own in the next few chapters. In passing we note that we can use a similar argument to that in the Parseval result to find the mean square error due to approximating a function by a truncated Fourier expansion; see Exercise 7.4.

   We defer discussion of the Fourier transform to the appendix 7.1, where we examine one or two samples. The interested reader is urged to look at the appendix, as it does give an insight into the aliasing phenomenon.

7.6 THE DISCRETE FOURIER TRANSFORM (DFT)

In discrete time we have a very similar set of orthogonal relations to those forming the basis of Fourier series:

$$\sum_{t=0}^{N-1} \cos(\omega_j t) = 0 \qquad j \neq 0$$

$$\sum_{t=0}^{N-1} \sin(\omega_j t) = 0$$

for any integer $N > 0$ and any $\omega_j = 2\pi j/N$, that is, a Fourier frequency.

$$\sum_{t=0}^{N-1} \cos(\omega_j t)\cos(\omega_k t) = \begin{cases} N/2 & \text{if } j = k \neq 0 \text{ or } N/2 \\ N & j = k = 0 \text{ or } N/2 \\ 0 & j \neq k \end{cases}$$

$$\sum_{t=0}^{N-1} \cos(\omega_j t)\sin(\omega_k t) = 0$$

$$\sum_{t=0}^{N-1} \sin(\omega_j t)\sin(\omega_k t) = \begin{cases} N/2 & \text{if } j = k \neq 0 \text{ or } N/2 \\ 0 & \text{otherwise.} \end{cases} \tag{7.7}$$

These results are not difficult to derive if one uses the fundamental result for a finite sum of complex exponentials:

$$\sum_{j=a}^{b} e^{i\omega j} = e^{i\omega\left(\frac{b+a}{2}\right)} \frac{\sin\left\{\omega \frac{(b-a+1)}{2}\right\}}{\sin\left(\frac{\omega}{2}\right)} \qquad \omega \neq 0$$

$$= b - a + 1 \qquad\qquad\qquad \omega = 0. \tag{7.8}$$

These relations are also invaluable for many problems; for example, we can simply find solutions to problems such as our regression problem discussed in Chapter 1. If we have

$$E[X_t] = \mu + \sum_{j=1}^{m} \left\{ \alpha_j \cos(\omega_j t) + \beta_j \sin(\omega_j t) \right\}$$

then the least squares solutions to the problem of estimating the coefficients are

$$\hat{\mu} = \frac{1}{N} \sum_{t=1}^{N} X_t$$

$$\hat{\alpha}_j = \frac{2}{N} \sum_{t=1}^{N} X_t \cos(\omega_j t)$$

$$\beta_j = \frac{2}{N} \sum_{t=1}^{N} X_t \cos(\omega_j t)$$

where ω_j denotes a Fourier frequency, that is, one of the frequencies $2\pi j/N$, $j = 0, 1 \ldots$. Evidently quantities of the form

$$\frac{2}{N} \sum_{t=1}^{N} X_t \sin(\omega_j t) \qquad \text{and} \qquad \frac{2}{N} \sum_{t=1}^{N} X_t \cos(\omega_j t)$$

are very useful and are quite often required, so, as is usual in much of mathematics, to make life a little simpler we consider the complex form

$$\frac{2}{N} \sum_{t=1}^{N} X_t e^{i\omega_j t}$$

or, for simplicity,

$$\frac{2}{N} \sum_{t=1}^{N} X_t W_N^{-tj} \tag{7.9}$$

where $W_N = \exp\{2\pi i/N\}$. The orthogonality relations for these complex series are rather similar to the sine and cosine ones, rather as one might expect. Explicitly,

$$\sum_{u=0}^{N-1} W_N^{uv} W_N^{-ku} = \sum_{u=0}^{N-1} e^{i\frac{2\pi}{N}(v \cdot k)} \begin{matrix} = N \text{ if } k = v \,(\mathrm{mod}\, N) \\ = 0 \text{ otherwise.} \end{matrix} \tag{7.10}$$

Recall that $k = v \bmod N$ if $k - v$ is a multiple of N.

We begin a systematic look at the use and manipulation of these sums. Since they transform *discrete* sequences, they are often known as *Discrete Fourier transform* or DFTs, especially by engineers, and are used to transform data segments of length N.

Consider the sequence $a_1, a_2, ..., a_N$, then we define the DFT $A(\omega)$ as

$$A(\omega) = \sum_{t=0}^{N-1} a_t e^{-i\omega t} \qquad 0 \leq \omega \leq 2\pi. \tag{7.11}$$

The quantity $A(\omega)$ *is the discrete Fourier transform of the input series* $a_1, a_2, ..., a_N$. As for the usual Fourier transform, we have an inverse transform. Using the results above, *the discrete Fourier transform of the quantity* $A(\omega_j)$ is

$$a_t = \frac{1}{N} \sum_{j=0}^{N-1} A(j) e^{i\omega_j t}. \tag{7.12}$$

As it is usual to consider the $A(\omega)$ only at the Fourier frequencies

$$\omega_j = \frac{2\pi j}{N}, \qquad j = 0, 1, ..., N-1,$$

we can use the obvious notation

$$A\left(\frac{2\pi j}{N}\right) = A(j).$$

From the relations above we can show that there is a transform pair

$$A(j) = \sum_{t=0}^{N-1} a_t W_N^{-jt} \qquad j = 0, 1, 2, ..., N-1$$

and

$$a_t = \frac{1}{N} \sum_{j=0}^{N-1} A(j) W_N^{jt} \qquad t = 0, 1, 2, ..., N-1,$$

so given the $a_1, a_2, ..., a_N$ we can deduce the $A(j)$, and vice versa. The justification is not difficult even if the algebra is a little messy, and the reader should attempt to check that the assertion is indeed true.

The reader might like to think of the DFT as a truncated Fourier representation at the *Fourier frequencies*. It is instructive to look at some examples.

Example 7

Suppose that $a_0 = 1$, $a_1 = 1$, and $a_j = 0$ otherwise as in Fig. 7.11. Then

$$A(\omega) = 1 + e^{-i\omega} = e^{-i\omega/2}\left[e^{i\omega/2} + e^{-i\omega/2}\right] = 2e^{-i\omega/2}\cos\left(\frac{\omega}{2}\right)$$

for any ω which is a Fourier frequency. See Figs 7.12 and 7.13.

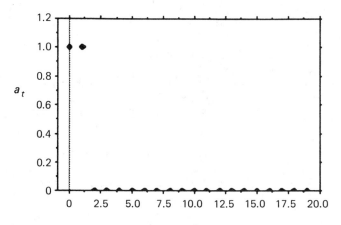

Fig. 7.11. Example 7.

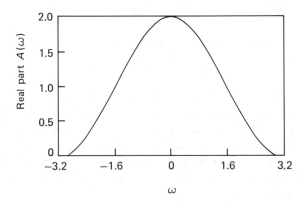

Fig. 7.12. Example 8.

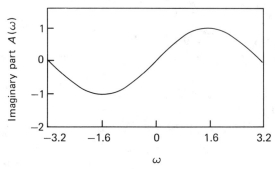

Fig. 7.13. Example 9.

Example 8

Suppose that $a_t = 1/R$, $t = 0, 1,\ldots, R-1$. Then

$$A(\omega) = \frac{1}{R}\left\{1 + e^{-i\omega} + e^{-2i\omega} + \ldots + e^{-i\omega(R-1)}\right\} = 1 \qquad \text{when } \omega = 0$$

and

$$= \frac{1}{R}\frac{1 - e^{-i\omega R}}{1 - e^{-i\omega}} = \frac{1}{R}e^{-i\omega R/2}\left\{\frac{\sin\left[\omega\frac{R}{2}\right]}{\sin(\omega/2)}\right\} \qquad \text{otherwise.}$$

Example 9

Suppose that we now take $a_t = e^{-i\theta t}$, $t = 0, 1,\ldots, N-1$, then

$$A(\omega) = \sum_{t=0}^{N-1} e^{-(\omega-\theta)t} = N \qquad \text{when } \omega = \theta$$

$$= e^{-i(\omega-\theta)(N-1)/2}\left\{\frac{\sin\left[(\omega-\theta)\frac{N}{2}\right]}{\sin[(\omega-\theta)/2]}\right\} \qquad \text{otherwise.}$$

The transform $A(\omega)$ thus has a large peak when ω takes the value θ, and is small in comparison otherwise. We can conclude that *a cyclic term in the series gives rise to a large peak in the DFT*. This is an important result, as we shall see later.

As we have seen, the form of the discrete sequence $\{a_t\}$ is reflected in the characteristic form of the transformed function $A(\omega)$. As we shall see in later chapters, this is the key to the frequency approach.

We are also interested in the *algebra* of transformations. Define the DFT pair

$$A(j) = \sum_{t=0}^{N-1} a_t W_N^{-jt} \qquad j = 0,1,2,\ldots, N-1$$

and

$$a_t = \frac{1}{N}\sum_{j=0}^{N-1} A(j)W_N^{jt} \qquad t = 0,1,2,\ldots, N-1,$$

and another pair

$$B(j) = \sum_{t=0}^{N-1} b_t W_N^{-jt} \qquad j = 0,1,2,\ldots, N-1$$

and

$$b_t = \frac{1}{N}\sum_{j=0}^{N-1} B(j) W_N^{jt} \qquad t = 0,1,2,\ldots, N-1,$$

then we can show that

(1) the DFT of the sum $xa_t + yb_t$ is just $xA(\omega) + yB(\omega)$
(2) the DFT of

$$c_t = \sum_{j=0}^{N-1} a_j b_{t-j},$$

say $C(\omega)$, is just the product $C(\omega) = A(\omega)B(\omega)$, and that

the DFT of $d_t = a_t b_t$ is $D(\omega)$, where $D(k) = \frac{1}{N}\sum_{j=0}^{N-1} A(j)B(k-j).$

This last result is the *discrete convolution* of two sequences, which as we shall see is important, as it has the same form as the correlation function. *Note*: In the convolution definitions we use a circular definition for the sequence, viz.

$$a_u = a_{kN+u} \qquad \text{so} \quad a_{-1} = a_{N-1} \quad \text{and} \quad a_{-38} = a_{N-38}.$$

Before we move on to the z-transform it should be pointed out that we need only compute the DFT $A(j)$ for $j = 0, 1,\ldots, [N/2]$ since the higher values of j only duplicate the lower j values. Thus for even N

$$A\left(j+\frac{N}{2}\right) = \sum a_t \exp\left\{-i\left(j+\frac{N}{2}\right)\frac{2\pi t}{N}\right\} = \sum a_t \exp\left\{-ij\frac{2\pi t}{N} - i\pi\right\};$$

however, $e^{-i\pi} = -1$, so that

$$A\left(j+\frac{N}{2}\right) = -\sum a_t \exp\left\{-ij\frac{2\pi t}{N}\right\} = -A(j).$$

This makes for some computational savings.

7.7 THE z-TRANSFORM

Like the DFT above, we can define the *z-transform* of a sequence of a function. If we
have a function $a(t)$ defined at $t = 0, \pm1, \pm2,\dots$, then the z-transform of $a(t)$ is just

$$A(z) = \sum_{t=-\infty}^{\infty} a_t z^{-t},$$

and *we do not have to assume that z is one of the complex roots of unity.* Thus if, as in the
examples, $a_t = 1/R$, $t = 0, 1,\dots, R-1$, then we have

$$A(z) = \frac{1}{R}\left\{1 + z^{-1} + z^{-2} + \dots + z^{-(R-1)}\right\} = \frac{1}{R}\frac{1-z^{-R}}{1-z^{-1}}.$$

Alternatively, suppose that $a_t = \alpha^t$ for $|\alpha| < 1$, $t = 0, 1, 2,\dots, N-1$, then

$$A(z) = \sum_{0}^{N-1}\left(\frac{\alpha}{z}\right)^t = \frac{1 - \left(\frac{\alpha}{z}\right)^N}{1 - \frac{\alpha}{z}} = \frac{z^N - \alpha^N}{\alpha z^{N-1} - z^N}.$$

Some readers might recognize the z-transform as the Laplace transform, and there is a
good deal known about such standard expressions of this form. Thus, for instance, such
transforms are unique if they exist in an interval containing the origin and there is an
inverse transform

$$a(t) = \frac{1}{2\pi i}\int A(z)z^{n-1}\,dz$$

where the integral is around the unit circle. Fortunately we do not have to study or
evaluate such integrals; in most cases we can look up the necessary transform. In most of
what follows we only make use of the z-transform as an operational convenience; however, it can be a very useful tool. We digress to give a simple example of an application
from geophysics.

A seismologist sends a (sound) signal from a vessel through water and the ocean bed.
The reflected signal is recorded for later analysis. Unfortunately, the received signal
consists of the reflection from the stratum of interest together, with reflections from other
layers. In the simplest case, let us just consider reflections from the sea bed. So we have a
primary signal and a series of ghosts, as in Fig. 7.14.

If we think of the signal taken at unit time intervals with the primary as 1 at time zero
and a ghost signal at time d, we might regard the received signal as $\mathbf{y} = (1, 0, 0, 0,\dots, k)$,
that is, a combination of primary and surface reflections. Note that $|k| < 1$ since the
energy must be less than the primary. We would like to disentangle the two signals so as
to get a better view of the primary.

The z-transform of the signal is $Y(z) = 1 + kz^{-d}$, using $\mathbf{y}$ above as our sequence. If we
want a clear view we could multiply our signal by another, whose z-transform is $F(z)$, so
as to get $Y(z)F(z) = 1$. Then clearly

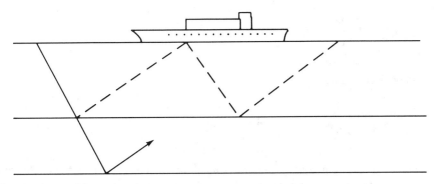

Fig. 7.14. Seismological sounding.

$$F(z) = \frac{1}{1 + kz^{-d}} = 1 - kz^{-d} + k^2 z^{-2d} - \dots$$

the z-transform of $(1, 0, \dots, -k, 0, \dots, k^2, 0, \dots, -k^3, 0, 0 \dots)$. The *discrete convolution* of these two sequences gives $(1, 0, 0, \dots)$, removing the ghosts. Thus we can find a factor to remove the unwanted reflections—in some sense at least.

7.8 THE FAST FOURIER TRANSFORM (FFT)

When we wish to compute the DFT

$$A(j) = \sum_{t=0}^{N-1} a_t e^{-i\omega_j t},$$

then it is easily done by computing the two real sums

$$\sum_{t=0}^{N-1} a_t \cos(\omega_j t) \qquad \text{and} \qquad \sum_{t=0}^{N-1} a_t \sin(\omega_j t),$$

which can be rather a slow process, especially when the value of N is large. Thus if one is taking a reading every centimetre on several kilometres of railway track, then the corresponding transforms can take considerable computation. There are some tricks one can use to speed up computation such as precalculating the trigonometric terms and using the relations

$$\sin(2\pi k + \theta) = \sin \theta, \qquad k \text{ an integer}$$

but the computations are still extensive. Cooley & Tukey (1965) discovered (or perhaps rediscovered) an ingenious method for computation, which is very much faster and which is known as an FFT. We will not spend very much time on the details, but FFTs are so central to much of time series that it is worth digressing to spell out the main details.

The DFT of the sequence $a_0, a_1, a_2, \dots, a_{n-1} A(\omega)$ is defined as

$$A(\omega) = \sum_{0}^{N-1} a_t \, e^{-i\omega t}$$

so at the Fourier frequency

$$A(j) = \sum_{0}^{N-1} a_t W_N^{-tj} \qquad j = 0,1,2,\dots N-1.$$

The obvious direct computation requires something of the order of N^2 operations; our aim is to do better. The idea we use is simple but ingenious. Define two sequences $a_t(1) = a_{2t}$ and $a_t(2) = a_{2t+1}$. Then we can easily show that

$$
\begin{aligned}
A(j) &= \sum_{t \text{ even}}^{N-1} a_t W_N^{-jt} + \sum_{t \text{ odd}}^{N-1} a_t W_N^{-jt} \\
&= \sum_{t=0}^{N/2-1} a_{2t} W_N^{-2jt} + \sum_{t=0}^{N/2-1} a_{2t+1} W_N^{-(2t+1)j}.
\end{aligned}
$$

But since

$$W_N^2 = \left(e^{2\pi i/N}\right)^2 = \exp\left(\frac{2\pi i}{N/2}\right) = W_{N/2}$$

we have (after some algebra) $A(j) = A_1(j) + W_N^{-j} A_2(j)$ where $A_1(j)$ and $A_2(j)$ are the DFTs of the odd and even sequences. Thus we can write a DFT of order N in terms of two DFTs of order $N/2$ and some 'twiddle' factors. If $N/2$ is even, we can split the DFTs down once again and recombine to get the DFT. For N a power of 2, say 2^p, then we can factorize the expression to DFTs of length 2 and recombine with the appropriate twiddle factor. A similar approach is possible when N has other prime factors, but the algebra is rather more messy and the gains are not so large. For $N = 2^p$ the technique is most efficient and the number of operations is $N \log N$, a considerable saving. On the computer the technique works like a charm and enables us to compute DFTs for long sequences in a reasonable time.

The scheme we have given above is not the only one; an alternative is to 'decimate in frequency'. In this case we suppose that $N = 2^p$, and we let

$$b_t = a_t \qquad t = 0,1,2,\dots, \frac{N}{2} - 1$$

$$c_t = a_{t+\frac{N}{2}} \qquad t = 0,1,2,\dots, \frac{N}{2} - 1.$$

Then

$$A(j) = \sum_{t=0}^{N/2-1} a_t W_N^{-jt} + \sum_{t=N/2}^{N-1} a_t W_N^{-jt}$$

$$= \sum_{t=0}^{N/2-1} b_t W_N^{-tj} + \sum_{t=0}^{N/2-1} c_t W_N^{-(t+N/2)j}$$

$$= \sum_{t=0}^{N/2-1} \left[b_t + e^{-\pi ji} c_t \right] W_N^{-jt}.$$

Now if we examine the even and odd DFTs $A(2t)$ and $A(2t+1)$ we can (after a little algebra) see that the DFT of our original series can be obtained from the two order $N/2$ DFTs of $b_t + c_t$ and $\{b_t - c_t\} W_N^{-t}$, $j = 0, 1, \ldots, N/2 - 1$. The two procedures are similar but differ in detail, for the first one computes the short DFTs and then adds the 'twiddle factors'; while in the second approach the 'twiddles' are done first.

While the details of the algorithms are of some interest, we leave the reader to pursue the matter further. Many algorithms have been published, and there is a good deal of code available on most computer systems. In practice, one would make use of the software available on the computer that one is using. This often means that the choice is between a powers of 2 FFT or a 'slow transform'. In such cases, one has to choose between truncating one's sequence to the nearest power of two or of 'padding with zeros'. In this case the sequence is extended to the next highest power of two by adding zeros to the end of the sequence.

7.9 A HEURISTIC SPECTRUM

In the next chapter we formally derive a spectrum for a stationary time series; however, at this point we can get a sketch of the main ideas without too much formalism by using the ideas above. Suppose that we have a fragment of time series $X_0, X_1, \ldots, X_N$ and we take the DFT

$$A(\omega) = \sum_0^{N-1} X_t e^{-i\omega t}.$$

If we assume a zero mean, or that we remove the mean before analysis, then the sample variance is just

$$s^2 = \frac{1}{N} \sum_{t=1}^{N} X_t^2.$$

If we use Parseval's theorem for DFTs (see Exercise 7) then we can see that, if we write $A(j)$ to denote $A(2\pi j/N)$, then

$$s^2 = \frac{1}{N} \sum_{t=1}^{N} X_t^2 = \frac{1}{N} \sum_{j=1}^{N} |A(j)|^2.$$

This has far reaching implications since it means that the variance of the series can be decomposed into contributions tied to a set of distinct frequencies. The values at each frequency are called the (power) spectrum, and give us an alternative way of looking at the series. It is not difficult to relate the coefficient to the covariances (see Exercise 7), and as we shall see, the information available in the covariances is also in the spectrum. The subject is important enough for us to study in detail in the next chapter.

We can use our heuristic ideas above in a very practical way with some thought. Suppose that we have an irregular series that we would like to 'smooth' in order to make a rather more careful study. Almost by definition, random variation due to noise will be short term, that is short period, and hence high frequency. We could take the DFT of the series, remove some of the high frequency terms, and transform back. The resulting series will then be smoother. The proof of the pudding is, however, in the eating, so we take an example.

Beveridge produced an index of annual wheat prices from 1500 to 1869. The first 256 years are plotted in Fig. 7.15.

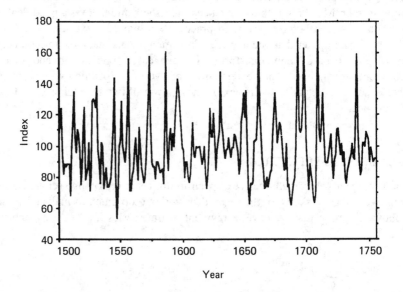

Fig. 7.15. Wheat price index (trend free).

Taking the FFT and setting the coefficient of values above $A(20)$ to zero we take the inverse transform. The result is given in Fig. 7.16, and shows a somewhat smoother series. The reverse operation, that is, setting to zero frequencies below 20 gives a much more irregular series, as shown in Fig. 7.17.

An artificial example may help here, so suppose that $X_t = \cos(4\pi t/127) + \text{noise}$, as plotted in Fig. 7.18. We take the DFT and set

(a)   all the terms at frequencies exceeding 20 to zero, giving series Y (Fig. 7.19)

(b)   all the terms at frequencies not exceeding 20 to zero, giving series Z (Fig. 7.20).

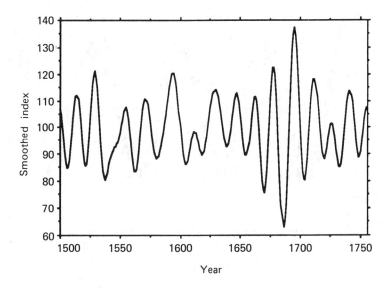

Fig. 7.16. Smoothed series: high frequencies removed.

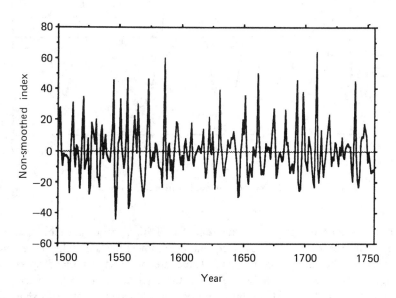

Fig. 7.17. Wheat price index (trend free) after filtering.

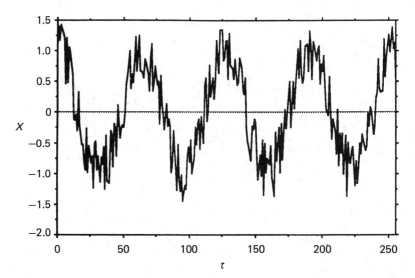

Fig. 7.18. Original series.

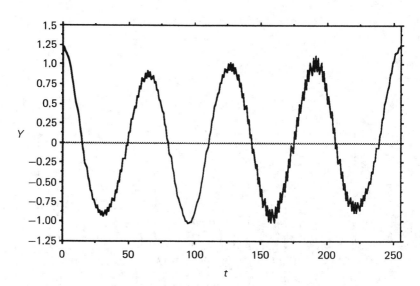

Fig. 7.19. Smoothed series: low frequencies remain.

As can be seen from Fig. 7.20 the removal of high frequencies makes the trace smoother, while the removal of low frequencies removes the 'smoothly changing' features and leaves the random component. There are more sophisticated approaches to smoothing, but we leave this to Chapter 8; in the interim we leave the reader with an example on real data. Fig. 7.21 displays the price of a Manchester brewery share for 256 successive days. As you can see, it is an irregular fluctuating function. If we smooth,

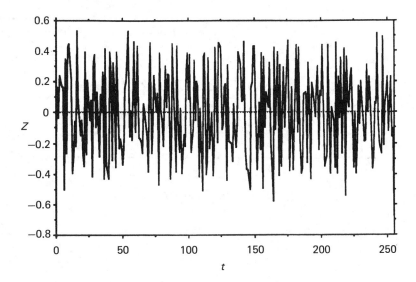

Fig. 7.20. Smoothed series: high frequencies remain.

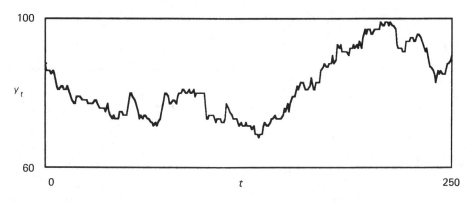

Fig. 7.21. Brewery share prices.

taking the FFT and setting frequencies above 30 to zero, we have Fig. 7.22. The smoothed version looks rather more tractable, while more severe truncation gives 7.23.

At this point we need to gain a rather deeper understanding of the role of the frequency domain in random series, and this is the aim of the next chapter.

EXERCISES

(1) An economist has a monthly record of the amount of money in circulation in the banking system. He discovers that there is a regular 13 week cycle caused by accounting practices in the bank. At what frequency will this appear in the monthly data?

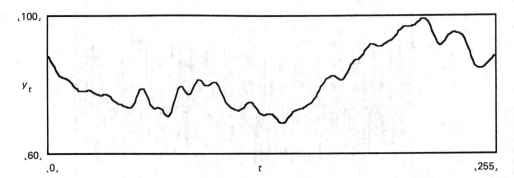

Fig. 7.22. Smoothed version of Fig. 7.21.

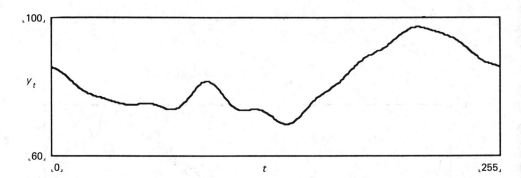

Fig. 7.23. Version with more severe truncation.

(2) Find Fourier series for

(i) $f(x) = 1 - x^2$, $-\pi < x < \pi$
(ii) $f(x) = 1 - x^2$, $-5 < x < 5$
(iii) $f(x) = |x|$, $-\pi < x < \pi$.

(3) Suppose that $f(x)$ is defined on the range $0 < x < \pi$. Define

$$F(x) = -f(x)   \quad -\pi < x < 0$$

$$f(x)   \quad 0 < x < \pi$$

and

$$G(x) = f(x)   \quad -\pi < x < 0$$

$$f(x)   \quad 0 < x < \pi.$$

Hence deduce that one can produce different Fourier expansions for $f(x)$ on $0 < x < \pi$.

(4) $f(x) = -x \quad -\pi < x \le 0$

$\qquad\quad x \quad\;\; 0 < x < \pi$

has a Fourier series

$$\frac{\pi}{2} - \frac{4}{\pi} \sum_{n=1}^{\infty} \frac{\cos(2n-1)x}{(2n-1)^2}.$$

(i)　Show that

$$\frac{\pi^4}{96} = 1 + \frac{1}{3^4} + \frac{1}{5^4} + \frac{1}{7^4} + \dots.$$

(ii)　Does the integral of $f(x)$ have a Fourier series?

(iii)　Does the derivative of the Fourier series for $f(x)$ equal $f'(x)$?

(iv)　By using Parseval, find an expression for

$$\int_{-\pi}^{\pi} f(x)^2 \, dx.$$

Hence show how to find an expression for

$$\int_{-\pi}^{\pi} |f(x) - S_m(x)|^2 \, dx$$

where $S_m(x)$ is truncated Fourier series of m terms.

(5) Suppose we define the sequence $\{x_t\}$ such that

$$x_t = -1 \quad t = n$$

$$\quad +1 \quad t = n + p$$

$$\quad\;\; 0 \quad \text{otherwise.}$$

Find the DFT of x and show that for suitably chosen integers n and p, this DFT will look like the DFT of a (ghost) sinusoid.

(6) Show how one might evaluate the simple correlation by using the FFT and the original series.

(7) Show that one may use Parseval's theorem with DFTs.

APPENDIX 7.1 FOURIER TRANSFORMS

The two integrals

$$F(t) = \int_{-\infty}^{\infty} f(x) \, e^{-2\pi i x} \, dx \quad \text{and} \quad f(x) = \int_{-\infty}^{\infty} F(t) \, e^{2\pi i x} \, dt$$

form a *transform pair* and $F(t)$ is known as the Fourier transform of $f(x)$, while $f(x)$ is known as the Fourier transform of $F(t)$. The connection between the two functions is via the integral, and we can think of this as a kind of black box $\mathscr{F}(f(x))$ which gives $F(t)$ while $\mathscr{F}^{-1}(F(t))$, the backwards transform, gives $f(x)$. There are many slight variations in the definition of a transform pair; we have chosen the one above, as it seems to be the simplest, but any author's definition should be examined.

There is a good deal of theory about Fourier transforms, much of it depending on facility with complex variables. The theory is very powerful and is capable of subtlety and beauty. We will look at two simple ideas. The convolution of two functions is defined as

$$h(t) = \int_{-\infty}^{\infty} f(x)g(t-x)\,\mathrm{d}x,$$

and we can show (after a little effort) that the transform $H(t)$ is related to the transforms of f and g by $H(t) = F(t)G(t)$.

Suppose that we look for a function f which satisfies

$$g(t) = \int_{-\infty}^{\infty} f(x)g(t-x)\,\mathrm{d}x,$$

for any function g. Then a reasonable starting point is

$$f_d(x) = \frac{1}{d} \qquad -d/2 \le x \le d/2$$
$$0 \qquad \text{otherwise.}$$

Then

$$g_d(t) = \int_{-d/2}^{d/2} \frac{1}{d} g(x-y)\,\mathrm{d}y,$$

and substituting $z = x - y$ we get

$$g_d(t) = \int_{x-d/2}^{x+d/2} \frac{1}{d} g(z)\,\mathrm{d}z.$$

This is the average value of the function g over the interval from $x - d/2$ to $x + d/2$. As d is made smaller and smaller, g_d gets closer to the function g. We define the limit of the function f_d as d tends to zero to be the delta function $\delta(x)$. This is rather an odd function, with the following properties:

(1) $\delta(x) = 0, x \ne 0$.
(2) $\delta(0)$ is infinite.

(3) $\displaystyle\int_{-\infty}^{\infty} \delta(x)\,\mathrm{d}x = 1$.

(4) $\displaystyle\int_{-\infty}^{\infty} \delta(x)g(x-y)\,\mathrm{d}y = g(x)$.

Thus the Fourier transform of the constant function is the delta function $\delta(x)$.

If we start from the other end, the transform of the square wave

$$f_d(x) = \begin{matrix} 1 & \text{if } -a \le x \le a \\ 0 & \text{otherwise} \end{matrix}$$

is

$$\int_{-\infty}^{\infty} f(x) \, e^{-2\pi i x} \, dx = \frac{\sin 2\pi a t}{\pi t}.$$

This function behaves like $\delta(x)$ as a tends to zero.

Most of the transforms and Fourier ideas have been based on ideas first used with the Fourier integral transform discussed in this appendix. If we wish to consider the effect of digitizing a continuous trace then we need to work in terms of the discrete Fourier transform rather than the integral. This means that we can manage with either Fourier series or DFTs.

In the next chapter we discuss the aliasing of the spectrum, and the concept is linked to the idea of approximating a continuous transform by a discrete one. Now we can define the correlation function for a continuous time series, and the relation with the spectrum is via Fourier integral transform

$$\gamma(u) = \int_{-\infty}^{\infty} e^{iut} f(t) \, dt.$$

If we replace u with $s\Delta t$ we can find a relation between the spectrum of the continuous series $f(\omega)$, defined over the whole real line, and the spectrum of the discrete series

$$f_d(\omega) = \sum_{-\infty}^{\infty} f\left(\omega + \frac{2\pi k}{\Delta t}\right) \qquad |\omega| < \frac{\pi}{\Delta t}.$$

The interested reader may like to see Fishman (1969) or Priestly (1981).

8

The spectrum

Don't panic.

R. Adams

8.1 INTRODUCTION

The first part of this book looked in some detail at the models and inferences that can be made about time series. The fundamental tools used were the second order moments. At the end of Chapter 7 we saw that the sample variance of a fragment of series could be decomposed, rather as in analysis of variance, into components attached to different frequencies. This idea is so valuable that we shall spend some time in this chapter in refining it and showing its use.

Suppose that we have a stationary series $\{X_t\}$ which is generated by

$$X_t = \sum_{j=1}^{p} \left\{ a_j \cos(\omega_j t) + b_j \sin(\omega_j t) \right\} \tag{8.1}$$

where the $\{a_j\}$ and $\{b_j\}$ are zero mean sequences of independent random variables having variances σ_j^2. This is very like the trigonometric regression model in Chapter 1 or the harmonic model of Chapter 2. We can regard a model of this form as an attempt to explain the signal X_t in terms of contributions at the 'frequencies' $\omega_1, \omega_2, \omega_3,\dots, \omega_p$. A close analogy is that of a musical instrument; a note played on such an instrument is the sum of harmonic vibrations at different frequencies. Since we work with discrete series it is sufficient to work with frequencies in the range $-\pi$ to π since with a unit time interval the Nyquist frequency is π.

From our examinations of the 'harmonic model' in Chapter 2 we have seen that it is not difficult to work out the correlation structure, but rather than do this again we shall write our series in terms of complex exponentials, an exercise which can be of immense value, as we shall see.

Suppose that we assume for simplicity that $\omega_p = \pi$ then, $\cos \omega + i \sin \omega = e^{i\omega}$ we may rewrite (8.1) as

$$X_t = \sum_{j=-p+1}^{p} z_j e^{i\omega_j t} \tag{8.2}$$

where

$$z_j = \tfrac{1}{2}(a_j - ib_j) \quad \text{and} \quad z_{-j} = \tfrac{1}{2}(a_j + ib_j) \qquad \text{for } 0 < |j| < p,$$

while at the end point $z_p = a_p$. The frequencies ω_{-j} are to be taken as $-\omega_j$, and if we take the obvious step of writing z_{-j} as $\bar{z}_j$, the complex conjugate of z_j, we have the nice equivalent form (assuming $\bar{z}_0 = 0$)

$$X_t = \sum_{j=-p+1}^{p} z_j\, e^{i\omega_j t}.$$

If we use this complex formulation, we can work out means without much trouble. From the definition of z_j we have

$$E[z_j] = 0$$

$$E[z_j \bar{z}_k] = 0 \quad j \neq k$$

notice we must use the *complex* form

$$\text{var}(z_j) = E[z_j \bar{z}_j] = \tfrac{1}{2}\sigma_j^2$$

and so

$$\gamma(s) = E[X_t X_{t+s}] = E \sum_{j=-p+1}^{p} \sum_{k=-p+1}^{p} \exp\{i\omega_j t - i\omega_k(t+s)\} z_j \bar{z}_k$$

$$= \sum_{j=-p+1}^{p} e^{-i\omega_j s}\sigma_j^2, \tag{8.3}$$

which reduces to

$$\gamma(s) = \sum_{j=1}^{p} \sigma_j^2 \cos(s\omega_j) \quad \text{and} \quad \gamma(s) = \text{var}(X_t) = \sum_{j=1}^{p} \sigma_j^2, \tag{8.4}$$

as before. Thus the variance of the process is made up of contributions which are distributed over the individual frequencies. In the same way as with probability distributions we can think of distributions of variance components (we shall use power as an abbreviation), and to this end we define the *cumulative spectral function* $F(\omega)$ as $F(\omega)$ = sum of contributions to the variance for frequencies less than or equal to ω with $F(-\pi) = 0$ and $F(\pi) = \text{var}(X_t)$. More formally

$$F(\omega) = \begin{cases} \displaystyle\sum_{\omega_j \leq \pi} \sigma_j^2 + \tfrac{1}{2}\sigma_p^2 & \omega = \pi \\[2ex] \displaystyle\sum_{\omega_j \leq \omega} \sigma_j^2 & 0 \leq \omega < \pi. \\[2ex] \tfrac{1}{2}\displaystyle\sum_{\omega_j \leq \omega} \sigma_j^2 & -\pi < \omega < 0 \\[2ex] 0 & \omega = -\pi. \end{cases} \tag{8.5}$$

Thus for the model we have been dealing with, the function F has the form given in Fig. 8.1. The jumps in F correspond to the frequencies contributing to the total variation, and the sizes of the jump give the magnitude of the contribution.

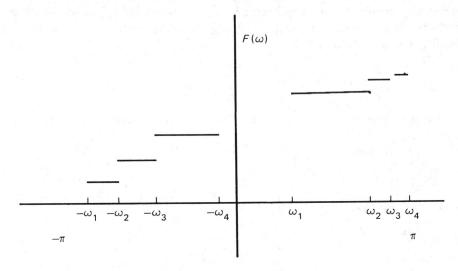

Fig. 8.1. Function F.

8.2 THE SPECTRUM

Suppose now that we imagine that the number of frequency points in our model becomes very large. Then the function F will become smoother until, in the limit, we will have a smooth function. This is an exact analogy to the cumulative distribution function of a continuous random variable. Then we must think of the contribution to the total variance made in a *frequency band* rather than at a specific frequency; thus the frequency band $[\omega, \omega + \delta\omega]$ contributes $F(\omega + \delta\omega) - F(\omega)$ to the total variation. Notice that we have assumed that there is not a dominant frequency contributing a large amount of power, and the contribution *from any point frequency* is zero. If in this limiting case $F(\omega)$ is differentiable, then the derivative $f(\omega)$ is define as

$$F(\omega) = \int_{-\pi}^{\omega} f(\lambda)\,d\lambda \qquad \text{or} \qquad f(\omega) = \frac{\partial F}{\partial \omega} \tag{8.6}$$

and is called the *power spectrum*. This function $f(\omega)$ is the analogue of the familiar probability density function in statistics, and gives the distribution of power over the frequency range. However, it should be borne in mind that the F *need not have a derivative*. If a frequency λ contributes a finite amount of power, then the cumulative spectrum will have a jump point at that frequency λ, as in Fig. 8.2.

The connection with the covariance function can be established directly by recalling that in the finite case (and rewriting the sum)

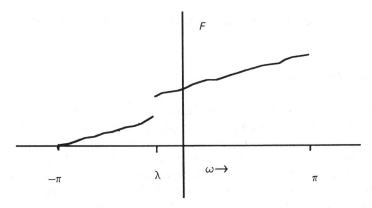

Fig. 8.2. Jump in power spectrum.

$$\gamma(s) = \tfrac{1}{2} \sum_{j=-p+1}^{p} e^{-i\omega_j s} \sigma_j^2 = \sum_{j=-p+1}^{p} e^{-i\omega_j s} \left\{ F(\omega_j) - F(\omega_{j-1}) \right\},$$

and following the same sort of limiting process as before we have for a differentiable function F

$$\gamma(s) = \int_{-\pi}^{\pi} e^{-i\omega s} f(\omega) \, d\omega, \tag{8.7}$$

and hence using the ideas of Fourier series we have the inverse relationship

$$f(\omega) = \frac{1}{2\pi} \sum_{s=-\infty}^{\infty} \gamma(s) \, e^{i\omega s},$$

and since $\gamma(s) = \gamma(-s)$ we have for *real* series the spectral density

$$f(\omega) = \frac{1}{2\pi} \sum_{s=-\infty}^{\infty} \gamma(s) \cos(s\omega), \tag{8.8}$$

and the spectral density is *symmetric* around $\omega = 0$.

While we have developed the equations in a quite informal way, one can, if one wished, check in a quite rigorous (and much more complex) way that they still hold. We summarize as follows:

For any stationary time series we can define a cumulative power spectrum $F(\omega)$ defined on a set of frequencies $-\pi \le \omega \le \pi$ and

(a)   The cumulative power spectrum $F(\omega)$ defines the amount of 'power' or the contribution to the total variance made by frequencies below ω.

(b)   When $F(\omega)$ is continuous, there is a spectral density function $f(\omega)$ which satisfies (8.8), that is,

$$f(\omega) = \frac{1}{2\pi} \sum_{s=-\infty}^{\infty} \gamma(s)\cos(s\omega).$$

It is sometimes useful to use the spectral density function which is the normalized function $f_n(\omega) = f(\omega)/\gamma(0)$. This function is exactly the same as a probability density function.

While we have started from a simple harmonic model it is possible to be very much more general and show that any second order stationary series has a spectral distribution $F(\omega)$. This function can be thought of as having the form $a_1F_1(\omega) + a_2F_2(\omega) + a_3F_3(\omega)$, where $F_1(\omega)$ is a discrete function, $F_2(\omega)$ is continuous, and $F_3(\omega)$ is a 'singular' component. In our work the function F will usually be continuous with possibly some jumps corresponding to pure sinusoids at a finite number of frequencies. In the continuous case the power spectrum $f(\omega)$ will satisfy (8.7) and (8.8).

8.3 EXAMPLES OF SPECTRA

At this point it is worth looking at some examples of spectra, and we begin with a white noise process.

Example 1
Suppose $\{\varepsilon_t\}$ is white noise, that is, has zero mean with correlation structure

$$\gamma(k) = \sigma^2 \qquad \text{for } k = 0$$
$$0 \qquad \text{otherwise.}$$

Then, using (8.8), we have

$$f(\omega) = \frac{\sigma^2}{2\pi} \qquad \text{for } -\pi < \omega < \pi$$
$$0 \qquad \text{otherwise.}$$

Example 2
For an autoregressive model $X_t = \phi X_{t-1} + \varepsilon_t$ where $\{\varepsilon_t\}$ is white noise as above, then for $|\phi| < 1$ we have

$$\gamma(k) = \phi^k \gamma(0) \qquad k = \ldots -2, -1, 0, 1, \ldots,$$

thus

$$2\pi f(\omega) = \gamma(0)\{1 + 2\phi\cos\omega + 2\phi^2\cos 2\omega + 2\phi^3\cos 3\omega + 2\phi^4\cos 4\omega + \ldots\},$$

which, after some algebra, gives

$$f(\omega) = \frac{\sigma^2}{2\pi(1+\phi^2 - 2\phi\cos\omega)} \qquad \text{for } -\pi < \omega < \pi$$

since $\gamma(0) = \sigma^2/(1-\phi^2)$.

Example 3
Consider a moving average process, say $X_t = \varepsilon_t - \theta\varepsilon_{t-1}$. We know that

$$\gamma(0) = (1+\theta^2)\sigma^2$$

$$\gamma(k) = -\theta\sigma^2 \qquad\qquad k = -1, +1$$

$$\gamma(k) = 0 \qquad\qquad\qquad \text{otherwise,}$$

thus we see that

$$f(\omega) = \frac{(1+\theta^2 - 2\theta\cos\omega)\sigma^2}{2\pi}.$$

You will no doubt be relieved to know that there is a rather simpler method of computing the spectrum, but before taking the technical side further we might look at the diagrams of the typical spectral shapes given in Fig. 8.3; we plot only half the range $-\pi, \pi$, as $f(\omega)$ is symmetric about $\omega = 0$.

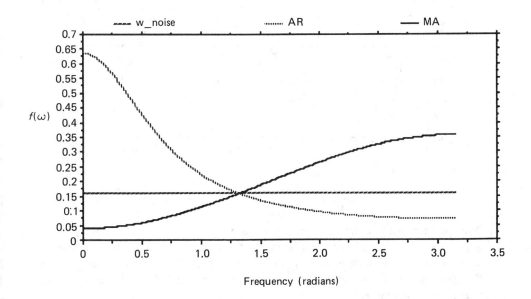

Fig. 8.3. Typical spectral shapes.

The flat white noise spectrum shows that the contributions to variance are equally distributed across the entire frequency range, while for the AR model, here with parameter 0.5, the contributions are greater from the low frequency and hence long period end. This would imply that there are rather weak short period effects, and in consequence we would expect a smoother series than white noise. The MA spectrum, again with a parameter of 0.5, shows the opposite effect; the power is concentrated towards the high frequency end of the frequency range, and in consequence we expect strong high frequency, that is, short period effects, giving an irregular appearance to a realization generated by such a model.

Example 4

Suppose that we have the AR(2) model of the type met in Chapter 3, say

$$X_t = \frac{3}{2} X_{t-1} - \frac{15}{16} X_{t-2} + \varepsilon_t.$$

This particular AR(2) model has been chosen to exhibit cyclic behaviour, which can be seen from the correlation plot given in Fig. 8.4.

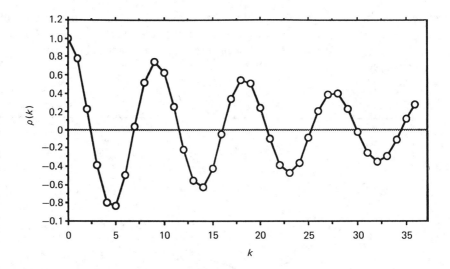

Fig. 8.4. Correlations for an AR(2) model.

The spectrum can be computed, and the plot is given in Fig. 8.5.

As we see, there is a large contribution to the power from frequencies around 0.7 radians/unit time, indicating behaviour which will look cyclic. There is *not a true cycle*, as the spectrum $F(\omega)$ *does not have a jump* and the peak in $f(\omega)$, while large, is still a peak and not a singular point.

8.4 THE SPECTRAL REPRESENTATION

At the beginning of this chapter we had written the series as a sum of complex random variables of the form

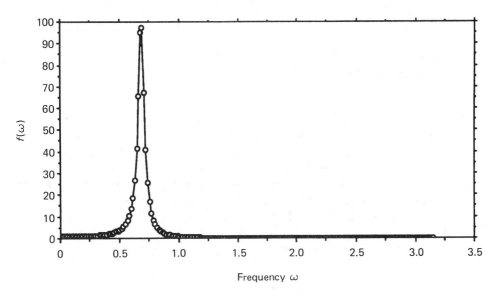

Fig. 8.5. Spectrum of an AR(2) model.

$$X_t = \sum_{j=-p+1}^{p} e^{i\omega_j t} z_j. \tag{8.9}$$

One might ask what happens to this as the number of individual frequencies becomes infinite? We can handle this by defining a stochastic process $Z(\omega)$ which is in some sense the accumulation of the z_j's up to frequency ω. While the mathematics is rather complex, and the new process is rather interesting, for our purposes we shall just think of $Z(\omega)$ as a complex process related to z_j via a limiting process

$$z_j \rightarrow Z(\omega_j) - Z(\omega_j - \delta\omega) \quad \text{as} \quad \delta\omega \rightarrow 0.$$

It can be shown that for intervals $[\omega_2, \omega_1]$ and $[\omega_4, \omega_3]$

$$E\Big[\{Z(\omega_1) - Z(\omega_2)\}\overline{\{Z(\omega_3) - Z(\omega_4)\}}\Big]$$

$$= F(\omega_1) - F(\omega_2) \qquad \text{when } \omega_1 = \omega_3 \text{ and } \omega_2 = \omega_4$$

$$= 0 \qquad\qquad\qquad \text{when the intervals do not overlap.}$$

$$= F(\omega_a) - F(\omega_b) \qquad \text{where } \omega_a, \omega_b \text{ is the overlap.}$$

For our purposes we shall just use the rather more simple relationships using $dZ(\omega) = Z(\omega + d\omega) - Z(\omega)$

$$E[dZ(\omega)\, dZ(\phi)] = \begin{matrix} 0 & \text{for } \omega \neq \phi \\ f(\omega)\, d\omega & \text{when } \omega = \phi \end{matrix} \tag{8.10}$$

or

$$E\left[|dZ(\omega)|^2\right] = f(\omega)\ d\omega. \tag{8.11}$$

We can thus take (informally) the limiting form of (8.9) as

$$X_t = \int_{-\pi}^{\pi} e^{i\omega t}\ dZ(\omega) \tag{8.12}$$

where the process $Z(\omega)$ satisfies (8.10) and (8.11).

While the full mathematical structure is difficult to derive, the formula above, known as the *spectral representation* or *the Cramer representation*, holds for *all* stationary processes, and as we shall see gives us a simple way to deal with the calculation of the spectra of linear models. It also gives insight into the very important idea of filters. While the study of $Z(\omega)$ itself is interesting, it falls beyond our remit. For the moment we will use the result to try to compute the spectra of some models, but first we check the connection with the autocorrelations.

$$\gamma(k) = E[X_t X_{t+k}] = E\left[\int_{-\pi}^{\pi}\int_{-\pi}^{\pi} e^{i\omega t}\ dZ(\omega)\ e^{-i\theta(t+k)}\ d\bar{Z}(\theta)\right].$$

Note the complex form of the correlation. Then using 8.10 and 8.11 this becomes

$$\begin{aligned}
\gamma(k) = E[X_t X_{t+k}] &= E\left[\int\int_{-\pi}^{\pi} e^{i\omega t}\ dZ(\omega)\ e^{-i\theta(t+k)}\ d\bar{Z}(\theta)\right]\\
&= E\left[\int_{-\pi}^{\pi} e^{-i\omega k}|dZ(\omega)|^2\right]\\
&= \int_{-\pi}^{\pi} e^{-i\omega k}\ dF(\omega)\\
&= \int_{-\pi}^{\pi} e^{-i\omega k} f(\omega)\ d\omega
\end{aligned}$$

as we might expect!

Example 5

First we recall that for a white noise process we have a flat spectrum $f_\varepsilon(\omega) = \sigma^2/(2\pi)$, then for the MA(1) model $X_t = \varepsilon_t - \beta\varepsilon_{t-1}$ we have in terms of the spectral representation

$$X_t = \varepsilon_t - \beta\varepsilon_{t-1} = \int_{-\pi}^{\pi}\left[e^{i\omega t} - \beta\ e^{i\omega(t-1)}\right] dZ_\varepsilon(\omega) = \int_{-\pi}^{\pi} e^{i\omega t}\ dZ_x(\omega),$$

hence using the obvious notation

$$dZ_x(\omega) = [1 - \beta\ e^{-i\omega}]\ dZ_\varepsilon(\omega)$$

and thence

$$f_x(\omega)\ d\omega = |dZ_x(\omega)|^2 = \left|[1 - \beta\ e^{-i\omega}]dZ_\varepsilon(\omega)\right|^2 = \left|1 - \beta\ e^{-i\omega}\right|^2 f_\varepsilon(\omega)\ d\omega,$$

giving

$$f_x(\omega) = \frac{\left|1 - \beta e^{-i\omega}\right|^2 \sigma^2}{2\pi} = \frac{\sigma^2}{2\pi}\{1 + \beta^2 - 2\beta\cos\omega\}.$$

Example 6

In the same way as for an AR(1) model $X_t = \alpha X_{t-1} + \varepsilon_t$ we have

$$\int_{-\pi}^{\pi}[e^{i\omega t} - \alpha e^{i\omega(t-1)}]\,dZ_x(\omega) = \int_{-\pi}^{\pi}e^{i\omega t}\,dZ_\varepsilon(\omega)$$

so

$$\left|dZ_\varepsilon(\omega)\right|^2 = \left|[1 - \alpha e^{-i\omega}]\,dZ_x(\omega)\right|^2$$

or

$$f_\varepsilon(\omega) = \frac{\sigma^2}{2\pi} = \left|1 - \alpha e^{-i\omega}\right|^2 f_x(\omega)$$

or

$$f_x(\omega) = \frac{\sigma^2}{2\pi\left|1 - \alpha e^{-i\omega}\right|^2} = \frac{\sigma^2}{2\pi\{1 + \alpha^2 - 2\alpha\cos\omega\}}.$$

The authors find this a rather simpler way to evaluate spectral densities when given a difference equation model.

In the general case any (non-deterministic) second order stationary model can be written in the general linear representation of Chapter 2, viz.

$$X_t = \sum_{0}^{\infty}\psi_j a_{t-j},$$

hence the spectrum of X_t is

$$f(\omega) = \frac{\sigma^2}{2\pi\left|\sum_{0}^{\infty}\psi_j e^{-ij\omega}\right|^2}.$$

Mathematicians know that this function, a polynomial in exponentials, can be well approximated by rational functions of the form

$$\frac{\sigma^2}{2\pi}\left|\frac{A(e^{-i\omega})}{B(e^{-i\omega})}\right|^2$$

where $A(z)$ and $B(z)$ are finite polynomials in z. This form is just the form of the spectrum of a typical ARMA model, perhaps indicating the reason why models of this form have been so successful.

8.5 LINEAR FILTERS

One very important reason for the utility of the spectral form of time series analysis is its value when studying linear transformations on time series. Suppose we have a series $\{X_t\}$ which passes into a 'black box' which produces $\{Y_t\}$ as output, rather as in the schematic in Fig. 8.6.

Fig. 8.6. Black box.

We could regard the effect of the box as an operation on the input giving output, say $Y_t = \mathcal{L}X_t$. This would model an enormous number of common situations; thus, for example, the impact of a bump on the road is modified by the suspension system to give an output to the car occupants. While the model is so general it is difficult to study in detail, we make two crucial restrictions

(1)   That the relationship is *linear*.
(2)   That the relationship is *invariant* over time.

While it is not obvious, these restrictions mean in effect that for any t, Y_t is a weighted linear combination of past and future values of the input, viz.

$$Y_t = \sum_{j=-\infty}^{\infty} a_j X_{t-j},\tag{8.13}$$

for details, see, for example, Koopmans (1974).

We call the relationship in (8.13) a *linear filter*, and much of time series analysis is based on the study of such filters. The only other condition we impose is that

$$\sum_{-\infty}^{\infty} a_j^2 < \infty,$$

so that the sum in (8.13) has a limit in mean square.

We can study filters in the time domain since from (8.13) we could turn our attention to estimating the coefficients; rather than do this, we look at the relationship between the input and output *spectra*. Suppose that the input series $\{X_t\}$ has a power spectrum $f_x(\omega)$, and the output $\{Y_t\}$ a corresponding spectrum $f_y(\omega)$; then we can use the spectral representation as follows.

$$Y_t = \int_{-\pi}^{\pi} e^{i\omega t} \, dZ_y(\omega) = \int_{-\pi}^{\pi} \sum_{j=-\infty}^{\infty} a_j \, e^{i\omega(t-j)} \, dZ_x(\omega),$$

thus

$$\left| dZ_y(\omega) \right|^2 = \left| \sum_{j=-\infty}^{\infty} a_j \, e^{-i\omega j} \, dZ_x(\omega) \right|^2,$$

and so

$$f_y(\omega) = \left| \sum_{-\infty}^{\infty} a_j \, e^{-i\omega j} \right|^2 f_x(\omega). \tag{8.14}$$

In consequence it is very easy to relate the input and output spectra of a linear filter; indeed the relation

$$Y_t = \sum_{-\infty}^{\infty} a_j B^j X_t$$

gives

$$f_y(\omega) = \left| \Gamma(\omega) \right|^2 f_x(\omega) \tag{8.15}$$

where

$$\Gamma(\omega) = \sum_{-\infty}^{\infty} a_j \, e^{-i\omega j}.$$

The function $\Gamma(\omega)$ is called the *transfer function* or the *frequency response function*, while $|\Gamma(\omega)|$ is often called the *amplitude gain*. The squared value $|\Gamma(\omega)|^2$ is known as the *gain* or the *power transfer function* of the filter. The argument $\arg\{\Gamma(\omega)\}$ is the *phase gain* or just the *phase*. There is rather a rich variety of nomenclature since filters are widely used in many fields, most especially in branches of engineering.

At this point we look at some simple filters to collect our ideas.

Example 7
Suppose that we apply a moving average to a series, say

$$Y_t = \tfrac{1}{5}(X_{t+2} + X_{t+1} + X_t + X_{t-1} + X_{t-2}),$$

then

$$5\Gamma(\omega) = e^{-2i\omega} + e^{-i\omega} + 1 + e^{i\omega} + e^{2i\omega} = 1 + 2\cos\omega + 2\cos 2\omega = \frac{\sin\left(\dfrac{5\omega}{2}\right)}{\sin\dfrac{\omega}{2}},$$

and as we can easily see, this function is zero when

$$\frac{5\omega}{2} = k\pi \quad \text{or} \quad \omega = \frac{2k\pi}{5}, \qquad k = \ldots -2, -1, 0, 1, \ldots .$$

If this filter is applied to a series with a cycle of period 5, that is frequency $2\pi/5$, the resulting output spectrum given by

$$f_y(\omega) = |\Gamma(\omega)|^2 f_x(\omega)$$

will have a zero at this frequency, and in consequence the output series will not contain this cyclic effect. See Fig. 8.7.

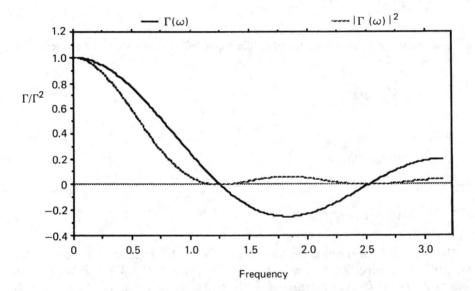

Fig. 8.7. Effect of a five point moving average.

Example 8

It is quite possible to introduce unexpected effects by transforming a series. Suppose we difference a series as $Y_t = X_t - X_{t-1} = (1 - B)X_t$, then $f_y(\omega) = f_x(\omega)|1 - e^{-i\omega}|^2$, so

$$f_y(\omega) = 4f_x(\omega)\sin^2\left(\frac{\omega}{2}\right).$$

If this process is repeated k times we have

$$f_y(\omega) = f_x(\omega)\left\{2\sin\left(\frac{\omega}{2}\right)\right\}^{2k}.$$

This will clearly suppress both the zero frequencies and the long term or fixed effects which correspond to frequencies around zero; however, it will also, if done to excess, introduce a peak at $\omega = \pi/4$. This will be entirely spurious. The introduction of such ghost cycles is known as the 'Slutsky effect'; see Granger (1964). Our next example is rather more realistic.

Example 9

Kuznets (1961) studies some economic series by applying two filters. Given $\{X_t\}$, the first was

$$Y_t = \sum_{s=-2}^{2} X_{t-s},$$

while the second was $W_t = Y_{t+5} - Y_{t-5}$. The gain for the first filter is, as we have seen, $\sin(5\omega/2)/5\sin(\omega/2)$, while the gain of the second is just

$$e^{-5i\omega} - e^{5i\omega} \quad \text{or} \quad -2i\sin(5\omega).$$

Notice that the second filter, *unlike* the first, introduces a change in phase of $\pi/2$, and the two filters in series have overall squared gain

$$|\Gamma(\omega)|^2 = \left| \frac{2\sin\left(\dfrac{5\omega}{2}\right)\sin(5\omega)}{5\sin\left(\dfrac{\omega}{2}\right)} \right|^2, \tag{8.16}$$

and this is plotted in Fig. 8.8.

As can be seen, this filter has a large peak at $\omega = 0.310$ (corresponding to 20.26 years for his study). One would thus beware of any assertion that 20 year cycles existed in the output series, as this filter has a large peak at a very similar frequency and damps out high frequency components, implying that the output would have cyclic type behaviour at 20.26 years and would also be smoothed at higher frequencies, removing or diminishing short term cycles. The study was an investigation of the existence of long period cycles!

8.6 FILTER DESIGN

The design of filters is of considerable importance, and much attention has been paid to the problems encountered. We illustrate one approach in Fig. 8.9, but readers would be well advised to consult more specialized works. Suppose that we specify some desirable action we wish the filter to undertake in the *frequency* domain, for example, as in Fig. 8.9,

$$\Gamma(\omega) = \begin{cases} 0 & |\omega| < \omega_0 \\ 1 & |\omega| \geq \omega_0 \end{cases}$$

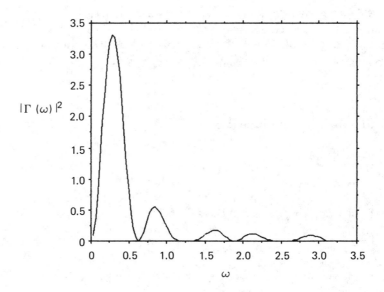

Fig. 8.8 Kuznet's filter: squared gain.

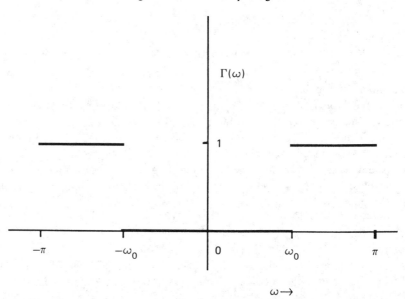

Fig. 8.9. Filter design.

a *high pass* filter and we wish to find coefficients $\{a_j\}$ such that

$$Y_t = \sum_{j=m}^{n} a_j X_{t-j}$$

has the appropriate gain. All things being equal we would also wish to minimize the number of coefficients a_j in the filter.

One approach is to use a least squares criterion to select the coefficients, that is, to minimize

$$\int_{-\pi}^{\pi} \left| \Gamma(\omega) - \sum_{j=m}^{n} a_j e^{-i\omega j} \right|^2 d\omega. \tag{8.17}$$

Standard results in Fourier theory assure us that if $\Gamma(\omega)$ has Fourier coefficients c_j, that is,

$$c_j = \frac{1}{2\pi} \int_{-\pi}^{\pi} \Gamma(\omega) e^{ij\omega} d\omega \quad \text{or} \quad \Gamma(\omega) = \sum_{-\infty}^{\infty} c_j e^{-i\omega j},$$

then (8.17) is minimized by choosing $a_j = c_j$, $j = m, m + 1, \ldots, n$. Naturally we have an approximate result since we are approximating $\Gamma(\omega)$ by a truncated Fourier series. We can in fact evaluate the gain of this approximate filter since its transfer function $\Gamma_A(\omega)$ is just given by

$$\Gamma_A(\omega) = \sum_{j=m}^{n} a_j e^{-i\omega j} = \frac{1}{2\pi} \sum_{j=m}^{n} e^{-i\omega j} \int_{-\pi}^{\pi} \Gamma(\phi) e^{i\phi j} d\phi. \tag{8.18}$$

This is a little tricky to evaluate, but using convolution ideas we get

$$\Gamma_A(\omega) = \frac{(n-m+1)}{2\pi} \int_{-\pi}^{\pi} \Gamma(\theta) \frac{\sin\left\{(n-m+1)\left(\dfrac{\omega-\theta}{2}\right)\right\}}{(n-m+1)\sin\left(\dfrac{\omega-\theta}{2}\right)} e^{-i\frac{(n+m)(\omega-\theta)}{2}} d\theta,$$

a good example of a solution which can be rather less than informative. A rather simpler way of gauging the approximation is to look at the numerical results. Let us look at our example where we want

$$\Gamma(\omega) = \begin{cases} 0 & |\omega| < \omega_0 \\ 1 & |\omega| \geq \omega_0 \end{cases},$$

so the Fourier coefficients are

$$c_j = \frac{1}{2\pi}\int_{-\pi}^{\pi}\Gamma(\omega)e^{ij\omega}\,d\omega = \frac{1}{\pi}\int_0^{\pi}\Gamma(\omega)\cos(j\omega)\,d\omega$$

$$= \frac{1}{\pi}\int_{\omega_0}^{\pi}\cos(j\omega)\,d\omega = -\frac{\sin(j\omega_0)}{\pi j},$$

so choosing $\omega_0 = \pi/2$ for simplicity we have $c_0 = \frac{1}{2}$, $c_1 = 1/\pi$, $c_2 = 0$, $c_3 = 1/3\pi,\dots$. The result of using a five coefficient and a thirty coefficient filter are illustrated in Fig. 8.10.

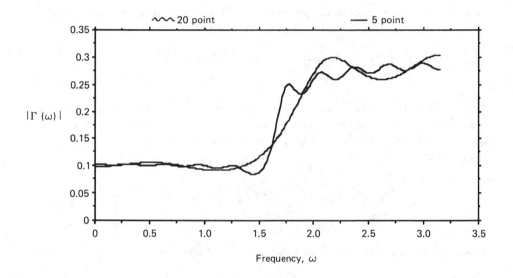

Fig. 8.10. Approximate high pass filters.

As we might expect, increasing the number of terms improves the approximation, but there are extra ripples in the transfer function. This is a consequence of the use of a truncated Fourier series and is known as the 'Gibbs phenomenon'. Bear in mind that we have chosen to approximate a discontinuous function by a continuous one, the worst possible case. It is possible to improve the filter performance by use of 'convergence factors', but this is rather technical and we refer the interested reader to the nice account in Bloomfield (1976).

8.7 FORECASTING

We take the opportunity at the end of this chapter to illustrate the central role of the spectrum in the analysis of stationary time series. We begin by looking at the problem of prediction. As in Chapter 2 we consider the expected mean square error of prediction one step ahead

$$\sigma_p^2 = E\left[\left\{X_{t+1} - X_{t+1|t}\right\}^2\right].$$

where $X_{t+1|t}$ is the optimum predictor at time t. The first question one might ask is under what conditions might σ_p^2 be zero? We know that if such a perfect prediction is possible, then $\{X_t\}$ is a deterministic series. In fact it is possible to go rather further and to show:

I   A necessary and sufficient condition for a stationary series to be deterministic is that

$$\int_{-\pi}^{\pi} \log f(\omega) \, d\omega = -\infty.$$

Indeed if the integral is bounded, then

$$\sigma_p^2 = \exp\left\{\frac{1}{2\pi}\int_{-\pi}^{\pi} \log 2\pi f(\omega) \, d\omega\right\}. \tag{8.19}$$

There is an even more detailed results as follows:

II   If

$$\int_{-\pi}^{\pi} \log f(\omega) \, d\omega > -\infty,$$

then

$$f(\omega) = \sigma_p^2 \left|A(e^{-i\omega})\right|^2,$$

where

$$A(e^{-i\omega}) = \sum_0^{\infty} a_j \, e^{-i\omega j}$$

is a *one sided* Fourier transform. This is equivalent to saying that the time series has an infinite moving average representation. Naturally we have assumed that the cumulative spectrum has a derivative $f(\omega)$. The equation (8.19) has been used as a means of estimating σ_p^2 by several authors, and the problem of finding $A(e^{-i\omega})$ has also been studied by many authors.

The prediction problem was solved by Kolmogorov (essentially the approach of Chapter 2) and Wiener at about the same time, but in rather different ways. Wiener's approach is rather different to the one that we have presented up to now, and we sketch the argument here. Interested readers should consult Whittle (1963) or Priestley (1981) for further details.

We start with some definitions, following Whittle (1963). Suppose

$$G(z) = \sum_{-\infty}^{\infty} g_j z^j,$$

then we define the one sided transforms

$$[G(z)]_+ = \sum_{0}^{\infty} g_j z^j, \quad \text{and} \quad [G(z)]_- = \sum_{-\infty}^{\infty} g_j z^j. \tag{8.20}$$

Wiener considered the predictor

$$X_{t+m|t} = \sum_{j=0}^{\infty} a_j X_{t-j}$$

for X_{t+m}, the mean squared error being

$$\sigma_p^2 = E\left[\left\{X_{t+m} - X_{t+m|t}\right\}^2\right].$$

One can expand this expression as

$$\gamma(0) - 2\sum_{j=0}^{\infty} a_j \gamma(m+j) + \sum_{j=0}^{\infty} \sum_{k=0}^{\infty} a_j a_k (j-k)$$

and then find equations

$$\sum_{j=0}^{\infty} a_j \gamma(k-j) = \gamma(k+m) \quad k = 0, 1, 2, \ldots \tag{8.21}$$

for a minimal solution. These are examples of Wiener–Hopf equations, but they are of limited use for us. We can get further by using the spectral representation in our expression for the mean square error. The error in prediction is just

$$X_{t+m} - X_{t+m|t} = \int_{-\pi}^{\pi} \left\{ e^{i(t+m)\omega} - A(e^{-i\omega})(e^{i\omega t}) \right\} dZ(\omega),$$

so then

$$\sigma_p^2 = \int_{-\pi}^{\pi} \left| e^{im\omega} - A(e^{-i\omega}) \right|^2 f(\omega) \, d\omega. \tag{8.22}$$

Our aim now is to find the function $A(\ )$ which will minimize the mean square error. Since for a non-deterministic series, $f(\omega) = \sigma^2 |\Gamma(e^{-i\omega})|^2$ we can write

$$\sigma_p^2 = \sigma^2 \int_{-\pi}^{\pi} \left| e^{im\omega} \Gamma(e^{-i\omega}) - A(e^{-i\omega})\Gamma(e^{-i\omega}) \right|^2 \, d\omega.$$

At this point we recall that Γ is a one sided (backward) transform, and so in consequence is $A(e^{-i\omega})\Gamma(e^{-i\omega})$. Suppose that we write

$$e^{im\omega}\Gamma(e^{-i\omega}) = [e^{-im\omega}\Gamma(e^{-i\omega})]_+ + [e^{-im\omega}\Gamma(e^{-i\omega})],$$

then it is possible to argue (after some algebra, see Priestley (1981, Chapter 10) for details) that

$$A(z) = \frac{[z^{-m}\Gamma(z)]_+}{\Gamma(z)} \qquad\qquad (8.23)$$

or

$$A(e^{-i\omega}) = \frac{\sum\limits_{k=0}^{\infty} e^{-i\omega k} \int_{-\pi}^{\pi} e^{i\theta(m+k)} \Gamma(e^{-i\theta})\, d\theta}{2\pi\Gamma(e^{-i\omega})}.$$

While these results give a solution to the prediction problem which is identical to the approach of Chapter 2, the thrust of the argument does appear to be less directly involved in the structure of the problem. The solutions, when in this form, do often give great insight, but one must first be able to factorize the spectrum, something which in itself is a difficult problem. We shall stick with our previous approach but leave the reader with an example of the Wiener approach.

Example 8

Suppose that we have a series $X_t = \varepsilon_t - \theta\varepsilon_{t-1}$ and we wish to make a one step prediction. In this case $f(\omega) = \sigma^2|1 - \theta e^{-i\omega}|^2/2$ so from (8.23)

$$A(z) = \frac{[z^{-m}\Gamma(z)]_+}{\Gamma(z)} = \frac{[z^{-1} - \theta]_+}{(1 - \theta z)} = -\theta(1 - \theta z)^{-1}$$

$$= -\theta\{1 + \theta z + (\theta z)^2 + (\theta z)^3 + \ldots\},$$

so the optimum predictor is $-\theta X_t - \theta^2 X_{t-1} - \theta^3 X_{t-2} - \ldots$, as we might expect. The derivation is rather slick, but the answer is exactly what we might obtain by other methods.

8.8 SAMPLING AND ALIASING

As we saw in the last chapter, sampling a continuous time series introduces an aliasing effect, and as we might expect this shows up in the spectrum. While we have avoided discussion of continuous time series it is quite possible to define autocorrelation and spectral functions for such series, provided that they are stationary. One major difference is that the spectrum of a continuous time series may be defined for all frequencies ω. If we sample such a continuous series we have an aliasing effect, which we summarize in the following theorem.

Theorem

Suppose that $\{X(t)\}$ is a continuous non-deterministic time series whose spectrum $f(\omega)$ is zero for $|\omega| > \Lambda$. Then the continuous series can be exactly reconstructed from its values at the points $\pi k/\Lambda$, $k = 0, \pm 1, \pm 2, \ldots$. For a proof and further details, see Koopmans (1974).

This shows us that if our original series has spectral power *outside* the frequency range $[-\Lambda, \Lambda]$, then some information is lost because of aliasing effects. Indeed if $X_t = X(t), t = 0, \pm\Delta t, \pm 2\Delta t,\ldots$, then the spectrum of the sample series $f_s(\omega)$ is given by

$$f_s(\omega) = \sum_{j=-\infty}^{\infty} f\left(\omega + \frac{2\pi j}{\Delta t}\right) \quad \omega \le \frac{\pi}{\Delta t};$$

see Fishman (1969, page 36). An experimenter is thus well advised to ensure that he finds a frequency value, say Λ, above which there is negligible power, that is the spectrum is negligible, and then chooses the sampling rate Δt to satisfy $\Delta t \le \pi/\Lambda$ or equivalently that the Nyquist frequency ω_N satisfies

$$\omega_N \ge \Lambda.$$

Any large frequency contributions exceeding the Nyquist frequency in the original (continuous) series will smear the lower frequencies in the spectrum of the sample series, causing distortion.

In the *discrete case* we can easily see the effect of sampling. Suppose we take a rather simple case where we have a stationary series $\{X_t\}$ with spectrum $f_x(\omega)$ and correlations $\gamma_x(k)$, and then define $Y_t = X_{3t}$.

Then

$$Y_t = \int_{-\pi}^{\pi} e^{i\omega t} \, dZ_y(\omega) = \int_{-\pi}^{\pi} e^{3i\omega t} \, dZ_x(\omega) = \int_{-3\pi}^{3\pi} e^{i\theta t} \, dZ_x\left(\frac{\theta}{3}\right),$$

and splitting up the range of the integral now gives

$$Y_t = \int_{-3\pi}^{-\pi} e^{i\theta t} \, dZ_x\left(\frac{\theta}{3}\right) + \int_{-\pi}^{\pi} e^{i\theta t} \, dZ_x\left(\frac{\theta}{3}\right) + \int_{\pi}^{3\pi} e^{i\theta t} \, dZ_x\left(\frac{\theta}{3}\right),$$

and changing the variable in the first and third integrals to make the limits $-\pi$ and π gives

$$Y_t = \int_{-\pi}^{\pi} e^{i\theta t} \, dZ_x\left(\frac{\theta + 2\pi}{3}\right) + \int_{-\pi}^{\pi} e^{i\theta t} \, dZ_x\left(\frac{\theta}{3}\right) + \int_{-\pi}^{\pi} e^{i\theta t} \, dZ_x\left(\frac{\theta - 2\pi}{3}\right),$$

hence

$$dZ_y(\omega) = dZ_x\left(\frac{\omega + 2\pi}{3}\right) + dZ_x\left(\frac{\omega}{3}\right) + dZ_x\left(\frac{\omega - 2\pi}{3}\right),$$

and in consequence

$$f_y(\omega) = \frac{1}{3}\left\{ f_x\left(\frac{\omega + 2\pi}{3}\right) + f_x\left(\frac{\omega}{3}\right) + f_x\left(\frac{\omega - 2\pi}{3}\right) \right\}.$$

This is easily extended for the case where $Y_t = X_{kt}$, provided that k is odd. The even case is rather more difficult; see Neave (1970) and Exercise 8.6. The moral is to take care that there is no real power in the spectrum which may reappear as an aliased component and mislead.

8.9 TRANSFORMATIONS AND THE COMBINATION OF SERIES

We conclude our survey of spectral theory with a brief look at the effects on the spectrum of transformations of series. We use transformations in a rather wide sense, and begin with an effect that is common in economic series, that of aggregation. Suppose that we have a series which is an aggregate of another, say

$$Y_t = \sum_{j=0}^{p} X_{t-j}.$$

What is the effect on the spectrum? From our knowledge of filters

$$f_y(\omega) = \left| \sum_{j=1}^{p} e^{-i\omega j} \right|^2 f_x(\omega),$$

so the transfer function is just

$$\Gamma(\omega) = \sum_{j=1}^{p} e^{-i\omega j} = e^{-i\omega p/2} \frac{\sin\left\{ \omega \left(\dfrac{p+1}{2} \right) \right\}}{\sin\left(\dfrac{\omega}{2} \right)}.$$

If we take a particular case, say $p = 11$, thus simulating the effect of annualizing monthly data, we have a filter gain of the form plotted in Fig. 8.11. This shows a marked drop off in high frequencies, rather as we would expect since we lose the detailed information on short term, that is, monthly effects.

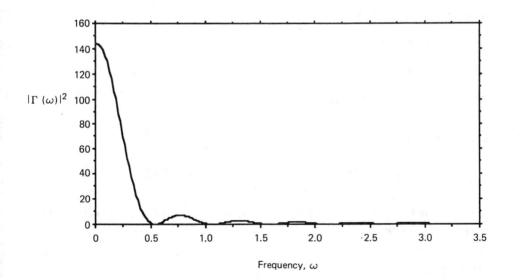

$|\Gamma(\omega)|^2$

Frequency, ω

Fig. 8.11. Aggregate filter, $p = 12$.

Another way of aggregating series is to add series with different correlation structures. Suppose that $\{X_t\}$ and $\{Y_t\}$ are independent time series, and that we define Z_t as the sum, that is, $Z_t = X_t + Y_t$. The correlation is easily evaluated, giving, with just a little abuse of notation, $\gamma_z(k) = \gamma_x(k) + \gamma_y(k)$. The spectra are thus related via $f_z(\omega) = f_x(\omega) + f_y(\omega)$. Suppose that we know that $\{X_t\}$ and $\{Y_t\}$ are both AR(1) models, that is $X_t = \alpha X_{t-1} + \varepsilon_t$ and $Y_t = \beta X_{t-1} + \eta_t$

$$f_z(\omega) = \frac{\sigma_x^2}{2\pi\left|1 - \alpha e^{i\omega}\right|^2} + \frac{\sigma_y^2}{2\pi\left|1 - \beta e^{i\omega}\right|^2}$$

$$= \frac{\sigma_x^2}{2\pi\{1 + \alpha^2 - 2\alpha\cos\omega\}} + \frac{\sigma_y^2}{2\pi\{1 + \beta^2 - 2\beta\cos\omega\}}.$$

This will, after multiplication, have the form of the spectrum of an ARMA(2, 1) model (see Chapter 5). This gives a relatively simple way of determining the model of the sums of series.

Once we move away from linear transformations of series we encounter considerable problems, and the general theory is complex. Some cases are possible; for example, suppose that we define

$$Y_t = X_t^2,$$

we can make some progress using a nice result due to Isserlis (1918) which assures us that for a multivariate normal family the moments of the random variables A, B, C, D satisfy

$$\mathrm{cov}(AB, CD) = E[AC]E[BD] + E[AD]E[BC]$$

for our case with $Y_t = X_t^2$ we have

$$\gamma_y(k) = \mathrm{cov}(X_t^2, X_{t-k}^2) = 2\gamma_x(k)^2.$$

Thus since

$$f_y(\omega) = \frac{1}{2\pi}\sum_{-\infty}^{\infty}\gamma_y(k)\cos(k\omega)$$

using the convolution theorem we have

$$f_y(\omega) = \frac{1}{2\pi}\sum_{-\infty}^{\infty}\gamma_x^2(k)\cos(k\omega) = 2\int_{-\pi}^{\pi}f_x(\omega - \lambda)f_x(\lambda)\,\mathrm{d}\lambda.$$

As we indicated, this is not a particularly easy form to handle, but it does enable us to at least attack the problem.

EXERCISES

(1) Suppose the series $\{X_t\}$ is defined by

$$X_t = \sum_{k=1}^{n} a_k \cos(\omega_k t + \phi_k)$$

where n, A_k, ω_k, $k = 1, 2,..., n$, are known constants and the ϕ_k, $k = 1, 2,..., n$ are independent random variables having a uniform distribution on $[-\pi, \pi]$.

Assuming that

$$\rho_s = \frac{\sum_{k=1}^{n} \left(\frac{1}{2} A_k\right)^2 \cos \omega_k s}{\sum_{k=1}^{n} \left(\frac{1}{2} A_k\right)^2} \qquad s = ..., -1, 0, 1, 2 ...$$

show that the cumulative spectrum $F(\omega)$ is a step function with jumps at ω_k, $k = 1, 2,..., n$. What are the magnitude of the jumps?

(2) The spectrum of $\{X_t\}$ is known to be

$$F(\omega) = \begin{cases} 0 & \omega < 0 \\ \frac{1}{2} & \omega \geq 0 \end{cases}.$$

Suggest a model for $\{X_t\}$.

(3) Assuming that $\{X_t\}$ is white noise, find the spectrum of $Y_t = e^{i\theta t} X_t$.

(4) Suppose that $X_t = \alpha X_{t-1} + \varepsilon_t$, where $\{\varepsilon_t\}$ is zero mean white noise and $Y_t = \beta Y_{t-1} - X_t$. Find the spectrum of $\{Y_t\}$ when

(i) $\alpha = 0$
(ii) $\alpha = \beta$
(iii) $\alpha \neq \beta$, $\alpha \neq 0$, and $\beta \neq 0$
(iv) $\alpha \neq 1$ and $\beta = 1$.

(5) Suppose that

$$Y_t = \frac{1}{P} \sum_{j=0}^{P-1} X_{t-Qj},$$

where $\{X_t\}$ is a stationary zero mean process and P, Q are constants. Calculate the transfer function of the filter and sketch the gain when $P = 4$ and $Q = 6$.

An economist has a time series with a strong 3 monthly cycle. How should one use the above filter to remove such a cycle?

(6) $\{X_t\}$ is stationary with a zero mean. Define $\{Y_t\}$ as $Y_t = X_{2t}$. Show that the spectral density of $\{Y_t\}$ is given by

$$f_Y(\omega) = \frac{1}{2}\left\{ f_X\left(\frac{\omega}{2}\right) + f_X\left(\frac{\omega}{2} - \pi\right)\right\}.$$

When $X_t = \theta X_{t-1} + \varepsilon_t$, where $\{\varepsilon_t\}$ is zero mean white noise, find the spectral density of $\{X_t\}$. Hence obtain the spectral density of $Y_t = X_{2t}$ and from it deduce a model for $\{Y_t\}$. Check your solution by evaluating the $\{Y_t\}$ model in the time domain.

9

Estimation in the frequency domain

An approximate answer to the right problem is worth a good deal more than an exact answer to an approximate problem.

J. Tukey.

Having seen how one can use the frequency domain to our advantage in theoretical problems, we now turn our attention to the problems of estimation. Suppose that given a stationary series, we wish to look at the power spectrum

$$f(\omega) = \frac{1}{2\pi} \sum_{s=-\infty}^{\infty} \gamma(s)\cos(s\omega). \tag{9.1}$$

An obvious approach is to replace the autocorrelations by their estimates $c(s)$, giving

$$\hat{f}(\omega) = \frac{1}{2\pi} \sum_{s=-m}^{m} c(s)\cos(s\omega)$$

where m is some suitable number of autocorrelations. At most m could be the number of observations minus one. This estimate is just a disguised version of the *periodogram*

$$I(\omega) = \frac{1}{N}\left| \sum_{t=1}^{N} X_t e^{-i\omega t} \right|^2,$$

since, as we shall see,

$$2\pi f(\omega) = \frac{1}{N}\left| \sum_{t=1}^{N} X_t e^{-i\omega t} \right|^2.$$

Sadly it is also known that this 'periodogram estimate' is not a very good one. It has several drawbacks as an estimate of the spectrum, the main one being that it is an erratic fluctuating function since, as we shall see, it is not a consistent estimator. The periodograms of a uniform noise series of length 100 and of a series comprising the number of Foxes trapped is plotted in Figs 9.1 and 9.2

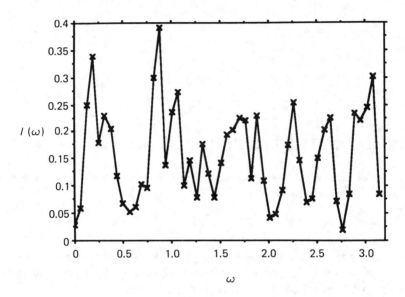

Fig. 9.1. Periodogram of noise.

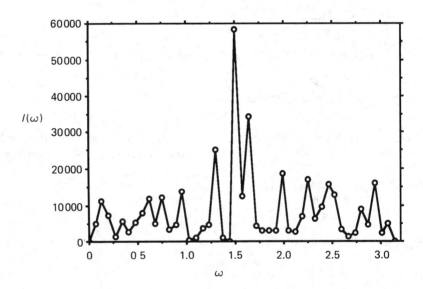

Fig. 9.2. Periodogram of Fox data.

As we can see, there is considerable variation, although a large peak is visible in the Fox periodogram.

Despite the variability of the periodogram it nevertheless has rather nice distributional properties, and in consequence is very useful. What is more, as we shall see, it is a thinly disguised DFT of the observed series. We will look at it in rather more detail in the next section. The reader who wishes to take our claims at face value may prefer to turn to the summary at the end of section 9.1.

9.1 THE PERIODOGRAM

Suppose we define the periodogram $I_N(\omega)$ as

$$I_N(\omega) = \frac{1}{N}\left|\sum_1^N X_t e^{-i\omega t}\right|^2,$$

(9.2)

then since

$$\left|\sum_1^N X_t e^{-i\omega t}\right|^2 = \sum_r \sum_s X_r X_s e^{-\omega(r-s)}$$

we have, on collecting up the terms,

$$\frac{1}{N}\left|\sum_1^N X_t e^{-i\omega t}\right|^2 = 2\sum_1^{N-1}\left\{\frac{N-k}{N}\right\}c_u(k)\cos(\omega k) + c_u(0)$$

where $c_u(k)$ is the unbiased estimate of the autocovariance at lag k, viz.

$$c_u(k) = \frac{1}{N-k}\sum_{s=1}^{N-k} X_s X_{s+k} \qquad k \geq 0.$$

This can be seen most easily in the tableaux

$$
\begin{array}{llll}
X_1 X_1 & X_1 X_2 e^{-i\omega} & \ldots & X_1 X_N e^{-i(N-1)\omega} \\
X_2 X_1 e^{i\omega} & X_2 X_2 & \ldots & X_2 X_N e^{-i(N-2)\omega} \\
X_3 X_1 e^{2i\omega} & X_3 X_2 e^{i\omega} & \ldots & X_2 X_N e^{-i(N-2)\omega} \\
& & \ldots & \\
X_N X_1 e^{(N-1)i\omega} & X_N X_2 e^{i(N-2)\omega} & \ldots & X_N X_N
\end{array}
$$

For N of reasonable size, $c(s) \approx c_u(s)$, and so

$$I_N(\omega) = \frac{1}{N}\left|\sum_1^N X_t e^{-i\omega t}\right|^2 = 2\pi\hat{f}(\omega) = \sum_{s=-N-1}^{N-1} c(s)\cos(s\omega)$$

To investigate the distribution of the periodogram let us begin with the simplest case, the periodogram of a white noise series, say, and for an ω which is a multiple of $2\pi/N$.

$$I_N(\omega, \varepsilon) = \frac{1}{N}\left|\sum_1^N \varepsilon_t e^{-i\omega t}\right|^2,$$

then

$$\left|\sum_1^N X_t e^{-i\omega t}\right|^2 = \left\{\sum_1^N \varepsilon_t \cos(\omega t)\right\}^2 + \left\{\sum_1^N \varepsilon_t \sin(\omega t)\right\}^2.$$

Now let

$$A(\omega) = \sum_1^N \varepsilon_t \cos(\omega t) \quad \text{and} \quad B(\omega) = \sum_1^N \varepsilon_t \sin(\omega t),$$

then as the noise has zero mean we have

$$E[A(\omega)] = E[B(\omega)] = 0,$$

while using our finite sums

$$\text{var}(A(\omega)) = \text{var}(B(\omega)) = \frac{N\sigma^2}{2}$$

while $A(\omega)$ and $B(\omega)$ are *uncorrelated*. This takes a little algebra. If we appeal, for simple fixed ω, to the central limit theorem then we can conclude that $A(\omega)$ and $B(\omega)$ are approximately normal. Now the periodogram is the sum of squares of two approximately normal and uncorrelated variables, so it seems not unreasonable to assume that $(2/\sigma^2)I_N(\omega, \varepsilon)$ is chi-squared with two degrees of freedom. Notice that at the ends of the ranges we have only one sum to square, and the distribution is chi-square with just one degree of freedom. This heuristic argument can be made quite precise!

This is all very well for noise, but what about a series with some correlation structure? Suppose that $\{X_t\}$ is stationary with zero mean, then the periodogram is

$$I_N(\omega, x) = \frac{1}{N}\left|\sum_1^N X_t e^{-i\omega t}\right|^2.$$

Since $\{X_t\}$ is stationary, we can write it as an infinite moving average

$$X_t = \sum_{j=0}^{\infty} b_j \varepsilon_{t-j}$$

since as you may recall this is always possible for a stationary non-deterministic process. Now

$$I_N(\omega, \varepsilon) = \frac{1}{N} \left| \sum_1^N \varepsilon_t e^{-i\omega t} \right|^2 ,$$

so

$$I_N(\omega, x) = \frac{1}{N} \left| \sum_{j=0}^{\infty} \sum_{t=1}^{N} b_j \, \varepsilon_{t-j} e^{-i\omega t} \right|^2 ,$$

which we may approximate, after some algebra, to

$$\frac{1}{N} \left| \sum_{j=0}^{\infty} b_j e^{-i\omega j} \right|^2 I_N(\omega, \varepsilon),$$

hence

$$I_N(\omega, x) \approx 2\pi f(\omega) I_N(\omega, \varepsilon). \tag{9.3}$$

since

$$f(\omega) = \frac{\sigma^2}{2\pi} \left| \sum_{j=0}^{N} b_j e^{-i\omega j} \right|^2 .$$

Thus we may deduce that the variance of $I_N(\omega, x)$ *does not tend* zero as N increases, and in consequence $I_N(\omega, x)$ is *not* a consistent estimator of $f(\omega)$. We can summarize the properties of the periodogram as follows.

Properties of the periodogram

If $\{X_t\}$ is stationary mean μ with an absolutely convergent covariance function, then as $N \to \infty$

(1) $E[I_N(\omega)] \to 2\pi f(\omega)$ $\omega \neq 0$

   $E[I_N(\omega)] \to 2\pi f(0) + N\mu^2$ $\omega = 0$

(2) $I_N(\omega, x) \approx 2\pi f(\omega) I_N(\omega, \varepsilon)$

(3) $I_N(\omega_1), I_N(\omega_2),..., I_N(\omega_k)$ are independent for distinct Fourier frequencies $\omega_1...., \omega_k$.

(4) $I_N(\omega)/[\pi f(\omega)]$ is distributed as χ^2 with two degrees of freedom when $\omega \neq 0, \pi$ and as χ^2 with one degree of freedom at the end points, 0 and π. This means that $I_N(\omega)$ is exponential mean $2\pi f(\omega)$, where $\omega \neq 0, \pi$.

NB Take care, as definitions of the periodogram do vary!

Series with means

It seems clear that most series will have a non-zero mean, and an obvious approach is then to work with the mean removed series $Y_t = X_t - \overline{X}$. This causes slight problems for the periodogram at zero frequency, since

$$I_N(0,x) = \frac{1}{N}\left|\sum_1^N (X_i - \overline{X})\right|^2 = 0. \tag{9.4}$$

There are two possibilities: one can either use the covariance expression to estimate the periodogram at zero frequency or use the periodic nature of the definition. Thus we might set

$$I_N(\omega_0,x) = I_N(\omega_1,x)$$

and then, using the average,

$$\overline{I}_N(\omega_0,x) = \tfrac{1}{5}[I_N(\omega_{-2},x) + I_N(\omega_{-1},x) + I_N(\omega_0,x) + I_N(\omega_1,x) + I_N(\omega_2,x)],$$

and using the periodic property we have

$$\overline{I}_N(\omega_0,x) = \tfrac{1}{5}[I_N(\omega_0,x) + 2I_N(\omega_1,x) + 2I_N(\omega_2,x)],$$

which becomes

$$\overline{I}_N(\omega_0,x) = \tfrac{1}{5}[3I_N(\omega_1,x) + 2I_N(\omega_2,x)].$$

A similar trick can be used at other frequencies.

9.2 APPLICATIONS OF THE PERIODOGRAM

Perhaps the main reason for initial interest in the periodogram was its value in the detection of periodicities. Recall that the DFT of a sinusoid with period p gives a large peak at the corresponding frequency, so that we expect a jump in the periodogram at frequency p. Thus if we look at the sunspot periodogram, there is a peak at around frequency $2\pi/10$ or π/s, angular, (or $\frac{1}{10}$), i.e. $k = 10$, as can be seen in Fig. 9.3.

The actual values of I_N are in order of frequency

0	8459.9512	8688.3291	255.7898	1099.3683
291.6404	354.3439	6030.2944	4463.1904	9515.7939
13663.6240	1192.7418	7552.8057	800.0388	1390.6996
100.9256	231.3764	1186.1600	786.2261	312.5396
153.5964	543.6401	438.7755	293.6582	332.5356
8.5699	262.9199	96.8114	28.8712	50.4806
4.8045	67.8224	38.9794	50.9368	136.9395
1.0063	32.8274	45.1697	0.7913	1.5814
7.9836	11.0189	5.5124	7.1539	4.1187
15.1212	19.7161	36.0719	14.0139	6.7716

Note that the mean was removed!

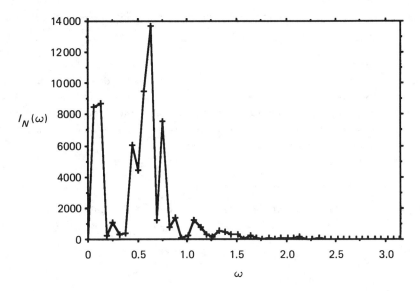

Fig. 9.3. Periodogram of sunspots (short series).

The periodogram is, however, an erratic and peaky function, and in consequence we may have problems in deciding if any given peak is real. A test for just this problem was devised by Fisher, and works as follows.

Assume that the series is noise plus a mean level and suppose, for simplicity, that we exclude frequencies 0, π, and let $E_k = I_N(\omega_k)/[\pi f(\omega_k)]$, $k = 1, 2, \ldots, m$, for some suitable value m. Since the E_k are independent, each having a chi-squared distribution, then we can find the distribution of $\sum_1^m E_k$. Given that, say, E_j is the largest peak, then we compute $M_j = E_j \bigg/ \sum_1^m E_k$.

Fisher (1929) showed that

$$P(M_k > x) = \sum_{j=1}^{k} (-1)^{j-1} \binom{m}{j} (1 - jx)^{m-1};$$

where $\binom{m}{j}$ denotes a combination; for details, see Wilks (1962). We will discuss alternatives later in this section. For the sunspots, the maximum is 13663.624 at lag 10, and the sum of the non-zero frequencies is 67768.9, giving $M_k = 0.20$. Then, $P(M_k > 0.20) = 0.001$, indicating a seasonal effect. Here we have calculated the probability, but tables of the statistic are available.

This conclusion is not quite so clear cut as you might think, since our test assumes for the null hypothesis that the series is *noise*. In the case of the sunspots we do not known if this is true (it is not), and so we need to modify our procedure. See, for example, Priestley (1981), Chapter 8.

A test for a white noise

Testing to see if a series is white noise is a well known and rather difficult problem. The principal difficulty is that the alternatives to white noise can be so different. Many tests have been devised, especially by those who test random number generators, and the literature provides grim warnings of the possibilities of failure. A rather neat test based on the periodogram is possible, and works as follows.

If a series $\{X_t\}$ is noise, then if we consider the general linear form

$$X_t = \varepsilon_t + b_1 \varepsilon_{t-1} + b_2 \varepsilon_{t-2} + b_3 \varepsilon_{t-3} + \ldots,$$

with $E[\varepsilon_t] = 0$ and $\mathrm{var}(\varepsilon_t) = \sigma^2$, then the hypothesis of randomness implies that $b_j = 0$ *for all j*. Since $\mathrm{var}(X_t) = \sigma^2 \{1 + b_1^2 + b_2^2 + b_3^2 + b_4^2 + \ldots\}$, this is equivalent to testing

$$H_0 : \sigma^2 = \mathrm{var}(X_t) \quad \text{against} \quad H_1 : \sigma^2 < \mathrm{var}(X_t).$$

Kolmogorov (1939) proved that

$$\log \sigma^2 = \frac{1}{2\pi} \int_{-\pi}^{\pi} \log 2\pi f(\omega)\, d\omega,$$

so a test can be based on the comparison of this with

$$\mathrm{var}(X_t) = \int_{-\pi}^{\pi} f(\omega)\, d\omega.$$

For details, see Davis & Jones (1968) or Janacek (1974).

By using asymptotic results we can derive a standard normal test statistic

$$z = \frac{\log s^2 - \log \sigma^2}{\sqrt{\dfrac{\phi'(1)}{n} - \phi'\left(\dfrac{N-1}{2}\right)}}$$

where

$$n = \left[\frac{N}{2}\right] \quad \text{and} \quad s^2 = \frac{1}{n} \sum_{1}^{n} I_N(\omega),$$

while

$$\log \sigma^2 = \frac{1}{n} \sum_{1}^{n} \log I_N(\omega) - c_1.$$

Here, $c_1 = \log 2 - \phi'(1)$ and $\phi(z)$ is the derivative of $\log \Gamma(z)$, the 'psi-gamma function'.

A rather more statistical approach is to ignore the end points, thus giving a set of periodogram values $I_N(\omega_i)$. If the series is random, then the spectrum should be flat and the periodograms should be *identically distributed*, so that we can now perform a likelihood ratio test using the fact that $Y_i = I_N(\omega_i)/[\pi f(\omega_i)]$ is chi squared with two degrees of freedom, so $I_N(\omega_i)$ is exponential with mean λ_i, say.

The likelihood ratio statistic is then

$$\frac{\Pi\{I_N(\omega_i)\}}{\left\{\sum_1^m \frac{I_N(\omega_i)}{m}\right\}^m},$$

which is essentially Bartlett's test for homogeneity of variances.

The above procedures and their refinements seem to be the most satisfactory of the available white noise tests, and we are surprised that they have not been more readily used.

9.3 ESTIMATING THE SPECTRUM: NON-PARAMETRIC ESTIMATES

As we have seen, the periodogram is not a very usable spectral estimate. One possibility is to modify the periodogram so as to remove the drawbacks which we have identified. This approach, which we shall refer to as the *non-parametric* or *windowed* approach, is well established, and we shall spend some time discussing the approach.

As the periodogram fluctuates wildly, one possibility is to smooth the function so as to make it more tractable. Thus a possible estimate is $h(\omega)$, where

$$h(\omega) = \frac{1}{2\pi} \int_{-\pi}^{\pi} W(\omega - \theta) I_N(\theta)\, d\theta \qquad (9.5)$$

where $W(\theta)$ is a suitably chosen function, usually with a sharp peak. By this we mean a function which is concentrated around zero and which approaches zero as $|\omega|$ becomes large. In fact since the periodogram is calculated at discrete frequency points we should really have a sum,

$$h(\omega) = \frac{1}{N} \sum_{j=1}^{N} W(\omega - \omega_j) I_N(\omega_j),$$

the idea being to average the periodogram ordinates near the frequency of interest ω. It is rather convenient, however, to use the integral form as a notation.

The problem now is to select the window function $W(\theta)$ so as to ensure a reasonable estimate. For a sharply peaked function we can approximate crudely as follows:

$$E[h(\omega)] \approx \frac{1}{2\pi} E[I_N(\omega)] \int_{-\pi}^{\pi} W(\theta)\, d\theta \approx f(\omega) \int_{-\pi}^{\pi} W(\theta)\, d\theta$$

$$\operatorname{var}(h(\omega)) \approx \frac{2\pi}{N} \int_{-\pi}^{\pi} W^2(\omega - \theta) f^2(\theta)\, d\theta$$

$$\operatorname{cov}(h(\omega) h(\phi)) \approx \frac{2\pi}{N} \int_{-\pi}^{\pi} W(\omega - \theta) W(\phi - \theta) f^2(\theta)\, d\theta.$$

We shall simply ignore any correction required for the end frequencies 0, π, at which the variances double.

In fact since we shall evaluate the periodogram only at the Fourier frequencies, it is, as we said above, more reasonable to express the equations above as Riemann sums, but the expressions are rather more messy.

From these equations it is now clear that for useful windows

$$\int_{-\pi}^{\pi} W(\theta)\, \mathrm{d}\theta = 1.$$

In addition since

$$\mathrm{var}(h(\omega)) \approx \frac{2\pi}{N}\int_{-\pi}^{\pi} W^2(\omega - \theta) f^2(\theta)\, \mathrm{d}\theta \approx \frac{2}{N} f^2(\omega)\int_{-\pi}^{\pi} W^2(\omega - \theta)\, \mathrm{d}\theta$$

we see that the variance of the estimate depends on the shape of the function W. There have been many suggestions as to the form of this function. Thus, for example, the Parzen or Frejer window, parameter M (Fig. 9.4).

$$W(\omega) = \frac{6}{\pi M^3}\left\{\frac{\sin\left(\dfrac{M\omega}{4}\right)}{\sin\left(\dfrac{\omega}{2}\right)}\right\}^4. \tag{9.6}$$

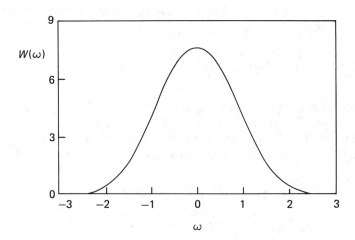

Fig. 9.4. Parzen window, $M = 4$.

These results can be sharpened quite considerably; see, for example, Priestley (1981). Thus, for example, the bias in the windowed estimate is approximately

$$\frac{1}{2}f''(\omega)\int_{-\pi}^{\pi}\omega^2 W(\omega)\, d\omega.$$

Concentrating the window around the frequency of interest gives the greatest weight near this frequency, which is generally a good idea. If the window has subsidiary peaks, so called 'side lobes', then the estimate at ω may be contaminated by effects at other frequencies. The resulting distortion is often called leakage. To get some feel for the parameters we require, we must define the peakedness or bandwidth of the window function. There are many definitions of bandwidth, all slightly different, but all giving much the same answer. To keep matters simple, we define the bandwidth B_w as the width of a rectangular window having the same maximum height as $W(\omega)$ and the same area. Thus

$$B_w = \frac{1}{W(0)}\int_{-\pi}^{\pi} W(\theta)\, d\theta,$$

but the area of the window is unity, so that

$$B_w = \frac{1}{W(0)}.$$

Thus we wish to make B_w small. Note that the window must be a periodic function, so we need only consider one part of the range. Other definitions of bandwidth are not uncommon. We stick to the above for simplicity. Since too much averaging of periodogram ordinates would smooth narrow peaks we aim to make our window bandwidth as small as is feasible. But as we shall see, it is not quite so simple. Note that we shall also refer to the *bandwidth* of an interesting peak in the spectrum, the definition being the area (to the first zeros) divided by the max.

The distribution of the weighted estimate is clearly a sum of chi-squared variables, and an approximation to the distribution is the chi-squared distribution itself. Since for chi-squared the degrees of freedom is $2(\mu/\sigma)^2$ we define the equivalent degrees of freedom (EDF) in the same way.

We take four of the many possible windows: the Unit, the Bartlett, the Tukey–Hanning, and the Parzen.

(1) Unit $\qquad\qquad W(\omega) = 1 \qquad -\left[\left(\frac{(M-1)}{2}\right)\right] \le \omega \le \left[\frac{M}{2}\right]$

(2) Bartlett $\qquad\qquad W(\omega) = \dfrac{1}{2\pi M}\dfrac{\sin^2\left(\dfrac{M\omega}{2}\right)}{\sin^2\left(\dfrac{\omega}{2}\right)}$

(3) Tukey–Hanning

$$W(\omega) = \frac{1}{2\pi} \left\{ \frac{\sin\left[\left(M + \frac{1}{2}\right)\omega\right]}{\sin\left(\frac{\omega}{2}\right)} \right.$$

$$\left. + \frac{1}{2}\left[\frac{\sin\left[\left(M + \frac{1}{2}\right)\left(\omega + \frac{\pi}{M}\right)\right]}{\sin\left(\frac{\omega}{2} - \frac{\pi}{M}\right)} + \frac{\sin\left[\left(M + \frac{1}{2}\right)\left(\omega - \frac{\pi}{M}\right)\right]}{\sin\left(\frac{\omega}{2} - \frac{\pi}{M}\right)} \right] \right\}$$

(4) Parzen $$W(\omega) = \frac{6}{\pi M^3} \left\{ \frac{\sin\left(\frac{M\omega}{4}\right)}{\sin\left(\frac{\omega}{2}\right)} \right\}^4 .$$

These have differing bandwidths etc., as can be seen from Table 9.1.

Table 9.1. Table of bandwidths.

Window	Bandwidth	Variance $f^2(\omega)$	EDF	Bias
Unit	$2\frac{\pi}{M}$	$2.00\frac{M}{T}$	$\frac{N}{M}$	no simple form
Bartlett	$2\frac{\pi}{M}$	$\frac{2M}{3N}$	$\frac{3N}{M}$	$-\frac{1}{M}f^{[1]}(\omega)$
Tukey	$\frac{2\pi}{M}$	$0.75\frac{M}{N}$	$2.7\frac{N}{M}$	$\frac{\pi^2}{4M^2}f''(\omega)$
Parzen	$\frac{8\pi}{3M}$	$0.54\frac{M}{N}$	$3.7\frac{N}{M}$	$\frac{6}{N^2}f''(\omega)$

Here, $f^{[1]}(\omega) = \frac{1}{2\pi}\sum_{k=-\infty}^{\infty}|k|c(k)\,e^{-i\omega k}$.

At first sight it would seem that the small bandwidth of the Unit window disqualifies the other windows. It does, however, have larger variance and its blockiness gives large side lobes. Bandwidth and variance cannot alone be criteria for the choice of window. The shape of the window is important if the average we choose is to give a *well resolved* estimate. By this we mean it does not change very much over the bandwidth of the window. There have been many arguments over the choice of window and the resulting estimate. We will choose to use the Parzen window out of choice, primarily because we find it reasonable and it must give non-zero estimates. This is not true of the commonly used Tukey–Hanning window. As we shall see when we discuss the FFT variants, the computational problems may determine the choice of window.

The choice of M is more problematical. Obviously we would like to make M as large as possible so as to decrease the bandwidth. If we do so, then the variance of the estimate at any frequency must increase. Thus we need to find some compromise value for M. The usual pragmatic approach is to try a value of M between $N/3$ and $N/5$ to select a suitable value. As M increases, the estimate becomes smoother, and we choose a value that seems 'smooth enough'. This is rather vague, but it essentially means that there is a peak in the spectrum which has the minimum bandwidth of interest, say B_f, that we wish to resolve. If we specify this, then we can choose the bandwidth of the smoothing window, say B_w, to fit this desired resolution. We require $B_w < B_f$ and we take as a reasonable choice $B_w = \frac{1}{2}B_f$.

Without a minimum bandwidth B_f, any choice of the parameter M is somewhat arbitrary. It is important to realize that for a fixed length of realization the requirements of bandwidth and variance are contradictory. If one decreases, the other increases, and since the amount of information contained in any data segment is finite, this is only reasonable, and we need to come to some sensible compromise. This is exactly the same as the problems of statistical testing, where one has two error probabilities. In the optimal case one chooses the length of realization to achieve the required bandwidth and variance; this may not always be possible, in which case compromise is essential.

9.4 LAG WINDOWS

We can look at these estimates in a rather different light if we assume that

$$W(\omega) = \frac{1}{2\pi} \sum_{-\infty}^{\infty} \lambda_j \, e^{-i\omega j},$$

for in this case from Parseval's theorem

$$h(\omega) = \frac{1}{2\pi} \sum_{j=-M}^{M} \lambda_j c(j) \, e^{-i\omega j} \tag{9.7}$$

for some parameter $M < N$. As we see, this is a weighted sum of estimated autocorrelations, the weight sequence $\{\lambda_s\}$ being known as the *lag window*. For the windows we have discussed so far, the corresponding lag windows are given in Table 9.2.

We can, in consequence, think of the smoothed periodogram as a weighted sum of covariances, the trick being to choose a suitable sequence $\{\lambda_s\}$ or window $W(\omega)$. Parzen in a series of papers in the 1960s, see Parzen (1967), studied this form of estimator and derived some theory which gave an indication of the design parameters. Since we restrict ourselves to sequences having transforms, we will select M according to the properties of W.

Table 9.2. Comparison of lag windows.

Window	λ_s	
Unit	1	$\|s\| \leq M$
	0	$\|s\| \leq M$
Bartlett	$1 - \|s\|/M$	$\|s\| \leq M$
	0	$\|s\| > M$
Tukey–Hanning	$\frac{1}{2}\left(1 + \cos(\|s\|/M)\right)$	$\|s\| \leq M$
	0	$\|s\| > \mathrm{M}$
Parzen	$1 - 6\left(\|s\|/M\right)^2 + 6\left(\|s\|/M\right)^3$	$\|s\| \leq M/2$
	$2\left(1 - \|s\|/M\right)^3$	$M/2 \leq \|s\| < M$
	0	$\|s\| > M$

This lag window approach has fallen into disfavour, the main reason being a computational one. The periodogram is essentially a DFT, and in consequence can be computed very quickly by using an FFT. This being so, the obvious approach is to compute the periodogram and then to smooth it. Nevertheless the lag window approach does have some virtues, especially for short data lengths. Indeed we have often used this approach to compute spectra, even on a desktop machine. If one stores the sines and cosines it can prove to be quite efficient for shortish ($N < 300$) data lengths. The computations are much easier, and this may be important if one is using a macro in a package like MINITAB.

As we said above, since the 'square root of $I_N(\omega)$',

$$J(\omega) = \frac{1}{\sqrt{N}} \sum_0^N X_t \, e^{-i\omega t} \tag{9.8}$$

is essentially a DFT, it makes sense to compute the transformation and hence the periodogram by using an FFT. Given the periodogram, then a unit or similar window becomes attractive since we work directly with $W(\theta)$. The correlations can also be computed by using an FFT, since the autocovariances are just the Fourier transforms of the spectrum. Most available programs use the FFT approach, since it can be considerably faster. There are some practical problems, especially when N is not a nice product of powers of primes, say 2^n. In this case the computational advantage of the FFT is smaller. One possibility is to 'pad' the series with zeros in order to make N a 'nice number', viz.

$$Y_t = X_t \qquad t \leq N$$

$$Y_t = 0 \qquad t = N+1, N+2, \ldots, 2^n.$$

This brings in other complications, one of which is the 'ringing' introduced by the Fourier transform of the sharp corner created by the series going to zero.

9.5 SAMPLING PROPERTIES OF THE SMOOTHED SPECTRAL ESTIMATE

Given that the estimates we have considered are weighted sums of periodograms and the periodograms are independent chi-squared variables, we would expect to be able to approximate the distribution of our spectral estimates by a chi-squared distribution. It can be shown that the chi-squared approximation is a reasonable one, if not quite correct, and we can summarize the result as follows.

Theorem
1 The spectral estimate $h(\omega)$ has a distribution which is approximately chi-squared with ν degrees of freedom. More precisely, $h(\omega)/f(\omega)$ is $a\chi_\nu^2$. The *equivalent degrees of freedom* (EDF) ν is defined as

$$\nu = 2\frac{\{E[h(\omega)]\}^2}{\text{var}(h(\omega))},$$

with $a = 1/\nu$, since for a chi-squared variable with ν degrees of freedom the mean is ν and the variance 2ν. As can be seen from Table 9.1, the higher the degrees of freedom, the smaller the variance, and the greater the smoothing of the periodogram.
2 Spectral estimates at least one bandwidth apart will be assumed to be independent.

Given this approximate distribution, it is easy to produce confidence intervals for the $h(\omega)$. If we are given α, then we select the $\alpha/2$ quantiles of the chi-squared distribution with ν degrees of freedom, say

$$p(\chi^2 \le a) = p(\chi^2 \ge b) = \frac{\alpha}{2},$$

then

$$p\left(a \le \nu\frac{h(\omega)}{f(\omega)} \le b\right) = \alpha,$$

so the $(1 - \alpha)100\%$ confidence interval is

$$\left\{\frac{\nu h(\omega)}{b}, \frac{\nu h(\omega)}{a}\right\}. \tag{9.9}$$

This gives a *pointwise* estimate rather than a confidence interval over a frequency band. For most cases this will suffice. One can find a band over all frequencies, and in this case the reader is referred to Priestley (1981, Chapter 6).

Some authors have used central limit theorem arguments to use a normal approximation for the distribution of $h(\omega)$. In the limit, one can 'prove' that $h(\omega_1), h(\omega_2)... h(\omega_k)$

have a joint normal distribution with variances and covariances of the forms shown earlier in this chapter. In this case the $(1 - \alpha)100\%$ confidence interval for $f(\omega)$ is

$$h(\omega)\left\{1 \pm z_{1-\alpha/2}\sqrt{\frac{2}{\nu}}\right\} \qquad (9.10)$$

where $z_{1-\alpha/2}$ is the $1 - \alpha/2$ quantile of the standard normal distribution.

The problem with these expressions is that they depend on the value of $f(\omega)$ at frequency ω. It is rather more satisfactory to consider $\log f(\omega)$. The corresponding confidence intervals to (9.9) are

$$\left\{\log h(\omega) + \log\left(\frac{\nu}{b}\right), \log h(\omega) + \log\left(\frac{\nu}{b}\right)\right\} \qquad (9.11)$$

have uniform width and are much easier to handle. There are advantages to the plotting of the log spectrum, and this is commonly done by engineers. One would often use such bands when searching the frequency range for spikes in the spectrum, a common method of finding periodicities.

9.6 SOME EXAMPLES

We looked at the Fox series of 93 annual observations. We use a Parzen window, and M values of $0.1N$, $0.2N$, and $0.3N$ i.e. 9, 18, and 28. The spectra obtained are plotted in Fig. 9.5. (NB. Unless we say so explicitly, each spectral plot is of a scaled spectrum.)

As we can see, as the truncation point decreases, we have, as we expect, a smoother estimate. The $0.1N$ seems rather too smooth, so we concentrate on the $0.2N$ value. We are being rather arbitrary, but having no background information it is not possible to set up any bandwidth arguments to select the appropriate smoothness. We have an apparent peak at $\omega = 1.5709$ and a subsidiary one at $\omega = 2.4588$.

Now frequency $\omega = 1.5709$ or $f = 0.251$ means an effect of period 3.98, say 4 years. If we use a filter to remove this 4 yearly cycle, we have Fig. 9.6. Here it is clear that the peak has vanished and the seasonal effects have been removed by the filter. The blip at $\omega = 2.4588$, period 2.6, remains.

If we select the 20% truncation point $(M = 0.2N)$ we may then add the chi-squared confidence intervals. In this case the equivalent degrees of freedom is $3.7\,N/M = 3.7*5 = 18.5 \approx 19$, and the 95% confidence interval (Fig. 9.7) is

$$\left\{\frac{19h(\omega)}{32.85}, \frac{19h(\omega)}{8.907}\right\}.$$

Other truncation points are easily catered for.

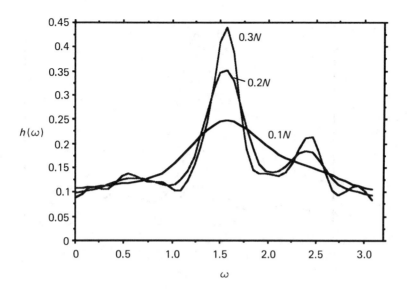

Fig. 9.5. Spectra using a Parzen window and 3 truncation points.

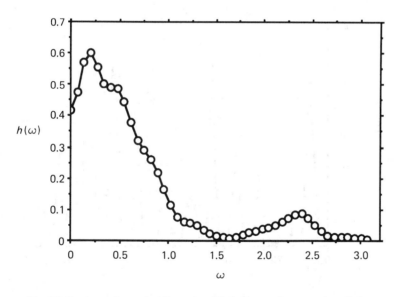

Fig. 9.6. Spectrum of smoothed Fox series with 4 point moving average applied.

Lynx series

We now consider a famous series, the number of lynx trapped per year in the Mackenzie River region of Northern Canada. There are 114 successive observations as reported by Campbell & Walker (1977), and these are displayed in Fig. 9.8 and correlations in Fig.

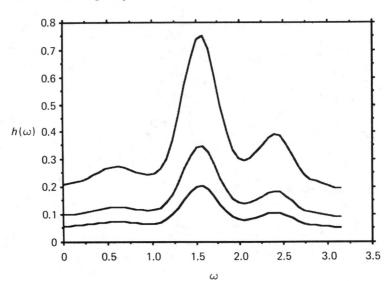

Fig. 9.7. 95% chi-squared confidence intervals.

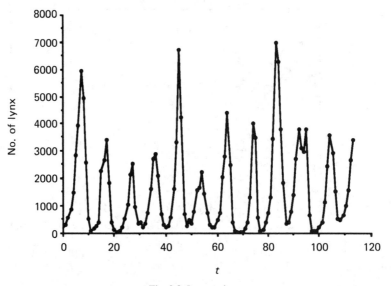

Fig. 9.8. Lynx series.

9.10. As is fairly obvious, the data appear to have a strong cyclic component, and the spectrum shows a distinct peak at $\omega = 0.6732$ corresponding to a period of 9.3 (Fig. 9.9).

To investigate further, we see that if we take a 10 point moving average, we would expect to eliminate the sharp peak (Fig. 9.9), and as we see from the spectrum of the moving average, the sharp peak is removed (Fig. 9.11). The resulting process has most

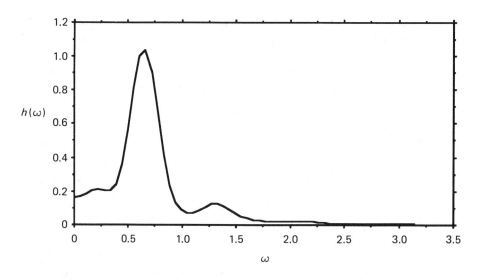

Fig. 9.9. Spectrum of lynx series.

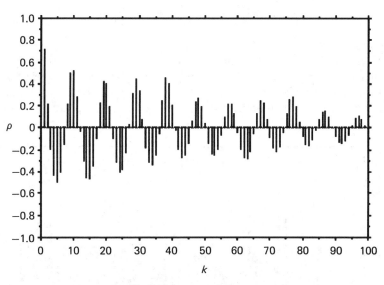

Fig. 9.10. Lynx correlations.

power in the lower frequencies, and as we might expect, as it will be a good deal smoother. The spectral shape might tempt one to suggest a purely sinusoidal model, say

$$X_t = A + B\cos\left\{\left(\frac{2\pi t}{9.63}\right)\right\} + C\cos\left\{\left(\frac{2\pi t}{9.63}\right)\right\} + \varepsilon_t$$

where ε_t is noise, and A, B, and C are unknown constants. This has been proposed by several authors, and an excellent description can be found in Campbell & Walker (1977).

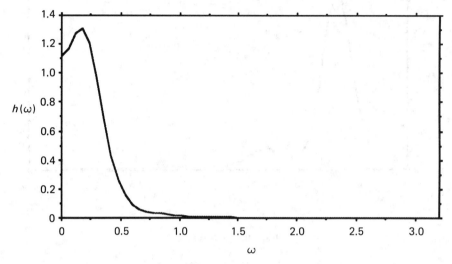

Fig. 9.11. Spectrum of moving average of lynx series.

Rainfall series
249 observations of annual rainfall are shown in Fig. 9.12(a). The trace appears fairly random, and the Parzen spectrum (Fig. 9.12(b)) has a largish peak, but appears to have an erratic fluctuating appearance. The peak at $\omega = 2.614$ is equivalent to period $= 2.4$, perhaps this indicates some power here and a tentative two yearly effect.

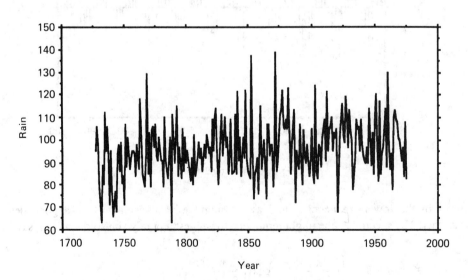

Fig.9.12(a). Annual rainfall.

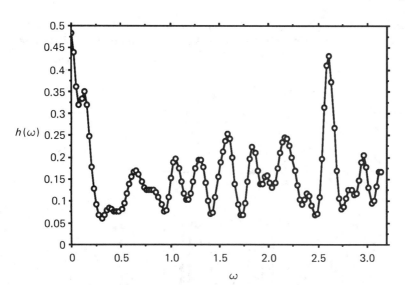

Fig. 9.12(b). Parzen spectrum of rainfall.

Wheat price

Beveridge (1921) introduced an annual time series index of wheat prices in Western and Central Europe for the period 1500–1869 (Fig. 9.13). His original intention was to detect cyclical movements, and later suggested a 15 year cycle. This data set has been studied by many workers.

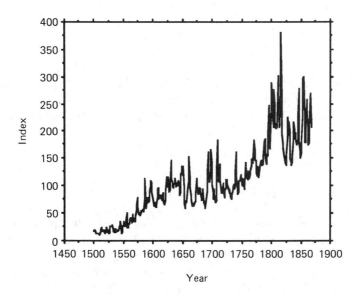

Fig. 9.13. Beveridge's original index.

The original index is clearly non-stationary, and to remove the non-stationary effects, Beveridge constructed an index of fluctuations, a trend-free index (Fig. 9.14) using

$$Y_t = \frac{X_t}{\dfrac{1}{31} \displaystyle\sum_{j=-15}^{15} X_{t-j}}.$$

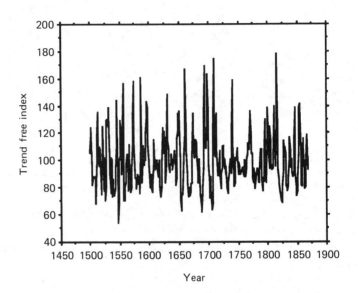

Fig. 9.14. Trend-free index.

The spectrum of the trend-free index can be seen in Fig. 9.15 with peaks at $\omega = 0.386$, 1.067, and 1.837, corresponding to periods of 16.3, 5.89 and 3.42 years. Granger & Hughes (1971) examined the effect of the trend removal filter and studied the series in some detail.

British industrial production
Crafts, Leybourne, & Mills (1989) constructed and analysed annual indices of British industrial production for the years 1700–1913. This series was also studied by Newbold & Agiaklogou (1991), and a Harvey model was fitted to the entire series in Chapter 6. The series is plotted in Fig. 9.16, and is clearly not stationary. A study of the histogram and of the series in general suggests that it may be more profitable to investigate the log of the index (Fig. 9.17), and we shall concentrate on this. To this end the log series was differenced, and the result (Fig. 9.18) appears reasonably stationary.

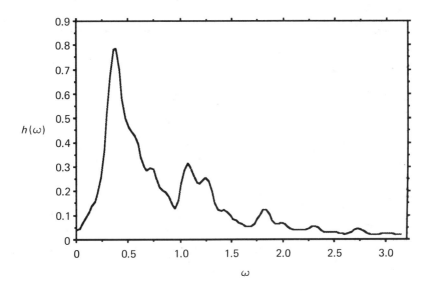

Fig. 9.15. Spectrum of wheat price index.

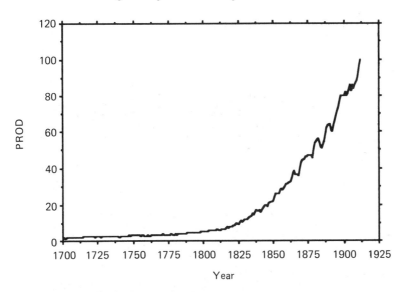

Fig. 9.16. Index of British industrial production.

Crafts, Leybourne, & Mills suggest that the series should be considered in three parts, 1700–83, which we call period 1, 1784–1814, period 2, and 1815–1913, period 3. The middle period, corresponding to the Napoleonic wars, we shall ignore, and we concentrate on periods 1 and 3. As a first comparison we overplot the two periods as in Fig. 9.19, and there appears to be some plausible reason for assuming a different model in each case.

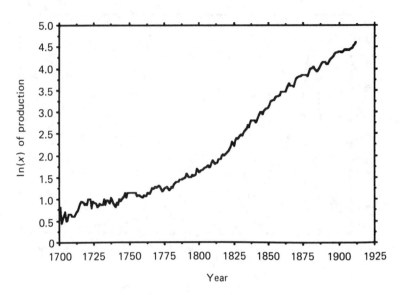

Fig. 9.17. Log of index of British industrial production.

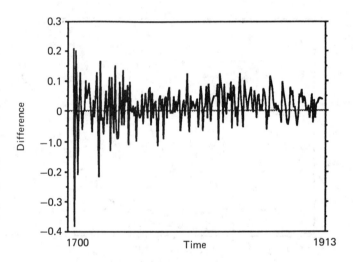

Fig. 9.18. Difference of ln(x) of industrial production.

As both series are clearly non-stationary, as before we take the first differences and examine the differenced series (Figs 9.20(a) and 9.20(b))

The power spectra are plotted in Figs 9.21 and 9.22. The two (normalized) spectra do look quite different. For period 1 we have a major peak at 2.15 which, with a series length of 83, indicates a period of 2.96, while period 3 has peaks at 0.785 and 2.356, which for a series of 97 corresponds to periods of 8.00 and 2.67. Since both series are short, we must view these peaks with a certain amount of scepticism.

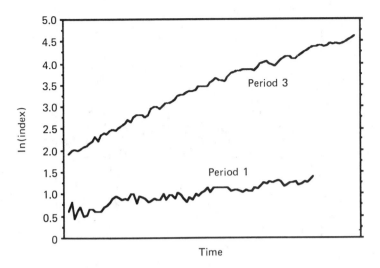

Fig. 9.19. Plot of ln (index) for the first and last periods.

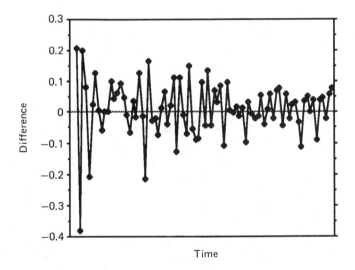

Fig. 9.20(a). Difference of period 1.

As is evident, the two sections exhibit quite different behaviour, the curious feature being the peaks at broadly similar periods. We are tempted to compare the values over these frequency ranges.

A fairly simple procedure is to look at the ratio of the spectral estimates. Since they are independent and chi-squared, we would expect the ratio to have an F distribution. For the Parzen window, we have used the equivalent degrees of freedom $3.7N/M$, which in our case is $3 \times 3.7 \sim 10$. Taking the five adjacent spectral values, that is, the two before the peak and the two after, *unscaled*, gives

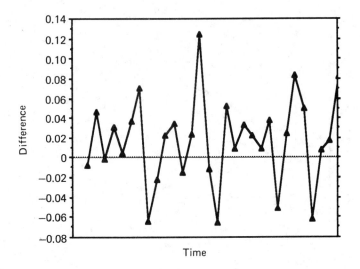

Fig. 9.20(b) Difference of period 2.

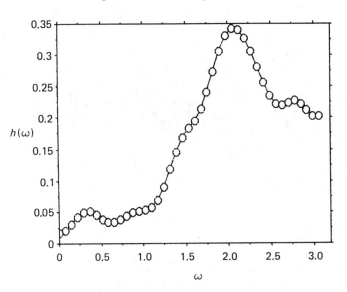

Fig. 9.21. Industrial production: first period.

Last data period	First data period	Ratio
0.049000	0.000405	120.978128
0.098000	0.000781	125.461195
0.147000	0.001326	110.900929
0.196000	0.001773	110.569239
0.245000	0.001830	133.901666

The ratios indicate that the spectral values are very different, although the pattern of a peak is similar, if shifted.

Newbold & Agiaklogou (1991) suggest ARIMA models for the series; the best fits, using MINITAB for their suggestions (the reader may wish to consult Chapter 5 §5) are summarized as

Period 1

       Final estimates of parameters

Type	Estimate	St. Dev.	t-ratio
MA 1	0.4922	0.0980	5.02

       Differencing: 1 regular difference
       No. of obs.: Original series 84, after differencing 83
       Residuals: SS =0.522939 (backforecasts excluded)
               MS = 0.006377 DF = 82
       Modified Box–Pierce chi-squared statistic

Lag	12	24	36	48
Chi-square	13.6 (DF = 11)	25.3 (DF = 23)	47.8 (DF = 35)	62.1 (DF = 47)

Period 3

       Final estimates of parameters

Type	Estimate	St. Dev.	t-ratio
AR 1	−0.4809	0.4917	−0.98
MA 1	−0.7161	0.4868	−1.47
MA 2	−0.2104	0.1620	−1.30
MA 3	−0.1723	0.1034	−1.67

       Differencing: 1 regular difference
       No. of obs.: Original series 98, after differencing 97
       Residuals: SS = 0.24296 (backforecasts excluded)
               MS = 0.002610 DF = 93

As suggested by the spectral analysis, the models are rather different, and there seems little reason to suspect any seasonal effect. This confirms the impression obtained from the spectral examination.

9.7 PARAMETRIC SPECTRAL ESTIMATES[†]

Since any non-deterministic time series can be written in the form of a general linear model

$$X_t = \sum_{j=0}^{\infty} \psi_j \varepsilon_{t-j},$$

the spectrum can be regarded as a function of some time domain model. Indeed, if we restrict ourselves to *rational spectra* of the form $|\theta(e^{-i\omega})/\phi(e^{-i\omega})|^2$ it seems only

---

† The reader may benefit from a prior reading of Chapter 5.

reasonable to estimate the parameters in the time domain. There are several approaches to this problem, and we shall discuss a few of these.

The first popular parametric estimate for the spectrum was the so called 'autoregressive estimates'. These were obtained by fitting an autoregressive model $\phi(B)X_t = \varepsilon_t$ and using as a spectral estimate

$$f(\omega) = \frac{\sigma^2}{2\pi|\phi(e^{-i\omega})|^2}$$

with the model estimates of σ and the autoregressive coefficients. A criterion is of course required to select the order of the autoregression, and AIC is often used. Parzen (1974) suggested an alternative CAT criterion defined as follows. For AIC, see Chapter 3 §5.

For each model, say of order m, based on a series of length N, we have a residual variance σ^2 which we might write as v_m. Then

$$\text{CAT}(m) = \frac{1}{N}\sum_{j=1}^{m}\frac{1}{v_j} - \frac{1}{v_m}$$

with $\text{CAT}(0) = -1 - 1/N$.

The model order we then select is that which minimizes the CAT. Another possibility proposed by Akaike (1969) is to select the order which minimizes the FPE (final prediction error) given by $(1 + (m + 1)/N)v_m$, while Rissanen (1983) suggests

$$\text{MDL}(m) = N \log v_m + m \log N.$$

There is little useful theory to help one choose a criterion. Jones (1976) suggests that the FPE underestimates the model order, while MDL and AIC are not consistent (statistically) as N tends to infinity. On balance we prefer AIC, but there appears to be little difference between the criteria. Note that the criteria may lead to different model orders. Experience shows that the procedures tend to select AR orders in the range $N/3$ to $N/2$ for reasonable results.

A relatively simple approach is to use the Yule–Walker equations and solve the system

$$\gamma(1) = \phi_1\gamma(0) + \phi_2\gamma(1) + \phi_3\gamma(2) + \ldots + \phi_p\gamma(p-1)$$
$$\gamma(2) = \phi_1\gamma(1) + \phi_2\gamma(0) + \phi_3\gamma(1) + \ldots + \phi_p\gamma(p-2)$$
$$\ldots$$
$$\gamma(k) = \phi_1\gamma(k-1) + \phi_2 + (k-2) + \gamma_3(k-3) + \ldots + \gamma_p\gamma(k-p)$$

for $k = 1, 2,\ldots$ to obtain estimates for the model

$$X_t = \phi_1 X_{t-1} + \phi_2 X_{t-2} + \phi_3 X_{t-3} + \ldots + \phi_p X_{t-p} + \varepsilon_t$$

and then to estimate σ^2 using the 'top' equation (see also § 5.2)

$$\gamma(0) = \phi_1\gamma(1) + \phi_2\gamma(2) + \phi_3\gamma(3) + \ldots + \phi_p\gamma(p) + \sigma^2.$$

While it is preferable to use available software, we have found that it is rather difficult to find a program which does not limit the AR order. Thus the scheme above has the virtue of simplicity. If one is constructing a purpose-built procedure, then naturally we might peruse an alternative. We illustrate our methods on the lynx series.

The log of the lynx series was the one chosen for analysis, and we obtained the values displayed in Table 9.3. As can be seen the model order suggested by AIC is 11, which is confirmed by the other criteria. The least squares estimates give a set of model parameters and an AR(11) model of the form

$$X_t - 1.139X_{t-1} + 0.508X_{t-2} - 0.213X_{t-3} + 0.270X_{t-4} - 0.113X_{t-5}$$
$$+ 0.124X_{t-6} - 0.068X_{t-7} + 0.040X_{t-8} - 0.134X_{t-9}$$
$$- 0.185X_{t-10} + 0.311X_{t-11} = \varepsilon_t$$

with residual variance 0.226. The resulting spectrum is then

$$f(\omega) = \frac{0.226}{2\pi}\left|1 - 1.139e^{-i\omega} + 0.508e^{-i2\omega}0.213e^{-i3\omega} \ldots + 0.311e^{-i11\omega}\right|^{-2},$$

which is quite spiked, as may be seen in Fig. 9.24 below. The contrast with the non-parametric estimate is characteristic of the method.

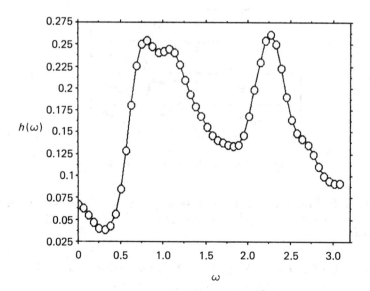

Fig. 9.22. Spectrum for industrial production, period 3.

Table 9.3. Log of lynx series.

Model order	AIC	FPE	CAT	σ^2
2	−132.231	0.314	−3.203211	0.303
3	−132.589	0.313	−3.212645	0.297
4	−135.541	0.305	−3.297717	0.284
5	−135.064	0.306	−3.282183	0.280
6	−133.882	0.309	−3.245351	0.278
7	−136.911	0.301	−3.335082	0.266
8	−136.520	0.302	−3.320686	0.262
9	−135.732	0.304	−3.293641	0.260
10	−137.784	0.299	−3.355086	0.251
11	*−147.378*	*0.275*	*−3.671070*	*0.226*
12	−146.422	0.277	−3.633710	0.224
13	−145.498	0.279	−3.597062	0.222
14	−143.645	0.284	−3.527979	0.222
15	−141.700	0.289	−3.455982	0.222
16	−141.377	0.290	−3.439364	0.219
17	−139.380	0.295	−3.365193	0.219
18	−139.410	0.295	−3.359866	0.215
19	−137.854	0.299	−3.299971	0.214
20	−136.479	0.303	−3.246141	0.213

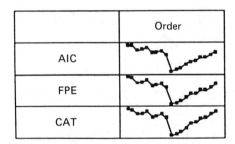

Fig. 9.23. Criteria plots versus order length.

For the trend-free Beveridge wheat price series, we have the values of Table 9.4, and the order 8 autoregressive model seems appropriate.

The model is

$$X_t - 0.711X_{t-1} + 0.338X_{t-2} - 0.041X_{t-3} + 0.300X_{t-4} - 0.005X_{t-5}$$
$$+ 0.620X_{t-6} + 0.027X_{t-7} + 0.137X_{t-8} = \varepsilon_t,$$

with a spectrum as shown in Fig. 9.25, which points up the peak around period 5.

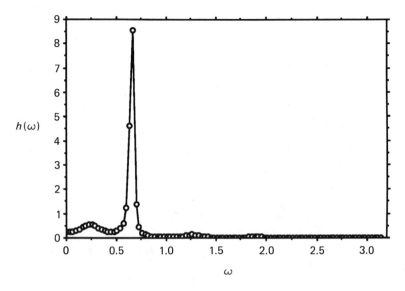

Fig. 9.24. AR spectrum for log (lynx) data.

Table 9.4. Trend-free Beveridge wheat prices.

Model order	AIC	FPE	CAT	σ^2
2	2054.262	257.768	−0.003880	254.996
3	2055.810	258.849	−0.003864	254.685
4	2057.417	259.976	−0.003847	254.415
5	2058.477	260.722	−0.003836	253.769
6	2055.922	258.928	−0.003862	250.664
7	2051.898	256.128	−0.003905	246.616
8	*2046.875*	*252.674*	*−0.003959*	*241.979*
9	2048.874	254.044	−0.003937	241.979
10	2050.675	255.284	−0.003917	241.848
11	2051.932	256.154	−0.003903	241.363
12	2052.474	256.531	−0.003897	240.414
13	2054.430	257.893	−0.003875	240.385
14	2056.296	259.198	−0.003855	240.298
15	2058.295	260.605	−0.003833	240.298
16	2059.331	261.337	−0.003821	239.672
17	2060.174	261.936	−0.003812	238.924
18	2061.450	262.845	−0.003797	238.457
19	2062.818	263.822	−0.003782	238.050
20	2064.816	265.254	−0.003760	238.049

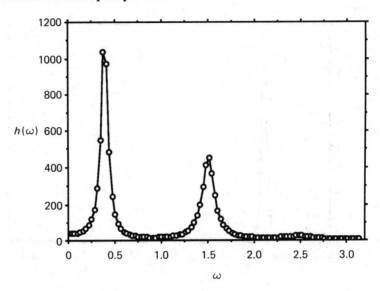

Fig. 9.25. AR spectrum wheat price index.

As one might expect, very sharp peaks are not always the order of the day, as can be seen from the AR spectrum of the sunspot (short) series in Fig. 9.26.

Many authors use the Durbin–Levinson recursions (Appendix 5.2) to compute the solutions to the equations, since this is rather faster. This can cause some problems near the boundaries of the stationary region where instabilities arise. In fact our lynx

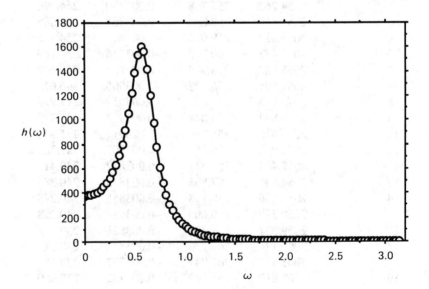

Fig. 9.26. Sunspot series AR(2) spectrum.

calculations were carried out on a desktop machine, and unless very large orders are contemplated, the direct approach appears rather more satisfactory.

Least squares is commonly used to estimate the parameters; however, a variant known as 'maximum entropy' spectral estimation due to Burg (1968) minimizes

$$\sum_{t=1}^{N-m}\left\{[X_t - \theta_1 X_{t+1} - \dots \theta_m X_{t+m}]^2 + [X_{t+m} - \theta_1 X_{t+m-1} - \theta_2 X_{t+m-2} \dots \theta_m X_t]^2\right\},$$

and the estimates are constrained to follow the Levinson recursion. This latter condition is dropped in some variants. There is some evidence—see Beamish & Priestley (1981)—that the unconstrained Burg method is rather better for cases with AR roots near the unit circle and for short series. The constrained version is known to suffer from 'line splitting', where a sharp peak in the spectrum is replaced by two or more closely spaced peaks. In addition the Burg estimate may give problems if the signal has a sinusoid, as it is sensitive to the phase of the sinusoid and a frequency dependent bias may be introduced.

There has been less work done on MA estimates of the spectrum of the form $F(\omega) = (\sigma^2/2\pi)|\theta(e^{-i\omega})|^2$. Brockwell & Davis (1985) give details and the distribution theory for such estimates. Given the time and effort we have expended on fitting the ARMA model it seems only reasonable to use the ARMA model to obtain the spectrum. This is easily done, since

$$f(\omega) = \frac{\sigma^2 \left|\theta(e^{-i\omega})\right|^2}{2\pi \left|\phi(e^{-i\omega})\right|^2}.$$

These estimates have been less popular, perhaps because they are less automatic. Other spectral techniques are available, but the main ones are as given above. Readers with more esoteric tastes might consult Priestley (1981).

At the end of the day we need to choose our method of estimation. The central question is the use to which the spectral estimates are to be put. As we tried to think of them as complementary to a time domain model, this does imply that a non-parametric approach is sensible. If the spectrum is the aim, and a time domain development is of little interest, then a non-AR estimate may be preferable.

9.8 ESTIMATION IN THE FREQUENCY DOMAIN

As we have seen, there can be problems in estimating coefficients in the time domain. In some circumstances estimation may be simpler in the frequency domain. After all, for any set of parameters θ, our likelihood function can be expressed in terms of the periodogram and the theoretical spectrum expressed in terms of θ. Such procedures often require less computation and have the advantage that they can be based on only part of the periodogram, thus enabling one to avoid undesirable features, such as seasonal fluctuations. On the other hand we do need an appreciable data set for efficiency.

We outline a simple approach to the estimation procedure. Suppose we have N observations from a stationary series $\{X_t\}$ with power spectrum $f(\omega, \theta)$ and we wish to estimate the parameter vector θ. We take the periodogram $I_N(\omega_j)$ at the frequencies $\omega_j = 2\pi j/N, j = 0, 1, 2,..., [N/2]$, and recall that if the ω_j correspond to the Fourier frequencies, then the values are independent. Indeed, if we ignore the end points, $Y_j = I_N(\omega_j)/[\pi f(\omega_j, \theta)]$ is chi-squared with two degrees of freedom. Then the pdf of $I_N(\omega_j)$ is

$$g(x) = \frac{1}{\pi f(\omega_j, \theta)} \exp\left\{ \frac{x}{\pi f(\omega_j, \theta)} \right\},$$

and so we may write the log-likelihood as

$$l(\theta) = \text{constant} - \sum \ln\left\{ f(\omega_j, \theta) \right\} - \sum \frac{I_N(\omega_j)}{\pi f(\omega_j, \theta)}.$$

The procedure for estimating the parameters is now conventional, using a suitable optimization procedure. Notice that the periodogram values are used as weights only in the likelihood, and in consequence only need to be used once. The form of the likelihood is quite simple, and good examples of its use are to be seen in Harvey (1989).

One nice property of the likelihood in the frequency domain is that one is not obliged to use the whole frequency range. Thus if the frequencies in a band are thought to be contaminated in some way—perhaps there is a cyclic term—then that frequency band can be omitted from the likelihood. The only drawback is the loss of data. This feature can be used to advantage in fitting long memory models, as we shall see in Chapter 10.

EXERCISES

(1) Using Parseval's theorem to evaluate

$$\int_{-\pi}^{\pi} W^2(\theta)\, d\theta.$$

Hence find the variance of the spectral estimate of $f(\omega)$ using a Parzen window. Show that the variance tends to zero as the sample length or the truncation point tends to infinity.

(2) Suppose we wish to estimate the spectrum of a time series and we know that there is a well defined peak in the spectrum whose bandwidth is $\pi/30$. Using this as the bandwidth of the spectral estimate we are to use, find the truncation point M for a sample of size N. If we decide that we can manage with a bandwidth of $\pi/20$, what value of M (in terms of N) is now required?

(3) In the problem in Exercise 2 we also impose the condition that the variance of the spectral estimate at $\pi/4$ must not exceed c, for some known constant c. Use this information to find the minimum sample length required in each case.

(4) The minimum mean square error of prediction σ^2 is known to satisfy

$$\ln(\sigma^2) = \frac{1}{2\pi} \int_{-\pi}^{\pi} \ln\{2\pi f(\omega)\} \, d\omega$$

for a non-deterministic series. Find an estimate of $\ln \sigma^2$ based on the periodogram, and assuming that one can use the central limit theorem (in fact one can), find the approximate distribution of your estimate.

(5) Using the distribution of the periodogram, devise a likelihood ratio test of

$$H_0: f(\omega) \equiv \text{constant}   \text{against}   H_1: f(\omega) \neq \text{constant}.$$

Suggest an extension of this test to decide between

$$H_0: f(\omega) \equiv f_0(\omega)   \text{against}   H_1: f(\omega) \neq f_0(\omega)$$

for some known $f_0(\omega)$. You may omit $\omega = 0, \pm\pi$ from the frequency range.

(6) Generate a time series using an AR(2) model designed to give a pseudo-cyclic effect. Estimate the spectrum using

(1)   an AR spectral estimator
(2)   a smoothed periodogram estimator.

(7) Repeat the procedure in Exercise 6, but in this case use a harmonic model of the form

$$X_t = 2\cos(\omega_1 t) + \cos(\omega_2 t) + \varepsilon_t$$

where ω_1 and ω_2 are suitably chosen constants.

(8) Using your series in Exercise 6, estimate the spectrum using the Parzen and Tukey windows with

(1)   comparable bandwidths
(2)   comparable variances.

10

Odds and ends: a taste of some more advanced topics

What we call the beginning is often the end
And to make an end is to make a beginning.
The end is where we start from.

T.S. Eliot, *Little Gidding*, Part 5.

10.1 INTRODUCTION

This chapter provides a brief introduction to some more advanced topics in time series analysis which are beyond the scope of this book. We have endeavoured to give the reader some idea of the nature of each topic and to provide references for further reading.

10.2 TRANSFORMATIONS

As in all areas of statistics, a little judicious data transformation can work wonders. We have already seen how we can remove both trend and seasonal effects, but we may encounter situations where the variance also changes with time. To overcome this common problem and 'stabilize' the variance, authors often try data transformations. The log transform $Y_t = \log X_t$ or the more general Box–Cox transformation

$$Y_t = \frac{(X_t + m)^\theta - 1}{\theta} \tag{10.1}$$

with parameters m and θ can be used to construct a series with more constant variance. Usually θ is constrained to lie between 0 and 1, and $\theta \to 0$ implies a log transformation. An example of this transformation has been seen in the industrial production figures described in Chapter 9. If the mean level of the series changes with time, the log transform is always worth a try. For more complex cases we attempt to find the transform which best allows us to fit a simple model to the transformed data. Thus a simple model could be fitted to the Y_t in (10.1), and the parameters m and θ chosen to minimize the residual sum of squares from this model. Thus for the last period (post-1815) of the industrial production series in Chapter 9 a log transformation is suggested. Applying the Box–Cox formula to the Rubella data of Montgomery & Johnson (1976) plotted in Fig. 10.1 we get suggested values of $\theta = 0.25$ and $m = 0$. We choose this transformation to stabilize the variance.

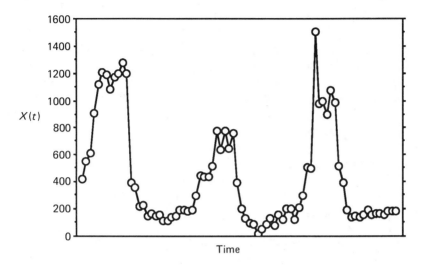

Fig. 10.1. Rubella cases.

Anderson (1982) goes rather further and suggests that both the transformation and the model should be estimated at the same time. This should cause no theoretical problem since the likelihood is available and numerical optimization can be used to estimate both the model and the transformation parameters. For a more comprehensive view, see Granger & Newbold (1986). If we have a series whose marginal distribution is known to be non-normal, then we can obviously fall back on the classic transformations long used by statisticians such as log or square root. The interested reader is well advised to consult McCullagh & Nelder (1989) or Harvey (1989).

In the case where the data appear to exhibit a particular (non-normal) marginal distribution, Janacek & Swift (1990, 1991) have proposed a two stage method of estimating the parameters of the transformation and the model and forecasting, using orthogonal polynomials.

10.3 COPING WITH MISSING VALUES

In practice it is quite possible that some of the data in a time series are missing. An observation may not be made at a particular time owing to faulty equipment, records may be lost, or a mistake may be made which cannot be rectified later. When one or more observations (which may be consecutive) are missing we would like to be able to estimate the model and also to obtain estimates of the missing data.

Suppose that we have N observations as usual, but that these have been observed at times $t_1, t_2,..., t_N$, where $0 < t_1 < t_2 < ... < t_N$ and all the t_τ's are integer. As before, the likelihood is the joint probability $f(X_1, X_2,..., X_N)$ regarded as a function of the unknown parameters $\boldsymbol{\theta}$ and is the product of the conditional distributions of each observation given the previous observations, that is,

$$L(\boldsymbol{\theta}) = \prod_{\tau=1}^{N} f(X_\tau | \mathbf{X}_{\tau-1}),$$

where $\mathbf{X}_\tau$ represents the observations up to and including X_τ.

The mean of the conditional distribution of X_τ given $X_{\tau-1}$ is the $t_\tau - t_{\tau-1}$ step forecast $X_{\tau|\tau-1}$ and its variance is the corresponding forecast error. When more than one observation is missing between $X_{\tau-1}$ and X_τ the step length $t_\tau - t_{\tau-1}$ will be greater than one.

When the model is in state space form and we are using the Kalman filter, the k-step predictor is $X_{t+k|t} = \mathbf{H}\boldsymbol{\phi}^k \mathbf{a}_t$ and has variance given by (4.18). Such predictors can be produced automatically by the Kalman filter recursions as follows. Suppose that X_{t-1} is observed but the observation at time t is missing. The prediction equations of the Kalman filter are still valid and give $\mathbf{a}_{t|t-1} = \boldsymbol{\phi}\mathbf{a}_{t-1}$ and prediction error variance

$$F_t = \mathbf{H}\mathbf{C}_{t|t-1}\mathbf{H}^{\mathrm{T}} + \sigma_\varepsilon^2.$$

As no observation is available at time t, the updating equations (4.12), (4.13) cannot be processed but can be replaced by $\mathbf{C}_t = \mathbf{C}_{t|t-1}$ and $\mathbf{a}_t = \mathbf{a}_{t|t-1}$. If a second consecutive missing observation is encountered, that is X_{t+1} is also missing, the prediction equations can be processed again to give

$$\mathbf{a}_{t+1|t} = \boldsymbol{\phi}\mathbf{a}_t = \boldsymbol{\phi}^2 \mathbf{a}_{t-1},$$

$$\mathbf{C}_{t+1|t} = \boldsymbol{\phi}\mathbf{C}_t\boldsymbol{\phi}^{\mathrm{T}} + \mathbf{K}\boldsymbol{\Sigma}\mathbf{K}^{\mathrm{T}}$$

$$= \boldsymbol{\phi}\mathbf{C}_{t|t-1}\boldsymbol{\phi}^{\mathrm{T}} + \mathbf{K}\boldsymbol{\Sigma}\mathbf{K}^{\mathrm{T}}$$

$$= \boldsymbol{\phi}(\boldsymbol{\phi}\mathbf{C}_{t-1}\boldsymbol{\phi}^{\mathrm{T}} + \mathbf{K}\boldsymbol{\Sigma}\mathbf{K}^{\mathrm{T}})\boldsymbol{\phi}^{\mathrm{T}} + \mathbf{K}\boldsymbol{\Sigma}\mathbf{K}^{\mathrm{T}}$$

which from (4.18) is the two step prediction error variance. This extends to any number of consecutive missing observations. When the next available observation X_τ becomes available, the updating equations can be calculated in the usual way, and the resultant V_τ and F_τ will represent the $t_\tau - t_{\tau-1}$ step prediction error and variance.

The log-likelihood of the series can therefore be written

$$\log L(\boldsymbol{\theta}) = -\frac{N}{2}\log 2\pi - \frac{1}{2}\sum_{\tau=1}^{N} \log F_\tau - \frac{1}{2}\sum_{\tau=1}^{N} \frac{V_\tau^2}{F_\tau}.$$

Notice that this is the same as (4.4) except that the prediction errors V_τ and their variances F_τ may be for multiple step predictions.

To summarize, the Kalman filter equations are easily adapted to cope with missing observations. When a missing observation is encountered at time t the prediction equations (4.5), (4.6) are processed as usual, but the updating equations (4.12), (4.13) are replaced by $\mathbf{C}_t = \mathbf{C}_{t|t-1}$ and $\mathbf{a}_t = \mathbf{a}_{t|t-1}$. The terms corresponding to missing observations are omitted from the log-likelihood.

We have already seen that a sensible way of choosing starting values for the Kalman recursions is to start with a large $\mathbf{C}_0$ matrix and an arbitrary $\mathbf{a}_0$ and omit the first d (where d is the state dimension) observations from the likelihood (section 4.4). Problems will arise if any of the first d observations are missing. Kohn & Ansley (1986) give a more general state space algorithm which can cope with such circumstances.

If lots of adjacent observations are missing from the series and the series is stationary, $\mathbf{a}_{t+j|t-1}$ will approach $\mathbf{a}_0$ as $j \to \infty$ and $\mathbf{C}_{t+j|t-1}$ will tend to the (unconditional) variance of $\mathbf{a}_0$. This mean and variance are the desirable starting values for a stationary series (see section 4.4), and so at the end of the missing block of data the recursions are in effect restarted as might be expected.

The second issue when data are missing is the estimation of the missing observations themselves. Again the Kalman recursions provide the solution. If the recursions have been run as described above we can use the resultant $\mathbf{a}_t$'s and $\mathbf{C}_t$'s in the smoothing equations (4.16), (4.17) to obtain estimates of the missing observations given all N observations. Other smoothing algorithms are available and may be more efficient when only a few data are missing; see Harvey & Pierce (1984).

Harvey (1989, page 326 onwards) gives a more detailed overview of the treatment of missing data, and discusses the implications for model selection and diagnostics. Priestley (1981, page 585) considers spectral estimation when there are missing observations.

10.4 INCORPORATING EXPLANATORY VARIABLES IN THE TIME SERIES MODEL

In our work so far we have always assumed that the time series of interest can be modelled in terms of some combination of a trend or seasonal component and past values of the series itself. Such a series is termed *autoprojective*. In reality, however, the series may also depend on values of one or more other time series. For instance, a monthly time series of the number of first-time mortgage advances may depend on the current interest rate and on the number of home building starts in the previous few months, as well as advances in recent months. The other variables required to explain the series of interest in this way are called *explanatory* or exogenous variables, as in regression.

Suppose that the values of the explanatory variables at time t are contained in the vector $\mathbf{z}_t$. The simplest way of incorporating these into the state space model is to assume that the relationship between the observed series and the explanatory variables is linear. The measurement equation of the state space model (4.1) now includes an additional term and becomes

$$X_t = \mathbf{H}\boldsymbol{\alpha}_t + \varepsilon_t + \mathbf{z}_t^{\mathrm{T}}\boldsymbol{\delta} \tag{10.2}$$

where $\boldsymbol{\delta}$ is a vector containing the coefficients of the explanatory variables and $\mathrm{var}(\varepsilon_t) = \sigma_\varepsilon^2$ as usual. For example, the structural time series model which is additive in the trend and seasonal components $X_t = \mu_t + \gamma_t + \varepsilon_t$ becomes $X_t = \mu_t + \gamma_t + \varepsilon_t + \mathbf{z}_t^{\mathrm{T}}\boldsymbol{\delta}$

when explanatory variables are included in this way. The state equations describe the generation of $\boldsymbol{\alpha}_t$ and remain the same as (4.2), that is,

$$\boldsymbol{\alpha}_t = \boldsymbol{\phi}\boldsymbol{\alpha}_{t-1} + \mathbf{K}\boldsymbol{\eta}_t \tag{10.3}$$

where the covariance matrix of $\boldsymbol{\eta}_t$ is $\boldsymbol{\Sigma}$.

Notice that our time series model with explanatory variables can be regarded as a regression model with autocorrelated error terms, and that if there is no autoprojective component then our model reduces to a linear regression.

The vector $\boldsymbol{\delta}$ usually contains unknown parameters, and needs to be estimated. Estimates of $\boldsymbol{\delta}$ can be obtained automatically as part of the Kalman filter procedure by defining an augmented state vector which incorporates $\boldsymbol{\delta}$ as follows. Let the augmented state be

$$\boldsymbol{\alpha}_t^+ = \begin{pmatrix} \boldsymbol{\alpha}_t \\ \boldsymbol{\delta}_t \end{pmatrix},$$

then the measurement equation (10.2) becomes

$$X_t = \left(\mathbf{H}\mathbf{z}_t^T \right)\boldsymbol{\alpha}_t^+ + \varepsilon_t$$

and the state equations (10.3) are augmented to

$$\begin{pmatrix} \boldsymbol{\alpha}_t \\ \boldsymbol{\delta}_t \end{pmatrix} = \begin{pmatrix} \boldsymbol{\phi} & \mathbf{0} \\ \mathbf{0} & \mathbf{I} \end{pmatrix}\begin{pmatrix} \boldsymbol{\alpha}_{t-1} \\ \boldsymbol{\delta}_{t-1} \end{pmatrix} + \begin{pmatrix} \boldsymbol{\eta}_t \\ \mathbf{0} \end{pmatrix}$$

where variance $(\varepsilon_t) = \sigma^2$ and the covariance matrix of

$$\begin{pmatrix} \boldsymbol{\eta}_t \\ \mathbf{0} \end{pmatrix} \quad \text{is} \quad \begin{pmatrix} \boldsymbol{\Sigma} & \mathbf{0} \\ \mathbf{0} & \mathbf{0} \end{pmatrix}.$$

Notice that the augmented state equations include the relation $\boldsymbol{\delta}_t = \boldsymbol{\delta}_{t-1}$, as we are assuming that the coefficient vector $\boldsymbol{\delta}$ is time invariant.

As the observation matrix of this augmented model includes $\mathbf{z}_t$, it is time varying. This does not present a problem, as the Kalman filter equations (4.5), (4.6), (4.8), (4.12), (4.13) remain valid so long as the appropriate observation matrix, say $\mathbf{H}_t$, is used in place of $\mathbf{H}$ at each iteration. (In fact the Kalman filter equations are valid so long as the parameter matrices $\mathbf{H}$, $\boldsymbol{\phi}$, $\mathbf{K}$, $\boldsymbol{\Sigma}$ are known at time t.)

The maximum likelihood estimators of the augmented model can therefore be found via Kalman in the usual way, and the final state estimate

$$\mathbf{a}_N^+ = \begin{pmatrix} \mathbf{a}_N \\ \mathbf{d}_N \end{pmatrix}$$

at the MLEs of the parameters will include $\mathbf{d}_N$, the minimum mean square estimate of $\boldsymbol{\delta}$ based on all the observations. The augmented model can be used directly for prediction, taking care that $\mathbf{H}_t$ is used to calculate forecasts of X_t. The corresponding prediction error variances will take into account the error attributable to the estimation of $\boldsymbol{\delta}$.

As in regression analysis the explanatory variables may take the form of dummy variables. A well known time series application requiring a crucial dummy variable is the study of the series of numbers of car drivers injured in road traffic accidents before and after the introduction of the seat belt law in the UK in 1983 (Harvey & Durbin 1986). The model includes a dummy variable which takes the value of zero before the introduction of the seat belt law and 1 afterwards.

10.5 MODELLING MORE THAN ONE TIME SERIES: THE TIME DOMAIN

All our work so far has been on univariate time series models: that is, we have been interested in the observation of only one variable X_t at each time t, even if we have employed another series as an explanatory variable as described in section 10.4. While such models are often quite adequate, two or more series may be interdependent, and our forecasts may improve when the series are considered together. When more than one time series is of interest, so that we observe two or more variables at each time t, such sets of data are called *multivariate*, *multiple*, or *vector* time series. We have already unwittingly met a model for such a series. Recall the state equation of the state space model (4.2) $\alpha_t = \phi \alpha_{t-1} + K \eta_t$. The state vector α_t is d-dimensional, and so if $d > 1$ the state equation is a vector time series model.

Many of the ideas of univariate modelling have a natural extension to multivariate models, although the analysis of multiple time series is much more complicated, and often the practicalities of application are difficult. We do not have the space here to do more than outline some approaches to the study of multiple series and to supply some references for further reading. Some key texts which include multiple models are Harvey (1989) for structural models, Priestley (1981) for spectral analysis, Granger & Newbold (1986) especially for bivariate series, and Box–Jenkins for transfer functions. Hannan (1970) includes much of the theory for multiple models.

Suppose, in general, that at time t we make an r-variate observation $X_t = (X_{1t}, X_{2t}, ..., X_{rt})^T$. As our emphasis has been on the state space model as a general class of time series model we will start by considering the multivariate state space model. The general state space model for such a multiple series X_t is

$$X_t = H \alpha_t + \epsilon_t \tag{10.4}$$

$$\alpha_t = \phi \alpha_{t-1} + K \eta_t \tag{10.5}$$

where again H, ϕ, K are parameter matrices. The measurement equation now requires that H is an $r \times d$ matrix, where d is the state dimension and ϵ_t is a vector white noise process with covariance matrix Σ_ϵ. The state equation (10.5) is exactly the same as (4.2) for the univariate case except that the state space noise η_t need have dimension no more than r for a stochastic, normally distributed model, so K is a $d \times r$ matrix. The covariance matrix of η_t is Σ.

The number of parameters in a multiple model can easily become prohibitively large, and so there is an even stronger case for identification than for univariate models. In section 4.3 we showed that we could linearly transform the state of a univariate model into $\alpha_t^* = T\alpha_t$, where T is a non-singular square matrix, to obtain an input–output equivalent model. The same argument applies to multiple models, that is, the model

$$X_t = H^*\alpha_t^* + \epsilon_t, \quad \alpha_t^* = \phi_t^*\alpha_{t-1}^* + \eta_t$$

where $H^* = HT^{-1}$, $\phi^* = T\phi T^{-1}$ and $K^* = TK$ is an equivalent system to (10.4), (10.5) in the sense that the same set of random noise 'inputs' η_t and ϵ_t will produce the same set of 'outputs' X_t. One model from each equivalence class can be chosen b y stipulating the structure, known as the *canonical* form of the matrices H, ϕ, K.

To describe such a canonical form the state vector is usually split into r partitions of $d_1, d_2,..., d_r$ elements respectively, where $d_1 + d_2 + ... + d_r = d$. For one such form the H matrix is

$$H = \begin{pmatrix} 1 & \vdots & 0 & \vdots & 0 & \vdots & ... & \vdots & 0 \\ L_{21} & \vdots & 1 & \vdots & 0 & \vdots & ... & \vdots & 0 \\ L_{31} & O & \vdots & L_{32} & O & \vdots & 1 & O & \vdots & ... & \vdots & 0 & O \\ \vdots & & \vdots & \vdots & & \vdots & \vdots & & \vdots & \vdots & \vdots \\ L_{r1} & \vdots & L_{r2} & \vdots & L_{r3} & \vdots & ... & \vdots & 1 \end{pmatrix} \quad (10.6)$$

where the first block contains d_1 columns, the second d_2, etc., and so on. The transition matrix ϕ is subdivided into blocks ϕ_{ij} which correspond to the partitioning of the state vector so ϕ_{ij} will have dimension $d_i \times d_j$. The i,jth block where $i \neq j$ takes the form

$$\begin{pmatrix} \phi_{ij1} & \\ \phi_{ij2} & O \\ \phi_{ij3} & \\ \vdots & \\ \phi_{ijd_i} & 0 & 0 & ... & 0 \end{pmatrix} \quad (10.7)$$

and the diagonal blocks have the form

$$\begin{pmatrix} \phi_{ii1} & \\ \phi_{ii2} & I_{d_i-1} \\ \phi_{ii3} & \\ \vdots & \\ \phi_{iid_i} & 0 & 0 & ... & 0 \end{pmatrix} \quad (10.8)$$

where I_{d_i-1} is a $d_i - 1$ square identity matrix. Some more parameters of the canonical form can be set to zero according to the following rules. In (10.6), $L_{i,j} = 0$ if $d_i \geq d_j$ and $j < i$, and in (10.7), $\phi_{ijk} = 0$ if $1 \leq k \leq d_i - d_j$. Notice that if the d_i's are all equal, no further parameters will be zeroized. The K matrix has unspecified form for input–output equivalent identification, although further restrictions (equivalent to invertibility) can be made for identification under likelihood equivalence.

Any state space model (10.4), (10.5) can be transformed into an (input–output) equivalent canonical form (10.6), (10.7), (10.8). A method for finding this canonical form is given by Denham (1974) or Denery (1971), for instance.

When two stochastic state space models have the same $\mathbf{K\Sigma K}^T$, they will be likelihood equivalent, and so the number of parameters in the model can be reduced further by either (i) fixing $\mathbf{\Sigma} = \mathbf{I}$ and constraining the top rows in each partition of $\mathbf{K}$ to form a lower triangular matrix, or (ii) allowing $\mathbf{\Sigma}$ to be any $r \times r$ covariance matrix but set the top rows in each partition of $\mathbf{K}$ to the identity matrix.

Most of the properties of univariate state space models generalize to multivariate models. For instance, as before, a multiple state space model is stationary if all the eigenvalues of the transition matrix lie inside the unit circle.

The autocovariance at lag k, $\boldsymbol{\gamma}(k)$, of a stationary multiple model is defined as

$$E\left\{(\mathbf{X}_t - \boldsymbol{\mu})(\mathbf{X}_{t-k} - \boldsymbol{\mu})^T\right\},$$

where $\boldsymbol{\mu}$ is the mean vector $E(\mathbf{X}_t)$. (An alternative definition is

$$\boldsymbol{\gamma}(k) = E\left\{(\mathbf{X}_t - \boldsymbol{\mu})(\mathbf{X}_{t+k} - \boldsymbol{\mu})^T\right\}$$

but we prefer the first definition because, as we will see later, the autocovariances exhibit the same triangular structure to ARMA coefficients when there is unidirectional causality.)

The autocovariances are therefore $r \times r$ matrices, and the autocovariance matrix at lag k is the transpose of the covariance matrix at lag $-k$. Element i, j of the corresponding autocorrelation matrix $\boldsymbol{\rho}(k)$ is defined as

$$\rho_{ij}(k) = \frac{\gamma_{ij}(k)}{\sqrt{\gamma_{ii}(0)\gamma_{jj}(0)}}$$

where $\gamma_{ij}(u)$ denotes the i,jth element of $\boldsymbol{\gamma}(u)$. For the multiple state space model (10.4), (10.5) the autocovariance at lag k is still

$$\boldsymbol{\gamma}(k) = \mathbf{H}\boldsymbol{\phi}^k(\mathbf{KK}^T + \boldsymbol{\phi}\mathbf{KK}^T\boldsymbol{\phi}^T + \boldsymbol{\phi}^2\mathbf{KK}^T\boldsymbol{\phi}^{2T} + \ldots)\mathbf{H}^T,$$

as in the univariate case.

Sample estimates of the autocovariances and autocorrelations are calculated as might be expected, that is,

$$\mathbf{c}(k) = \frac{1}{N}\sum_{t=k+1}^{N}(X_t - \overline{X})(X_{t-k} - \overline{X})^T.$$

Approximate standard errors of the elements of the autocorrelation matrices for large samples have been derived by Bartlett, but are usually further approximated by $1/\sqrt{N}$ (see Granger & Newbold (1986), page 246). There is a danger, however, that two series may appear to be highly correlated simply because each individual series is highly autocorrelated, so some caution should be exercised when interpreting the cross-correlations.

Model selection for multivariate series is even more haphazard than for univariate models, although the autocorrelation matrices may provide the odd clue. For instance, if the elements of the autocorrelation matrices do not become small for large lags, then one or more series can be differenced individually, although with state space methods a non-stationary model can be fitted directly.

We can establish the likelihood function using exactly the same reasoning as for the univariate case (section 4.4). We will repeat the bare bones. The likelihood of a multivariate series can still be represented in terms of one step conditional distributions

$$L(\boldsymbol{\theta}) = f(\mathbf{X}_1, \mathbf{X}_2, \ldots, \mathbf{X}_N) = \sum_{t=1}^{N} f\left(\mathbf{X}_t | \mathbf{X}_{t-1}, \mathbf{X}_{t-2}, \mathbf{X}_{t-3}, \ldots, \mathbf{X}_1\right).$$

Assuming that the noise vectors $\boldsymbol{\epsilon}_t$ and $\boldsymbol{\eta}_t$ each have a multivariate normal distribution, the observed series will also be multivariate normal, as will the one step conditional distributions. The mean and variance of each one step conditional distribution will therefore be the one step prediction $\mathbf{X}_{t|t-1}$ and its variance matrix $\mathbf{F}_t$.

The Kalman filter equations still apply to the multivariate model, the only difference being that $\mathbf{F}_t$, the prediction error variance, is no longer a scalar. The one step prediction errors $\mathbf{V}_t = \mathbf{X}_t - \mathbf{X}_{t|t-1}$ and the corresponding prediction error variance matrices $\mathbf{F}_t$ can therefore be produced as for the univariate model. The Kalman filter equations for the multivariate model parallel (4.5), (4.6), (4.8), (4.12), (4.13), (4.7), and are given below

The prediction equations:

$$\mathbf{a}_{t|t-1} = E\left(\boldsymbol{\alpha}_t | \mathbf{X}_1, \mathbf{X}_2, \ldots, \mathbf{X}_{t-1}\right) = \boldsymbol{\phi}\mathbf{a}_{t-1}$$
$$\mathbf{C}_{t|t-1} = \boldsymbol{\phi}\mathbf{C}_{t-1}\boldsymbol{\phi}^{\mathrm{T}} + \mathbf{K}\boldsymbol{\Sigma}\mathbf{K}^{\mathrm{T}}$$

The updating equations:

$$\mathbf{F}_t = \mathbf{H}\mathbf{C}_{t|t-1}\mathbf{H}^{\mathrm{T}} + \boldsymbol{\Sigma}_\varepsilon$$
$$\mathbf{C}_t = \mathbf{C}_{t|t-1} - \mathbf{C}_{t|t-1}\mathbf{H}^{\mathrm{T}}\mathbf{F}_t^{-1}\mathbf{H}\mathbf{C}_{t|t-1}$$
$$\mathbf{a}_t = \mathbf{a}_{t|t-1} + \mathbf{C}_{t|t-1}\mathbf{H}^{\mathrm{T}}\mathbf{F}_t^{-1}(\mathbf{X}_t - \mathbf{H}\mathbf{a}_{t|t-1})$$

and:

$$\mathbf{V}_t = \mathbf{X}_t - \mathbf{H}\mathbf{a}_{t|t-1}.$$

The log-likelihood of the multivariate series is therefore analogous to (4.4) and is

$$\log L(\boldsymbol{\theta}) = -\frac{N}{2}\log 2\pi - \frac{1}{2}\sum_{t=1}^{N}\log \mathbf{F}_t - \frac{1}{2}\sum_{t=1}^{N}\frac{\mathbf{V}_t^2}{\mathbf{F}_t}. \tag{10.9}$$

As for the univariate recursions, the first few observations can be used to set up starting values and can be omitted from the likelihood function so that it is the multivariate analogue of (4.14).

The Kalman filter smoothing equations (4.16), (4.17) also apply to multivariate models, and can be used to estimate missing data as described in section 10.3.

We can generalize the univariate ARMA model (5.1) to a multiple ARMA model

$$\mathbf{X}_t = \phi_1 \mathbf{X}_{t-1} + \phi_2 \mathbf{X}_{t-2} + \dots + \phi_p \mathbf{X}_{t-3} + \theta_q \boldsymbol{\epsilon}_{t-q}$$
$$+ \dots + \theta_2 \boldsymbol{\epsilon}_{t-2} + \theta_1 \boldsymbol{\epsilon}_{t-1} + \boldsymbol{\epsilon}_t \qquad (10.10)$$

where $\boldsymbol{\epsilon}_t$ is now an r dimensional white noise vector with variance $\boldsymbol{\Sigma}$ and each coefficient ϕ or θ is now an $r \times r$ matrix. We can say that the autoregressive order of (10.10) is p and the moving average order is q, and we write $\phi(B)\mathbf{X}_t = \theta(B)\boldsymbol{\epsilon}_t$, where $\phi(z)$ and $\theta(z)$ are now the *matrix polynomials* $(\mathbf{I} - \phi_1 B - \phi_2 B^2 \dots - \phi_p B^p)$ and $(\mathbf{I} + \theta_1 B + \dots + \theta_q B^q)$ respectively.

The simplest way of placing the multiple ARMA model (10.10) into a state space form is shown in (10.11), where $m = \max(p, q+1)$. If p is less than $q+1$, $|q+1-p|$ of the higher ϕ_i matrix coefficients, or final θ_i matrix coefficients will be zero.

$$\mathbf{X}_t = (\mathbf{I} \quad \mathbf{0} \quad \dots \quad \mathbf{0})\boldsymbol{\alpha}_t \quad \boldsymbol{\alpha}_t = \begin{pmatrix} \phi_1 & \mathbf{I} & \mathbf{0} & \dots & \mathbf{0} & \mathbf{0} & \mathbf{0} \\ \phi_2 & \mathbf{0} & \mathbf{I} & \dots & \mathbf{0} & \mathbf{0} & \mathbf{0} \\ \vdots & \vdots & \vdots & \dots & \vdots & \vdots & \vdots \\ \phi_{m-1} & \mathbf{0} & \mathbf{0} & \dots & \mathbf{0} & \mathbf{0} & \mathbf{I} \\ \phi_m & \mathbf{0} & \mathbf{0} & \dots & \mathbf{0} & \mathbf{0} & \mathbf{0} \end{pmatrix} \boldsymbol{\alpha}_{t-1} + \begin{pmatrix} \mathbf{I} \\ \theta_1 \\ \theta_2 \\ \vdots \\ \theta_{m-1} \end{pmatrix} \boldsymbol{\eta}_t.$$

$$(10.11)$$

For instance, the model

$$\mathbf{X}_t = (\mathbf{I} \quad \mathbf{0} \quad \mathbf{0})\boldsymbol{\alpha}_t \quad \boldsymbol{\alpha}_t = \begin{pmatrix} \phi_1 & \mathbf{I} & \mathbf{0} \\ \phi_2 & \mathbf{0} & \mathbf{I} \\ \phi_3 & \mathbf{0} & \mathbf{0} \end{pmatrix} \boldsymbol{\alpha}_{t-1} + \begin{pmatrix} \mathbf{I} \\ \theta_1 \\ \theta_2 \end{pmatrix} \boldsymbol{\eta}_t$$

where $\mathbf{I}$, ϕ_i, $\mathbf{0}$, θ_i are $r \times r$ submatrices, and $\boldsymbol{\eta}_t$ is an r-variate white noise process with covariance matrix $\boldsymbol{\Sigma}$ can be multiplied out in an analogous way to the univariate ARMA model in state space form (section 4.1(ii)) to give the multivariate ARMA model

$$\mathbf{X}_t = \phi_1 \mathbf{X}_{t-1} + \phi_2 \mathbf{X}_{t-2} + \phi_3 \mathbf{X}_{t-3} + \theta_2 \boldsymbol{\eta}_{t-2} + \theta_1 \boldsymbol{\eta}_{t-1} + \boldsymbol{\eta}_t.$$

Properties of multiple ARMA models can either be established directly from the difference equation (10.10) or obtained from the equivalent state space representation. We will state some of the main results.

A multiple ARMA model is stationary if and only if the *determinant of $\phi(B)$* has all its roots outside the unit circle (see Hannan 1970). Similarly, the invertibility condition requires that all the roots of the determinant of $\theta(B)$ lie outside the unit circle.

The sample partial autocorrelation coefficient matrices are the estimated coefficients ϕ_k of a multiple AR model of order k, as in the univariate case. They exhibit similar properties to their univariate counterparts. Multivariate Yule–Walker estimates are often used to calculate the sample partial correlations, and a multivariate version of the Levinson–Durbin equations is available (Ansley & Newbold 1979).

As a rough guide, if the model is really of order $p < k$, the kth sample partial autocorrelation coefficient can be taken to have a standard error of $1/\sqrt{N}$.

The autocorrelations of a multiple moving average only model of order q are zero for lags greater than q, and the partial autocorrelations of an AR only model of order p are zero for lags greater than p. Effects corresponding to the sinusoidal or exponential patterns of the univariate autocorrelations are more obscure, as we are now dealing with matrices.

As in the univariate case we can invert the multiple ARMA model to give the infinite moving average representation $\mathbf{X}_t = \phi^{-1}(B)\theta(B)\epsilon_t$, which will converge if the model is stationary. As $\phi(B)$ is a matrix (in which the elements are functions of B) we can write its inverse as

$$\phi^{-1}(B) = \frac{1}{\det(\phi(B))} \ \mathrm{adj}(\phi(B))$$

where 'det' denotes the determinant, and 'adj' denotes the adjoint matrix. $\det(\phi(B))$ will be a scalar polynomial and $\mathrm{adj}(\phi(B))$ will be a matrix, so the model can be written

$$\det(\phi(B))\mathbf{X}_t = \mathrm{adj}(\phi(B))\theta(B)\epsilon_t. \tag{10.12}$$

If we take each equation in (10.12) separately, we obtain r models for $\mathbf{X}_1, \mathbf{X}_2, ..., \mathbf{X}_r$ respectively. Notice that the right hand side of each of these univariate models will be a linear combination of MA processes. It can be shown (consider the autocorrelation function) that each linear combination is likelihood equivalent to an MA process in which the order is the maximum of the MA orders of the component processes. This means that each series can be modelled as a univariate ARMA model with AR polynomial $\det \phi(B)$, although the models will have the same AR polynomials and the random terms in different models will be correlated.

Tiao & Box (1981) give a good outline and examples of multivariate ARMA model fitting, and Terasvirta (1985) gives a further example.

We should point out that the model (10.11) is not in general a canonical form for the multiple ARMA model. Even when the θ parameters are constrained to be invertible, further conditions are required. Priestley (1981, page 802) summarizes the conditions for identifiability.

We can usually reduce the number of parameters in an ARMA model to be estimated by using the state space form as follows. Consider the canonical state space form (10.6), (10.7), (10.8). We can produce an input–output equivalent model, by reordering the states taking the first from each partition first, then the second from each partition, and so on. As the d_i's are not necessarily equal, sometimes the kth state of a partition will not exist, in which case we introduce a new (zero) state. To correspond with this reordering, both the columns and the rows of the ϕ matrix must be reordered in this way, as well as the rows of the $\mathbf{K}$ matrix and columns of the $\mathbf{H}$ matrix. A zero row or column must be inserted to correspond to a zero state, and a 1 (the coefficient of the zero state in the transition equation) in the zero column of ϕ, r rows above the corresponding row of zeros.

For example, if the model is bivariate with $d_1 = 3$ and $d_2 = 2$, the canonical state space model can be reordered to give

$$\mathbf{H} = \begin{pmatrix} 1 & 0 & 0 & 0 & 0 & 0 \\ L_{21} & 1 & 0 & 0 & 0 & 0 \end{pmatrix}$$

$$\phi = \begin{pmatrix} \phi_{111} & 0 & 1 & 0 & 0 & 0 \\ \phi_{211} & \phi_{221} & 0 & 1 & 0 & 0 \\ \phi_{112} & \phi_{122} & 0 & 0 & 1 & 0 \\ \phi_{212} & \phi_{222} & 0 & 0 & 0 & 1 \\ \phi_{113} & \phi_{123} & 0 & 0 & 0 & 0 \\ 0 & 0 & 0 & 0 & 0 & 0 \end{pmatrix} \quad \mathbf{K} = \begin{pmatrix} 1 & 0 \\ 0 & 1 \\ \theta_{111} & \theta_{121} \\ \theta_{211} & \theta_{221} \\ \theta_{112} & \theta_{122} \\ 0 & 0 \end{pmatrix} \quad \text{and} \quad \text{var}\boldsymbol{\eta}_t = \boldsymbol{\Sigma}.$$

$$(10.13)$$

Notice that after transformation, the ϕ and $\mathbf{K}$ matrices correspond to the state space representation of the ARMA model in (10.11), so the first two vector states, say, $\boldsymbol{\alpha}_t^{(1)}$ of (10.13) are generated by a multiple ARMA model. In general, for an r-variate model, the first r states of our canonical state space model transformed in this way are generated by

$$\boldsymbol{\alpha}_t^{(1)} = \phi_1\boldsymbol{\alpha}_{t-1}^{(1)} + \phi_2\boldsymbol{\alpha}_{t-2}^{(1)} + \dots + \phi_p\boldsymbol{\alpha}_{t-p}^{(1)} + \theta_q\boldsymbol{\eta}_{t-q} + \dots + \theta_2\boldsymbol{\eta}_{t-2} + \theta_1\boldsymbol{\eta}_{t-1} + \boldsymbol{\eta}_t.$$

Notice also, from the observation equation of (10.13), that $\mathbf{X}_t = \mathbf{L}\boldsymbol{\alpha}_t^{(1)}$, where $\mathbf{L}$ is the lower triangular matrix formed from the non-zero columns of the canonical $\mathbf{H}$ matrix in (10.6). We can therefore write

$$\mathbf{L}^{-1}\mathbf{X}_t = \phi_1\mathbf{L}^{-1}\mathbf{X}_{t-1} + \phi_2\mathbf{L}^{-1}\mathbf{X}_{t-2} + \dots + \phi_p\mathbf{L}^{-1}\mathbf{X}_{t-p} + \theta_q\boldsymbol{\eta}_{t-q} + \dots$$
$$+ \theta_2\boldsymbol{\eta}_{t-2} + \theta_1\boldsymbol{\eta}_{t-1} + \boldsymbol{\eta}_t$$

or

$$\phi_0^*\mathbf{X}_t = \phi_1^*\mathbf{X}_{t-1} + \phi_2^*\mathbf{X}_{t-2} + \dots + \phi_p^*\mathbf{X}_{t-p} + \theta_q\boldsymbol{\eta}_{t-q} + \dots$$
$$+ \theta_2\boldsymbol{\eta}_{t-2} + \theta_1\boldsymbol{\eta}_{t-1} + \boldsymbol{\eta}_t \qquad (10.14)$$

where $\phi_0^* = \mathbf{L}^{-1}$, which is lower triangular, and $\phi_i^* = \mathbf{L}^{-1}\phi_i$. Recall from the canonical form that if the d_i's are all equal, $\mathbf{L}$ is the identity matrix, so (10.14) is the multiple ARMA model (10.10). If the d_i's are not all equal, (10.14) gives an equivalent model to a multiple ARMA model, whereby $\mathbf{X}_t$ has a coefficient matrix ϕ_0 which is lower triangular with 1s on the diagonal. Premultiplication throughout (10.14) by $\mathbf{L}$ would give the usual ARMA model (10.10). Hence for efficient estimation the parameters of canonical state space model can be estimated and then transformed as described above into an ARMA difference equation.

In (10.14) we could say that the ith variable has AR order p_i if row i of $\boldsymbol{\phi}_k$ is zero for all $k > p_i$, and has MA order q_i if row i of $\boldsymbol{\theta}_k$ is zero for all $k > q_i$, where p_i, q_i have a natural interpretation as the autoregressive and moving average 'orders' of the ith variable in the model respectively. The number of states in the ith corresponding canonical state space partition is $d_i = \max(p_i, q_i + 1)$. If the orders p_i, q_i, $i = 1, \ldots, r$, are known, the number of parameters for estimation may be greatly reduced. Model selection algorithms have been devised for non-explosive models which attempt to ascertain these orders p_i, q_i, $i = 1, \ldots, r$, from the data; see Akaike's canonical correlations analysis (1976), Swift (1990), or Tsay (1989), for instance.

Not much work has been done on diagnostic checking for multiple time series, but see Hosking (1980).

An important issue in multivariate modelling is whether a subset of the observed series, say A, causes another (mutually exclusive) subset of observed variables B, B causes A, or both, or neither. Granger & Newbold (1986) consider causality in some detail, especially for the bivariate case.

We will introduce the concept of causality by considering the bivariate case, that is, $\mathbf{X}_t = (X_{1t}, X_{2t})^T$. The correlation between the two series is represented by the off-diagonal terms of the autocorrelation matrices. As $\rho(k) = \rho(-k)^T$ we need only look at the autocorrelation matrices for $k = 0, 1, 2, \ldots$. If, for instance, the autocorrelation matrices at positive lags are upper triangular, then it could be said that X_{2t} causes X_{1t}, but not vice versa, and there is said to be *unidirectional causality*.

Alternatively, by noting that $\rho_{12}(k) = \rho_{21}(-k)$, where the subscripts denote the elements of the $\boldsymbol{\rho}_k$ matrix, the *cross-correlations* $\rho_{12}(k)$, $k = \ldots -1, 0, 1, \ldots$, entirely describe the correlation between the two series. Computer software often gives the cross-correlations of bivariate series. If $\rho_{12}(k)$ is non-zero for $k > 0$, X_{1t} is related to $X_{2\,t-k}$, and past X_2's are useful in predicting X_1. Similarly, if the cross-correlations are non-zero for negative lags k, past X_1's are predictors of X_2.

The idea of causality extends naturally to more than two variables. When inspection of the sample autocorrelations or *a priori* information seems to indicate that the causality is unidirectional, a suitable state space model might be the canonical multivariate state space representation of (10.6), (10.7), (10.8), but with the ϕ_{ijk} parameters in the lower triangle of blocks, that is, where $j > i$ set to zero. The model in the first variable will now be self-contained, the model in the second variable will involve past values of the first and second variables only, and so on, and the model will exhibit unidirectional causality. The noise terms may still be correlated, and it may be necessary to zeroize the corresponding 'lower triangular' terms of the canonical $\mathbf{K}$ matrix as well. For instance, unidirectional bivariate data might be modelled by

$$\boldsymbol{\phi} = \begin{pmatrix} \phi_{111} & 1 & \phi_{121} & 0 \\ \phi_{112} & 0 & \phi_{122} & 0 \\ 0 & 0 & \phi_{221} & 1 \\ 0 & 0 & \phi_{222} & 0 \end{pmatrix} \quad \text{and} \quad \mathbf{K} = \begin{pmatrix} 1 & 0 \\ \theta_{112} & \theta_{212} \\ 0 & 1 \\ 0 & \theta_{222} \end{pmatrix} \quad \text{var}(\boldsymbol{\eta}_t) = \boldsymbol{\Sigma}.$$

The bivariate ARMA model $\boldsymbol{\phi}(B)\mathbf{X}_t = \boldsymbol{\theta}(B)\boldsymbol{\epsilon}_t$ can be written in terms of scalar polynomials as follows:

$$\begin{pmatrix} \phi_{11}(B) & \phi_{12}(B) \\ \phi_{21}(B) & \phi_{22}(B) \end{pmatrix} \begin{pmatrix} X_{1t} \\ X_{2t} \end{pmatrix} = \begin{pmatrix} \theta_{11}(B) & \theta_{12}(B) \\ \theta_{21}(B) & \theta_{22}(B) \end{pmatrix} \begin{pmatrix} \varepsilon_{1t} \\ \varepsilon_{2t} \end{pmatrix},$$

and in general such a model will exhibit 'two-way' causality. If, however, $\phi_{21}(B) = 0$ and $\theta_{21}(B) = 0$, the model becomes

$$\begin{pmatrix} \phi_{11}(B) & \phi_{12}(B) \\ 0 & \phi_{22}(B) \end{pmatrix} \begin{pmatrix} X_{1t} \\ X_{2t} \end{pmatrix} = \begin{pmatrix} \theta_{11}(B) & \theta_{12}(B) \\ 0 & \theta_{22}(B) \end{pmatrix} \begin{pmatrix} \varepsilon_{1t} \\ \varepsilon_{2t} \end{pmatrix}, \qquad (10.15)$$

so each matrix coefficient is upper triangular, and we have a suitable model for unidirectional causality.

To illustrate the foregoing work we will use the methods outlined above to fit a model to some bivariate data from a papermaking machine. Our first variable is the height of a gate on the machine, and the second is the deviation of paper output weights from a target value, and as such can be assumed to have zero mean. These data were originally analysed by Tee & Wu (1972). A plot of the heights (less their mean) and weights (deviations) is shown in Fig. 10.2, and to show the relationship between the two series more clearly, a plot of a section of data is shown in Fig. 10.3.

The variance of series 1 is 0.1909 and of series 2 is 0.5469. The cross-correlations are

$$\mathbf{r}(0) = \begin{pmatrix} 1 & -0.14 \\ -0.14 & 1 \end{pmatrix} \qquad \mathbf{r}(1) = \begin{pmatrix} 0.025 & 0.236^* \\ -0.141 & 0.895^* \end{pmatrix}$$

$$\mathbf{r}(2) = \begin{pmatrix} -0.031 & 0.188^* \\ -0.140 & 0.802^* \end{pmatrix} \qquad \mathbf{r}(3) = \begin{pmatrix} -0.111 & 0.135 \\ -0.01 & 0.723^* \end{pmatrix}$$

and

$$\mathbf{r}(4) = \begin{pmatrix} -0.090 & 0.072 \\ -0.076 & 0.664^* \end{pmatrix}$$

where * denotes a significant autocorrelation or cross-correlation. The significant statistics form upper triangular autocorrelation matrices indicating that series 2 may cause series 1 but not vice versa. The autocorrelation function of series 2 does not appear to cut off after finite lag so a moving average only model seems unsuitable. The sample partial autocorrelation matrices were calculated by estimating successively larger orders of autoregressive model using state space methods. The significant elements of these matrices up to lag 4 formed upper triangular matrices, and the partial autocorrelations did not appear to decay, so an autoregressive only model seemed unlikely.

We fitted the one way causality canonical form of (arbitrary) dimensions $d_1 = d_2 = 2$, using state space methods. After zeroizing any non-significant parameters one by one we obtained the 9 parameter model

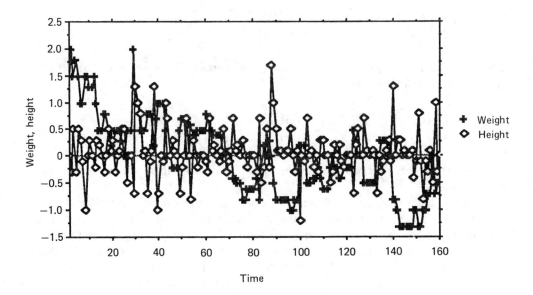

Fig. 10.2. Two series from a paper production process.

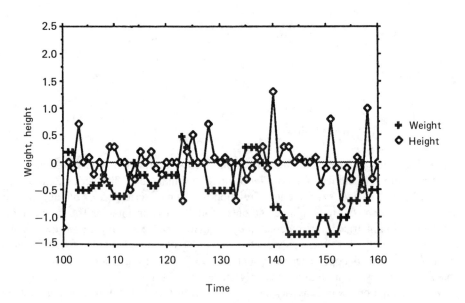

Fig. 10.3. A closer look at a section of the papermaking series in Fig. 10.2.

$$\phi = \begin{pmatrix} 0.7169 & 1 & 0.9959 & 0 \\ 0 & 0 & -0.8919 & 0 \\ 0 & 0 & 0.9052 & 1 \\ 0 & 0 & 0 & 0 \end{pmatrix} \quad \text{and} \quad K = \begin{pmatrix} 0.4011 & 0 \\ -0.0684 & 0 \\ -0.2590 & -0.1466 \\ 0 & 0.0632 \end{pmatrix}$$

$$\text{var}(\boldsymbol{\eta}_t) = I \quad \text{and} \quad H = \begin{pmatrix} 1 & 0 & 0 & 0 \\ 0 & 0 & 1 & 0 \end{pmatrix}.$$

This had a maximum likelihood (omitting the first two observations) of -0.844112 and a prediction error variance of

$$\begin{pmatrix} 0.1609 & -0.1039 \\ -0.1039 & 0.0886 \end{pmatrix}.$$

A competing model with one additional parameter was

$$\phi = \begin{pmatrix} 0.77729 & 1 & 0.49899 & 0 \\ 0 & 0 & -0.44399 & 0 \\ 0 & 0 & 0.88698 & 1 \\ 0 & 0 & 0 & 0 \end{pmatrix} \quad \text{and} \quad K = \begin{pmatrix} 0.40863 & 0 \\ -0.23264 & 0 \\ -0.26572 & -0.14709 \\ 0 & 0 \end{pmatrix}$$

$$\text{var}(\boldsymbol{\eta}_t) = I \quad \text{and} \quad H = \begin{pmatrix} 1 & 0 & 0 & 0 \\ 0 & 0 & 1 & 0 \end{pmatrix}$$

where the prediction error variance was

$$\begin{pmatrix} 0.16698 & -0.10858 \\ -0.10858 & 0.09225 \end{pmatrix}.$$

This had log-likelihood -4.268039, so the AIC is lower. Of course the above models are easily transformed into an ARMA form. For instance, the 9 parameter model has ARMA representation

$$X_t = \begin{pmatrix} 0.7169 & 0.9959 \\ 0 & 0.9052 \end{pmatrix} X_{t-1} + \begin{pmatrix} 0 & -0.8919 \\ 0 & 0 \end{pmatrix} X_{t-2}$$

$$+ \begin{pmatrix} -0.0684 & 0 \\ 0 & 0.0632 \end{pmatrix} \epsilon_{t-1} + \begin{pmatrix} 0.4011 & 0 \\ -0.2590 & -0.1466 \end{pmatrix} \epsilon_t,$$

where $\text{var}(\epsilon_t) = I$.

Box–Jenkins (1970) developed a class of bivariate models specifically to model unidirectional causality. Suppose again that X_{2t} causes X_{1t}, but not vice versa. Then we could model the current X_{1t} as a linear function of current and past X_{2t}'s plus error, and write $X_{1t} = V(B)X_{2t} + e_t$, where $V(B)$ is a polynomial in the backward operator and e_t is an error term which is uncorrelated with $X_{2t-k}, k = \dots -1, 0, 1, \dots$. As in our ARMA work, to produce a more parsimonious model we can approximate the series $M_t = V(B)X_{2t}$ by using two small order polynomials $\omega(B)$ and $\delta(B)$. Suppose M_t is generated by $\delta(B)M_t = \omega(B)X_{2t}$ so that we can write $M_t = (\omega(B)/\delta(B))X_{2t}$. We also allow the error term e_t to follow an ARMA model, that is $\phi(B)e_t = \theta(B)\varepsilon_{1t}$, where ε_{1t} is white noise as usual. In this way we can write our model as

$$X_{1t} = \frac{\omega(B)}{\delta(B)} X_{2t} + \frac{\theta(B)}{\phi(B)} \varepsilon_{1t}. \tag{10.16}$$

We assume also that the X_{2t} series is generated by a univariate ARMA model $\phi_2(B)X_{2t} = \phi_2(B)\varepsilon_{2t}$. This completes our *transfer function* model.

An advantage of transfer function models is that Box & Jenkins (1970) devised a complete methodology for model selection, fitting, and diagnostic checking. The selection procedure is called *prewhitening*. Briefly, they fit a univariate ARMA model to X_{2t} and calculate the residuals from this, say $\{Y_t\}$. Then they apply the *same* ARMA model to the X_{1t} series to obtain another set of residuals which we shall call $\{Z_t\}$. It can be shown that when the true univariate ARMA is known the cross-correlations $\rho_{zy}(j)$ between Z_t and Y_{t-j} are proportional to the transfer function coefficients V_j, and so give clues to the possible orders of $\omega(B)/\delta(B)$. The ARMA part of the model can be found by estimating the parameters of the model

$$X_{1t} = \frac{\omega(B)}{\delta(B)} X_{2t} + e_t$$

as if the e_t was white noise and then fitting an ARMA model to the residuals of this model.

Granger & Newbold (1986) and Box & Jenkins (1970) give least squares algorithms for estimation of the transfer function model, and diagnostic checking can be performed on the X_{1t} series just as if a univariate ARMA had been fitted. Tee & Wu (1972) fit a transfer function to the papermaking data by using these methods. Their final model is

$$X_{1t} = 1.0991X_{2t} + \frac{1}{1 - 0.8511B} \varepsilon_{1t}$$

where the prediction error variance is estimated as 0.19277 and the univariate model for the second series was $X_{2t} = 0.89809X_{2t-1} + \varepsilon_{2t}$.

The bivariate ARMA model with unidirectional causality (10.15) is a special case of (10.16) in which $\delta(B)$ and $\phi(B)$ are the same. To see this, observe that the first equation is $\phi_{11}(B)X_{1t} = -\phi_{12}(B)X_{2t} + \theta_{12}(B)\varepsilon_{2t} + \theta_{11}(B)\varepsilon_{1t}$ so that

$$X_{1t} = \frac{-\phi_{12}(B)}{\phi_{11}(B)} X_{2t} + \frac{\theta(B)}{\phi_{11}(B)} \zeta_t,$$

as $\theta_{12}(B)\varepsilon_{2t} + \theta_{11}(B)\varepsilon_{1t}$ is the sum of two moving average terms of orders q_1, q_2 respectively, and can be equivalently represented by a moving average model $\theta(B)\zeta_t$ of order max (q_1, q_2). The second equation in (10.15) gives the univariate model for the independent variable, in this case X_{2t}. Conversely, we can place the transfer function into a unidirectional bivariate ARMA model (10.15) by multiplying (10.16) by the $\delta(B)$ and

$\phi(B)$ to obtain the first equation of the ARMA model and using the univariate model for X_{2t} as the second equation.

Harvey (1989, Chapter 8) talks about a class of multiple structural models which he calls *seemingly unrelated time series equations* (SUTSEs). These assume that each series has its own equation, but that the influences on each series are similar (for instance, the weather or the economy), so the noise terms of different series may be correlated. In this way one series does not *cause* any of the other series. The simplest SUTSE model is the multivariate random walk model $\mathbf{X}_t = \boldsymbol{\mu}_t + \boldsymbol{\epsilon}_t$, $\boldsymbol{\mu}_t = \boldsymbol{\mu}_{t-1} + \boldsymbol{\eta}_t$, where the covariance matrices of the vector noise variables $\boldsymbol{\epsilon}_t$ and $\boldsymbol{\eta}_t$ are $\boldsymbol{\Sigma}_\epsilon$ and $\boldsymbol{\Sigma}_\eta$ respectively, which need not be diagonal. The series may also have factors, such as the trend component, in common. By choosing less general models than the MVARMA model or canonical state space form, Harvey is able to establish more theory and methodology, although, of course, the models themselves are less versatile.

Chapter 15 of West & Harrison (1989) discusses multivariate versions of the Bayesian models that we mentioned in section 6.8. The dynamic linear model (6.5), (6.6) extends in an obvious way to a vector observation $\mathbf{Y}_t$, in which case $\mathbf{F}_t$ will be a matrix and $\mathbf{V}_t$ a covariance matrix. When $\mathbf{V}_t$ and $\mathbf{W}_t$ are known, in the univariate case equations, the Kalman recursions obtain the posterior point estimator of the state from the previous point estimator of the state. If, however, $\mathbf{v}_t$ is assumed to be multivariate normal with unknown variance matrix $\mathbf{V}_t$, there is no neat analysis for the multivariate dynamic linear model involving conjugate prior distributions.

West and Harrison select a wide class of models which extend the dynamic linear model. They assume that each of several similar series can be modelled as a univariate dynamic linear model, and that these models have a common $\mathbf{F}$, $\mathbf{G}$ and $\mathbf{W}$, but may have different measurement noise variance matrices $\mathbf{V}$. Such models might arise, for example, when modelling the prices of several shares. Covariances are allowed between the observation errors of different series and between their state noises. This can be represented in one large model with a vector of observations but requires a matrix of state parameters.

In general, the study of multivariate models is much more complicated than univariate models, and we have only attempted to introduce some of the issues for modelling vector time series.

10.6 MULTIPLE SERIES: THE FREQUENCY DOMAIN

We have seen how we can model more than one series by using extensions of our time domain methods. It is also possible to extend our spectral techniques, and as in the time domain we get a rich and interesting theory. For simplicity we begin with the bivariate case, that is, with a stationary series $\mathbf{X}_t = (X_{1t}, X_{2t})^{\mathrm{T}}$ with a zero mean and covariance matrix $\boldsymbol{\gamma}(k)$.

We define the *spectral density matrix* $\mathbf{F}(\omega)$ as

$$\mathbf{F}(\omega) = \begin{pmatrix} f_{11}(\omega) & f_{12}(\omega) \\ f_{22}(\omega) & f_{21}(\omega) \end{pmatrix} = \frac{1}{2\pi} \sum_{k=-\infty}^{\infty} \boldsymbol{\gamma}(k)\, e^{ik\omega}$$

with

$$\gamma(k) = \left\{ \gamma_{ij}(k) \right\} = \left(E[X_{it}, X_{jt+k}] \right).$$

$f_{11}(\omega)$ and $f_{22}(\omega)$ are the *univariate* or *autospectra*, while $f_{12}(\omega)$ is the *cross-spectrum*. From the definition,

$$f_{12}(\omega) = \frac{1}{2\pi} \sum_{k=-\infty}^{\infty} \gamma_{12}(k)\, e^{ik\omega},$$

and since

$$\gamma_{ij}(k) = E[X_{it}, X_{jt+k}] = E[X_{ir-k}, X_{jr}] = \gamma_{ji}(-k),$$

we have

$$f_{12}(\omega) = \frac{1}{2\pi} \sum_{k=-\infty}^{\infty} \gamma_{12}(k)\, e^{ik\omega} = \frac{1}{2\pi} \sum_{k=-\infty}^{\infty} \gamma_{21}(-k)\, e^{ik\omega} = \bar{f}_{21}(\omega),$$

so we see that $f_{12}(\omega)$ and $f_{21}(\omega)$ are complex conjugates. This implies that the spectral matrix **F** is Hermitian. Since we are dealing with a complex-valued quantity $f_{12}(\omega)$, if we are interested in the relationship between the series, it is natural to work in one of the traditional representations of complex numbers, either

(a) $f_{12}(\omega) = c_{12}(\omega) - iq_{12}(\omega)$

where c_{12} is known as the *co-spectrum* and q_{12} as the *quadrature spectrum*.

or

(b)   The alternative polar form, we prefer, which gives

$$f_{12}(\omega) = \alpha_{12}(\omega)\, e^{i\phi_{12}(\omega)}$$

where here $\alpha_{12}(\omega)$ is the *amplitude spectrum* and $\phi_{12}(\omega)$ the *phase spectrum*.
    Our last but important major definitions are the (complex) *coherency spectrum*

$$c(\omega) = \frac{f_{12}(\omega)}{\sqrt{f_{11}(\omega)f_{22}(\omega)}} \quad \text{and the gain} \quad G_{12}(\omega) = \frac{|f_{12}(\omega)|}{f_{11}(\omega)}.$$

    We use the cross-spectrum in its various guises to gain insight into the relationship between series.
    The modulus of the coherence measures the strength of relationships between corresponding frequency components of the two series in almost exactly the same way as a correlation coefficient. The gain is the analogue of the regression of the frequency ω component of the first series on the second. The lead or lag of this relationship is measured by the slope of the phase.
    To see how this follows, we proceed to some mathematics. The simplest mathematical device is to generalize the spectral representation in Chapter 8, giving

$$X_{1t} = \int_{-\pi}^{\pi} e^{-i\omega t}\, dZ^1(\omega) \quad X_{2t} = \int_{-\pi}^{\pi} e^{-i\omega t}\, dZ^2(\omega)$$

where the Z processes are not only orthogonal but *cross-orthogonal*

$$E\left|dZ^1(\omega)\right|^2 = f_{11}(\omega)\, d\omega$$

$$E\left|dZ^2(\omega)\right|^2 = f_{22}(\omega)\, d\omega$$

$$E\left|dZ^1(\omega)\, d\bar{Z}^2\omega)\right| = f_{12}(\omega)\, d\omega$$

$$E\left|dZ^i(\theta)\, d\bar{Z}^j(\omega)\right| = 0 \quad \omega \neq \theta.$$

From this, it is easily shown that the coherence is unchanged under linear transformations. If Y_t is a filtered version of X_t as below

$$Y_t = \begin{pmatrix} a_{11}(B) \\ a_{22}(B) \end{pmatrix} X_t$$

the new spectral matrix becomes

$$F_y(\omega) = \begin{pmatrix} \left|a_{11}(e^{-i\omega})\right|^2 f_{11}(\omega) & a_{12}(e^{-i\omega})f_{12}(\omega) \\ a_{21}(e^{-i\omega})f_{21}(\omega) & \left|a_{22}(e^{-i\omega})\right|^2 f_{22}(\omega) \end{pmatrix},$$

with $a_{12}(B) = a_{11}(B)a_{22}(B)$ and $a_{21}(B) = a_{12}(B)$. We see that from the definition the coherency does not involve any of the filter functions. For a rather simpler case, suppose

$$X_{1t} = \beta X_{2t-d} + \varepsilon_t,$$

then it is easy to show that $\phi_{12}(\omega) = -\omega d$. This illustrates the important point that when there is a time delay the phase spectrum is a linear function of frequency, with the slope representing the size of the delay. For further details, see Priestley (1981).

Before we look at some examples of cross-spectra, we mention one important application to linear relationships with extra noise.

Suppose that we have

$$Y_t = \sum_{s=-\infty}^{\infty} g_s X_{t-s} + \eta_t,$$

then by taking Fourier transforms we have

$$f_{yx} = G_{yx}(\omega)f_{xx}(\omega)$$

where G_{yx} is the gain defined above.

In addition if X_t and the noise series are uncorrelated, then

$$f_{yy}(\omega) = \left|G_{yx}(\omega)\right|^2 f_{xx}(\omega) + f_{\eta\eta}(\omega).$$

Now $\phi_{yx}(\omega) = \tan^{-1}\{f_{yx}(\omega)\}$, while the gain $|f_{yx}(\omega)|$ is $|G_{yx}(\omega)|f_{xx}(\omega)$. Thus the transfer function, *complete with the gain and the phase information*, can be computed from the spectral matrix. Indeed, we can prove that the filter that best approximates Y_t in the mean square sense has coefficients given by

$$g_s = \int_{-\pi}^{\pi} \frac{f_{yx}(\omega)}{f_{xx}(\omega)} e^{ik\omega} \, d\omega,$$

while the residual variance is bounded by

$$\sigma^2 = \int_{-\pi}^{\pi} \left\{ 1 - |c(\omega)|^2 \right\} f_{xx}(\omega) \, d\omega$$

where $c(\omega)$ is the coherency. In other words, if we fit a linear relationship between two variables, then the residual variance will at best equal this value.

As one might expect, there are rather more problems involved in estimating the spectral matrix than the univariate spectral density function. The individual autospectra can be handled by the methods developed in Chapter 9 and consistent estimates obtained. We can also apply a smoothed window technique to the estimate cross-spectrum, and for simplicity we shall assume that the same smoothing, both window and degree, is applied for each spectral estimate. This is a simplification, but a very welcome one. Given our estimate

$$\hat{f}_{ij}(\omega) = \frac{1}{2\pi} \sum_{-m}^{m} \lambda(k) c_{ij}(k) e^{i\omega k}$$

we have the unusual problems that we discussed in the estimation of univariate spectra, and one more. This one, *the alignment* problem, arises as the behaviour of cross-covariances and autocovariances are very different in one respect; the cross-covariance is not necessarily an even function, hence its maximum need not occur at the zero lag. Since we are using a symmetric lag window designed for the autospectra, this introduces inefficiencies. A pragmatic solution is to use

$$\hat{f}_{ij}(\omega) = \frac{1}{2\pi} \sum_{-m}^{m} \lambda(k - k_0) c_{ij}(k) e^{i\omega k},$$

and the consequent adjustment of the window (or the two series) is known as *alignment*. We seek the value of k_0 which gives the maximum cross-correlation at the maximum of the weighting sequence $\{\lambda(k)\}$; for details, see Priestley (1981).

The distribution theory of the estimates is also complex, in more ways than one. Goodman (1957) introduced the complex Wishart distribution, and from this we can answer, to some extent, distributional questions. For details the reader is advised to consult Koopmans (1974) or Priestley (1981).

Naturally, the two series can be generalized into a multivariate series problem with a spectral matrix **F**. Partial and multiple coherences can be defined and have properties analogous to those of the partial and multiple correlations in regression analysis. There are also applications of standard multivariate techniques such as canonical correlation analysis and principal components.

As an example we look at the spectra of the papermaking data studied earlier in this chapter. The coherence is plotted in Fig. 10.4, and we can see that away from zero frequency it is large.

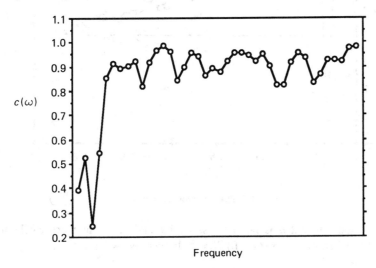

Fig. 10.4. Coherency plot.

The phase spectrum, Fig. 10.5, gives a rather nice linear decline, indicating a lagged relationship.

As you might expect, some problems are easier to tackle in the frequency domain and some in the time domain, thus investigations of causality could perhaps be more profitably studied in the time domain. Nevertheless, there is a rich structure available whichever domain is chosen.

10.7 NON-LINEAR AND NON-STANDARD MODELS

As we have seen, the sort of models we have fitted to time series frequently assume that the correlations die away fairly rapidly, at least after trend and seasonal effects are removed. While this is quite reasonable there are some types of series which appear to exhibit long-term dependence; see Hurst (1951) or MacLeod & Hipple (1978). While these long memory series can in theory be represented by an ARMA model of large order, in fact the orders become so large that estimation is quite difficult. A rather attractive alternative is to extend the form of the model so that it displays the long memory characteristics required.

Suppose we take the standard ARIMA form

$$(1-B)^d \phi(B)X_t = \theta(B)\varepsilon_t,$$

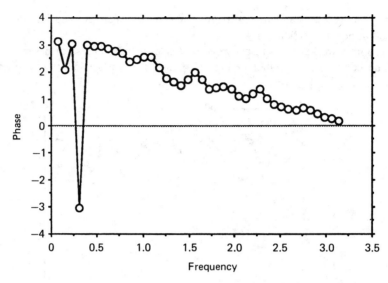

Fig. 10.5. Phase plot for paper data.

but with the extension that d is not necessarily integral. We can more easily see the implications for the simpler form $(1 - B)^d X_t = \varepsilon_t$. In this case we have

$$X_t = \sum_{j=0}^{\infty} \psi_j B^j \varepsilon_t$$

$$= \left\{ 1 + (-d)B + \frac{(-d)(-d-1)B^2}{2!} + \frac{(-d)(-d-1)(-d-2)}{3!} B^3 + \dots \right\} \varepsilon_t.$$

If we use the Gamma function, then

$$\psi_j = \frac{\Gamma(j+d)}{\Gamma(j+1)\Gamma(d)},$$

and after some algebra the autocorrelations can be shown to be

$$\rho(k) = \frac{\Gamma(k+d)\Gamma(1-d)}{\Gamma(d)\Gamma(k-d+1)}.$$

If we apply Stirling's formula and some hefty approximations we get

$$\rho(k) = k^{2d-1} \frac{\Gamma(1-d)}{\Gamma(d)}.$$

As this decays rather slowly, we have a process with long memory. If $|d| > 0.5$, then the series above are not convergent! For details of the more general case, see Brockwell & Davies (1985, Chapter 12). The actual form we have looked at was first considered by

Granger & Joyeux (1980) and Hosking (1981). Granger & Joyeux (1980) looked at the problem via the spectrum, since in terms of filters we can think of the 'spectrum' of the series as

$$f(\omega) = \frac{\left|\theta(e^{-i\omega})\right|^2}{\left|\phi(e^{-i\omega})\right|^2 \left|1 - e^{-i\omega}\right|^{2d}},$$

which near zero has the form $f(\omega) = \text{constant} \times \omega^{-2d}$. This has prompted Granger & Joyeux (1980), Janacek (1983), and Geweke & Porter-Hudack (1983) to examine the behaviour of the estimated spectrum, or rather its log, in the neighbourhood of the origin. Since $\log f(\omega) = -2d \log \omega + \text{constant}$ near zero, a regression method is an obvious approach, and has been explored by Geweke & Porter-Hudack (1983), although Janacek (1983) took a slightly different view, using the Fourier expansion of the log spectrum.

There is also obvious scope with these models for direct estimation in the frequency domain, since the forms are closed and we do not have the problems of the long orders that we do in the time domain. Readers might consult Li & McLeod (1986), while for applications there is the interesting paper of Haslett & Raftery (1989).

Another approach to the generalization of standard time series models has been the 'threshold model' introduced and developed by Tong (1990). In the simplest case we could have an autoregressive model which changes its form when the series crosses a threshold. Thus the TAR(1) (threshold autoregressive model order 1) might be

$$X_t + \phi_1 X_{t-1} = \varepsilon_t \quad \text{if} \quad X_{t-1} < d \quad \text{and} \quad X_t + \phi_2 X_{t-1} = \eta_t \quad \text{if} \quad X_{t-1} \geq d.$$

Here, $\{\varepsilon_t\}$ and $\{\eta_t\}$ are white noise and ϕ_1, ϕ_2 are constants, while the parameter d is the threshold. The model class is easily extended to cases with several thresholds and higher order autoregressions. In state space form we have

$$\boldsymbol{\alpha}_t = \boldsymbol{\phi}^{(i)} \boldsymbol{\alpha}_{t-1} + \mathbf{K}^{(i)} \quad \text{if} \quad \boldsymbol{\alpha}_t \text{ is in region } R_i, i = 1, 2, \dots m$$
$$X_t = \mathbf{H}\boldsymbol{\alpha}_t + \varepsilon_t.$$

These threshold models have some interesting properties; perhaps the most important is that they may give rise to 'limit cycles' in almost exactly the same way as do differential equations; see Tong (1983). By this we mean that the state vectors eventually fall on a closed curve, the limit cycle, and consequently the model exhibits a cycle. This is difficult to envisage in several dimensions, so one usually plots only two, or perhaps three components of the state vector. Such plots can be very informative! Thus we cite Tong's example

$$X_t - X_{t-1} = \begin{cases} 0.7 - 0.2 X_{t-3} & \text{if } X_{t-2} \leq 3.1 \\ -(1.2 X_{t-2} - 2.0) + 0.5 X_{t-1} & \text{if } X_{t-2} > 3.1 \end{cases}$$

which has a limit cycle which we can illustrate by plotting X_t against X_{t-1} as in Fig. 10.6.

For cyclic data the limiting behaviour of threshold models makes them a very attractive choice for modelling, especially as these models can give rise to asymmetric cycles and in consequence to a clear time directional effect. Estimation is a variation on AR

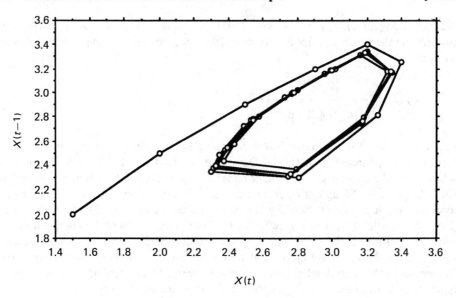

Fig. 10.6. Example of a limit cycle.

estimation, using AIC as a fitting criterion; for details, see Tong (1983). For examples of these models applied to data sets, see Tong (1990).

A major departure from the linear model classes discussed in this book is the *bilinear model* which first appeared in control theory. A general discrete bilinear model is

$$X_t + \sum_{s=1}^{p} \phi_s X_{t-s} = \sum_{s=1}^{q} \theta_s \varepsilon_{t-s} + \sum_{r=1}^{m} \sum_{s=1}^{k} b_{rs} X_{t-r} \varepsilon_{t-s}$$

where, as usual, $\{\varepsilon_t\}$ is a white noise process. As we can see, this differs from the usual ARMA model in that we have extra terms of the (bilinear form) $X_{t-r}\varepsilon_{t-s}$. These models were introduced to time series by Granger & Anderson (1978), and a comprehensive account is given in Subba Rao & Gabr (1984) and Priestley (1988). These non-linear models appear to be very successful, and promising results have been reported. Space does not permit the development of these models in detail, and the reader is referred to the comprehensive discussion in Subba Rao & Gabr (1984).

As the spectrum is a transformation of the second order moments of a series it naturally reflects this limitation in its inability to tell us much about the non-linear or non-normal characteristics of a series. If this is our interest, then we should contemplate taking the Fourier transforms of not just the second order moments but of the higher order moments. The resulting transforms, known as polyspectra, appear to have been introduced by Shiryaev (1960) and studied by Brillinger (1965) and Brillinger & Rosenblatt (1967). The concept is simple, for a series stationary to order $r \geq k$, the kth order polyspectrum is, if it exists, just $f_k(\omega_1, \omega_2, \omega_3, \ldots, \omega_{k-1})$, where

$$f_k(\omega_1, \omega_2, \omega_3, \ldots, \omega_{k-1}) =$$

$$\left(\frac{1}{2\pi}\right)^{k-1} \Sigma \ldots \Sigma C(s_1, s_2, s_3, \ldots, s_{k-1}) \exp\left\{-i(\omega_1 s_1 + \omega_2 s_2 + \ldots + \omega_{k-1} s_{k-1})\right\}$$

and $C(s_1, s_2, s_3, \ldots, s_{k-1})$ is the joint kth order cumulant of the series.

The commonest polyspectrum is the bispectrum

$$f_k(\omega_1, \omega_2) = \left(\frac{1}{2\pi}\right) \Sigma \Sigma C(s_1, s_2,) \exp\left\{-i(\omega_1 s_1 + \omega_2 s_2)\right\}$$

or the third order polyspectrum. Since for a Gaussian process the polyspectra all vanish for order 3 and higher orders, since the joint cumulants of the multivariate normal distribution are zero, the polyspectra give us a method of measuring non-linearity. For a comprehensive discussion and examples of the spectra, the interested reader should read Subba Rao & Gabr (1984). For cross-polyspectra, see Priestley (1988).

Somehow I knew it would always work out that way. Time is the great author.
Always writes the perfect ending.

Charles Chaplin learning he has lost Claire Bloom to Sydney Chaplin in Charles
Chaplin's *Limelight*. (Original screenplay by Charles Chaplin.)

References

Akaike, H. (1969) 'Fitting autoregressive models for prediction', *Annals of the Inst. of Statistical Maths.* **21,** 243–247.

Akaike, H. (1976) 'Canonical correlation analysis of time series and the use of an information criterion', In: R. K. Mehra and D. G. Lainiotis (Eds), *Systems Identification: Advances and Case Studies*, Academic Press, New York, pp. 27–96.

Anderson, A. (1982) 'An empirical examination of Box–Jenkins forecasting', *J. Roy. Statist. Soc.* **145**(4), 472–498.

Ansley, C. F. & Newbold, P. (1979) 'Multivariate partial autocorrelations', *Proc. Bus. Econ. Stat. American Statistical Association*, pp. 349–353.

Bartlett, M. S. (1946) 'On the theoretical specification of a sampling properties of autocorrelated time series', *J. Roy. Statist. Soc. Supp.* **8,** 27–41.

Beamish, N. & Priestley, M. B. (1981) 'A study of autoregressive estimation', *Applied Statistics* **30**, 41–58.

Beveridge, W. H. (1921) 'Weather and harvest cycles', *Econ. J.* **31**, 429–452.

Bloomfield, P. (1976) *Fourier Analysis of Time Series*, Wiley, New York.

Box, G. E. P. & Jenkins, G. (1970) *Time Series Analysis: Forecasting and Control*, Holden-Day, San Francisco. [Reprinted 1976.]

Box, G. E. P. & Pierce, D. A. (1970) 'Distribution of residual autocorrelations in autoregressive integrated moving average models', *J. Am. Stat. Assoc.* **65**, 1509–1526.

Brillinger, D. R. (1965) 'An introduction to polyspectra', *Annals. Math. Statist.* **36**, 1351–1374.

Brillinger, D. R. & Rosenblatt, M. (1967) 'Computation and interpretation of kth order spectra', In: B. Harris (Ed.), *Spectral Analysis of Time Series*, Wiley, New York, pp. 189–232.

Brockwell, P. J. & Davis, R. A. (1987) *Time Series: Theory and Methods*, Springer, New York. Second edition 1990.

Brown, R. G. (1963) *Smoothing Forecasting and Prediction of Discrete Time Series*, Prentice-Hall, New Jersey.

Burg, J. P. (1968) *Maximum Entropy Spectral Analysis*. Reprinted: *Modern Spectrum Analysis* (Ed. D. G. Childers), IEEE Press, New York.

Campbell, M. & Walker, A. (1977) 'A survey of statistical work on the Mackenzie River Series of Annual Lynx Trappings for the years 1821–1934 and a new analysis', *J. Roy. Statist. Soc. A* **140**, 411–432.

Champeney, D. (1987) *A Handbook of Fourier Theorems*, Cambridge University Press, Cambridge.

Chatfield, C. (1978) 'The Holt Winters forecasting procedure', *Applied Statistics* **27**(3), 264–279.

Cooley, J. & Tukey, J. (1965) 'An Algorithm for the machine calculation of complex Fourier series', *Math. Comp.* **19**, 297–301.

Crafts, N., Leybourne, S. & Mills, T. (1989) 'Trends and cycles in British industrial production 1700–1913', *J. Roy. Statist. Soc. A* **152**, 43–60.

Davis, H. & Jones, R. (1968) 'Estimation of the innovation variance of a stationary time series', *J. Am. Statist. Assn* **63**, 141-149.

Denery, D. G. (1971) 'An identification algorithm which is insensitive to initial parameter estimates', *American Institute of Aeronautics and Astronautics* **9**, 371–377.

Denham, M. J. (1974) 'Canonical forms for the identification of multivariable linear systems', *IEEE Trans. of Automatic Control* **19**, 646–656.

Fisher, R. (1929) 'Tests of significance in harmonic analysis', *Proc. Roy. Soc. London Ser. A* **125**, 54–59.

Fishman, G. S. (1969) *Spectral Methods in Econometrics*, Harvard University Press, Cambridge, Mass.

Gardner, G. A., Harvey, A. C., & Phillips, G. D. A. (1980) 'An algorithm for exact estimation of ARMA models by means of Kalman filtering', *J. Applied Statistics* **29** Algorithm AS154, 311–322.

Geweke, J. & Porter-Hudack, S. (1983) 'The estimation and application of long-memory series models', *J. Time Series Anal.* **4**, 221–238.

Goodman, N. R. (1957) 'On the joint estimation of the spectra, cospectrum and quadrature spectrum of a two dimensional stationary Gaussian process', *Sci. Paper 10*, Engineering Statistical Lab, New York University.

Granger, C. (1964) *Spectral Analysis of Economic Time Series*, Princeton University Press, Princeton.

Granger, C. & Anderson, A. P. (1978) *An Introduction to Bilinear Time Series Models*, Vandenhoek and Ruprecht, Gottingen.

Granger, C. & Hughes, A. (1971) 'A new look at some old data: the Beveridge wheat price series', *J. Roy. Statist. Soc. A* **134**, 413–428.

Granger, C. & Joyeux, R. (1980) 'An introduction to long memory time series', *J. Time Series Anal.* **1**, 15–29.

Granger, C. & Nelson, H. (1978) 'Experiences using the Box–Cox transformation when forecasting economic time series', Working Paper 78(1), Department of Economics, U.C.S.P.

Granger, C. & Newbold, P. (1977) *Forecasting Economic Time Series*, Academic Press, New York.

Granger, C. & Newbold, P. (1986) *Forecasting Economic Time Series*, 2nd edn, Academic Press, London.

Hannan, E. J. (1970) *Multiple Time Series*, Wiley, New York.

Harrison, P. J. & Stevens, C. F. (1976) 'Bayesian forecasting', *J. Royal Statistical Society* **38**, 3.

Harvey, A. C. (1981a) *Time Series Models*, Philip Allan, Oxford.

Harvey, A. C. (1981b) 'Finite sample prediction and overdifferencing', *J. Time Series Analysis* **2**, 221–238.

Harvey, A. C. (1989) *Forecasting Structural Time Series Models and the Kalman Filter*, Cambridge University Press, Cambridge.

Harvey, A. C. & Durbin, J. (1986) 'The effects of seat belt legislation on British road casualties: a case study in structural time series modelling', *J. Roy. Statist. Soc. Series A* **149**, 187–227.

Harvey, A. C. & Pierce, R. G. (1984) 'Estimation of missing observations in economic time series', *J. Amer. Statist. Assoc.* **79**, 125–131.

Harvey, A. C. & Todd, P. H. J. (1983) 'Forecasting economic time series with structural and Box–Jenkins models', *J. Business and Economic Statistics* **1**, 299–315.

Haslett, J. & Raftery, A. E. (1989) 'Space time modelling with long memory dependence: assessing Ireland's wind power resource', *Applied Statistics* **38**, 1–50.

Hosking, J. R. M. (1980) 'The multivariate portmanteau statistic', *J. Amer. Statist. Assoc.* **75**, 602–608.

Hosking, J. R. M. (1981) 'Fractional differencing', *Biometrica* **68**(1), 165–176.

Hurst, H. (1951) 'Long-term storage capacity of reservoirs', *Trans. Am. Soc. Civil Engineers* **116**, 778–808.

Isserlis, L. (1918) 'On a formula for the product moment correlation coefficient of any order of a normal frequency in any number of variables', *Biometrika* **12**, 134.

Janacek, G. (1974) 'Estimation of the mean square error of prediction', *Biometrika* **62**, 175–180.

Janacek, G. (1983) 'Determining the degree of differencing for time series via the log spectrum', *J. Time Series Analysis* **3**, 177–184.

Janacek, G. J. & Swift, A. L. (1990) 'A class of models for non-normal time series', *J. Time Series* **11**, 19–32.

Jazwinski, A. H. (1970) *Stochastic Processes and Filtering Theory*, Academic Press, New York.

Jones, R. (1976) 'Autoregressive order selection' *Geophysics* **41**, 771–773.

Kalman, R. E. (1960) 'A new approach to linear filtering', *Trans. ASME J. of Basic Engineering* **82**, 35–45.

Kendall, M. (1973) *Time Series*, Griffin, London.

Knuth, D. E. (1981) *The Art of Computer Programming Volume 2: Semi-numerical Algorithms,* Addison-Wesley, Reading, MA.

Kohn, R. & Ansley, C. F. (1986) 'Estimation, prediction, and interpolation for ARIMA models with missing data', *J. Am. Statist. Assoc.* **81**, 751–761.

Kolmogorov, A. (1939) 'Sur l'interpretation et extrapolation des suites stationaries', *Comptes Rendus Ac. Sci. Paris* **208**, 2043–2045.

Koopmans, L. (1974) *The Spectral Analysis of Time Series*, Academic Press, New York.

Kuznets, S. S. (1961) 'Capital and the American economy: its formation and financing', Nat. Bureau of Economic Research, New York.

Li, W. & McLeod, A. (1986) 'Fractional time series modelling', *Biometrika* **73**, 217–221.

Ljung, G. M. & Box, G. E. P. (1970) 'On a measure of lack of fit in time series models', *Biometrika*, **65**, 297–303.

Mann, H. B. & Wald, A. (1943) 'On the statistical treatment of linear stochastic difference equations', *Econometrica* **173**, 173–220.

McCullagh, P. & Nelder, J. (1989) *Generalized Linear Models*, 2nd ed, Chapman and Hall, London.

McLeod, A. I. & Hipel, K. W. (1978) 'Preservation of the rescaled range', *Water Re sources Research* **14**(3), 491–518.

Montgomery, D. C. & Johnson, A. L. (1976) *Forecasting and Time Series Analysis*, Addison-Wesley, Reading, Mass. USA.

Nash, J. C. (1979) *Compact Numerical Methods for Computers: Linear Algebra and Function Minimisation*, Adam Hilger, Bristol.

Neave, H. (1970) 'An improved formula for the asymptotic variance of spectrum estimates', *Ann. Math. Statist.* **41**, 70–77.

Newbold, P. & Agiaklogou, C. (1991) 'Looking for evolving growth rates and cycles in British industrial production', *J. Roy. Statist. Soc. A* **154**(2), 341–349.

Newton, H. (1989) *Timeslab: A Times Series Analysis Laboratory*, Wadsworth and Brooks Cole, Pacific Grove.

Parzen, E. (1967) *Time Series Analysis Papers*, Holden-Day, San Francisco.

Parzen, E. (1974) 'Some recent advances in time series modelling', *IEEE Trans. Automatic Control* **19**, 723–730.

Piggot, J. L. (1980) 'The use of Box–Jenkins modelling for the forecasting of daily gas demand', Paper presented to the Royal Statistical Society.

Press, W. H., Flannery, B. P., Teukolsky, S. A. & Vetterling, W. T. (1986) *Numerical Recipes*, Cambridge University Press, Cambridge.

Priestley, M. B. (1981) *Spectral Analysis and Time Series*, Volumes 1 and 2, Academic Press, New York.

Priestley, M. B. (1988) *Non-linear and Non-stationary Time Series Analysis*, Academic Press, London.

Rissanen, J. (1983) 'A universal prior for the integers and estimation by minimum description length', *Ann. Statist.* **11**, 417–431.

Shiryaev, A. N. (1960) 'Some problems in the spectral theory of higher order moments 1', *Theor. Prob. Appl.* **5**, 265–284.

Shumway, R. H. (1988) *Applied Statistical Time Series Analysis*, Prentice-Hall, Englewood Cliffs, NJ.

Stephenson, G. (1973) *Mathematical Methods for Science Students*, Longman, London.

Subba Rao, T. & Gabr, M. M. (1984) *An Introduction to Bispectral Analysis and Bilinear Time Series Models*, Springer, Lecture Notes in Statistics 14.

Swift, A. L. (1990) 'Orders and initial values for non-stationary multivariate ARMA models', *J. Time Series* **11**, 349–360.

Tee, L. H. & Wu, S. M. (1972) 'An application of stochastic and dynamic models for the control of a papermaking process, *Technometrics* **14**, 481–498.

Terasvirta, T. (1985) 'Mink and muskrat interaction: a structural analysis', *J. Time Series Analysis* **6**, 171–180.

Tiao, G. C. & Box, G. E. P. (1981) 'Modeling multiple time series with applications', *J Am. Statist. Assoc.* **76**, 802–816.

Tong, H. (1983) *Threshold Models in Non-Linear Time Series Analysis*, Springer, Lecture Notes in Statistics 21.

Tong, H. (1990) *Non-linear Time Series: a Dynamical Systems Approach*, Oxford University Press.

Tsay, R. S. (1989) 'Parsimonious parameterization of vector autoregressive moving average models', *J. Business and Economic Statistics* **7**, 327–351.

Tunnicliffe-Wilson, G. (1969) 'Factorization of the generating function of a pure moving average process', *SIAM J. Num. Analysis*.

Tunnicliffe-Wilson, G. (1979) 'Some efficient computational schemes for high order ARMA models', *J. Statist. Comp. Simul.* **8**, 301–309.

West, M. & Harrison, J. (1989) *Bayesian Forecasting and Dynamic Methods*, Springer-Verlag, New York.

Whittle, P. (1963) *Prediction and Regulation by Linear Least Squares Methods*, English Universities Press. [Reprinted, Blackwell, Oxford, 1984.]

Wichmann, B. A. & Hill, I. D. (1982) 'An efficient and portable random number generator', *Applied Statistics* **31**, 188–190.

Wilks, S. S. (1962) *Mathematical Statistics*, Wiley, New York.

Wold, H. (1938) *A Study of the Analysis of Stationary Time Series*, Almqvist and Wiksell, Stockholm.

Data appendix

We enclose listings of some of the series which were used in this book. In each case the reader should read along the line for the correct time sequence.

Airline passenger series $N = 144$ (monthly, 1949–1960)

112	118	132	129	121	135	148	148	136	119
104	118	115	126	141	135	125	149	170	170
158	133	114	140	145	150	178	163	172	178
199	199	184	162	146	166	171	180	193	181
183	218	230	242	209	191	172	194	196	196
236	235	229	243	264	272	237	211	180	201
204	188	235	227	234	264	302	293	259	229
203	229	242	233	267	269	270	315	364	347
312	274	237	278	284	277	317	313	318	374
413	405	355	306	271	306	315	301	356	348
355	422	465	467	404	347	305	336	340	318
362	348	363	435	491	505	404	359	310	337
360	342	406	396	420	472	548	559	463	407
362	405	417	391	419	461	472	535	622	606
508	461	390	432						

Beveridge wheat price index—trend free $N = 212$

106	118	124	94	82	88	87	88	88	68
98	115	135	104	96	110	107	97	75	86
111	125	78	86	102	71	81	129	130	129
125	139	97	90	76	102	100	73	86	74
74	76	80	96	112	144	80	54	69	100
103	129	100	90	100	123	156	71	71	81
84	97	105	90	78	112	100	86	77	80
93	112	131	158	113	89	87	87	79	90
90	87	83	85	76	110	161	97	84	106
111	97	108	100	119	131	143	138	112	99
97	80	90	90	80	77	81	98	115	94
93	100	99	100	94	88	92	100	82	73
81	99	124	106	106	121	105	84	97	109
148	114	108	97	92	97	98	105	97	93
99	99	107	106	96	82	88	116	122	134
119	136	102	72	63	76	75	77	103	104
120	167	126	108	91	85	73	74	80	74

Brewery share price—daily from 01–02–85, first 330 observations

88	86	86	86	85	86	85	82	81	81	82
82	81	81	82	80	79	78	77	77	79	79
79	78	78	78	78	77	77	77	77	78	78
77	76	76	76	76	75	77	75	74	73	74
73	73	73	75	75	74	74	74	76	80	80
79	78	77	75	73	74	73	74	74	73	73
72	72	71	72	71	72	73	75	78	80	80
79	77	77	78	78	77	79	80	80	81	81
80	80	81	80	80	81	79	80	80	80	80
80	80	73	73	74	74	74	74	72	73	73
73	72	72	73	77	76	75	74	73	73	73
72	71	72	71	71	72	71	71	71	70	71
69	69	68	69	69	71	72	71	71	72	73
73	74	73	73	73	73	74	76	75	77	75
77	79	79	79	82	81	83	83	83	81	81
81	82	84	81	81	83	83	83	86	87	88
87	87	88	88	90	88	89	93	92	93	91
91	91	91	90	92	92	93	92	93	92	94
92	95	97	96	97	97	96	96	97	97	97
97	99	98	98	99	99	98	99	98	98	97
93	92	92	92	91	91	94	94	94	95	95
94	94	96	96	95	94	93	91	92	90	87
87	86	85	83	86	85	86	85	85	85	88
88	89	90	92	94	96	95	93	96	95	95
95	95	95	94	94	92	91	91	91	90	90
90	89	89	88	87	88	88	92	94	93	93
93	94	94	94	94	94	94	95	96	99	99
99	98	96	95	97	99	102	101	106	107	111
109	118	125	121	119	124	125	126	125	127	132

Fox series $N = 92$

78	159	29	104	82	148	28	256	355	47
214	12	34	285	9	23	85	151	29	15
100	152	38	5	24	127	15	27	81	105
75	21	30	337	34	11	59	48	116	23
161	234	147	70	19	123	383	37	158	151
27	31	55	33	29	67	261	97	27	90
119	173	101	90	17	30	50	157	67	10
39	254	207	10	70	162	144	4	77	83
424	51	74	189	133	0	48	125	91	51
122	309								

UK primary energy consumption (coal equivalent)

Fuel data $N = 84$

874	679	616	816	866	700	603	814	843	719
594	819	906	703	634	844	952	745	635	871
981	759	674	900	957	760	649	891	915	780
683	949	995	809	705	970	881	781	706	954
932	752	630	883	959	752	654	933	980	796
691	917	983	979	690	920	1076	830	713	938
1001	759	969	871	919	720	633	900	927	704
630	857	912	725	635	847	938	692	925	946
974	746	670	874						

Industrial production data $N = 213$

1.82	2.24	1.53	1.87	2.03	1.65	1.69	1.92	1.93
1.82	1.82	1.82	2.01	2.10	2.24	2.46	2.58	2.55
2.38	2.47	2.43	2.76	2.72	2.19	2.59	2.52	2.47
2.29	2.32	2.48	2.38	2.43	2.72	2.39	2.67	2.64
2.46	2.86	2.70	2.47	2.27	2.50	2.39	2.74	2.62
2.81	2.90	3.16	2.83	3.12	3.14	3.13	3.18	3.14
3.18	2.88	2.98	2.96	2.90	2.86	3.02	2.90	2.93
3.11	3.05	3.27	3.54	3.39	3.59	3.51	3.60	3.72
3.60	3.21	3.33	3.50	3.51	3.65	3.33	3.46	3.63
3.56	3.78	4.08	4.06	4.03	4.22	4.21	4.34	4.36
4.52	4.85	4.55	4.45	4.55	4.71	4.64	4.75	5.38
5.32	4.98	5.25	5.30	5.48	5.60	5.65	5.87	5.58
5.72	6.22	6.54	6.15	6.20	6.31	6.85	6.70	7.32
7.62	7.37	7.56	7.88	8.30	8.75	9.22	10.10	9.19
10.40	11.10	10.70	11.70	11.90	11.80	12.50	13.20	13.70
15.10	14.30	15.60	16.90	16.60	16.80	160.00	16.90	19.10
20.00	20.00	19.00	21.00	21.70	21.70	22.60	24.00	26.00
26.40	26.30	28.10	29.10	28.50	30.00	31.70	31.70	32.40
32.50	35.00	37.30	38.70	36.400	36.40	35.80	40.20	43.50
44.80	45.30	46.40	46.70	47.50	47.4	47.30	45.60	50.30
53.50	55.70	56.50	54.40	52.10	51.00	55.10	58.30	62.40
63.30	64.10	61.00	60.00	63.50	66.50	71.40	73.40	77.00
80.10	80.10	80.30	81.70	80.00	81.00	85.70	82.50	85.60
83.80	86.00	88.60	92.10	96.10	100.00			

Lynx data $N = 114$

269	321	585	871	1475	2821	3928	5943	4950
2577	523	98	184	279	409	2285	2685	3409
1824	409	151	45	68	213	546	1033	2129
2536	957	361	377	225	360	731	1638	2725
2871	2119	684	299	236	245	552	1623	3311
6721	4245	687	255	473	358	784	1594	1676
2251	1426	756	299	201	229	469	736	2042
2811	4431	2511	389	73	39	49	59	188
377	1292	4031	3495	587	105	153	387	758
1307	3465	6991	6313	3794	1836	345	382	808
1388	2713	3800	3091	2985	3790	674	81	80
108	229	399	1132	2432	3574	2935	1537	529
485	662	1000	1590	2657	3396			

UK migration series $N = 23$

284	302	309	278	293	291	240	233	246	269
238	210	209	192	189	229	233	259	185	164

Mud thickness in lake Saki in mm, $N = 420$ observations

25.0	33.1	24.0	37.1	19.6	15.2	16.7	27.3	24.6	32.0
23.3	25.3	32.0	19.3	22.0	35.8	18.8	20.1	15.5	18.0
24.4	21.5	16.0	14.4	14.7	14.7	12.6	19.0	16.9	15.4
11.4	10.7	11.0	15.3	17.5	10.8	17.1	11.9	17.1	18.6
14.2	14.2	16.2	9.3	11.5	17.4	16.1	15.1	9.3	11.5
11.5	10.0	8.9	7.8	9.9	12.0	9.0	11.1	12.7	25.3
13.3	11.3	14.2	14.7	10.7	17.4	7.4	9.9	9.5	12.7
9.0	10.0	12.2	15.1	6.2	11.5	17.2	13.2	15.8	9.1
9.2	10.3	11.7	11.9	11.8	8.0	10.0	11.2	10.2	8.0
10.8	8.7	8.6	8.7	10.7	11.2	9.6	11.1	14.3	12.9
12.3	10.3	8.8	8.5	12.8	9.2	12.2	12.1	13.6	15.0
9.9	9.3	12.0	10.8	9.4	11.1	9.7	8.6	8.9	9.0
15.1	10.4	11.9	13.4	16.0	18.4	9.7	12.9	13.7	8.2
8.2	8.8	10.1	9.1	8.8	11.3	10.7	9.5	14.9	12.1
12.9	18.3	10.6	13.2	12.7	13.4	11.9	10.2	16.0	17.7
19.6	16.3	10.9	12.9	13.0	11.7	12.3	10.3	9.5	10.4
14.4	12.4	15.1	12.1	11.6	11.2	12.7	10.5	12.4	11.0
7.6	11.2	10.5	10.1	9.6	8.7	10.1	13.6	10.5	11.3
9.6	13.1	12.1	13.2	10.9	12.3	8.9	9.7	10.7	9.8
11.0	9.4	14.9	12.6	12.7	17.8	21.0	5.4	12.9	9.1
7.9	9.4	8.7	12.4	11.6	13.1	14.7	12.8	15.6	11.9
10.1	10.2	12.7	9.3	9.6	13.0	11.0	16.9	8.7	11.2
9.0	15.2	15.6	13.2	10.5	12.4	13.7	15.2	16.0	13.8
9.8	9.1	10.7	11.2	12.4	11.5	14.0	8.2	11.3	13.5
10.5	14.3	13.5	16.1	21.6	17.1	10.4	9.7	11.9	11.6
13.3	11.7	12.4	12.4	15.1	9.7	9.1	12.6	9.2	13.0
12.0	9.8	9.6	10.4	14.7	12.1	9.4	12.5	8.9	13.1
13.8	12.4	15.3	12.5	12.4	11.9	12.8	11.6	13.4	11.7
12.7	8.6	12.6	13.1	11.9	14.7	13.0	11.2	14.5	13.2
11.7	10.2	10.8	10.5	9.1	11.8	11.0	10.9	13.4	10.0
11.3	10.4	12.7	12.8	11.9	13.5	12.4	11.4	12.7	20.6
37.9	14.0	13.4	15.7	17.5	19.4	13.7	16.6	14.5	10.1
10.4	17.5	17.7	13.2	15.2	11.8	17.9	13.0	12.8	15.5
12.6	21.7	12.4	18.4	16.1	12.6	12.3	15.6	16.4	17.8
17.7	27.6	18.6	18.8	24.6	24.9	21.1	20.1	20.8	18.7
21.7	13.6	17.4	19.6	25.2	18.2	15.7	20.2	12.2	13.4
13.1	14.8	11.5	13.4	12.8	12.8	12.2	14.6	18.6	19.9
14.7	12.9	11.6	17.8	20.8	14.7	22.4	13.0	15.7	10.1
14.5	23.7	13.2	13.9	13.5	17.6	15.0	13.9	14.3	12.1
17.1	17.7	14.2	17.0	10.7	13.7	19.0	12.9	14.1	12.6
21.9	13.9	12.3	10.3	21.9	21.8	19.9	18.5	11.0	21.7
13.7	13.7	18.6	17.3	10.8	12.2	15.1	20.4	19.8	24.8

Purse snatching data $N = 71$

10	15	10	10	12	10	7	17	10	14
8	17	14	18	3	9	11	10	6	12
14	10	25	29	33	33	12	19	16	19
19	12	34	15	36	29	26	21	17	19
13	20	24	12	6	14	6	12	9	11
17	12	8	14	14	12	5	8	10	3
16	8	8	7	12	6	10	8	10	5
7									

Papermaking data $N = 160$

Series 1: height (less mean)

0.0	-0.3	0.5	-0.3	0.5	0.3	-0.1	-1.0	0.0	0.3
0.0	-0.2	0.3	0.2	0.0	-0.3	0.0	0.5	0.1	0.3
-0.3	0.0	0.1	0.5	0.5	-0.5	0.0	0.0	-0.7	1.3
1.0	0.8	0.0	0.1	-0.7	-0.1	0.1	1.3	-1.0	-0.7
0.0	-0.1	1.0	0.7	0.0	0.3	0.1	0.0	-0.7	-0.2
0.0	0.7	0.0	-0.8	0.3	0.0	-0.2	0.0	0.0	-0.1
-0.3	0.7	0.1	0.2	0.0	-0.1	0.1	0.5	-0.3	-0.1
0.1	0.7	0.1	0.2	0.0	0.3	0.0	-0.2	0.0	0.0
0.0	-0.3	0.7	-0.5	-0.2	0.5	-0.2	1.7	1.0	0.5
0.1	0.1	0.0	0.1	0.1	0.5	0.0	-0.3	0.1	-1.2
0.0	-0.1	0.7	0.0	0.1	-0.2	0.0	-0.3	0.3	0.3
0.0	0.0	-0.5	-0.3	0.2	0.0	0.2	-0.1	-0.2	0.0
0.0	0.0	-0.7	0.2	0.5	0.0	0.0	0.7	0.1	0.0
0.1	0.0	-0.7	0.0	-0.3	-0.1	0.1	0.3	-0.1	1.3
0.0	0.3	0.3	0.0	0.1	0.0	0.0	0.1	-0.4	-0.1
0.8	-0.1	-0.8	-0.1	-0.3	0.1	-0.5	1.0	-0.3	0.0

Series 2: weight

33.5	34.0	33.5	33.8	33.5	33.0	33.0	33.5	33.5	33.3
33.3	33.5	33.0	32.5	32.5	32.8	32.8	32.5	32.5	32.2
32.5	32.5	32.5	32.3	32.0	32.5	32.5	32.5	34.0	33.3
33.0	32.5	32.5	32.5	32.8	32.8	32.8	32.2	32.7	33.0
33.0	33.0	32.5	32.0	32.0	31.8	31.8	31.8	32.5	32.7
32.7	32.0	32.0	32.6	32.4	32.4	32.5	32.5	32.5	32.5
32.8	32.5	32.5	32.4	32.4	32.4	32.4	32.0	32.1	32.1
32.1	31.6	31.6	31.5	31.5	31.2	31.2	31.4	31.4	31.4
31.4	31.6	31.2	31.8	32.2	32.0	32.3	32.0	31.5	31.2
31.2	31.2	31.2	31.2	31.2	31.0	31.0	31.2	31.2	32.2
32.2	32.2	31.5	31.5	31.5	31.6	31.6	31.8	31.6	31.4
31.4	31.4	31.8	32.0	31.8	31.8	31.6	31.6	31.8	31.8
31.8	31.8	32.5	32.3	32.0	32.0	32.0	31.5	31.5	31.5
31.5	31.5	32.0	32.0	32.3	32.3	32.3	32.0	32.0	31.2
31.2	31.0	30.7	30.7	30.7	30.7	30.7	30.7	31.0	31.0
30.7	30.7	31.0	31.0	31.3	31.3	32.0	31.3	31.5	31.5

Rainfall (annual) series 1797–1975

95	106	98	79	63	89	80	112	95	106
92	71	95	78	66	77	68	94	98	86
99	81	84	71	107	88	101	87	92	95
95	94	84	98	92	87	118	103	85	79
93	129	85	103	79	104	106	97	107	93
91	101	91	91	79	110	91	86	83	94
101	63	111	90	102	115	84	97	90	83
105	86	101	90	95	86	82	92	80	102
84	87	92	99	92	96	86	98	92	102
99	94	97	86	109	95	110	114	92	80
101	111	93	101	110	97	101	85	93	109
85	86	111	85	121	91	101	84	93	101
92	122	91	86	83	137	94	74	85	87
92	76	97	115	87	100	88	74	107	107
93	98	98	79	93	139	86	91	111	113
122	106	105	109	105	123	103	85	98	113
72	95	91	87	107	91	80	104	93	90
98	84	91	105	85	81	124	86	83	98
96	88	101	109	91	121	95	105	106	110
95	103	101	105	68	102	109	116	102	99
119	111	97	113	105	100	78	92	109	105
106	95	109	98	93	91	90	97	90	114
89	103	85	110	120	97	82	117	85	94
97	114	88	130	97	87	94	78	110	113
109	108	101	100	91	97	84	108	83	

Rubella series $N = 78$, observations biweekly

420	550	610	910	1115	1210	1190	1080	1175	1195
1280	1200	395	360	220	230	150	165	150	160
110	110	140	150	190	195	180	195	300	445
440	435	520	775	640	775	650	760	390	200
130	100	90	20	50	90	130	80	160	120
202	200	125	210	300	505	500	1500	980	1000
900	1075	990	520	395	190	140	150	140	155
194	154	162	164	160	180	185	181		

Simulated data from ARMA(2, 1) (Fig. 5.13) $N = 200$

1.96856	3.46100	0.40183	2.56100	-0.09434	3.84189
-0.22183	0.20878	2.36408	0.98304	0.57140	0.20447
2.32745	-1.69392	2.56774	-1.04496	-0.48353	0.83992
-1.86672	0.75570	-0.47162	-0.56487	1.05950	-1.51171
-0.35161	0.66809	-0.15788	-1.02134	-0.65486	1.09831
-2.05903	0.87201	-0.16319	0.54675	-0.46915	0.97921
1.05625	-0.47127	-0.13975	1.68293	0.31367	-1.78751
0.12870	0.20572	-0.95924	0.48429	-0.53770	0.37789
-0.90995	0.43197	-0.09793	1.20082	-0.26873	1.43542
-0.58360	2.17358	0.73848	-0.18956	4.24151	0.28602
3.08449	2.15544	0.23372	4.73565	1.93650	2.97048
0.46059	3.18544	0.58868	2.47705	0.45415	-0.00840
2.87355	-1.41275	0.75572	-0.90303	-0.00966	-1.50760
0.72965	-2.08217	-1.10086	-0.71557	-1.78392	-0.53458
-1.70561	0.47334	-1.82401	0.21585	-0.41153	-2.08935
3.12382	-1.95905	1.46370	-0.28035	2.05824	0.91357
1.74739	-0.05307	2.14730	0.32958	1.34653	-0.04815

Simulated data from ARMA(2, 1) (Fig. 5.13) (continued)

1.94694	-0.89561	1.23703	0.16746	0.50658	1.22151
0.13189	0.62463	-0.99246	3.67675	-1.07049	1.32746
-0.38079	2.52017	0.38138	2.09868	-0.67839	2.65327
1.82270	0.77235	0.29227	2.47381	1.58111	2.15595
2.80943	1.80200	0.77876	3.31014	1.77253	1.62289
1.47341	2.23646	1.05285	0.81602	0.96746	1.55069
0.57321	0.44259	0.60779	-0.73593	-1.89147	0.95306
-0.74375	-0.85613	-3.21718	-0.66795	1.71258	-2.68771
0.61421	-0.97969	-0.64207	0.59015	-0.32519	0.71084
-1.98232	2.04099	-1.09449	0.92746	-0.67680	1.72461
1.65165	-0.55204	1.65238	3.47023	0.34663	2.70491
0.78850	0.73785	2.63842	1.15330	1.33541	0.59211
1.44474	0.55622	1.97609	0.08706	-0.12935	1.09230
-2.06838	0.81665	-1.77224	0.12763	-2.79750	-0.18016
1.87449	-2.35266	0.71078	0.28287	0.50359	-1.29541
1.90587	-0.50497	-0.65378	-1.63421	0.54719	-1.62579
0.54499	0.08903				

Temperature data $N = 366$

-1.49	-1.62	5.20	6.23	6.21	5.86	4.09	3.18	2.62	1.49
1.17	0.85	-0.35	0.24	2.44	2.58	2.04	0.40	2.26	3.34
5.09	5.00	4.78	4.11	3.45	1.65	1.29	4.09	6.32	7.50
3.89	1.58	5.21	5.25	4.93	7.38	5.87	5.81	9.68	9.07
7.29	7.84	7.55	7.32	7.97	7.76	7.00	8.35	7.34	6.35
6.96	8.54	6.62	4.97	4.55	4.81	3.68	4.16	6.30	8.05
7.53	5.90	3.33	4.92	5.33	6.86	5.67	6.13	6.82	5.76
7.59	7.10	4.36	4.12	3.37	3.57	2.92	3.89	1.68	0.98
0.74	2.42	4.51	6.81	6.74	7.18	8.21	7.42	6.92	7.20
8.52	8.09	7.41	7.04	8.21	8.40	8.89	8.22	6.60	7.47

8.67	9.59	11.25	13.50	13.06	14.19	13.91	11.08	11.72	9.35
6.51	8.01	9.42	9.76	9.61	7.85	8.31	9.49	8.70	8.40
8.39	9.79	9.22	8.37	8.87	8.05	7.61	7.74	7.23	8.87
11.77	14.27	16.53	16.58	14.77	13.96	14.42	13.98	15.46	16.40
11.27	12.42	10.73	10.95	11.50	11.96	12.84	12.78	10.73	9.63
10.88	10.19	12.69	14.21	17.96	21.14	17.81	14.77	13.69	13.58
14.91	14.26	13.00	15.14	16.23	14.08	14.94	13.54	13.48	15.19
13.25	12.12	12.46	11.37	11.61	12.20	13.01	13.03	13.08	12.89
14.19	12.78	12.38	14.98	15.11	14.20	13.78	13.49	13.56	13.14
13.02	12.86	13.70	13.10	13.60	13.24	12.68	13.52	13.11	14.86

14.87	12.63	13.70	16.31	17.43	17.68	20.74	17.91	17.57	19.49
18.42	16.85	16.45	16.93	17.84	18.03	17.34	16.31	16.38	17.19
15.04	15.68	17.44	15.77	14.21	18.28	18.98	17.86	17.33	16.99
15.88	15.41	18.15	15.15	13.52	12.85	13.34	15.16	16.31	17.19
17.10	15.75	14.71	14.90	16.66	16.98	17.05	15.84	14.37	15.89
16.68	14.69	13.02	14.71	15.15	14.58	13.99	14.78	16.07	15.71
14.09	15.42	16.57	16.12	16.03	15.33	15.11	13.40	13.30	14.53
14.35	12.85	13.26	13.21	13.01	11.24	11.76	11.26	10.71	12.25
9.05	8.42	7.92	6.70	8.28	7.92	8.97	9.22	8.29	7.21
7.28	5.68	7.05	8.45	11.31	12.90	10.13	9.13	8.65	12.16

Temperature data $N = 366$ (continued)

15.34	12.42	8.79	6.12	7.36	6.91	4.11	3.37	4.72	4.51
5.29	4.05	5.00	4.86	5.16	4.55	4.50	7.45	9.61	12.34
12.02	11.31	7.13	10.98	11.91	12.17	12.84	12.50	11.33	5.83
3.51	5.70	1.93	1.53	1.03	2.22	5.14	3.14	5.30	7.20
2.50	0.46	1.55	5.59	10.17	9.72	10.36	10.00	8.44	4.82
5.54	7.91	3.94	3.19	4.72	4.84	9.78	10.63	9.99	5.37
3.23	2.41	6.98	9.19	9.20	7.73				

Wolfer sun spot numbers $N = 100$

101	82	66	35	31	7	20	92	154	125
85	68	38	23	10	24	83	132	131	118
90	67	60	47	41	21	16	6	4	7
14	34	45	43	48	42	28	10	8	2
0	1	5	12	14	35	46	41	30	24
16	7	4	2	8	17	36	50	62	67
71	48	28	8	13	57	122	138	103	86
63	37	24	11	15	40	62	98	124	96
66	64	54	39	21	7	4	23	55	94
96	77	59	44	47	30	16	7	37	74

Index

MATHEMATICS AND ITS APPLICATIONS

Series Editor: G. M. BELL

Emeritus Professor of Mathematics, King's College London, University of London

MATHEMATICS AND ITS APPLICATIONS

Series Editor: G. M. BELL,
Emeritus Professor of Mathematics, King's College London, University of London

Toth, G.	HARMONIC AND MINIMAL MAPS AND APPLICATIONS IN GEOMETRY AND PHYSICS
Townend, M.S.	MATHEMATICS IN SPORT
Townend, M.S. & Pountney, D.C.	COMPUTER-AIDED ENGINEERING MATHEMATICS
Twizell, E.H.	COMPUTATIONAL METHODS FOR PARTIAL DIFFERENTIAL EQUATIONS
Twizell, E.H.	NUMERICAL METHODS, WITH APPLICATIONS IN THE BIOMEDICAL SCIENCES
Vein, R. & Dale, P.	DETERMINANTS AND THEIR APPLICATIONS IN MATHEMATICAL PHYSICS
Vince, A. and Morris, C.	DISCRETE MATHEMATICS FOR COMPUTING
Warren, M.D.	FLOW MODELLING IN INDUSTRIAL PROCESSES
Webb, J.R.L.	FUNCTIONS OF SEVERAL REAL VARIABLES
Willmore, T.J.	TOTAL CURVATURE IN RIEMANNIAN GEOMETRY
Willmore, T.J. & Hitchin, N.	GLOBAL RIEMANNIAN GEOMETRY

Statistics, Operational Research and Computational Mathematics
Editor: B. W. CONOLLY,
Emeritus Professor of Mathematics (Operational Research), Queen Mary College, University of London

Abaffy, J. & Spedicato, E.	ABS PROJECTION ALGORITHMS: Mathematical Techniques for Linear and Nonlinear Equations
Beaumont, G.P.	INTRODUCTORY APPLIED PROBABILITY
Beaumont, G.P.	PROBABILITY AND RANDOM VARIABLES
Beaumont, G.P. & Knowles, J.D.	STATISTICAL TESTS: An Introduction with Minitab Commentary
Bunday, B.D.	STATISTICAL METHODS IN RELIABILITY THEORY AND PRACTICE
Conolly, B.W.	TECHNIQUES IN OPERATIONAL RESEARCH: Vol. 1, Queueing Systems
Conolly, B.W.	TECHNIQUES IN OPERATIONAL RESEARCH: Vol. 2, Models, Search, Randomization
Conolly, B.W.	LECTURE NOTES IN QUEUEING SYSTEMS
Conolly, B.W. & Pierce, J.G.	INFORMATION MECHANICS: Transformation of Information in Management, Command, Control and Communication
Doucet, P.G. & Sloep, P.B.	MATHEMATICAL MODELING IN THE LIFE SCIENCES
French, S.	SEQUENCING AND SCHEDULING: Mathematics of the Job Shop
French, S.	DECISION THEORY: An Introduction to the Mathematics of Rationality
Goult, R.J.	APPLIED LINEAR ALGEBRA
Griffiths, P. & Hill, I.D.	APPLIED STATISTICS ALGORITHMS
Griffiths, H.B. & Oldknow, A.	MATHEMATICAL MODELS OF CONTINUOUS AND DISCRETE DYNAMIC SYSTEMS
Hartley, R.	LINEAR AND NON-LINEAR PROGRAMMING
Janacek, G. & Swift, L.	TIME SERIES: Forecasting, Simulation, Applications
Jolliffe, F.R.	SURVEY DESIGN AND ANALYSIS
Jolliffe, I.T. & Jones, B.	STATISTICAL INFERENCE
Kapadia, R. & Andersson, G.	STATISTICS EXPLAINED: Basic Concepts and Methods
Lindfield, G. & Penny, J.E.T.	MICROCOMPUTERS IN NUMERICAL ANALYSIS
Lootsma, F.	OPERATIONAL RESEARCH IN LONG TERM PLANNING
Moscardini, A.O. & Robson, E.H.	MATHEMATICAL MODELLING FOR INFORMATION TECHNOLOGY
Moshier, S.L.B.	METHODS AND PROGRAMS FOR MATHEMATICAL FUNCTIONS
Norcliffe, A. & Slater, G.	MATHEMATICS OF SOFTWARE CONSTRUCTION
Oliveira-Pinto, F.	SIMULATION CONCEPTS IN MATHEMATICAL MODELLING
Ratschek, J. & Rokne, J.	NEW COMPUTER METHODS FOR GLOBAL OPTIMIZATION
Schendel, U.	INTRODUCTION TO NUMERICAL METHODS FOR PARALLEL COMPUTERS
Schendel, U.	SPARSE MATRICES
Sehmi, N.S.	LARGE ORDER STRUCTURAL EIGENANALYSIS TECHNIQUES: Algorithms for Finite Element Systems
Sewell, G.	COMPUTATIONAL METHODS OF LINEAR ALGEBRA
Sharma, O.P.	MARKOVIAN QUEUES
Smith, D.K.	DYNAMIC PROGRAMMING: A Practical Introduction
Späth, H.	MATHEMATICAL SOFTWARE FOR LINEAR REGRESSION
Stoodley, K.D.C.	APPLIED AND COMPUTATIONAL STATISTICS: A First Course
Stoodley, K.D.C., Lewis, T. & Stainton, C.L.S.	APPLIED STATISTICAL TECHNIQUES
Thomas, L.C.	GAMES, THEORY AND APPLICATIONS
Vajda, S.	FIBONACCI AND LUCAS NUMBERS, AND THE GOLDEN SECTION
Whitehead, J.R.	THE DESIGN AND ANALYSIS OF SEQUENTIAL CLINICAL TRIALS: Second Edition
Woodford, C.	SOLVING LINEAR AND NON-LINEAR EQUATIONS